KT-367-014

Outdoor Leadership

THEORY AND PRACTICE

Bruce Martin

Christine Cashel

Mark Wagstaff

Mary Breunig

HUMAN KINETICS

Library of Congress Cataloging-in-Publication Data

Martin, Bruce, 1969-
 Outdoor leadership : theory and practice / Bruce Martin ... [et al.].
  p. cm.
 Includes bibliographical references and index.
 ISBN 0-7360-5731-5 (hard cover)
 1. Recreation leadership. 2. Outdoor recreation. I. Title.
 GV181.4.M27 2006
 790'.06'9--dc22   2005022006

ISBN-10: 0-7360-5731-5

ISBN-13: 978-0-7360-5731-8

Copyright © 2006 by Bruce Martin, Christine Cashel, Mark Wagstaff, and Mary Breunig

All rights reserved. Except for use in a review, the reproduction or utilization of this work in any form or by any electronic, mechanical, or other means, now known or hereafter invented, including xerography, photocopying, and recording, and in any information storage and retrieval system, is forbidden without the written permission of the publisher.

The Web addresses cited in this text were current as of October 2005, unless otherwise noted.

Acquisitions Editor: Gayle Kassing, PhD; **Developmental Editor:** Ray Vallese; **Assistant Editor:** Derek Campbell; **Copyeditor:** Alisha Jeddeloh; **Proofreader:** Kathy Bennett; **Indexer:** Marie Rizzo; **Permission Manager:** Carly Breeding; **Graphic Designer:** Bob Reuther; **Graphic Artist:** Yvonne Griffith; **Photo Manager:** Sarah Ritz; **Cover Designer:** Keith Blomberg; **Photographer (cover):** Mark Radel and Wildwater Expeditions; **Photographers (interior):** Sarah Ritz, unless otherwise noted; photos on pages 3, 5, 7, 9, 11, 13, 98, 169, 172, 193, 199, 202, 203, 215, 216, 219, 220, 249, and 261 courtesy of Bruce Martin; photos on pages 25, 42, 53, 58, 66, 129, 139, 140, 149, 152, 153, 157, 158, 162-164, 179, 183, 232, 247, 263, 270, 276, 278, 282, and 283 courtesy of Mark Wagstaff; and photos on pages 20, 31, 32, 106, 108, 136, and 144 courtesy of Christine Cashel; **Art Manager:** Kelly Hendren; **Illustrators:** Keri Evans (figures on pages 78 and 160) and Al Wilborn; **Printer:** Sheridan Books

Printed in the United States of America.   10

The paper in this book is certified under a sustainable forestry program.

Human Kinetics
Web site: www.HumanKinetics.com

United States: Human Kinetics
P.O. Box 5076
Champaign, IL 61825-5076
800-747-4457
e-mail: humank@hkusa.com

Canada: Human Kinetics
475 Devonshire Road, Unit 100
Windsor, ON N8Y 2L5
800-465-7301 (in Canada only)
e-mail: info@hkcanada.com

Europe: Human Kinetics
107 Bradford Road
Stanningley
Leeds LS28 6AT, United Kingdom
+44 (0)113 255 5665
e-mail: hk@hkeurope.com

Australia: Human Kinetics
57A Price Avenue
Lower Mitcham, South Australia 5062
08 8372 0999
e-mail: info@hkaustralia.com

New Zealand: Human Kinetics
P.O. Box 80
Mitcham Shopping Centre, South Australia 5062
0800 222 062
e-mail: info@hknewzealand.com

This book is dedicated to everyone who has helped us in our own development as outdoor leaders, including our mentors, our colleagues, our families and friends, and especially our students.

B. M., C. C., M. W., and M. B.

Contents

PART III Teaching and Facilitation   101

Preface

One of the traditional roles of higher education is to prepare students for participation in the various professional roles that are available in society. Outdoor leadership is no exception. Several colleges and universities offer basic professional training in the field of outdoor leadership. A number of programs have developed over the past 30 to 40 years that are designed specifically to prepare individuals for professional positions in outdoor leadership. One of the challenges facing college instructors of outdoor leadership during this time has been the task of finding a suitable textbook for use in introductory college courses on outdoor leadership. The authors of this text have yet to find a text that ideally suits their needs as instructors. This book is designed to meet this need. It is intended to serve as a primary textbook in an introductory course in outdoor leadership. It can be complemented by secondary texts on skills-based instruction in particular outdoor pursuits, such as backpacking, rock climbing, and kayaking.

When we began to write this book, we hoped to accomplish three goals. The first goal was to create a textbook at a level more appropriate for undergraduate study than some of the more theory-laden books that are currently available in the field. The second goal was to develop a textbook more comprehensive in nature than many of the more field-oriented texts that are also currently available. The third goal was to create a text that balances theory and practice in its consideration of the practice of outdoor leadership. We wanted to find a middle ground between theory and practice that does not appear to exist in the texts that are currently available for use in the introductory-level college course on outdoor leadership.

This text is based on a core-competencies approach to outdoor leadership. We have identified eight core competencies that we consider to be essential to the practice of outdoor leadership.

These core competencies provide the conceptual basis of this book. They define the parameters of outdoor leadership and consequently the parameters of this text. The book's introduction describes these competencies and helps the reader to understand how the competencies serve as a conceptual foundation for the text. The text is only loosely structured around these competencies, yet they help tie the text together. The introduction draws connections between the competencies and the topics addressed in the text.

The chapters in this text are arranged into four parts. Part I focuses on the foundations of outdoor leadership, including the general purpose, historical development, and current state of the profession. Part II considers general leadership theory as it is applied within the context of outdoor leadership. It also considers judgment and decision making and values and ethics as elements of outdoor leadership. Part III considers the role of teaching and facilitation in outdoor leadership. Part IV considers resource and program management in outdoor leadership.

Each chapter opens with a vignette that illustrates the concepts addressed in the chapter. The purpose of these vignettes is to bring the chapter concepts to life in the minds of readers. We adopted this technique in writing the book to help meet our goal of bridging theory and practice.

An example of the vignettes is the story of Gabriela, a leader of a 2-week expedition on federally managed lands in the Colorado Rockies. Gabriela and her group were greeted by a ranger in the parking lot of a trailhead at the start of their expedition route. Despite diligent planning, Gabriela's expedition was thwarted. She and her group did not have a permit to use the area. The ranger refused to grant an exception to Gabriela and her group, even though she had been told by a representative of the land management agency nearly a year earlier during the planning phase of her trip that she and her group did not need a permit. This vignette opens the chapter on parks and protected areas. It illustrates the importance of being aware of the agencies that are responsible for our parks and protected areas. Natural areas provide the physical context in which we practice outdoor leadership. Most of the areas that we use are managed by federal, state, or local government. The vignette also illustrates the importance of being aware of the rules and regulations that govern use of these areas. We refer to each of these vignettes throughout their respective chapters to illustrate the relevance of the material to the reader.

This textbook encourages self-assessment on the part of the reader throughout the text through the use of a professional-development portfolio. Though this text can be used by the seasoned professional as a resource guide for continued professional development (we are all lifelong learners), the text is written to facilitate the development of the aspiring outdoor leader. It is written to foster the development of outdoor leaders in the various areas of expertise—the core competencies—addressed in the text. An essential aspect of personal and professional development is self-awareness. Accurately assessing one's knowledge, skills, and dispositions is essential to mapping out areas for continued growth and development. To assist the reader in doing this, we have developed a series of professional-development activities. Taken together, these activities constitute a professional-development portfolio. This portfolio can be used as a valuable assessment tool not only for the reader but also for the instructor.

An example of the activities in the professional-development portfolio is the learning style inventory in chapter 12, Teaching Strategies. In this activity, readers are asked to complete a learning style inventory to determine their preferred learning styles. The importance of determining one's preferred learning style is based on the fact that individuals are inclined to teach according to their preferred learning style. Making prospective outdoor leaders aware of the different ways in which individuals learn is essential to ensuring that they learn to teach to those different styles.

Though this text is written specifically for use in an introductory course on outdoor leadership, it should be useful to a broad audience. In addition to serving teachers and students of outdoor leadership, the book should serve as a useful resource to anyone involved in leading groups into the outdoors. This includes outdoor leaders new and old, ecotourism operators, outdoor program administrators, camp directors, and laypeople, to name a few. Anyone interested in engaging in safe, enjoyable, and ecologically responsible excursions into the wild outdoors will benefit from this book.

Acknowledgments

Following are notes of acknowledgment from each of the authors of the text and then a collective note of acknowledgment from all of the authors.

This book is a culmination of sorts for me in my development as an outdoor leader. As such, I would like to acknowledge all who have contributed to my development as an outdoor leader. In particular, my parents, Fred and Diane Martin, whetted my appetite for adventure and the outdoors early in my life. Greg Eliot inspired me to embark on my journey as a professional outdoor leader. Ryan Madden of Sheldon Jackson College in Sitka, Alaska, challenged me to write this book. Finally, I acknowledge my coauthors. This book is the product of a truly collaborative endeavor among us. Thank you for your selfless dedication to the book and to the profession.

—*Bruce Martin*

I would like to acknowledge all my students, past and present, who make me proud by excelling past their teacher. I value the time I have spent with every person in the mountains, on the sea, or in the desert. You have made me a better person by knowing you. My family and friends have supported me through all of my days in the field and let me tell stories of my adventures. I love you all!

—*Chris Cashel*

The inspiration and drive to create this text stem from my students. I would like to thank those students who have journeyed into the outdoor classroom with me to study the art of outdoor leadership. My students have taught and challenged me to be a better professional outdoor leader. Their excitement and passion inspired me to articulate our experiences for the benefit of future professionals.

—*Mark Wagstaff*

I would like to acknowledge my parents, Patricia and LaVern Breunig, and my family for teaching me the leadership values of hard work, honesty, and integrity. I would like to acknowledge two of my most influential mentors, the late Richard Chernov and his wife Barbara Chernov, camp directors of Camp Birch Trail, for their early influence on my career as an outdoor leader. I am grateful to the many trip participants, coleaders, teachers, students, and friends who have taught me many lessons over the years and with whom I have shared many wonderful trips. I am particularly grateful to my husband, Tim O'Connell, for his constant support of me and of this book.

—*Mary Breunig*

All of the authors would like to thank the Human Kinetics staff for unwavering assistance and enthusiasm during the creation of this text. In particular, we thank Gayle Kassing for her guidance and extra efforts to meet with our team as we hashed out our vision for the book. We also praise Ray Vallese for his ability to organize and juggle thousands of details to turn the manuscript into a useful learning tool. Others from Human Kinetics who contributed in varying capacities include Derek Campbell, Bob Reuther, Sarah Ritz, Kelly Hendren, Keith Blomberg, and Yvonne Griffith. Thank you all for helping us to achieve a successful result in writing this book.

Introduction

BUILDING CORE COMPETENCIES

© Lynn Seldon

" There are hundreds of combinations of character, personality, and knowledge that make for good outdoor leadership. . . . For our purposes, leadership is defined as the ability to plan and conduct safe, enjoyable expeditions while conserving the environment. "
—**Paul Petzoldt**

This text takes a core-competencies approach to understanding the practice of outdoor leadership. This approach is not new; it was developed through the collective efforts of a number of leaders in the field during the past 25 years (Priest and Gass 1997; Priest 1984; Raiola 1986; Buell 1981; Swiderski 1981). The authors of this text have identified eight **core competencies** essential to the practice of outdoor leadership:

- Foundational knowledge
- Self-awareness and professional conduct
- Decision making and judgment
- Teaching and facilitation
- Environmental stewardship
- Program management
- Safety and risk management
- Technical ability

These competencies provide the essential framework for the text. They illustrate the multifaceted nature of outdoor leadership.

Core Competencies

This section of the text outlines and describes each of the core competencies (see figure I.1). It also illustrates the way in which the competencies serve as a basis for the text. Once we have described the competencies, we will draw connections between the chapters in the text and each of the competencies. We will show how each of the core competencies is incorporated as a foundational concept in the text. Each competency is denoted with *CC* followed by a number. This denotation will be used later in connecting the dots between core competencies and the chapters for which they serve as foundational concepts. Following are the competencies and their descriptions.

Foundational Knowledge (CC-1)

Foundational knowledge is the first of the eight core competencies. It consists of four elements: sense of purpose, sense of heritage, knowledge of the breadth of the profession, and understanding of leadership theory.

Sense of Purpose

Sense of purpose refers to the general philosophy on which the practice of outdoor leadership is based. Why do we do what we do in the field of outdoor

leadership? What value does outdoor leadership hold for society? What am I as an outdoor leader trying to accomplish through my work? These are questions that help us develop a sense of purpose as outdoor leaders. They also help us develop an understanding of the general purpose of outdoor leadership. These questions will be addressed in chapter 1, but they also represent the broader focus of the text.

Sense of Heritage

Sense of heritage refers to the history of the profession. In understanding what outdoor leadership is as a profession, we need to understand its origins. Good outdoor leaders know the general roots of the profession, they have a sense of future trends in the profession, and they feel a sense of place within the tradition of the profession. Chapter 2 will take an in-depth look at the history of outdoor leadership as a profession.

Breadth of the Profession

Breadth of the profession refers to the various ways in which outdoor leadership is practiced. Outdoor leadership is broad in scope. It is practiced in a variety of contexts, from traditional wilderness programs to public schools to national parks. Good outdoor leaders are aware of the professional contexts that help constitute the profession, and they are aware of the organizational contexts in which outdoor leadership is practiced. Chapter 3 will provide a sense of the scope of outdoor leadership.

Understanding of Leadership

One of the primary goals of outdoor leadership is to serve as a source of transformation in the lives of people. This can be accomplished only through effective leadership. Consequently, competency in the theory and practice of leadership is essential to outdoor leadership. Chapters 4 and 5 will address the theory and practice of leadership.

Self-Awareness and Professional Conduct (CC-2)

Self-awareness and professional conduct is the second core competency. It includes the following elements: acting mindfully as an outdoor leader, having an accurate sense of one's abilities and limitations, having knowledge and sensitivity about how we influence others, and having a strong sense of personal and professional ethics. This competency is integral to many of the other competencies.

Core Competencies in Outdoor Leadership

CC-1: Foundational knowledge	Sense of purpose Sense of heritage Breadth of the profession Understanding of leadership theory
CC-2: Self-awareness and professional conduct	Acting mindfully Knowing one's abilities and limitations Knowing how we influence others Behaving ethically
CC-3: Decision making and judgment	Decision making as a conscious process Role of judgment in decision making Available resources in decision making
CC-4: Teaching and facilitation	Effective facilitation skills Effective teaching skills Experiential learning
CC-5: Environmental stewardship	Environmental ethics Ecological literacy Parks and protected areas management
CC-6: Program management	Planning skills Organizational skills Management skills
CC-7: Safety and risk management	Participant safety Preparation and planning Legal aspects of safety and risk management Assessing abilities and limitations
CC-8: Technical ability	Proficiency in particular activities Experience-based competency Professional certifications

Figure I.1 Eight core competencies that are essential to effective outdoor leadership.

Acting Mindfully

Good outdoor leaders are always mindful in their actions. This means that they are intentional in all of their actions. They act with regard to the ultimate goals of a group experience. At times, this means being attentive to the needs of group members. At other times, it means being attentive to tasks that must be accomplished. Nonetheless, every action involves mindfulness and specific intent.

Knowing One's Abilities and Limitations

One aspect of acting mindfully and intentionally involves having an accurate sense of your abilities and limitations as a leader. This means "knowing thyself," or, as Paul Petzoldt used to frequently exclaim, "Know what you know, and know what you don't know!" Without a clear sense of their own abilities and limitations, outdoor leaders can hardly begin to define appropriate levels of challenge for their program participants. Without a clear sense of their abilities and limitations, outdoor leaders may set the bar too high, jeopardizing the emotional and physical safety of their participants. In such cases, leaders may actually become a danger to the group, and at the very least, they diminish the quality of an experience.

Influencing Others

Another aspect of acting mindfully and intentionally involves knowing how we affect others. In what ways do you typically influence a group?

What effect does your personality typically have on others within a group? Without a clear sense of the influence that leaders have within a group, they can hardly begin to consciously fashion experiences for the group that are psychologically rewarding. On the contrary, they might come across as a social oaf serving only to hinder group development.

Behaving Ethically

Yet another aspect of acting mindfully and intentionally is principled behavior. Leaders without moral scruples serve as negative influences within groups. Having a strong sense of personal and professional ethics is essential to effective leadership. The leader who bends or breaks rules or allows others to bend or break rules undermines the quality and value of an experience.

Decision Making and Judgment (CC-3)

Decision making and judgment are considered by many to be one of the most crucial elements of effective leadership. Good outdoor leaders realize that decision making should be a conscious process, exercise good judgment as an integral aspect of the decision-making process, and are aware of available resources in making decisions. This competency will be addressed extensively in chapter 6.

Decision Making as a Conscious Process

Many decisions in our lives are snap decisions that we make without much conscious thought. This approach to decision making is acceptable when the decisions are simple and the consequences are not great. In situations where decisions are complex, uncertainty is high, and the difference in consequences may mean the difference between life and death, this approach is unacceptable. Good decision making is a conscious process that involves weighing options as well as consequences of the options in choosing a course of action.

Role of Judgment

Judgment becomes part of the decision-making process when the consequences of a particular decision are unclear or unknown and you as a leader must make a best guess about a course of action. Judgment is defined as an estimation of the likely consequences of such a decision or course of action. Effective judgment relies on past experience and knowledge as a basis for estimating likely consequences.

Awareness of Available Resources

Conducting an inventory of available resources is essential to effective decision making. This inventory includes physical resources in the surrounding environment, physical resources within the possession of the group such as equipment, and human resources—knowledge, experience, and expertise—both within and outside of the group. This inventory is aimed at ascertaining the resources that are available to you in making a decision or choosing a certain course of action.

Teaching and Facilitation (CC-4)

A primary goal of outdoor education and recreation is personal and interpersonal growth among program participants. This goal involves psychomotor development among program participants (i.e., learning technical skills related to outdoor pursuits, or how to perform a given activity). It involves cognitive development (i.e., learning new information related to outdoor pursuits). It also involves affective development (i.e., gaining a better sense of one's self and one's relationship to others). This goal is accomplished through effective facilitation skills, effective teaching skills, and an emphasis on experiential learning. Facilitation skills will be addressed in chapters 8, 9, and 10, while teaching skills will be addressed in chapter 12.

Facilitation Skills

A common approach to facilitation in the early days of outdoor leadership was to let the experience speak for itself. Outdoor leaders took a hands-off approach when it came to the broader lessons that participants might gain from an experience. Eventually, however, outdoor leaders began to realize that they were forgoing an opportunity to make a difference in the lives of their participants. They began to frame experiences in ways that would help participants gain as much as possible from an experience. This process, known as facilitation, enhances the quality of experiences for individuals and groups. It involves assisting individuals and groups in gaining insights that they may not gain on their own.

Teaching Skills

Outdoor leaders commonly find themselves offering direct instruction to course participants. Whether it is teaching participants basic wilderness living skills, climbing or paddling techniques, or safety and rescue skills, outdoor leaders are instructors. To become an effective instructor, outdoor leaders must learn how to teach. This means learning how to create lesson plans and activities. It entails developing an understanding of different instructional and learning styles. It also entails learning how to model effective technique and how to coach others in developing effective technique.

Teaching Experientially

Outdoor leaders place a great deal of emphasis on learning by doing. Experiential education is the method by which outdoor leaders deliver their educational content. Every lesson should involve a degree of explanation, a degree of demonstration, and a greater degree of practice. This means giving participants an opportunity to learn skills in a hands-on manner. In teaching a group how to operate camp stoves, for instance, an outdoor leader should explain the process of operating a camp stove, demonstrate the process, and then give the students the chance to actually practice operating the stoves.

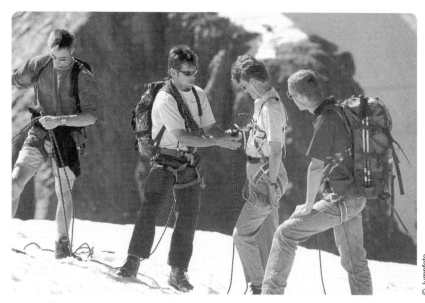

The ability to teach technical skills is an essential competency among outdoor leaders.

Environmental Stewardship (CC-5)

Environmental stewardship includes a strong sense of environmental ethics, high level of ecological literacy, and knowledge of parks and protected areas management. This competency will be addressed in chapters 13 and 14.

Environmental Ethics

Ethics is defined as a moral code or rules of conduct. Environmental ethics is the moral code or rules of conduct that we follow in our relationship with the natural environment. Outdoor leaders typically follow the code of conduct represented by the seven principles of Leave No Trace. Developed by the Leave No Trace Center for Outdoor Ethics, these principles serve as the basis for ecologically responsible interactions with the natural environment. Leave No Trace will be discussed in detail in chapter 14.

Ecological Literacy

One of the goals of outdoor leadership is to develop environmental or ecological literacy in individuals so that they can engage in intelligent action regarding their relationship with the natural environment. Ecological literacy entails thinking and acting critically in an environmen-

tal context, especially when it comes to making decisions and exercising judgment regarding environmental problems.

Parks and Protected Areas Management

Our classroom in the field of outdoor leadership is the outdoors. We rely on natural areas as a setting for teaching and programming. Many of the areas that we use are managed by national, state, and municipal agencies. In using these areas, it is important to know the rules and regulations under which they are managed. It is also important to know the management principles and practices of the agencies managing these areas. Finally, it is important to be familiar with issues that are of particular importance to the areas into which we travel for outdoor education and recreation experiences.

Program Management (CC-6)

Program management includes planning skills, organizational skills, and management skills. This competency will be addressed in chapter 15, on program management, and chapter 17, on expedition planning.

Planning Skills

Planning skills are applied in developing a program design or structure. Program design includes program goals and objectives, procedures and operations, and activities and services. Planning skills are also applied in developing trip, activity, and lesson plans. Trip plans include such components as emergency management plans, contingency plans, time control plans, energy control plans, and so forth. Proper planning is essential to effective outdoor leadership.

Organizational Skills

Once a plan has been established, the ability to implement the plan is largely contingent on the organizational skills of a leader. Implementation involves creating a system for getting things done and requires the ability to orchestrate the various components of a plan so that it comes together to create a unified whole.

Management Skills

Management skills involve the ability to direct the collective efforts of people in accomplishing program goals and objectives. It includes supervision and administration skills.

Safety and Risk Management (CC-7)

Safety and risk management includes ensuring the physical and psychological safety of program participants, preparing adequately, understanding legal aspects of safety and risk management, and assessing your abilities and limitations. This competency, one of the most important in outdoor leadership, will be addressed in chapter 16.

Participant Safety

A primary goal of outdoor leadership is to ensure the safety of individuals venturing into natural settings for outdoor education and recreation experiences, including both physical and psychological safety.

Preparation and Planning

One of the reasons program planning is considered a core competency in outdoor leadership is the implications of program planning in ensuring the safety of program participants. The old adage, "An ounce of prevention is worth a pound of cure," holds true here. Poorly planned programs are more prone to mistakes and mishaps than well-planned programs. In outdoor education and recreation, the slightest mishap can compromise the safety of participants.

Legal Aspects of Safety and Risk Management

Safety and risk management in outdoor leadership must be considered from a legal perspective as well as a practical perspective. Outdoor leaders can potentially be held liable for any injury or loss that may befall a participant. To be held liable, the outdoor leader or program for which the leader works must be proven negligent of their duty to provide a certain standard of care to the program participant. The program participant must also show that the injury or loss was actually a result of the leader's failure to provide that standard of care. In any case, a leader or a program that is shown to be negligent can be held financially responsible for injuries or losses. Program planning is as much about ensuring that participants engage in a safe and quality experience as it is about ensuring that you as a leader are adhering to the standard of care in the industry.

Assessing Abilities and Limitations

As mentioned, the ability to accurately self-assess as a leader is significant not only in determining your own limitations but also in determining the limitations of your followers. As an outdoor leader, the safety of your participants is often in your hands. Knowing your and your followers' limitations is crucial to ensuring your safety and the safety of your group.

Technical Ability (CC-8)

Technical ability includes proficiency in particular outdoor activities as well as experience-based competency and professional certification. There are at least two compelling reasons for the development of technical competency as an outdoor leader. First, how can you teach skills you do not know how to perform? This is especially true when you consider the importance of skills demonstration in the instructional process. Second, how can you ensure the safety of your program participants in an environment in which you cannot competently perform? A kayak instructor who plans to teach an introduction to white-water kayaking class should be able to kayak competently in at least intermediate-level white water. This ensures a level of mastery on the part of the kayak instructor in introductory-level white water both in terms of paddling technique and rescue ability. The same is true for any other sport or activity.

This text is not designed as a resource for developing technical abilities. However, a variety of other resources can complement this text for this purpose, including *The Backpacker's Field Manual* by Rick Curtis, *The Coastal Kayaker's Manual* by Randel Washburne, *How to Rock Climb* by John Long, and *Mountaineering: The Freedom of the Hills* edited by Don Graydon and Kurt Hanson.

Proficiency in Outdoor Activities

Outdoor leaders must possess technical competency in a variety of areas. The most basic of these areas is backcountry living skills. Backcountry living skills include stove operation and use, cooking, navigation using a map and compass, animal-encounter prevention techniques, latrine construction and use, and so forth. In addition to backcountry living skills, outdoor leaders should develop expertise in different activity areas or modes of travel. These may include canoeing, kayaking, rafting, sailing, technical rock climbing, mountaineering, backcountry skiing or snowboarding, and mountain biking. The ability to operate a challenge ropes course represents another set of technical skills that is important for outdoor leaders. Challenge ropes courses are only a small part of outdoor education and recreation, but because they are so common in the industry, competency in their operation and use is necessary for all outdoor leaders.

Experience-Based Competency

Technical proficiency in outdoor activities can only be gained through experience. The more experience individuals gain, the more competent they generally become. A common joke among many river guides when introducing themselves to their guests is, "Don't worry. I watched a video about white-water rafting last night, and I'm sure I can get you down the river safely today." Fortunately, this is only a joke. Outdoor leaders who fall out of practice in a given technical activity should refresh their knowledge and skills before leading individuals in those activities. A common practice among white-water rafting companies is to have their returning guides perform at least two refresher runs at the beginning of each rafting season on the rivers on which they will be guiding. Beginning guides must complete extensive technical training programs before being allowed to work as guides. Outdoor leaders should do their best to stay up to date in the areas in which they lead others.

Professional Certification

Professional certifications are one indicator of competence in different areas of expertise. Certifications signify only a minimal level of competence; nonetheless, they do indicate competence. Certifications also typically represent the industry norm or standard of care in technical activities. Examples of professional certifications in the field of outdoor education and recreation include the American Mountain Guide Association's instructor and guide certifications in rock climbing and mountaineering and the American Canoe Association's instructor certifications in canoeing and kayaking.

Connecting the Dots

This text is based on a core-competencies approach to outdoor leadership. The actual content of the book, however, is only loosely organized according to these competencies. The following information is intended to help you to draw connections between the structure of the book and the core competencies just described (see figure I.2). The book is organized into four parts: Foundations of Outdoor Leadership, Outdoor Leadership Theory, Teaching and Facilitation, and Resource and Program Management.

Part I: Foundations of Outdoor Leadership

Part I offers insight into the nature of outdoor leadership as a profession. Chapter 1, The Journey Begins, relates primarily to CC-1 and CC-2. The chapter is intended to give aspiring outdoor leaders a sense of the purpose of the profession and thus help outdoor leaders act more mindfully or intentionally than they otherwise would.

Chapter 2, History of Outdoor Leadership, relates primarily to CC-1 and CC-2. It is intended to provide aspiring leaders with basic knowledge of the heritage of outdoor leadership. In doing so, it should help leaders develop an awareness of their place within this heritage. Understanding professional heritage enhances self-awareness among outdoor leaders and their ability to act mindfully as they help to direct the future course of the profession.

Chapter 3, Professional Development, relates primarily to CC-1 and CC-2. It outlines the breadth of the profession, illustrating the various settings in which outdoor leaders work. It also picks up where chapter 2 leaves off in considering the development of the profession, offering a look at the current state of the profession through the consideration of the various contexts in which outdoor leaders currently work.

Part II: Outdoor Leadership Theory

Part II offers insight into the nature of leadership. Chapter 4, Theories of Leadership, relates primarily to CC-1. It is intended to provide aspiring

Connecting the Dots

Chapter 1: The Journey Begins	CC-1: Foundational knowledge CC-2: Self-awareness and professional conduct
Chapter 2: History of Outdoor Leadership	CC-1: Foundational knowledge CC-2: Self-awareness and professional conduct
Chapter 3: Professional Development	CC-1: Foundational knowledge CC-2: Self-awareness and professional conduct
Chapter 4: Theories of Leadership	CC-1: Foundational knowledge
Chapter 5: Leadership in Practice	CC-1: Foundational knowledge CC-2: Self-awareness and professional conduct
Chapter 6: Judgment and Decision Making	CC-3: Decision making and judgment
Chapter 7: Values and Ethics	CC-2: Self-awareness and professional conduct CC-3: Decision making and judgment
Chapter 8: Understanding Facilitation	CC-1: Foundational knowledge CC-2: Self-awareness and professional conduct CC-4: Teaching and facilitation
Chapter 9: Facilitating Personal Development	CC-1: Foundational knowledge CC-2: Self-awareness and professional conduct CC-4: Teaching and facilitation
Chapter 10: Facilitating Group Development	CC-1: Foundational knowledge CC-3: Decision making and judgment CC-6: Program management
Chapter 11: Challenge Course Leadership	CC-1: Foundational knowledge CC-2: Self-awareness and professional conduct CC-4: Teaching and facilitation CC-6: Program management
Chapter 12: Teaching Strategies	CC-1: Foundational knowledge CC-2: Self-awareness and professional conduct CC-4: Teaching and facilitation
Chapter 13: Parks and Protected Areas Management	CC-1: Foundational knowledge CC-5: Environmental stewardship CC-6: Program management
Chapter 14: Environmental Stewardship	CC-2: Self-awareness and professional conduct CC-3: Decision making and judgment CC-4: Teaching and facilitation CC-5: Environmental stewardship
Chapter 15: Program Management	CC-6: Program management CC-7: Safety and risk management
Chapter 16: Safety and Risk Management	CC-2: Self-awareness and professional conduct CC-6: Program management CC-7: Safety and risk management
Chapter 17: Expedition Planning	CC-6: Program management CC-7: Safety and risk management CC-8: Technical ability

Figure I.2 Drawing connections between the chapters that follow and the eight core competencies.

leaders with a sense of leadership theory and its heritage.

Chapter 5, Leadership in Practice, relates primarily to CC-1 and CC-2. It focuses on the application of leadership theory within the practice of outdoor leadership. It is intended to give aspiring leaders a sense of their potential influence as leaders.

Chapter 6, Judgment and Decision Making, relates primarily to CC-3. It is intended to help aspiring leaders develop effective decision-making skills through an understanding of the decision-making process.

Chapter 7, Values and Ethics, relates primarily to CC-2 and CC-3. Developing a strong sense of personal and professional ethics is essential to effective outdoor leadership. It is also essential to acting mindfully as a leader.

Part III: Teaching and Facilitation

Part III offers insight into the nature of facilitation and teaching as part of outdoor leadership. Outdoor education and recreation ultimately focus on facilitating personal and interpersonal growth among individuals. As such, facilitation and teaching are vital aspects of outdoor leadership.

Chapter 8, Understanding Facilitation, relates primarily to CC-1, CC-2, and CC-4. The chapter is intended to help the aspiring leader develop an understanding of the goals of facilitation, the process of facilitation, and challenges to effective facilitation. The chapter focuses on one of the primary methods through which outdoor leaders attempt to help program participants gain meaning from program experiences.

Chapter 9, Facilitating Personal Development, relates primarily to CC-1, CC-2, and CC-4. As we will see in chapter 1, one of the primary goals of outdoor leadership is to create opportunities for growth and development among people. This chapter details developmental theory as well as the outdoors as a context for fostering human development.

Chapter 10, Facilitating Group Development, relates primarily to CC-1, CC-3, and CC-6. The chapter focuses on group development theory, group development processes, and expedition behavior.

Chapter 11, Challenge Course Leadership, relates primarily to CC-1, CC-2, CC-4, and CC-6. It is intended to provide aspiring leaders with basic theories and concepts related to challenge course leadership, standards for professional conduct in leading challenge course programs, and knowl-edge and skills for planning and implementing challenge course programs.

Chapter 12, Teaching Strategies, relates primarily to CC-1, CC-2, and CC-4. It is intended to assist aspiring leaders in developing knowledge and ability to teach effectively in the outdoors.

Part IV: Resource and Program Management

Part IV offers insight into resource and program management as an aspect of outdoor leadership. Chapter 13, Parks and Protected Areas Management, relates primarily to CC-1, CC-5, and CC-6. The chapter focuses on the agencies that are responsible for managing our parks and protected areas and the rules and regulations under which these areas are managed. It is intended to provide aspiring leaders with an understanding of the rules and regulations governing use of parks and protected areas, the obligation to help preserve parks and protected areas, and the professional opportunities that are available in parks and protected areas management.

Chapter 14, Environmental Stewardship, relates primarily to CC-2, CC-3, CC-4, and CC-5. It focuses on our responsibility as outdoor leaders to preserve and protect natural resources through our work as educators. This involves developing an awareness of our relationship with the natural environment, especially our impact on that environment. It involves developing good decision-making skills regarding our relationship with the natural environment. And, it involves developing an ability to teach others how to be ecologically responsible in their relationship with the natural environment.

Chapter 15, Program Management, relates primarily to CC-6 and CC-7. It focuses on the duties and skills involved in planning and implementing outdoor programs.

Chapter 16, Safety and Risk Management, relates primarily to CC-2, CC-6, and CC-7. Effective risk management involves accurate estimation of your abilities and limitations. Knowing your limitations helps you avoid getting in over your head.

Chapter 17, Expedition Planning, relates primarily to CC-6, CC-7, and CC-8. Expedition planning involves effective organization skills, quality risk-management skills, and technical ability.

Finally, the text includes an appendix of outdoor leadership organizations and a glossary to help the reader understand the terms used within the text.

Drawing Connections

While the content of the text is organized according to a different logic and sequence than that represented in the core competencies, the core competencies are the conceptual basis of the book. At the beginning of each chapter, we have noted each of the competencies to which the chapter primarily relates. This is a reminder of the relationship of the material to the competencies that comprise the practice of outdoor leadership. The reader may begin to draw connections between the competencies and the text that the authors have not articulated. The connections that we have drawn are not necessarily all-encompassing. They are meant simply to draw the most obvious connections between chapter content and the core competencies.

Selected References

Buell, L.H. 1981. The identification of outdoor adventure leadership competencies for entry-level and experience-level personnel. Unpublished doctoral dissertation, University of Massachussets.

Curtis, R. 1998. *The backpacker's field manual: A comprehensive guide to mastering backcountry skills.* New York: Three Rivers Press.

Graydon, D., and K. Hanson, eds. 1997. *Mountaineering: The freedom of the hills.* 6th ed. Seattle: Mountaineers.

Long, J. 2003. *How to rock climb!* 4th ed. Guilford, CT: Falcon.

Priest, S. 1984. Effective outdoor leadership: A survey. *Journal of Experiential Education* 7(3): 34-36.

Priest, S., and M.A. Gass. 1997. *Effective leadership in adventure programming.* Champaign, IL: Human Kinetics.

Raiola, E.O. 1986. Outdoor wilderness education—A leadership curriculum. Unpublished doctoral dissertation. Antioch, OH: Union Graduate School.

Swiderski, M.J. 1981. Outdoor leadership competencies identified by outdoor leaders in five western regions. Unpublished doctoral dissertation, University of Oregon.

Washburne, R. 1998. *The coastal kayaker's manual: The complete guide to skills, gear, and sea sense.* 3rd ed. Guilford, CT: Globe Pequot.

PART I

Foundations of Outdoor Leadership

To study the foundations of a given profession or practice is to study the value of that profession or practice to society. The value of a profession to society can be considered from a variety of theoretical perspectives. An economist might ask what financial benefit a profession holds for society. A sociologist might ask what benefit a profession holds in addressing contemporary social problems. A psychologist might ask what benefit a profession holds for improving the psychological welfare of members of society. An ecologist might ask what benefit the profession holds in addressing environmental concerns. Studying the foundations of a profession is the act of asking why we do what we do in a given profession. This section focuses on the value of outdoor leadership as a professional practice.

Chapter 1, The Journey Begins, defines the nature of the practice. It is intended to give a sense of the general purpose of outdoor leadership and, in doing so, a sense of the potential value of outdoor leadership to society. The chapter also describes outdoor education and outdoor recreation as contexts in which outdoor leadership is practiced.

Chapter 2, History of Outdoor Leadership, gives an overview of the development of outdoor leadership as a profession. Outdoor leadership is a young and growing profession. This chapter is intended to give a sense of the professional heritage of outdoor leaders.

Chapter 3, Professional Development, gives an overview of the professional opportunities that are currently available in the field of outdoor leadership. This chapter is intended to give a sense of the scope of the profession through an overview of the professional associations that influence the field and the professional settings in which outdoor leadership is currently practiced. It offers a contemporary view of the profession of outdoor leadership.

chapter 1

The Journey Begins

" I only went out for a walk and finally concluded to stay out till sundown, for going out, I found, was really going in. " —John Muir

Chapter Concepts

- Purpose of outdoor leadership—Outdoor leaders must understand the nature of the profession and its value to society.
- Outdoor leadership in context—Outdoor leadership is practiced primarily within the context of outdoor education and outdoor recreation.
- Outdoor leadership as a professional journey—Outdoor leaders embark on a journey that leads to continual growth and development.

The chapter concepts relate to the following core competencies:

- Foundational knowledge (CC-1)—Outdoor leaders must have a clear sense of purpose in their work.
- Self-awareness and professional conduct (CC-2)—One of the most important aspects of outdoor leadership is recognizing one's abilities and limitations and defining areas for future growth.

As a sophomore in college, Bill agonized over career options. His grandfather had been a lawyer and his grandmother had always encouraged him to pursue law as a career. Bill seriously considered it but decided that being a lawyer was not for him. His other grandfather had been a medical doctor, but Bill knew that he didn't want to be a doctor. He had also considered following in his father's footsteps as a director of a youth services program. Bill had been active in the program while growing up. He had attended the program's summer camp nearly every summer as a child, and he worked as a camp counselor at the same camp during college. Bill could envision himself in that kind of career, but he just wasn't sure. Bill's mother worked as an activity director at a nursing home. Bill thought about that type of career but could not envision himself working in a nursing home. His favorite subject in school was history, but he could not envision himself working in a museum or teaching history. And he definitely could not envision himself in a confined office space working for an insurance company or some other corporation. Bill knew that he wanted to work with people in a helping profession. It was not until he became involved in his college's outdoor adventure program that he finally realized what he wanted to do.

One of Bill's friends invited him to an open house that the college outdoor adventure program was hosting to introduce students to the program. The program offered single- and multiday trips hiking, backpacking, rock climbing, caving, canoeing, kayaking, rafting, hang gliding, and bicycling. One of the features of the program that excited Bill the most was that many of its trips were student-led—in addition to recruiting students to participate in the program's activities, the program director was recruiting students to become leaders in the program. Bill excitedly introduced himself to the program director, expressing his interest in becoming a student leader. He recounted to the program director his summer camp experiences and his many family canoeing and camping outings. After hearing all of this, the program director put his arm around Bill's shoulders and exclaimed, "Well, Bill, we've got a training program for you!" To his chagrin, Bill realized that becoming a leader in the program was not as simple as that. There were some hoops through which he would have to jump first. The first of these was a course in outdoor leadership. This course served as the cornerstone of the outdoor adventure program's student leadership development process and as the cornerstone of the college's degree program in outdoor leadership. Bill eagerly signed up for the course, thus beginning his career in the field of outdoor leadership.

By the time Bill finished his undergraduate degree in outdoor leadership, he had become a senior leader in the college's outdoor adventure program, specializing in caving, canoeing, and white-water rafting. The program director had become a close friend and mentor, and Bill had decided that he wanted to be a director of a college outdoor program, too. Bill couldn't believe the news when he was offered his first professional position as an outdoor leader. What a long way he had come! The job that he was offered upon graduation was that of an assistant director in a college outdoor program at a small private college.

Is there an innate need in humans to explore? What is it that inspires us to explore? To begin, there are certainly political and economic motives for exploration. European explorers sailing westward across the Atlantic did so in search of a new trade route to the East. Lewis and Clark's expedition was driven largely by the desire of the United States government for political and economic control of a large swath of North America. Our current space exploration program began as a result of political and military competition between the United States and the Soviet Union during the Cold War. Today, the program is driven largely by a desire for scientific discoveries and technological developments that can lead to the development of new industries here on earth.

Learning to kayak on Clear Creek in Golden, Colorado.

There are also personal motives for exploration. Explorers are often drawn by a desire for the honor and glory that follows from exploration, or even by sheer curiosity about what lies beyond the next horizon. Explorers are also often drawn by a more fundamental reason, the desire to better know themselves.

Exploration and self-discovery are one of the underlying themes in this textbook. Exploration and self-discovery represent the spirit of **outdoor leadership.** Outdoor leaders are drawn to the profession not just for the opportunities that the outdoors provides for adventure in a traditional sense but also for the opportunities for the adventure of looking inward and getting to know yourself. One of the things that Bill found most appealing about the outdoors as a leader is that it offered him constant challenges that compelled

him to continually grow and develop as a leader and as a person. Once he began his professional journey, he quickly realized that his career choice represented just that, a journey filled with opportunities for self-discovery and growth. He also realized that his career choice would allow him to help others make similar journeys as participants in his programs. He would be able to help others experience not only the joy and adventure that can be found in nature but also the joy and adventure that can be found in getting to know themselves better.

This book is an introductory textbook on outdoor leadership. It is intended for those who are just beginning their professional journey in the field of outdoor leadership and for those who are considering outdoor leadership as a potential professional pursuit, whether on a full-time or part-time basis. This text explores the theory and practice of leadership as it applies to the fields of **outdoor education** and **outdoor recreation.**

Learning Activity 1.1

Reflect on past adventure experiences in your life. Describe one of those experiences to your classmates. How did you get involved in the experience? What was the experience like? Why was it adventurous? What did you gain from the experience? Did the experience change you in any way? Would you engage in such an experience again?

What Is Outdoor Leadership?

Outdoor leadership is the practice of leading individuals and groups into natural settings via a variety of modes of transportation: walking, biking, canoeing, caving, kayaking, and mountaineering, to name a few. Three primary goals define the practice of outdoor leadership (Petzoldt 1984):

- Outdoor leaders aim to ensure the safety of individuals engaging in outdoor education and recreation experiences.

- Outdoor leaders aim to ensure the protection and preservation of the natural environments into which people venture for outdoor education and recreation experiences.

- Outdoor leaders aim to enhance the quality of outdoor experiences for individuals with whom they are working.

Paul Petzoldt (1984), who had a hand in the establishment of Outward Bound in the United States, the National Outdoor Leadership School, and the Wilderness Education Association, suggests that a number of elements comprise effective leadership in the outdoors. One of the most important of these elements is recognition and acceptance of one's abilities and limitations as a leader. Outdoor leaders do not necessarily have to be the most knowledgeable or experienced people in a particular outdoor pursuit, but they should recognize their limitations and not get themselves and their groups in over their heads. An outdoor experience that results in discord within groups; physical discomfort from blisters, cold, and hunger; unfulfilled personal and group goals; and injury or harm to participants are all indicators of poor leadership. If your leadership results in conditions such as these, you are doing something wrong as a leader. The goal of this text is to inform you of the elements that comprise effective leadership in the outdoors. Integral to your journey through this text is a process of self-reflection intended to assist you in assessing your abilities and limitations and identifying areas for growth as an outdoor leader.

Understanding Leadership in Outdoor Education and Recreation

Outdoor leadership is practiced within a variety of contexts. These contexts will be discussed extensively in chapter 3 to give an idea of the professional opportunities that are available in the field of outdoor leadership. Most of these contexts fall within two categories: outdoor education and outdoor recreation. Though similar in many ways, outdoor education and recreation are different disciplines. Outdoor education is part of the broader field of education, while outdoor recreation is part of the broader field of recreation and leisure. To develop a better understanding of the professional contexts in which outdoor leadership is practiced, we offer definitions of these different disciplines.

Recreation and Leisure

In defining outdoor recreation, it is necessary to define the broader framework within which it is situated. When the term **recreation** is used today, it is typically used synonymously with **leisure** (Jordan 1999; Russell 1996). However, there is a distinction between the two terms. Recreation is considered leisure, that is, recreation occurs during leisure time, but leisure is a broader concept than recreation.

Leisure is nonwork activity into which people enter voluntarily for enjoyment's sake, but this does not mean that leisure is purposeless. Russell identifies some of the potential benefits of leisure as "relaxation, diversion, refreshment, and re-creation" (1996, p. 34). She gives the following description of leisure:

> Although the psychological condition of leisure suggests it is simply a matter of "feeling good," the connotation goes beyond this. Leisure is an entire way of being—an opportunity for building purpose into life—capable of providing opportunities for self-expression, self-achievement, and self-actualization. Leisure is engaging in flights of imagination, developing talents, looking at things in new ways, and being ourselves. (p. 35)

Wall states that a psychological definition of leisure and recreation "reminds us that we are not providing opportunities to recreate in and for themselves; rather we are making available the chance to achieve a wide range of satisfactions, which vary from individual to individual, from activity to activity, and from place to place" (1989, p. 4). Kelly notes, "Leisure is not in the time or the action but in the actor. . . . The leisure attitude is a way of life, a philosophy about living, a psychological condition" (1982).

The Greeks used the terms *scol, schole,* or *skole,* from which the modern term *school* is derived, to refer to leisure. The modern term *leisure* is derived from the Latin term *licere,* which means "to be free." As such, leisure time is considered to be time free from obligation to work, family, community, and so forth.

Aristotle was the first major Western thinker to consider the nature of leisure. He divides leisure into three components: amusement, recreation, and contemplation. Amusement represents a passive form of leisure in which individuals exert little energy in the activity. Going to the movies is a form of amusement. The couch potato who spends time in front of the television watching sports or soap operas is engaged in an amusement activity. The spectator who sits in the stands watching a college football game or a NASCAR race is engaged in an amusement activity. Amusement activities are activities in which the spectator is enthusiastically engaged, but the activities are physically passive in nature.

Recreation, a term that is derived from the Latin *recreare*, which means "to regenerate, refresh, or re-create," represents a form of leisure in which individuals exert energy through some form of physical activity (Jensen 1995). Rather than simply watching others play for the sake of amusement, recreation entails participation in the activity. White-water rafting in a paddle raft is considered a recreation activity, for example, because everyone in the raft has a paddle and contributes to the movement of the raft down the river. Hiking and backpacking are likewise considered to be recreation activities because of the level of physical exertion they require.

Contemplation, in Aristotle's view, is the highest form of leisure. Aristotle considered contemplation a luxury afforded only during leisure time. The importance of contemplation within the Greek tradition is based on its role in ascertaining knowledge and understanding. In Aristotle's mind, to live in a state of knowledge and understanding was to live in a state of happiness. Aristotle considered contemplation to be the route to happiness, or humanity's highest good. Consequently, Aristotle considered contemplating life's great questions to be the highest form of leisure. Leisure was viewed within the Greek tradition as a means for self-cultivation.

Aristotle disdained amusement because of its passive and unproductive nature but appreciated

Mountain-biking among the aspens in Golden Gate Canyon National Conservation Area.

recreation because of the positive benefits it holds for the human body (Murphy 1981). Kurt Hahn, the founder of Outward Bound, also held little appreciation for amusement as a form of leisure activity. He considered "spectatoritis" to be one of the many ills afflicting our society (James 1995, p. 61).

While the concept of leisure developed within the Greek tradition, its meaning for the Greeks is different than its meaning in contemporary society. According to Neulinger (1981), there is no single definition of leisure but, rather, different understandings of leisure. Like the idea of happiness, leisure can mean different things to different people. Noting this divergence of opinion regarding the character of leisure experience, Neulinger writes, "To one person it may mean something good, to another something bad, to one something active, to another, something passive, still to another something noble and worthwhile, while to another something to be frowned upon, nay, immoral" (p. 1).

Neulinger's point is that there is an element of subjectivity in leisure experience. One person's work may well be another person's play. One person may cook solely for the sake of feeding a family. Cooking in this case is likely perceived as a chore. Another person may cook not merely for the sake of eating or feeding the hordes but for the simple pleasure of cooking. The same is true for gardening, home improvement, or any other activity, including outdoor activities. Outdoor recreation activities may represent leisure experience for some, but they can represent drudgery for others. Outdoor recreation activities are not always pleasurable even to the outdoor enthusiast because of the strain of carrying a backpack, enduring rain and cold, and so forth. The idea, though, is that by being in the outdoors, we open ourselves to the possibility of the rewards that outdoor recreation can yield.

Despite this element of subjectivity, three elements are common to all contemporary definitions of leisure. First, all leisure involves an element of perceived freedom; second, all leisure involves an element of intrinsic motivation; and third, all leisure experiences are aimed at some positive outcome.

Outdoor Recreation

Just as recreation is one aspect of leisure, outdoor recreation is one aspect of recreation. While recreation is considered to be the physically active side of leisure, outdoor recreation is considered to be recreation activities that occur in natural settings. Ford (1981) defines outdoor recreation as "All those leisure experiences in the out-of-doors that are related to the use, understanding, or appreciation of the natural environment or those leisure activities taking place indoors that use natural materials or are concerned with understanding and appreciation of the out-of-doors" (p. 18).

Outdoor recreation is an applied discipline that developed during the mid-20th century in response to growing concerns about the recreational use of natural areas throughout the United States, Canada, and other countries around the world (Manning 1986). It is viewed as an applied discipline because it arose to address specific needs in society, unlike conventional theoretical disciplines such as philosophy, history, and mathematics. Outdoor recreation opportunities grew tremendously during the 1950s along with the rise in economic prosperity in the United States, Canada, and other Western nations. Increased economic prosperity resulted in more leisure time. With the introduction of "automobile tourism" (Carley 2001) and the interstate highway system, America's historically remote and pristine areas suddenly became more accessible. The environmental effects of the increased use of natural areas served as the impetus for the development of outdoor recreation as a field of study.

The first significant study of concerns related to outdoor recreation was conducted by the Outdoor Recreation Resource Review Commission (ORRRC), a federal advisory board created by President Dwight Eisenhower in 1958 to assess the state of outdoor recreation in the United States and to make recommendations for its future development. The findings of the commission were published in 1962 in a report entitled *Outdoor Recreation in America.* This report revealed an absence of literature on outdoor recreation. Manning (1986) notes that the Library of Congress' card catalog system held no subject heading for outdoor recreation at the time and that there were fewer than 10 entries in the system with the phrase "outdoor recreation" in the title. The ORRRC's recommendations resulted in the Outdoor Recreation Act of 1963 and the Land and Water Conservation Fund Act of 1965. These two acts of Congress provided two of the primary instruments through which the goals laid out in the ORRRC report were accomplished. The acts provided federal money for the development and maintenance of outdoor recreation areas nationwide and they framed outdoor recreation as a social need that should be provided for the public good. Participation in outdoor recreation steadily increased during the past century and it continues to grow in the 21st century.

Outdoor recreation is considered to be a multidisciplinary field of study because of the wide array of concerns that it addresses. For example, natural scientists such as biologists and ecologists are concerned with the environmental effects of outdoor recreation. Economists are interested in the commercial value of an industry created by the pursuit of outdoor recreation activities. Psychologists are interested in the value that outdoor recreation activities offer to individuals in terms of life satisfaction. The list goes on.

According to Jensen (1995), outdoor recreation is unique from other forms of recreation because of its reliance on the natural resource base. Outdoor recreation activities, he contends, are those recreation activities that occur in natural outdoor settings typically removed from the daily home environment. Outdoor recreation and recreation in general involve more than just the activity itself. A series of phases constitute the overall outdoor recreation experience:

- Anticipation
- Planning
- Participation
- Recollection

This series of stages can be applied to any activity, leisure activity or not. The sense of anticipation in outdoor recreation experiences, however, tends to be heightened due to the nature of the activity, and planning for outdoor recreation activities is typically more involved and complex. The sense of fulfillment that the participant experiences once the activity is concluded, moreover, is also heightened because of the level of exhilaration and sense of accomplishment generated through participation in the activity.

Outdoor Education

Outdoor education is comprised of two primary disciplines: **environmental education** and **adventure education** (Priest and Gass 1997). Outdoor educators serve as environmental educators, adventure educators, or both. In addition to these two disciplines, **experiential education** is also discussed in this section because it serves as the primary basis for teaching in adventure education and environmental education.

Environmental Education

Priest and Gass (1997) state that environmental education is concerned with two types of relationships: **ecosystemic relationships** and **ekistic relationships.** Ecosystemic relationships refer to the "interdependence of living organisms in an ecological system." Ekistic relationships refer to "key interactions between human society and the natural resources of an environment. . . . In other words, how people influence the quality of the environment . . . and how, in turn, the environment influences the quality of their lives" (p. 17). Environmental educators teach people about the relationship of humans to the natural world. This involves developing an understanding of ecosystems and the place of humans within those systems. It also involves developing an understanding of issues in natural resources management, environmental preservation, and other areas of

Rappelling in the Colorado Canyons National Conservation Area.

concern in the field. Environmental educators do not simply teach about the environment for the sake of fulfilling the intellectual curiosity of their students. They focus on a much more fundamental concern: teaching about the environment for the sake of creating ecologically or environmentally literate members of society (Volk 1993; Golley 1998; Orr 1992). Project WILD, Project WET, Project Learning Tree, and the Leave No Trace Center for Environmental Ethics are all organizations that are designed to provide environmental education programming.

Adventure Education

Adventure educators provide opportunities for personal and interpersonal growth through adventure experiences. This can involve using the challenges of wilderness living and travel to develop greater self-confidence. It can also involve using the aesthetic beauty of natural environments as a source of spiritual enrichment. Or it can involve teaching individuals to use adventure sport to maintain a healthy, active lifestyle. These are a few of the ways in which adventure education can be used for personal growth.

Adventure education can also be used to teach people to work more effectively as groups. Outdoor expeditions provide a wonderful opportunity for addressing such concerns as communication, problem solving, and conflict resolution as they work to accomplish common goals and objectives. Challenge ropes courses provide another setting in which groups can work on such concerns. The skills that people develop in working with one another in adventure settings can be easily transferred to other areas of their lives. Corporate life is one segment of society that has embraced adventure programming as an effective tool for the development of teamwork among employees because increased teamwork equals increased productivity.

Experiential Education

The Association for Experiential Education (AEE), one of the primary professional associations in outdoor education and recreation, has defined experiential education as follows: "Experiential education is a philosophy and methodology in which educators purposefully engage with learners in direct experience and focused reflection in order to increase knowledge, develop skills, and clarify values" (AEE 2005). Outdoor education can be viewed both in terms of educational content and educational method. Experiential education is the primary method by which outdoor educators deliver educational content. Environmental education and adventure education are the basis of the content.

Sharp offers a definition of outdoor education that refers to the value of experiential education:

> That which can best be learned inside the classroom should be learned there. That which can best be learned in the out-of-doors through direct experience, dealing with native materials and life situations, should there be learned. This approach to education rests squarely upon the well-established and irrefutable principle of "learning by doing." (1957, p. ii; as cited in Ford 1981, p. 4)

Golley (1998) makes a pitch for experiential education as the best method for teaching students about the natural environment:

> Experience is the trigger for environmental literacy. It ignites curiosity and tests the muscles. It teaches us that we live in a world that is not of human making, that does not play by human rules. We call this world *nature*. To build environmental literacy we must go beyond books and libraries and experience nature directly. Only then do we gradually come to recognize a depth and complexity in nature that continually challenge and surprise us. . . . (p. x)

Smith and Williams (1999) also give a pitch for experiential education as the best method for teaching students about the natural environment. One of the key principles of environmental education is "the development of personal affinity with the earth and through the practice of an ethic of care" (p. 6). This personal affinity is best developed through direct experience with the natural environment, experience that allows students to develop an appreciation for and caring attitude toward that environment. Hunt (1990) also argues that experiential education is the best method for developing character in individuals. The best way to develop good character is through the development of proper habits. Habits can only be developed through repetitive practice—through experience.

Relationship of Outdoor Education to Outdoor Recreation

What is the difference between outdoor education and outdoor recreation? Considering the definitions just offered, there appears to be little difference between the two. When practiced properly, they are actually quite similar. The goal of each is the attainment of new knowledge, skills, and attitudes about the world. The Greek notion of recreation and leisure was centered on the concept of self-actualization, or the development of people to their fullest potential. The use of the term *schol* by the ancient Greeks to refer to the concept of leisure shows its similarity to our contemporary understanding of education.

Distinctions begin to arise between outdoor education and outdoor recreation, however, when considering the character of the broader disciplines within which each is based. Distinctions arise primarily when considering the two disciplines in a formal sense or the contexts and ways in which each is practiced. Education is often thought of in terms of schooling. Students go to the same place, a school building, each day for a specific amount of time to study a particular set of subjects. The goals of education are oriented toward the development of competence in these subject areas. Recreation, on the other hand, is often thought of in terms of nonschool and nonwork activity that occurs in a wide variety of settings, ranging from community recreation centers to day care programs. The goals of recreation are more loosely defined because of the participant-centered nature of recreation. Goals are framed by the nature of the program, and recreation leaders attempt to facilitate the achievement of goals throughout the course of the program.

The distinctions between the two disciplines fade when considering the practice of each in natural settings. The context in which outdoor education and outdoor recreation are practiced is the same. Each employs activities that are essentially the same. Specific goals and objectives may vary depending on the character of the particular program, but both outdoor education and outdoor recreation ultimately aim for growth and development among program participants. Outdoor leaders essentially are both recreation leaders and educators.

Teaching technical rock climbing in the Colorado Canyons National Conservation Area.

As Ford notes, "Only through education can one develop the skills, knowledge, and attitudes needed for the wise leisure use of the natural environment" (1981, p. 18). Not all outdoor recreation experiences include an educational component, but education is integral to developing the ability to competently engage in particular outdoor recreation activities. Not all outdoor education experiences are recreational in nature for program participants, but many are. In the case of physical education in particular, the goal is to teach students recreation activities, or adventure sports, in which they might engage for the sake of maintaining healthy, physically active lifestyles.

Professional-Development Portfolio

When Bill entered the outdoor leadership program at his college, he soon discovered that many of the professions that he had considered before deciding on outdoor leadership as his career were related in many ways to outdoor leadership. He discovered that he would have to develop wilderness first aid skills to be a competent outdoor leader, skills based in the field of medicine. He realized that he was not simply a leader in the outdoors but also a teacher as he began to instruct others in canoeing, kayaking, and other adventure sports. He discovered that he would get to indulge his interest in history by teaching program participants about the natural

and cultural heritage of the areas in which they traveled as part of their activities. He also realized that the process of becoming a competent outdoor leader would entail an extensive journey of professional development.

Personal and professional development is a process that never ends. The purpose of professional development is to help practitioners in the field progress from peripheral to full participation—to progress from being a novice to being an expert—in the profession. It is intended to help practitioners develop the mastery needed to be competent, qualified professionals.

One of the essential qualities of an effective outdoor leader is the ability to recognize one's abilities and limitations within a situation and define areas for personal and professional growth. This book offers you an opportunity to do just that. Each chapter includes professional-development exercises that comprise a professional-development portfolio. As you progress through each of the following chapters, you will be asked to assess where you are in your development as a leader. The professional-development portfolio exercises encourage you to assess your strengths and weaknesses in different areas of expertise, your motivations for becoming an outdoor leader, your attitudes about particular social and cultural issues, and your conceptions of leadership, morality, and cultural diversity, among other things. Most importantly, in this process you will be asked to identify areas for future growth and development.

Professional-Development Portfolio Activity

Write a short essay describing leadership experiences you have had in the past. They can be personal, professional, volunteer, or paid experiences. They can be experiences that have occurred within the context of outdoor education and recreation or within any other context.

Summary

Outdoor leadership is the practice of leading individuals and groups into what Petzoldt (1984) refers to as the "wild outdoors." Effective outdoor leadership ensures participant safety, preservation of the natural environment, and positive outcomes for group participants. Outdoor leadership is practiced primarily within the context of outdoor education and outdoor recreation. The goals of outdoor recreation are leisure oriented. Outdoor recreation activities are physically active leisure experiences that occur in the outdoors. The goals of outdoor education are twofold: to create opportunities for personal and interpersonal growth and to create opportunities for people to learn about the natural environment.

This text is focused on assisting you in becoming an effective outdoor leader, which involves a process of self-reflection that will help you determine areas of growth in your development as a leader. As Bill realized, one of the most exciting aspects of outdoor leadership is the opportunities that it provides not only for adventure in the traditional sense but also for the self-discovery and growth, both personal and professional, that go along with that adventure. Enjoy the journey!

Selected References

Aristotle. 1985. *Nichomachean ethics*. Trans. T. Irwin. Indianapolis: Hackett.

Association for Experiential Education. 2005. What is experiential ed? AEE Web site: www.aee.org.

Carley, R. 2001. *Wilderness A to Z: An essential guide to the great outdoors*. New York: Simon and Schuster.

Cordes, K.A., and H.M. Ibrahim. 1999. *Applications in recreation and leisure: For today and the future*. 2nd ed. Boston: WCB/McGraw-Hill.

Edington, C.R., D.J. Jordan, D.G. DeGraf, and S.R. Edington. 2002. *Leisure and life satisfaction: Foundational perspectives*. 3rd ed. Boston: McGraw-Hill.

Ewert, A.W. 1989. *Outdoor adventure pursuits: Foundations, models, and theories*. Columbus, OH: Publishing Horizons.

Ford, B., and Blanchard, J. 1993. *Leadership and administration of outdoor pursuits*. 2nd ed. State College, PA: Venture.

Ford, P. 1981. *Principles and practices of outdoor/environmental education*. New York: Wiley.

Golley, F. 1998. *A primer for environmental literacy*. New Haven, CT: Yale University Press.

Hunt, J.S. 1990. Philosophy of adventure education. In *Adventure education*, ed. J.C. Miles and S. Priest, 119-128. State College, PA: Venture.

James, T. 1995. The only mountain worth climbing: An historical and philosophical exploration of Outward Bound and its link to education. In *Fieldwork: An expeditionary learning Outward Bound reader, volume 1*, ed. E. Cousins and M. Rogers. Dubuque, IA: Kendall/Hunt.

Jensen, C.R. 1995. *Outdoor recreation in America*. 5th ed. Champaign, IL: Human Kinetics.

Jordan, D.J. 1999. *Leadership in leisure services: Making a difference*. State College, PA: Venture.

Kelly, J.R. 1982. *Leisure*. Englewood Cliffs, NJ: Prentice Hall.

Manning, R.E. 1986. *Studies in outdoor recreation: Search and research for satisfaction*. Corvallis, OR: Oregon State University Press.

Murphy, J.F. 1981. *Concepts of leisure*. 2nd ed. Englewood Cliffs, NJ: Prentice Hall.

Neulinger, J. 1981. *The psychology of leisure*. 2nd ed. Springfield, IL: Charles C Thomas.

Orr, D.W. 1992. *Ecological literacy: Education and transition to a post-modern world*. Albany, NY: SUNY Press.

Petzoldt, P. 1984. *The new wilderness handbook*. New York: Norton.

Phipps, M. 1985. Adventure, an inner journey to the self: The psychology of adventure expressed in Jungian terms. *Adventure Education Journal* 2(4/5): 11-17.

Priest, S., and M. Gass. 1997. *Effective leadership in adventure programming*. Champaign, IL: Human Kinetics.

Russell, R.V. 1996. *Pastimes: The context of contemporary leisure*. Chicago: Brown & Benchmark.

Smith, G.A., and D.R. Williams. 1999. Re-engaging culture and ecology. In *Ecological education in action: On weaving education, culture, and the environment*, ed. G.A. Smith and D.R. Williams, 1-20. New York: SUNY Press.

Volk, T. 1993. Educating for responsible environmental behavior. In *Environmental education teacher resource handbook: A practical guide for K-12 environmental education*, ed. R.J. Wilke. Millwood, NY: Kraus International.

Wall, G., ed. 1989. *Outdoor recreation in Canada*. Toronto: Wiley.

chapter 2

History of Outdoor Leadership

" There is properly no history; only biography. " —Ralph Waldo Emerson

Chapter Concepts

- Sense of heritage—Our heritage in the field of outdoor leadership is based on the accomplishments of those individuals and organizations who have helped shape the profession.
- Sense of purpose—Understanding the history of outdoor leadership helps us gain a sense of our own place and purpose within the profession as well as our potential to contribute to its development.
- Breadth of the profession—This chapter's historical sketch illustrates some of the contexts in which outdoor leadership takes place.

The chapter concepts relate to the following core competencies:

- Foundational knowledge (CC-1)—The chapter concepts are drawn directly from this competency. Sense of purpose, sense of heritage, and awareness of the breadth of the profession can all be gained from studying the history of the profession.
- Self-awareness and professional conduct (CC-2)—Understanding your history is an essential element in self-awareness, both personally and professionally.

Anna was enrolled in an introductory course on outdoor leadership. One of her assignments was to interview an established professional in the field of outdoor leadership. She selected Sylvia, a woman who had been a great source of inspiration to her while growing up and who had actually encouraged Anna to enroll in the course. The goal of Anna's interview was to find out how Sylvia had gotten to where she was professionally, what inspired her to enter the field of outdoor leadership, and what words of wisdom she might have for aspiring outdoor leaders.

In the interview Anna discovered that Sylvia had not taken a straightforward path to her current position and that she originally had not even planned on pursuing outdoor leadership as her profession. Sylvia had majored in art education in college but spent as much time in the outdoors leading rock-climbing and backpacking trips for her college's outdoor program as she spent studying for her degree. She was offered a position as a lead instructor for a company specializing in outdoor education when she graduated from college. Following her passion for the outdoors, she took the position and worked with the company for 2 years. She spent another 2 years working as an instructor with Outward Bound and 3 more years working for the National Outdoor Leadership School.

The life of an outdoor leader can sometimes seem like a shiftless affair. Outdoor leaders sometimes only find seasonal work, working for outdoor schools or guide services during the summer and working for ski resorts, going to school, or traveling during the winter. This was the case for Sylvia, and she had grown tired of it. She began to look for a full-time position that offered a stable income and full benefits. She went to work as an assistant education director for a conservation organization and eventually worked her way up to the director's position, the position that she currently held. Anna had met Sylvia while participating in an environmental education program sponsored by this organization.

In talking with Sylvia about what inspired her to get into outdoor leadership, Anna discovered that initially it was simply a passion for being in the outdoors that had led Sylvia to forgo art education in favor of outdoor education. As time passed, however, Sylvia's reasons for remaining in the profession had grown, and her ability to make a difference in the way that people perceive and interact with the natural environment eventually came to serve as her primary source of inspiration. In her current position, Sylvia was able to increase participants' awareness of their influence on the natural environment and to encourage them to protect the environment. Sylvia felt part of a larger movement of people working toward the common goal of environmental preservation. She felt part of a broader heritage that extended to the start of the conservation movement with the establishment of such organizations as the Appalachian Mountain Club, the American Canoe Association, and the Sierra Club. She felt as though she was carrying on the work of

(continued)

(continued)

some of the nation's great environmentalists—John Muir, Aldo Leopold, Rachel Carson, Edward Abby, and others—in her work as education director at her conservation organization. She felt as though she was a part of history.

In sharing her words of wisdom, Sylvia encouraged aspiring outdoor leaders to recognize and work to fulfill their potential as leaders. She encouraged them to recognize their ability to make a difference in the world around them. She noted that many of the most influential members of the profession were influential because they simply sought to make a difference through their work as outdoor leaders. For Sylvia, this was the point of outdoor leadership. She also encour-

aged aspiring leaders to recognize the tradition into which they were entering. She encouraged them to become aware of the heritage of the profession and to participate in shaping the profession as their predecessors had done.

Anna was more impressed than ever with Sylvia following the interview. Sylvia had given her some things to think about. Anna began to consider her own potential as an outdoor leader. She became curious about how she might become a part of the tradition in the profession. She also began to explore ways in which she might make contributions of the sort that Sylvia and others had made through their work as outdoor leaders.

Hunt (1999) argues that the roots of adventure education extend at least as far back as ancient Greece. He traces the ideas on which outdoor education and recreation are based to the ideas of Plato and Aristotle and those of subsequent thinkers in Western philosophy. While Hunt is accurate in this argument, this text begins with the more recent development of the field of outdoor education and recreation. It begins in the late 19th and early 20th centuries with the development of **dude ranches** and guide services in the western United States and Canada, the Boy Scouts and Girl Scouts, and the organized camping movement. It also considers more recent developments in the field: the development of Outward Bound and the National Outdoor Leadership School and the professionalization of outdoor leadership.

Before we start, it is important to note that this chapter does not cover the development of outdoor leadership during the past 25 years. The reason for this is that a more contemporary view of the profession is provided in chapter 3. Also, numerous organizations are not addressed in this chapter that could be in portraying the history of outdoor leadership. In particular, professional associations, such as the American Canoe Association and the American Mountain Guides Association; conservation organizations, such as the Appalachian Mountain Club and the Sierra Club; and governmental agencies, such as the National Park Service and the National Forest Service, that have been instrumental in the development of outdoor leadership as a field are not addressed in this chapter. The influence of these organizations on the field of outdoor leadership

is considered in subsequent chapters, especially chapters 3 and 13.

This chapter considers some of the more central aspects of the development of the field. It is intended to provide an overview of the key players and organizations that were instrumental in the development of the profession in the United States.

Dude Ranches and Guide Services

The history of guide services spans centuries. Daniel Boone began guiding hunting parties in the Watagua Valley of eastern Tennessee in 1761 (Carley 2001). Mountain guiding originated in Europe in the late 1700s as individuals sought to make the first ascents of Europe's famous peaks. In 1786, Michel-Gabriel Piccard and his guide, Jacques Balmat, became the first to summit Mount Blanc in the French Alps—the highest mountain in western Europe—marking the beginning of the golden age of mountaineering (Ewert 1989).

Dude ranches and guide services began to develop in the American West during the late 1800s and early 1900s in response to the demand of Easterners and Europeans touring the West. Hotels were in short supply, so tourists began looking to ranches for accommodation and entertainment. Ranchers not only provided their guests with room and board, they also entertained them by guiding them into the surrounding countryside. The term *dude* was used in the West to refer to people from cities, specifically in the East. Women were referred to as *dudines* and their children as *dudettes.* Carley states, "Accepting paying guests at a working ranch is a uniquely American enterprise. Some trace the seeds of the idea to Bill Sublette, who in 1844 agreed to take a group of easterners to Brown's Hole in Montana for the summer for a genuine taste of western wilderness" (2001, p. 99). She notes that the first dude ranch is thought to be the Custer Trail Ranch near the site of Custer's last stand at Little Bighorn near Medora, North Dakota.

An example of a guide service that emerged along with the emergence of tourism and dude ranches in the West is the American School of Mountaineering, which was established by Paul Petzoldt in 1929. This is a prominent example because of the influence of Petzoldt on the field of outdoor leadership over the course of his life. Petzoldt's guide service initially catered to guests of dude ranches in the area of Jackson Hole, Wyoming, during the early 20th century. At 16 years of age, Petzoldt and his friend Ralph Herron became the fourth group of climbers to summit the Grand Teton in Jackson Hole. It was a remarkable and harrowing feat for a couple of teenagers, a feat that gained the two a great deal of respect and notoriety among the folks of Jackson Hole. Soon after this accomplishment, Petzoldt found himself guiding friends to the summit of the Grand Teton. The following summer, he earned $100 guiding two dudes to the summit of the Grand Teton. Having earned the equivalent of a season's wages pitching hay as a ranch hand in a single trip to the summit of the Grand Teton, Petzoldt had found a new profession. When the Grand Teton National Park was established in 1929, Petzoldt was awarded the park's mountain guiding concession. He initially named his guide service the American School of Mountaineering. The name changed to the Petzoldt-Exum Climbing School in 1931 when he invited Glenn Exum to become his assistant.

Other guide services grew up during the late 19th and early 20th centuries to cater to the demands of tourists. Because tourists relied on dude ranches for accommodation, these guide services were often operated in conjunction with dude ranches. With the eventual development of resorts, lodges, and hotels throughout the West, dude ranches became less central to tourism and less central to guide services in marketing their product. Dude ranches enjoyed their greatest popularity during the 1920s. The Dude Ranchers' Association was formed in 1926 with 35 original members from the Yellowstone National Park and Jackson Hole area (Dude Ranchers' Association 2002). They experienced a decline during World War II, as did America's national parks, but that decline proved to be temporary. The association now includes more than 100 member ranches from around the western United States and Canada. Dude ranches have even been celebrated in such Hollywood movies as *City Slickers,* starring Billy Crystal.

Today, there are numerous guide services and guide associations throughout the United States. Rafting companies guide clients down such scenic rivers as the Colorado River through the Grand Canyon and the New River in West Virginia. Climbing companies offer guide services and instruction in rock and ice climbing in such places as Rocky Mountain National Park in Colorado, the Grand Tetons of Wyoming, and Seneca Rocks, West Virginia. Dive shops teach scuba diving and offer guided trips in such places as the Florida Keys and Hawaii. Commercial sport fishing companies take clients on guided fishing trips in such places as southeast Alaska and Cape Hatteras, North Carolina. Guide services in these and other pursuits are found throughout the United States and around the world. Incidentally, the American School of Mountaineering established by Paul Petzoldt continues to operate today. The school is now called Exum Climbing Guides.

The feats associated with these guide services were not limited to men. A notable female pioneer in mountaineering and skiing was Ruth Dyar Mendenhall (1912-1989). Mendenhall wrote *Women on the Rocks* (1987), which offers a detailed account of her experiences as a skier and climber as well as the activities of the Ski Mountaineers and Rock Climbing section of the Sierra Club beginning in 1937. She set up pioneering routes in the Sierras and in Taquitz Rock during a time when alpine techniques were just being introduced. She was a climber, an alpinist, a backpacker, and a ski mountaineer.

Organized Camping Movement

The organized camping movement began in 1861 when Frederick William Gunn, founder and headmaster of the Gunnery School for Boys in Washington, Connecticut, organized a 2-week camping trip for his students. The first church camp was established by the Reverend George W. Hinckley of West Hartford, Connecticut, a decade or so later, first on Gardner's Island in

Wakefield, Rhode Island, and then more permanently in Hinckley, Maine. The first institutional camp, organized by Sumner F. Dudley in 1887, was sponsored by the YMCA. Dudley's first camp was located at Pine Point on Orange Lake near Newburgh, New York.

Laura Mattoon, a pioneer in the field of camping, started one of the first summer camps for girls in the United States in 1902. The camp was named Camp Kehonka. As head of science at New York City's Veltin School, Mattoon "wished to show her students a kind of growth and adventure that only the outdoors could offer" (Camp Kehonka n.d.). She began her first camp with eight campers. They slept in tents, built their own furniture, and swam and hiked in New Hampshire's pristine lakes and mountains. They lived close to nature and each other. Miss Mattoon "insisted that the dining room encompass a pine tree and that the corners of porches be reserved for spiders. Meals were served family style, and campers joined in planning trips, activities, and plays. Miss Mattoon believed in camping as a means of building character. She taught her campers the pleasures, values, and skills of outdoor life" (Camp Kehonka n.d.). She shared her experiences and knowledge in the publication of the *Camper's Guidance Manual*, which emphasized character development and skills in outdoor activities, canoeing, swimming, hiking, arts and crafts, music, drama, and nature studies. Camp Kehonka has become one of the oldest and finest girls' camps in the United States.

The Camp Directors' Association of America was established in 1910 as the primary professional association in the organized camping movement. Its name changed to the American Camping Association (ACA) in 1935. The organization now operates as a nonprofit national organization whose mission is "to enhance the quality of the experience for youth and adults in organized camping, to promote high professional practices in camp administration, and to interpret the values of organized camping to the public" (Meier and Mitchell 1993, p. 23). The ACA, based in Bradford Woods, Indiana, sponsors an annual national conference, the publication of *Camping Magazine,* and an annual *Guide to Accredited Camps,* among other services. Laura Mattoon was elected as the first salaried executive of the Camp Directors' Association of America in 1924. She served as secretary of the ACA for 15 years.

The camping movement has grown by leaps and bounds since its beginnings. The ACA reports the following statistics:

- Over 12,000 day and resident camps currently exist in the United States.
- Over 10 million children and adults attend camp in the United States each year.
- Camps employ more than a million people annually to serve in various leadership roles within their organizations.
- Nearly two-thirds of camps in the United States are sponsored by nonprofit youth agencies and religious organizations.
- Nearly one-third of camps are privately sponsored for-profit operations.
- Approximately 60% of camps in the United States are resident camps.
- Approximately 40% of camps are day camps.
- Over half of ACA-accredited camps sponsor challenge course activities.
- Approximately one-third of ACA-accredited camps offer extended trips as a part of the camp experience.
- The number of day camps in the United States has increased by approximately 90% since the 1980s.

Organizations that sponsor camps include the YMCA, the YWCA, the YMHA, the YWHA, Boy Scouts, Girl Scouts, 4-H, Easter Seal Society, various religious groups, private schools, and private companies.

Initially, organized camping was intended to complement the sponsoring organization in fulfilling its goals, goals that were typically either educational or spiritual in nature. Eventually, camps began to develop for purely recreational purposes. Many sponsors wanted to channel the energies of boys and girls into positive, wholesome activities that the outdoors could provide. Camping has since taken on a broader purpose. Meier and Mitchell (1993) have characterized the camping movement as a progressive movement intended to encourage campers to develop social responsibility, independence, self-control, and self-reliance. The purpose of developing these qualities is to engender the democratic ideals in young people, qualities that are essential to participation in our society.

Scouting Movement

In 1907, Lord Robert Baden-Powell founded the Boy Scouts. Baden-Powell had become famous as the hero of Mafeking during the Boer War in South

Africa at the turn of the 20th century. The Boer War was fought between the British and descendents of Dutch settlers (Boers) in the region from 1899-1902. The Boers were fighting to maintain their independence from the British in South Africa. With military support from Germany, the Boers enjoyed several successes early in the war. They managed to lay siege to three British garrisons in the towns of Ladysmith, Mafeking, and Kimberly. Baden-Powell was responsible for the garrison at Mafeking. Though his command was both outgunned and outnumbered, Baden-Powell successfully held off the enemy for 217 days while awaiting relief. British reinforcements eventually arrived in early 1900 and ended the Boer sieges. Baden-Powell returned to Britain as one of its most popular war heroes.

After returning home from war, Baden-Powell revised a book that he had written on scouting for British soldiers, turning it into an outdoor skills manual for boys. He invited 22 boys to participate in an outing on Brownsea Island along the English coast, and, the event proving a success, the Scouting movement was begun.

Baden-Powell's primary reason for establishing the Boy Scouts was to address what he perceived to be a decline in the physical and moral character of the British population at the time (MacDonald 1993; Skidelsky 1969). Though the British prevailed in the Boer War, British troops in general did not perform very well during the war. They seemed to suffer the constant bedevilment of a generally inferior enemy. Baden-Powell developed the Boy Scouts to build character in boys, as a way to prepare them to be physically, mentally, and morally strong members of society. Primary goals of the organization include preparing boys for citizenship, service, and leadership through the development of strong ethical character. Baden-Powell hoped to appeal to boys' "romantic longings" for adventure to enlist them for "Higher Things" (Skidelsky 1969, p. 214). While Baden-Powell worked to dispel criticism that the Boy Scouts was established merely to prepare boys for Britain's next war, "it is clear that he initially aimed to create citizens who would be useful in fortifying and defending the walls of the British Empire" (Martin, unpublished manuscript).

The Scouting movement experienced phenomenal growth during its first years of existence through effective organization and marketing. It quickly spread throughout the world and made its way to the United States in 1910 thanks to William Boyce. A number of individuals played influential roles in the development of the Boy Scouts of America. A couple of these pioneers of the movement were Daniel Carter Beard and Ernest Thompson Seton. Both of these men were naturalists and outdoorsmen, and both had already established youth organizations of their own that held goals similar to those of the Boy Scouts. Seton had established an organization known as the Woodcraft Indians, and Beard had established an organization known as the Sons of Daniel Boone. Both of these men became involved with the Scouting movement in America, however, and soon merged their organizations with the Boy Scouts.

Along with establishing the Boy Scouts in Britain, Baden-Powell helped to establish an organization in 1911 known as the Camp Fire Girls. Juliette Gordan Low introduced the Camp Fire Girls in the United States in 1912. The Camp Fire Girls eventually became known as the Girl Guides in Great Britain and as the Girl Scouts in the United States.

The Boy Scouts of America (2005) reports that, including Cub Scouts, it had over 3 million total members in 2004. More than 1 million adults volunteered to serve the Boy Scouts in some leadership capacity in 2004 and nearly 1 million boys attended camps that the Boy Scouts sponsors around the United States in 2004. The Girl Scouts of the USA (2005) reports that it has nearly 2.8 million members. The organization also reports that nearly 1 million adult volunteers serve in leadership capacities in the organization each year.

Outward Bound Movement

Much of what is written on the history of Outward Bound portrays the organization's origins as a response to the high casualty rate among young British castaways during World War II. Laurence Holt, one of Britain's shipping tycoons, lamented the passing of the old square-rigged sailing vessels from contemporary shipping fleets. Contemporary seamen were mechanics, engineers, and technicians who seldom encountered the raw nature of the sea. Insulated within the walls of their modern steam frigates, they had little opportunity to practice the old craft of seamanship. When shipwrecked, those who were not trained to handle the raw elements of the sea fared far worse than the old salts who were tried and true on bygone sailing rigs. Younger sailors generally did not have the skill to navigate lifeboats when stranded at sea (Hogan 1968; Miner and Boldt 1981; Wilson 1981). Holt's concern stemmed from the constant dispatch of young sailors into the Atlantic, particularly during the Battle of the Atlantic between 1939 and 1945, and their likelihood of meeting hazards for which they were unprepared. He once remarked, "I would rather entrust the lowering of a lifeboat in mid-Atlantic to a sail-trained octogenarian than to a young sea technician who is competently trained in the modern way but has never been sprayed by salt water" (Miner and Boldt 1981, p. 32).

Another factor to which this high casualty rate was attributed was the general physical and moral weakness perceived to exist in the British population at the time. Younger castaways were considered less capable of bearing the hardships of the sea. Despair can quickly take root amid seemingly insurmountable obstacles. Moral fortitude and confidence can wane and give way to feelings of hopelessness; individual will can suffer paralysis amid hardships such as those endured by castaways in the Battle of the Atlantic (Hogan 1968; Miner and Boldt 1981; Wilson 1981).

Kurt Hahn provided Holt with a method for better preparing his merchant marines for the hardships of the sea. As Martin notes, "Hahn encouraged Holt to fund a sea school in Aberdovey, Wales, that would offer courses in which young men could confront physical challenges and survival situations that would test their character and give them the knowledge and confidence needed to carry on in similar situations" (unpublished manuscript). In 1941, with financing from Holt, Hahn established the first Outward Bound school. Outward Bound initially served as a survival school; however, it ultimately served a broader purpose. Holt illustrates this broader purpose: "The training at Aberdovey must be less a training *for* the sea than *through* the sea, and so benefit all walks of life" (Miner and Boldt 1981, p. 33). Outward Bound was a part of a broader educational movement. Hahn was engaged in a number of educational endeavors throughout

Sailboats used by Outward Bound are modeled after the lifeboats used on ships during World War II.

his lifetime that sought to provide students with the moral strength to serve as responsible and caring members of the broader society. As Miner and Boldt note, Hahn practiced an educational philosophy that was intended "to enable the student to make intelligent judgments and to develop the inherent strengths of selfhood . . . to build character, in the old-fashioned phrase" (1981, pp. 41-42).

Since its creation, Outward Bound has opened schools in numerous countries around the world. Charles Froelicher and Josh Miner introduced Outward Bound in the United States in 1962 with the creation of the Colorado Outward Bound school. Four other Outward Bound schools soon followed: the Hurricane Island Outward Bound school in Maine, the North Carolina Outward Bound school,

Learning Activity 2.1

Get in a group of three. Give a 10- to 15-minute presentation on a historical figure in the field of outdoor leadership. Give a biographical sketch of the person, identify the person's key contributions to the development of the profession, and consider the implications of these contributions. Why was this person important to the profession and to society? Where would the profession and society be without them?

1786—Michel-Gabriel Piccard and his guide, Jacques Balmat, become the first to summit Mount Blanc, marking the beginning of the golden age of mountaineering.

1861—Frederick William Gunn, founder and headmaster of the Gunnery School for Boys in Washington, Connecticut, organizes a 2-week camping trip for his students, initiating the organized camping movement.

1887—The YMCA sponsors the first institutional camp at Pine Point on Orange Lake near Newburgh, New York, under the direction of Sumner F. Dudley.

1902—Laura Mattoon founds Camp Kehonka for girls.

1907—The Boy Scouts are founded in Great Britain by Lord Robert Baden-Powell.

1910—Boy Scouts are brought to the United States by William Boyce.

1910—The Camp Directors' Association of America is established.

1911—The Camp Fire Girls, later known as the Girl Guides, are founded in Great Britain with the help of Baden-Powell.

1912—The Girl Guides, later known as the Girl Scouts, are introduced in the United States by Juliette Gordon Low.

1926—The Dude Ranchers' Association is established.

1929—Paul Petzoldt founds the American School of Mountaineering, now called Exum Climbing Guides.

1935—The Camp Directors' Association of America becomes the American Camping Association.

1941—The first Outward Bound school is founded by Kurt Hahn in Aberdovey, Wales.

1962—The Colorado Outward Bound school is founded by Josh Miner.

1965—National Outdoor Leadership School (NOLS) is founded by Paul Petzoldt.

1977—The Wilderness Education Association (WEA) is founded by Paul Petzoldt, Chuck Gregory, Robert Christie, and Frank Lupton.

Figure 2.1 Key moments in the development of the profession of outdoor leadership.

the Voyager Outward Bound school in Minnesota, and the Pacific Crest Outward Bound school in Oregon. The Colorado and Pacific Crest Outward Bound schools recently merged to become Outward Bound West. The schools are all overseen by an organization known as Outward Bound USA. The organization reports that it currently serves over 60,000 students per year and that it has served over 500,000 in its 42-year history (Outward Bound USA 2005).

Professionalization of Outdoor Leadership

Paul Petzoldt, who founded the American School of Mountaineering in the Grand Tetons in 1929, has arguably had a greater influence on the development of outdoor leadership as a profession in the United States than any other person. He was involved in the establishment of the first Outward Bound school in the United States, serving as its chief instructor during the early 1960s. He established the National Outdoor Leadership School (NOLS) in Lander, Wyoming, in 1965 to promote the development of outdoor leaders. The establishment of NOLS represented the first real attempt to promote outdoor leadership as a profession. Recounting his motivation for developing NOLS, Petzoldt states that, while working as chief instructor for the Colorado Outward Bound school, he was

> shocked into the realization that nobody had really trained outdoorsmen in America . . . we couldn't hire anyone that met my standards. We could hire

Paul Petzoldt.

people who knew how to do one thing well: climb mountains, fish, cross wild rivers, cook plain rations, recognize flora and fauna, read topographical maps, and teach and motivate. But we could not find a person who had been trained in all those things! They didn't exist. I thought the best thing I could do for American youth, if they were to use the wild outdoors, was to prepare better leaders for such experiences. (Ewert 1989, p. 29)

Petzoldt's promotion of outdoor leadership as a profession is one of his greatest contributions to the field. Since its establishment, NOLS has become one of the most reputable organizations of its kind in the United States and around the world. The organization reports that it has graduated over 75,000 students in its 40-year history and that it employs nearly 800 individuals worldwide (Wood 2005).

Petzoldt's promotion of outdoor leadership as a profession did not stop with the establishment of NOLS. In the mid-1970s, Petzoldt left NOLS due to conflicts with the NOLS board of trustees. Seeking new ways to promote the development of the profession, Petzoldt, along with Chuck Gregory, Robert Christie, and Frank Lupton, founded the Wilderness Education Association (WEA) in 1977. This organization was designed to offer nationally recognized professional certification in outdoor leadership. The mission of the WEA is to promote "the professionalism of outdoor leadership and to thereby improve the safety of outdoor trips and to enhance the conservation of the wild outdoors" (Berman and Teeters 2002). The organization is an affiliation of colleges and universities as well as other organizations around the country that seek to fulfill the organization's mission through the implementation of courses to train and certify outdoor leaders. The organization was born from a commitment to preserve the United States' natural areas through responsible use of these areas. The WEA was originally named the Wilderness Use Education Association to emphasize the role of education in responsible use. The name of the organization eventually changed, but the mission remains the same. The organization was born from a commitment to fulfill the need for leaders capable of taking groups into the outdoors without harming themselves or the surrounding environment. WEA is unique in that colleges, universities, and outdoor education programs form an affiliate network to offer outdoor leadership training courses. WEA's training programs are based on an 18-point curriculum found in their curriculum guide, *The Backcountry Classroom.*

The advantage of this organization in comparison to NOLS is that it is able to offer less expensive courses through its affiliate network. However, as a larger organization, NOLS can offer courses that are more diverse in activity options and course environments.

Summary

To tell the story of the development of outdoor leadership as a profession, we have focused on the stories of individuals and organizations that have helped to shape the profession. Only through the stories of these individuals and organizations can we get a sense of the development of the profession. As mentioned, it is impossible to cover the full scope of the history of the profession in a single chapter of this book. The story told here is far from fully inclusive. It focuses only on some of the primary personalities and organizations that have thus

Professional-Development Portfolio Activities

1. Write a short essay in which you describe people, places, and pieces of literature that have influenced your direction in life. How did their influence lead you to this course on outdoor leadership?

2. Interview an outdoor leader who has been working as a professional in the field for at least 10 years. Report the findings of your interview in a short essay. Focus on the career path that the interviewee followed in arriving at his or her current position in the field, why he or she got into the field, sources of inspiration in his or her work as an outdoor leader, and words of wisdom for prospective outdoor leaders.

far shaped the development of the industry and covers essential developments in the field.

The next chapter picks up where this chapter ends in describing organizations that have been influential in the development of outdoor leadership as a field. While the next chapter does not offer an extensive history of each of these organizations, it identifies the nature and the role of each in shaping the profession. It is intended to give a sense of the scope of outdoor leadership as well as the array of professional opportunities that are available in the field.

After her interview with Sylvia, Anna began to develop a sense of her own potential for participating in the development of the profession. She began to realize that, like Sylvia, she could become a part of the legacy that had been established by such people as Laura Matoon, Kurt Hahn, and Paul Petzoldt. After all, these people were only human, humans who had simply sought to make a difference in the world around them through their work. This sense of potential began to take shape as a primary motivation for Anna as she considered pursuing a career in outdoor leadership.

Selected References

Baden-Powell, R. 1909. *Yarns for Boy Scouts*. London: Pearson.

Berman, D., and C. Teeters, eds. 2002. *WEA affiliate handbook*. 7th edition. Bloomington, IN: WEA National Office.

Boy Scouts of America. 2005. Facts and figures. Boy Scouts of America National Council Web site: www.scouting.org.

Camp Kehonka. n.d. Laura Mattoon. Camp Kehonka Web site: http://kehonka.com/laura_mattoon.htm.

Carley, R. 2001. *Wilderness A to Z: An essential guide to the great outdoors*. New York: Simon & Schuster.

Drury, J.K., and B.F. Bonney. 1992. *The backcountry classroom: Lesson plans for teaching in the wilderness*. Merrillville, IN: ICS Books.

Dude Ranchers' Association. 2002. DRA info—origins of dude ranching. DRA Web site: www.duderanch.org.

Ewert, A.W. 1989. *Outdoor adventure pursuits: Foundations, models, and theories*. Columbus, OH: Publishing Horizons.

Girl Scouts of the USA. 2005. Who we are—Facts page. Girl Scouts of the USA Web site: www.girlscouts.org.

Hahn, K. 1947. Training for and through the sea. Address given to the Honourable Mariners' Company in Glasgow, February 10.

Hahn, K. 1965. Outward Bound. Address given to a Conference at Harrogate, May 9. Outward Bound Trust.

Hogan, J.M. 1968. *Impelled into experience: The story of the Outward Bound schools*. London: Educational Productions.

Hunt, J.S. 1999. Philosophy of adventure education. In *Adventure education*, 2nd ed., eds. J.C. Miles and S. Priest, 119-128. State College, PA: Venture.

James, T. 1989. *Outward Bound and public education*. Providence, RI: Education Department, Brown University.

James, T. 1990. Kurt Hahn and the aims of education. *Journal of Experiential Education*, 13(1): 6-13.

James, T. 1995. The only mountain worth climbing. In *Fieldwork: An expeditionary learning Outward Bound reader*, vol. 1, ed. E. Cousins and M. Rodgers. Dubuque, IA: Kendall/Hunt.

MacDonald, R.H. 1993. *Sons of the empire: The frontier and the Boy Scout movement, 1890 to 1918*. Toronto: University of Toronto Press.

Macleod, D.I. 1983. *Building character in the American boy: The Boy Scouts, YMCA, and their forerunners, 1870 to 1920*. Madison, WI: University of Wisconsin Press.

Martin, B. Ideology and adventure education: Crafting the ideal citizen. Unpublished manuscript.

Meier, J.F., and V.A. Mitchell. 1993. *Camp counseling: Leadership and programming for organized camp*. 7th ed. Long Grove, IL: Waveland Press.

Mendenhall, R.D. 1987, October. Women on the rocks, way back then. Unpublished essay.

Miner, J., and J. Boldt. 1981. *Outward Bound USA: Learning through experience in adventure-based education*. New York: Morrow.

Outward Bound USA. 2005. About Outward Bound. Outward Bound USA Web site: www.outwardbound.org.

Ringholz, R.C. 1997. *On belay! The life of legendary mountaineer Paul Petzoldt*. Seattle: Mountaineers.

Rosenthal, M. 1984. *The character factory: Baden-Powell and the origins of the Boy Scout movement*. New York: Pantheon Books.

Skidelsky, R. 1969. *English progressive schools*. Baltimore: Penguin Books.

Wilson, R. 1981. *Inside Outward Bound*. Charlotte, NC: East Woods.

Wood, H. 2005. NOLS history. NOLS Web site: www.nols.edu.

chapter 3

Professional Development

" Anyone can dabble, but once you've made that commitment, your blood has that particular thing in it, and it's very hard for people to stop you. " —**Bill Cosby**

Chapter Concepts

- Elements of a profession—People who work in the outdoors are professionals if they subscribe to the behaviors that comprise a profession.

- Places outdoor professionals work—There are many venues where outdoor professionals can seek employment. The range of opportunity fits most interests and abilities.

- Professional associations for outdoor professionals—Professional organizations create opportunities to share with like-minded people and to maintain up-to-date information about trends and issues.

The chapter concepts relate to the following core competencies:

- Foundational knowledge (CC-1)—Knowledge of how professions are established and where outdoor programs are located provides insight to the broad scope of opportunities involving outdoor leadership.

- Self-awareness and professional conduct (CC-2)—Awareness of what professionals do and how they can create quality programs in the outdoors is important for outdoor leaders.

Abby was excited. Her professor had invited her to attend an outdoor conference with several other students. The promise of meeting professionals and other students who aspired toward a future as outdoor leaders was the best opportunity she could imagine. On the way to the conference, they all chatted about their dreams, what to expect at the conference, and how to navigate as a group. Abby's professor assured all of them that she would introduce them to others as much as possible, but they should be prepared to introduce themselves and be willing to ask questions to make the most of the experience. After they arrived at the site, which was a large camplike facility, the group checked into their cabin and began walking around greeting other attendees. They ate together that first evening and began to talk with people from other groups. After the opening speeches the group was very excited about the days ahead and picked a variety of sessions to attend.

By the end of the second day, Abby was in tears. Everyone seemed to have more experience than she did. Her dream of being a professional in the outdoors seemed too daunting to manage and now she had no idea what she would do with her life. She had attended sessions, talked to others, and gone to the career center and everywhere she felt inadequate. It seemed to her that all the students at the conference knew more, had a lot of field experience, and were confident outdoor leaders.

Abby's professor sat with her before they left the conference. She tried to explain that everyone had to begin somewhere. Just because others already had

some experience did not exclude Abby from seeking a future position. She asked Abby if she still wanted to work as an outdoor leader and Abby said she could not picture herself doing anything else. Her professor told her that if being an outdoor leader was her dream, it was time to launch it! Looking at job descriptions, they began to list the type of experiences and credentials that Abby would need to enter the field. Some she could obtain at her university while others she could get by using her vacations, practicums, and internship experiences wisely. By starting with water-based activities, which Abby was most interested in, she could see that by the time she graduated she could probably be hired in an entry-level position. She participated in trainings, sought summer jobs and practicums that would help her obtain a variety of skills, and ultimately completed an internship in a large municipal recreation department in Colorado. The department had a unit that sponsored many different outdoor programs for the community. In this position, Abby could lead short outings in a safe environment. After graduation Abby was hired by a program for at-risk youth and she added to her skill base in leadership, rafting, and backpacking. After 2 years with the program, Abby moved on to a commercial rafting company in the southeast.

When she visited her professor, she was almost unrecognizable. The slightly overweight, unskilled, and overwhelmed girl had blossomed into a confident, fit, and talented raft guide. She loved her life and was anticipating going to international rivers with another company during the winter. Even though Abby had a moment of desperation and disappointment at the

(continued)

(continued)

conference, she committed herself to finding out what she needed to do, she invested in her future by creating a workable plan to acquire the skills and experiences necessary, and she continued to pay attention to current practices once she was in the field. She looked at jobs as ways to increase and improve her skills. She laughed with her teacher about that first outdoor conference she attended. Abby said that she seeks out students at conferences and passes along encouraging words. She is not sure if any of the students she has talked to over the years have been successful in following their dreams. What she is sure of is that she started out with no idea about what being an outdoor leader entailed and is now living her dream.

Being an outdoor professional involves more than being paid to do a job. It is more than an occupation or attitude. Being a professional requires knowledge of the field, a philosophy of the value of the field, and a vision for how individuals contribute to the field. Most professionals understand their responsibilities to their clients. In outdoor leadership the responsibilities are huge—we lead others through activities with an element of risk in an effort to help participants develop their potential as human beings. Certainly parents, family members, and friends expect an outdoor leader to provide a valuable experience for their loved one and trust us to lead others safely and enjoyably in the outdoors. However, if you ask the majority of people if outdoor leadership is a profession, they would answer no!

By examining what criteria establish a profession, we can determine if outdoor leadership falls in the parameters of a profession. The key concepts are the elements that make up a profession, the organizations that support outdoor leadership as a profession, and the issues concerning certification and accreditation, as well as how to begin developing yourself as a professional.

Elements of a Profession

Certain elements determine whether a discipline or a vocation is a true profession. These elements include the following:

- A body of knowledge that includes scientific bases, values, and applied skills.

- Organizations and institutions that transmit professional knowledge. This category includes colleges and universities, accrediting bodies, and professional organizations.

- Public sanction, meaning that the general population views the occupation as a profession. Certification enhances public opinion.

- Code of ethics, or values and behaviors that are supported by a particular group of professionals. Some view a code of ethics as a standard of conduct.

- Commitment to professional ideals, meaning that members of a profession accept rights, responsibilities, and obligations because they share common values about the field.

Achieving certifications is a step toward becoming a professional.

Elements of Outdoor Leadership as a Profession

The question remains of whether outdoor leadership is a profession. Using the elements of a profession as criteria for a profession, we can examine outdoor leadership.

Body of Knowledge

Outdoor leadership has a body of knowledge, but it is limited in size and scope. A body of knowledge is developed through scientific research and the subsequent development of theories. For the most part, knowledge about outdoor leadership comes from many other disciplines such as psychology, sociology, management, environmental science, education, recreation, geography, geology, meteorology, and philosophy. Using other bodies of knowledge is appropriate and advances the field considerably, but specific research on outdoor leadership is also important. In certain parts of the field there is a scientific basis for what we do. For example, much is known about human effects on land, flora, and fauna—too much traffic in one area degrades the environment. Leave No Trace skills are all based on scientific research. A variety of educational methods and theories are also applied to outdoor leadership. However, when it comes to examining the effects of an outdoor experience on a person, the effectiveness of outdoor leadership, or ethical behaviors in the outdoors, the research is limited. It is difficult to gather data when group sizes are small and researchers do not want to intrude on a course.

Organizations and Institutions

Organizations and institutions that transmit a profession's knowledge are a vital part of a profession. Educational organizations like Outward Bound, the National Outdoor Leadership School (NOLS), the Wilderness Education Association (WEA), the American Camp Association (ACA), the American Mountain Guide Association (AMGA), and the Association for Challenge Course Technology (ACCT) offer skill and leadership courses.

There are numerous professional organizations for outdoor leaders, including the Association for Experiential Education (AEE), the Association for Outdoor Recreation and Education (AORE), the National Association of Interpreters (NAI), the American Alliance for Health, Physical Education, Recreation and Dance (AAHPERD), the National Intramural-Recreational Sports Association (NIRSA), and the Association of College Unions International (ACUI).

Several organizations offer programs for accreditation, such as the AEE and AMGA. The ACA accredits camps. Professional associations serve in advocacy roles; provide educational opportunities, a community of professionals, and networking opportunities; promote standards; support research efforts; and recognize outstanding professionals.

Colleges and universities offer several avenues to pursue outdoor leadership. There are now undergraduate degree programs in outdoor leadership. Some colleges offer an emphasis in outdoor leadership through a recreation or physical education department. Related fields such as environmental education have also become popular. Graduate programs expand the possibilities with degrees in experiential education, counseling, natural resource management, and wilderness therapy as well as outdoor leadership. Many outdoor leaders have liberal arts degrees and have developed the technical skills needed to be successful in the field. There is no single path into the field.

Public Acceptance of Outdoor Leadership as a Profession

Does the public view outdoor leadership as a profession? Although no one wants to send their child into the outdoors with someone who is not qualified, most people probably would not categorize outdoor leadership as a profession. People outside the field often see outdoor leadership as a fun time and rarely think about or acknowledge all the training and responsibility that is involved. There is a host of certifications a person can acquire to demonstrate a minimum level of ability that enhances the view of their job. The WEA offers certification in outdoor leadership. The AMGA offers a series of certifications for climbing. Similarly, the American Canoeing Association offers flat-water and white-water certifications. There are certifications for scuba diving and sailing, wilderness medicine, and challenge course facilitation. With certifications and strict criteria for being an outdoor leader the public will eventually view the field differently and will respect the effort it takes to become an outdoor leader.

Code of Ethics

Many professions have a code of ethics that consists of written rules that members are supposed to follow. The code indicates a set of beliefs or a code of conduct that is supported by professionals in that field. There is no one code of ethics for all outdoor professionals. Many outdoor agencies incorporate appropriate behavior in their policies and procedures. However, there are no professional sanctions for anyone who makes an error in performing an outdoor leadership job. In a profession such as medicine or law if a person makes an ethical or professional error their license can be revoked. That is not the case in outdoor leadership because there is no uniform professional code of ethics or standards for behavior. Such dictums are left to individual organizations.

The National Recreation and Park Association (NRPA) has developed a code of ethics (see figure 3.1) to enhance the professionalism of the association and to assist its members in developing consistent responses to ethical issues (Clark 1995). A somewhat similar code of ethics exists for the therapeutic adventure professional who is a member of the AEE (see figure 3.2).

Ethical guidelines for outdoor leaders have been identified as one component of the AEE accreditation process (Williamson and Gass 1993). While these guidelines show that the field of outdoor leadership supports certain practices, they were not established as an ethical code of conduct. Development of such a code needs continued attention.

Commitment to Professional Ideals

Each profession has certain expectations for those engaged in it. Sometimes these expectations mean adding knowledge or a technique to existing practices. Sometimes they mean supporting and advocating for the group at community, state, or national levels. Sometimes they mean serving the profession in leadership roles, many of which are voluntary. Professions have a duty toward clients, other professionals, and society. Because outdoor leaders work in so many areas their obligation may be to a small part of the profession or to a specialized group of participants. For example, a person may only be interested in indoor climbing walls and not in mountaineering or outdoor climbing—a very specific part of the overall profession. In addition, duty can be an obligation to participants that is recognized by the legal system. Whether outdoor leaders are volunteers or professionals, their actions must be those of prudent professionals who take steps to protect the people they serve.

The National Recreation and Park Association (NRPA) has provided leadership to the nation in fostering the expansion of recreation and parks. NRPA has stressed the value of recreation, both active and passive, for individual growth and development. Its members are dedicated to the common cause of assuring that people of all ages and abilities have the opportunity to find the most satisfying use of their leisure time and enjoy an improved quality of life.

The association has consistently affirmed the importance of well-informed and professionally trained personnel to continually improve the administration of recreation and park programs. Members of NRPA are encouraged to support the efforts of the association and profession by supporting state affiliate and national activities and participating in continuing education opportunities, certification, and accreditation.

Membership in NRPA carries with it special responsibilities to the public at large and to the specific communities and agencies in which recreation and park services are offered. As a member of the National Recreation and Park Association, I accept and agree to abide by this Code of Ethics and pledge myself to do the following:

- Adhere to the highest standards of integrity and honesty in all public and personal activities to inspire public confidence and trust.
- Strive for personal and professional excellence and encourage the professional development of associates and students.
- Strive for the highest standards of professional competence, fairness, impartiality, efficiency, effectiveness, and fiscal responsibility.
- Avoid any interest or activity that is in conflict with the performance of job responsibilities.
- Promote the public interest and avoid personal gain or profit from the performance of job duties and responsibilities.
- Support equal employment opportunities.

Figure 3.1 The National Recreation and Park Association professional code of ethics.

Courtesy of the National Recreation and Park Association (NRPA).

The code of ethics for the Association for Experiential Education (AEE) includes these categories:

- Competence—Professionals provide services only within the boundaries of their competence based on education, training, supervision, experience, and practice. They also make efforts to maintain knowledge, practice, and skills they use.

- Integrity—Professionals are fair, honest, and respect others; they don't make false, misleading, or deceptive statements. They strive to be aware of their own belief systems, values, needs, and limitations and the effect of these on their work.

- Professional responsibility—Professionals uphold ethical principles of conduct, clarify their roles and obligations, accept responsibility for their behavior and decisions, and adapt their methods to the needs of different populations.

- Respect for people's rights and dignity—Professionals respect the fundamental rights, dignity, and worth of all people. These include the rights of individuals to privacy, confidentiality, and self-determination. Professionals strive to be sensitive to cultural and individual differences, including those due to age, gender, race, ethnicity, national origin, religion, sexual preference, disability, and socioeconomic status. Professionals do not engage in sexual or other harassment or exploitation of participants, students, trainees, supervisees, employees, colleagues, research subjects, and so on.

- Concern for welfare—Professionals are sensitive to real and ascribed differences in power between themselves and their participants and avoid exploiting or misleading other people during or after professional relationships.

- Social responsibility—Professionals are aware of their professional responsibilities to the community and society in which they work and live. Professionals also encourage the development of standards and policies that serve the interests of participants and the public.

Figure 3.2   The Association for Experiential Education code of ethics.

Printed with permission of the Association for Experiential Education (AEE). To learn more about AEE, go to www.aee.org.

A major concern in our field is determining professional competence and deciding who the client is: Is it the participant, the organization for which we work, or someone else?

Many areas related to becoming a profession still need to be discussed by practicing outdoor leaders. Following are a few areas that can contribute to building and maintaining a profession:

- Identifying professional incompetence and removing the culprits from service is a risk management concern.

- Researching what we do and possible consequences is important because proof of effects and understanding processes is essential to add credibility to the field.

- Scarcity of human and financial resources means finding qualified personnel is difficult. In addition, physical resources are becoming more difficult to access. Higher permit fees or a total ban on certain areas limits outdoor opportunities for programs.

People who work in outdoor pursuits have made great progress as members of an emerging profession, and for those who wish to work as professionals in the field, the future is bright. The field needs the best leaders, the best educators, and the best researchers, people who strive for excellence every day and who have a strong sense of integrity. Most of all the field needs people who have passion for the field and for sharing all that can be learned through, in, and about the outdoors. It is a unique combination of attributes that makes an outdoor leader. So if, like Abby, you dream about being an outdoor leader, it is time for you to take steps toward making that dream a reality. Like Abby's professor said, "Launch it!"

Steps Toward Professionalism

Outdoor leadership is a quickly emerging profession. It already meets many criteria that determine whether a field is a profession. The evolution of a field into a profession takes time and involves adding higher standards to demonstrate abilities. The practices of registration, certification, accreditation, and licensure, a hierarchy of standards, also contribute to the development of a profession.

Registration

Registration is simply a list of people who consider themselves professionals in the field. There may or may not be criteria for adding your name to the list. For example, being a paid member of a professional organization or working full time in the field may suffice.

Certification

Certification is evidence that a person has a minimum level of skill. Certification can be specific, like basic canoeing, or it can be more generalized. A professional organization backs the certification criteria to meet the standard. Certifications can be local—for example, you may be certified as a challenge course facilitator on a specific course—and they can also be at the state or national level. Certification for outdoor leaders is still contentious. Although the WEA certifies outdoor leaders based on their abilities, judgment, and leadership qualities and the ACA certifies leaders in various leadership roles, other organizations refuse to back a standard for outdoor leaders. Many in the field believe it does not make a difference, but almost everyone has an opinion about it. If you believe in moving outdoor leadership toward professional status, certification must be taken seriously. Specialized outdoor training programs offer certifications for certain technical skills. The AMGA offers a series of certifications such as top roping and rescue. The ACA has a similar series of certifications based on expertise in a variety of conditions. Wilderness medicine certifications are available through a variety of organizations.

The question of certifying outdoor leaders as generalists has loomed since the late 1970s when the WEA began certifying outdoor leaders after a 35-day program. The course of instruction centered on judgment and decision making. Initial arguments for certification centered on safety and reducing accidents as well as reducing human effects on the environment. At about the same time the AEE developed a manual of best practices. The practices became standards in the field that serve as criteria for measuring individuals and programs. The real concern with certification is the assessment methods—how assessors are trained, whether they are legally responsible for their decisions, and whether there is an appeal process for those who do not meet standards. Because of differences of opinions, most agencies that operate adventure programs are willing to take the stance that the person leading the group is responsible for any problems that arise during an adventure and the organization is responsible for the program. That stance covers the legal context for operating outdoor programs and satisfies most professionals in the field.

Accreditation

Accreditation is for a program or an agency. Standards regarding staff, facilities, programs, and **risk management** are established. Typically an agency begins the accreditation process by undergoing a self-study. An outside evaluator then visits the site to observe practices and determine whether the agency is doing what it says it does and how it complies with standards. Accreditation is somewhat like a seal of approval. Professional organizations like the ACA, AMGA, and AEE accredit agencies. This is another important step in the pursuit of professionalization.

Licensure

Licensing is for an individual or an agency. A state or legislative body establishes criteria and methods for proving abilities. For an individual such methods might be a written test, written and practical examinations, or an application and résumé. Licensure is based on educational background

Learning Activity 3.1

Choose a professional organization listed in the appendix of this book. Find out if it promotes a professional code of ethics and share your information with the class.

and experience. Think about becoming a teacher, for example. A person needs to graduate from an accredited college program and then meet test or experience standards to become licensed. Agencies that house, transport, and serve food to participants meet standards of operation based on state licensing rules. Several states require guide licenses for people who lead others for money. For example, states such as Idaho, Maine, and New York license their outdoor guides.

International Status

Other countries use certifications and skill levels to organize the training and advancement of outdoor leadership. Great Britain has a well-established system for developing technical skills in a variety of activities. Their system is used in many other parts of the world, including New Zealand, Australia, and Canada. They have a centralized system that offers basic and advanced training in mountain leadership, canoeing, snow sports, orienteering, climbing, and first aid.

Places That Use Outdoor Leaders

Outdoor leaders work in many settings. In park systems outdoor leaders work as backcountry rangers, interpreters, and advisers for outdoor experiences. Public and private treatment programs sponsored by such organizations as the Easter Seal Society, Outward Bound, and Project Adventure have been imitated by other organizations. Outdoor leaders often work as counselors, psychologists, and therapists who use adventure therapy to address the needs of individuals with psychological or developmental disabilities. Schools also hire outdoor leaders. Organized camps hire outdoor leaders for adventure programs in a wide variety of activities. In addition, there are outdoor recreation opportunities on almost every military base in the world. There are also specialized programs

for working with people who have disabilities and there are single-sex programs, adventure travel programs, and other commercial opportunities. Remember Abby? She was at the very beginning of her career and overwhelmed by the opportunities available and skills necessary to become an outdoor professional. By making a plan to acquire knowledge and technical experience she eventually became a successful river runner.

Park Systems

National, state, and municipal parks represent a context for the practice of outdoor leadership. Park employees at the national, state, and municipal levels are responsible for the management of public lands and facilities as a resource for outdoor education and recreation. Park employees are also responsible for the conservation of cultural and **natural resources** and the development of interpretive programs conveying the significance of those resources to the general public.

Schools

America's public and private schools are another important context in which outdoor leadership is practiced. One example is the Expeditionary Learning Outward Bound (ELOB) design being instituted in schools around the United States. This school design is one of the more innovative approaches to incorporating the principles of outdoor education into the United States' educational system. While much of its curriculum is delivered in a traditional school setting, other curriculum elements are delivered through field-based activities far removed from the classroom.

Adventure Therapy

Adventure therapy can be useful in addressing the needs of young people who lack basic developmental support. It can provide opportunities

Learning Activity 3.2

Determine what certifications are needed for an entry-level job in the outdoors. There are many: for example, a full-time challenge course instructor, raft guide, camp program director, or instructor of adventure activities. What certifications do you currently have?

for expression and interaction among physically, emotionally, or cognitively disabled populations.

Adventure therapy combines psychological counseling with adventure activities. Sometimes treatment is enhanced by immersing a client in a novel environment and using challenge course activities. Adventure activities are a means through which dramatic results can occur. Youth at-risk programs have thrived with adventure therapy. Challenge courses have been used to help psychiatric patients acquire feelings of success and mastery, demonstrate social skills, and develop metaphors for making appropriate decisions. Many drug and alcohol rehabilitation programs also use adventure as a medium. Adventure therapy is now used with almost any client group. It requires specialized training in psychology or counseling in addition to technical abilities.

National, state, and local parks employ outdoor professionals.

Nonprofit Organizations

Youth programs like 4-H, the YMCA, and Scouts use adventure activities. Philmont Scout Ranch in New Mexico is the largest camp in the world and hosts over 20,000 participants a year, engaging in a host of adventure-based activities. Similarly, Girl Scout camps, Camp Fire camps, and other camps regularly incorporate adventure-based activities to attract older campers and to develop leadership and other skills.

Outdoor Learning Centers

Outdoor learning centers and environmental learning centers use outdoor professionals as interpreters, educators, and guides. Outdoor centers can offer skills development in activities like skiing, snoeshoeing, kayaking, or caving and may host camplike experiences for organized groups. The Nantahala Outdoor Center in North Carolina, for example, specializes in water-based activities. Environmental learning centers offer self-education and guided experiences to relate and interpret environmental phenomena. For example, night hikes, learning about the stars,

and seeing the effects of certain behaviors on flora and fauna are interesting to many people of all ages. Environmental learning centers often work with school groups. Centers are found in communities and state and national recreation areas.

Military Recreation

The military has many opportunities for outdoor leadership. Almost every military base in the world has adventure-based activities. Morale, Welfare, and Recreation (MWR) offers activities on bases. Enlisted personnel might go on skiing trips, try mountain biking, acquire boat certifications, or travel in areas near the base to learn more about another culture. Most of the time the trips are inexpensive and offer challenge and adventure while personnel are on leave or off duty. These large, tax-funded programs offer a variety of opportunities for outdoor leaders and often provide training.

Regardless of the place of employment, an outdoor leader works in both the outdoors and indoors. Assessment, planning, initial teaching, and evaluation of the program are usually done indoors, and there is always planning related to staff, budget, marketing, transportation, equipment, and other details. In addition, outdoor leaders should like and understand all types of people, especially those who do not feel comfortable in the outdoors.

Professional Associations

There is a professional association to meet almost everyone's needs. Some organizations attract a wide range of professionals and have smaller sections that represent specific interest areas like outdoor leadership. Other organizations focus all of their efforts on outdoor leadership. As individuals develop professionally they will likely belong to several professional groups. Every professional organization has a mission statement, and it is worth reading to find out what an organization believes in before investing in a membership or attending a meeting. As stated, some organizations are narrow in scope and serve a limited range of professionals. Other organizations are large and outdoor leaders may be a small minority. Some organizations serve a local or state area while others are national or international in scope. You can find hundreds of outdoor-related organizations on the Internet. One site that has information on such organizations is www.cbel.com/outdoor_organizations. Also see the appendix for a list of professional organizations.

Participating with and in organizations connects professionals and provides opportunities to renew commitment to the field. People often comment when leaving a professional meeting that they are reenergized because they have spent time with like-minded people. In addition, current trends and knowledge are transmitted at conferences to keep professionals up to date. Giving something back to your profession by contributing to that knowledge can be very rewarding. Your personal and professional needs will change over time and you may change affiliation to a particular organization as a result. Think of that as growth!

Professional Practice

Self-awareness is needed to be a competent leader, starting with a clear idea of your own abilities and limitations. In addition, knowing how you influence others and how others influence you is an important aspect of self-awareness. Knowing yourself and what irritates you, what you tolerate, what you like, your needs for routine, and your time management abilities will all influence your ability as a leader. Insight into your willingness to put others' needs ahead of yours, your ability to make difficult decisions, and how you use your leader "power" are also needed. The list could go on and on. The point is, the better you know yourself and how you react in different environments and situations, the more effective you will be as an outdoor leader. You will be able to recognize when you are being challenged on a personal level and will be able to respond in a useful way.

Accurately reading a group's abilities, assessing the risks and challenges that are presented to the group, judgment and decision making, and following rules and regulations of the sponsoring organization and the managing agency of the outdoor resource are also necessary skills. A highly qualified leader is a unique commodity. Programs often use two or three leaders for every group to make sure that the leaders have the right skills in the field to manage a group safely. Competent leaders are generally selfless while leading others and many administrators of programs are looking for someone who has good judgment and decision-making ability on behalf of the group. Being highly skilled in an adventure activity does not mean a person has sound judgment in the field. NOLS, Outward Bound, and WEA have been mentioned as leadership schools. Private outing clubs like the Mountaineers in

Professionals continue learning at conferences.

Learning Activity 3.3

1. Debate the pros and cons of certification for outdoor leaders.
2. Debate accreditation as a benefit or detriment to organizations.

Seattle or the Sierra Club also train leaders. All such training programs seek to create leaders who are safe, competent, and effective at handling groups.

Over the years Buell (1981) and Cousineau (1977) each tried to identify competencies for outdoor leaders. Buell's work concluded that there are eight competencies, mostly involving technical skills and safety, necessary for entry-level leaders. For experienced outdoor leaders he noted about 60 skills. Cousineau found that outdoor leaders like people from a variety of backgrounds. He also determined that professionals should meet a certain level of competency in any skill area. In a smaller study, Cosgrove (1984) found that technical skills are most needed in human relations, with philosophical skills following in importance. None of the three studies agreed on what competencies and what level of ability are needed in any area.

Safety and risk management is the one common area of competence in every poll. Because safety and risk management are so important, higher levels of first aid training have become an industry standard, and most entry-level positions require at least wilderness first aid, with many more requiring the more involved Wilderness First Responder certification.

Experienced leaders who possess technical skills also need interpersonal and philosophical abilities. All abilities are important for the entry-level and experienced outdoor leader, but studies indicate that some abilities may be more important at different stages of a professional's development.

Starting a Career in Outdoor Leadership

Like any field, outdoor leadership blends academic and theoretical background with hands-on application. In the past outdoor leaders learned the field by practicing it. Today there are colleges that offer degrees in outdoor leadership, outdoor education, or environmental education or have recreation programs with an optional emphasis on outdoor recreation. The field attracts people from many disciplines. To get started, it would be useful to look at the AEE Jobs Clearinghouse (www.aee.org/customer/post/search.php) or jobs posted on an organization's Web site. You probably have an interest or experience in either land-based or water-based activities, and you can see in job postings that certain skills are required and others are recommended. Start with the requirements. They include participation in an extended trip through a well-known agency like NOLS, Outward Bound, or the Nantahala Outdoor Center. Land-based jobs may require the ability to carry a 40-pound (18-kilogram) pack a specified distance for a specified time. They may require the ability to lead climb at a certain level. Water-based positions probably require swift-water rescue certification. All will require at least wilderness first aid and most will require Wilderness First Responder certification.

Knowing what is required for entry-level positions is a good place to begin. After that, take classes, get certifications, and seek opportunities to speak in front of other people in any setting. Camp counseling experience is excellent for learning to think on your feet and work with small groups. Join an outing club, become a trip leader on campus, or be a challenge course facilitator. Begin to build an outdoor résumé that includes both professional and personal experience on land and on water. Do not worry about not having all skills. No one was born knowing how to do everything. It takes a big commitment to begin to develop the proper skills and experience to lead others in the backcountry. Every experience counts!

Attending professional conferences to meet like-minded people and seek advice from others in the field is a useful investment. Especially toward the end of college, a trip to a professional conference is valuable for networking and beginning to contact potential employers. AEE, International Conference on Outdoor Recreation and Education (ICORE), and WEA are student-friendly conferences. If a park job or military recreation position is appealing, NRPA and ICORE are good choices.

The National Association for Interpretation (NAI) conference attracts interpreters from many different outdoor centers. The Internet also has job postings and listings for almost any career choice.

Building a Professional-Development Portfolio

Seeking a professional position entails many components. Research about different jobs and organizations is a first step. A résumé or portfolio highlighting your experiences and background is a second step. In the outdoors you might create two résumés—one that indicates your education, work experience, and other highlights, and one that includes professional and personal outdoor experiences and training. Initially the résumés may be merged into one. It all depends on the setting you seek to work in. As a preprofessional with a little outdoor experience, a standard résumé will suffice and should include educational background, paid or volunteer experiences, and certifications. An outdoor résumé exclusively lists activities, training, and experiences related to the outdoors. For example, it would include the number of river miles you have completed, personal and professional trips that you have led, and the names and dates of peak ascents.

An outdoor résumé is different from any other type of résumé. In general, you will include the following:

- Name and contact information
- Objective
- Education and experience
  - Academic and educational experiences
  - Summary of training
  - Summary of professional experience and expeditions
  - Personal expeditions
- Mountaineeering
  - Mountaineering training
  - Professional mountaineering
  - Personal mountaineering
- Rock climbing
  - Rock-climbing training
  - Professional multipitch
  - Personal multipitch
- Rivers
  - River training
  - Professional river experience
  - Personal river trips

All categories need to be dated and described. Identifying the skills demonstrated and any other information is typical. Often details are displayed in a spreadsheet. Of course, you should only include the areas where your experiences can be documented. If you have no river experience, for example, that section would not be included.

A cover letter of application should accompany a résumé to a potential employer. The letter describes how you heard about the position and why you are interested in it. The letter also can highlight certain experiences that fit the job description. Finally, the letter informs the potential employers of your availability and contact information. While many students rely on the Internet for corresponding with agencies, a well-written letter along with a handsome résumé make a positive impression.

Once the letter and résumé show the potential employer that your skills match the job description, an interview may occur. This is the part of the hiring sequence where both the potential employer and employee determine if there is a match. Being able to articulate your philosophy, describe your abilities and limitations, and show your personality are important. Send a thank-you letter regardless of the interview's outcome.

In educational agencies, professional portfolios are becoming a popular way to organize information. A portfolio highlights the key areas of your professional life. The use of a ringed binder is advantageous, making it easy to add and subtract information in the portfolio as time goes on. The portfolio should be up to date, which requires a review about every 6 months. Adding pictures can enhance a presentation, but for the most part the portfolio needs to be legible, proofread, and organized. Most portfolios follow a format like the following:

- Table of contents
- Résumé
- List of references
- Recommendation letters
- Transcripts
- Educational philosophy
- Personal goals
- Photos of you in action
- Any paper or project that you have completed related to outdoor leadership

A teacher in school or a career counselor can assist you in preparing a résumé or portfolio. Once it is started it is relatively easy to maintain in the future. Use only copies of letters, transcripts, and projects. Keep the originals in a safe place.

Summary

Self-evaluation of outdoor leadership abilities is part of every chapter of this book. The exercises serve as a springboard to begin building an outdoor résumé or portfolio, helping you identify areas where your abilities need to be developed. Upon completion of the text you will have an accurate picture of your abilities and limitations at this moment in time. You can then develop a plan to acquire the skills and abilities necessary to enter the outdoors as a professional. The résumés that you will complete at the end of this chapter can be maintained in a computer file for easy access and updating.

This chapter also discussed the formation of professions, available opportunities for working in the outdoor leadership industry, and professional organizations. There is more to being a competent professional than leading others for a particular agency. Sharing knowledge, advocating for profes-

sional issues, and behaving in a positive way help our field gain the status it deserves.

Selected References

Buell, L. 1981. *Outdoor adventure leadership competencies for entry level and experienced level personnel.* Greenfield, MA: Environmental Awareness.

Clark, D. 1995. A new code of ethics for NRPA. *Parks and Recreation* 30(8): 38-43.

Cosgrove, M. 1984. Minimum skill competencies required for employment in a wilderness adventure program. Master's thesis, University of Southern Illinois.

Cousineau, C. 1977. A delphi consensus on a set of principles for the development of a certification system for educators in outdoor adventure programs. PhD dissertation, University of Northern Colorado.

Hunt, J.S., Jr., and S. Wurdinger. 1999. Ethics and adventure programming. In *Adventure programming,* ed. J.C. Miles and S. Priest, 123-131. State College, PA: Venture.

Priest, S., and M. Gass. 1999. Future trends and issues in adventure programming. In *Adventure programming,* ed. J.C. Miles and S. Priest, 473-478. State College, PA: Venture.

Williamson, J., and M.A. Gass. 1993. *Manual of program accreditation standards for adventure programs.* Boulder, CO: AEE.

Professional-Development Portfolio Activities

1

1. List the areas where you have documented abilities.
2. Prepare a current résumé.
3. Prepare an outdoor résumé following the guidelines on page 34.

2

1. Start a portfolio with copies of projects or papers you have completed for classes.
2. Think about developing your professional philosophy and write it down.
3. Use the guidelines found in this chapter to build your portfolio.

PART II

Outdoor Leadership Theory

Part II will provide background knowledge related to leadership theory. The goal is for you to develop a philosophical, historical, and theoretical understanding of leadership theory as a means to inform your practice as an outdoor leader.

Chapter 4, Theories of Leadership, begins with a brief history of leadership by exploring the meaning of leadership and the purpose of leadership theories. Early theories of leadership are presented as one component of this historical overview. The transformational potential of outdoor leadership is emphasized through a discussion of contemporary leadership theories.

Chapter 5, Leadership in Practice, examines the role of leadership traits and qualities as well as leadership skills and competencies. It responds to the query "Who will lead?" by exploring the role of leadership power. A number of leadership theory models are presented.

Chapter 6, Judgment and Decision Making, explores decision-making processes, decision-making models, and decision-making methods. Scenarios are presented throughout the chapter in addition to a number of activities that provide an opportunity to directly apply some of the theory that is presented.

Chapter 7, Values and Ethics, includes a discussion of ethical theories that will help you clarify your worldview and its influence on your practice. The differences between an ethic of care and an ethic of justice will be explained. The chapter concludes with a discussion of professionalism in outdoor leadership.

chapter 4

Theories
of Leadership

Martin Luther King, Jr. (© Empics)

Mother Theresa (© Empics)

Rachel Carson (© AP)

Winston Churchill (© Empics)

" The first thing you do is teach the person to feel that the vision is very important and nearly impossible. That draws out the drive in winners. "   —**Edwin Land**

Chapter Concepts

- History of leadership—A brief history will help you better understand leadership theory.

- Meaning of leadership—Leadership is both intentional, aiming toward the accomplishment of particular goals and outcomes, and interactional, involving relationships between two or more individuals in a particular situation.

- Transactional leadership—Transactional leadership is task-oriented, emphasizing the role of the leader to direct the group toward accomplishing a finite goal. Early theories of leadership exemplified transactional leadership.

- Transformational leadership—Transformational leadership can be found in contemporary leadership theories that emphasize the interactional nature of leadership and its transformative potential.

- Early theories of leadership—Early theories include trait and great men theories of leadership, charismatic and heroic leadership theories, style theory of leadership, situational leadership theory, and contingency leadership theory.

- Contemporary leadership theories—Contemporary theories include feminist leadership theory, authentic leadership theory, and servant leadership theory.

The chapter concepts relate to the following core competency:

- Foundational knowledge (CC-1)—A sense of heritage and an understanding of leadership theory are part of the foundation of outdoor leadership knowledge.

Michio had been working as a ropes course instructor for 6 months. He felt he had really progressed in his ability to facilitate ropes courses during this time. Although Michio worked mostly with school groups, he had instructed a number of programs for people with disabilities and a few other adult groups. He was looking forward to the opportunity to work with a corporate group soon. It would challenge him personally and he would receive twice the pay for the same amount of work. Michio's opportunity came when a large corporation signed up for a day of low and high ropes. Michio received a brief introduction from the lead instructor, who reviewed the group's goals, and was then assigned a small group of the employees to work with on his own.

Michio decided to start with the spider's web. It was a low element that he was comfortable facilitating. Because the element involved lifting people off the ground, Michio started with a trust sequence, encouraging the group members to do trust falls on the ground and in pairs. Michio was surprised at how the group reacted. They seemed more uncomfortable touching each other than the high school students with whom he typically worked. The group members were all joking around with each other and pretend-

ing like they were not going to catch each other. Very quickly, Michio realized that he was losing control of his group, so he stopped the sequence and asked the group to gather in a circle. He checked in with the group, asking members how they felt and how they thought the activity was going. A number of people voiced their opinion that the activity was just a silly exercise and that there was no way that this was going to help them build trust. From their comments, Michio learned that their daily work environment was contentious and competitive and that one of the executives thought that participation in the ropes course would be a good first step toward improving communication. None of the people in Michio's group agreed; in fact, the only thing that they could agree on was that they did not want to be there.

Michio tried not to show how panicked he felt. He was uncertain how to proceed. Should he just walk them through the paces and continue with the planned sequence or should he stop the group and try and address their needs? How could he address their needs? Michio looked around to see if any of the other facilitators were nearby so that he could quickly check in with someone else about what to do, but no one was around. Michio decided that the best course of

(continued)

action was to not proceed with his original plan. From past experience, Michio knew that there was transformative potential in the work that he was doing but that this type of learning would only occur if the participants were open to it. If he kept going with the ropes course, the group might achieve the intended purpose of the day in one sense, but ignoring the group's concern would mean that Michio was being inattentive to the real needs of the group.

Michio found a shady spot for the group and encouraged everyone to have a seat. He then queried the group as to how they felt about the day, how they felt about their work environment, and what steps they could take to improve communication. Michio sat and listened. He took notes and asked questions of the group. He reminded them that they should respond to each other in a supportive way.

The group finished the day and thanked Michio for his attentiveness. When the larger group came together for a final debriefing at the end of the day, the other groups shared stories of the activities they had done. Michio's group shared their story, telling the larger group about what they discovered about themselves, making suggestions for how to improve communication and workplace performance. It was clear to the other groups that while they experienced many fun activities over the course of the day, Michio's group had a truly transformational experience that would extend far past the day's activities.

James MacGregor Burns, regarded as both a political scientist and as a major social philosopher, has had an enormous influence on the field of leadership. In his seminal book, simply titled *Leadership* (1978), Burns maintains that leadership is one of the most observed and least understood phenomena on earth. He goes on to say that while people often know far too much about certain leaders, people know far too little about leadership itself. Think about this statement for a moment. When you think of the word *leadership,* what comes to mind? More than likely your thoughts do not turn to the actual theory of leadership: the definitions, leadership models, history of leadership, and theoretical concepts. Rather, your thoughts may turn to a particular experience that you have had or a person whom you regard as a leader.

That said, it can be argued that true comprehension of a concept only comes when a person knows and understands how and why something is the way that it is. In other words, having a particular person in mind whom you know to be a great leader is insufficient to understanding leadership. The development of knowledge and understanding begins with examining underlying thoughts, ideas, and theories about what makes something work. Understanding what makes a particular person a great leader therefore begins with the study of leadership theory.

In the field of outdoor leadership, there is widespread agreement that something may be known experientially. You may read about and develop a theoretical understanding of how to construct an ideal top-rope setup for a rock climb. But until you have actually gained some hands-on experience in setting up climbs, your comprehension of how to construct the setup is quite limited. Likewise, imagine if you were in a position where you lacked a theoretical understanding of redundancy and equalization and you were faced with a group of eager beginner climbers, trusting you to set up safe top-rope climbs, and you were forced to rely solely on intuition and common sense. True comprehension of any subject is enhanced by combining thoughts, ideas, and theories and using them to inform meaningful practice.

This chapter will introduce leadership models and theories in an attempt to provide a foundation of leadership knowledge. The focus of this chapter will be an overview of general leadership theory, including the history of leadership, the meaning of leadership, early theories of leadership, and contemporary theories of leadership. The chapter that follows will connect these general theories to outdoor leadership theory and will build on this effort to introduce theory as a means to inform practice.

History of Leadership

For at least two millennia, many philosophers grappled with the problems of the rulers versus the ruled. The Chinese classics written as early as 6th century b.c.e. are filled with advice to the country's leaders. Confucius urged leaders to set a moral example while Taoism emphasized that a leader's success was equivalent to his efforts (Bass 1990).

Long before modern sociology, Plato, Socrates, and Aristotle analyzed the influences of upbringing, social and economic institutions, and

Learning Activity 4.1

When you think of the terms *leader* and *leadership,* what comes to mind? Do you think of certain individuals? Who are they? What qualities make them a leader?

Leadership theory informs leadership practice.

responses of followers on leadership and rulers. Plato (360 b.c.e.) developed the first typology of political leaders. In *The Republic*, he regards the ideal leader as one who rules with order and reason and is virtuous. Aristotle (350 b.c.e.) was disturbed by the lack of virtue among leaders and pointed to the need to educate youth for such leadership. In *The Prince*, Machiavelli (1513) contends that a leader's main objective is to maintain authority and power, and leaders may need to resort to deceit, threat, and violence to achieve this end. However, Burns notes, "Long before Gandhi, religious thinkers were preaching nonviolence" (1978, p. 2).

Despite this rich history, leadership as a concept has dissolved into discrete and impractical meanings over time. Studies have turned up over 130 definitions of the word *leadership* (Burns 1978). Numerous types of leaders have been identified, including the autocrat, cooperator, elder statesman, eager beaver, pontifical type, muddled person, loyal staff person, philosopher, business expert, benevolent despot, child

protector, laissez-faire type, community-minded person, cynic, optimist, and democrat. There is, however, no school of leadership—intellectual, theoretical, practical, or otherwise. Some critics argue that the effects of leadership are in the eye of the beholder.

That said, the study of leadership does serve a number of purposes. As noted, the study of leadership theory informs leadership practice. Businesses require a higher level of leadership than ever before. Leadership is a critical factor in military successes, and on the political front, leadership style of world leaders contributes to legislation, policy, and programs. Academics, religious officials, parents, CEOs, heads of schools, executive directors, and heads of any number of organizations demonstrate the importance of leadership. We either lead or are being led in almost every interaction that we have.

Meaning of Leadership

With over 130 definitions, there are almost as many definitions of leadership as there are people who have attempted to define it. Bass tells us, "Although the Oxford English Dictionary noted the appearance of the word 'leader' in the English language as early as the year 1300, the word 'leadership' did not appear until the first half of the nineteenth century in writings about the political influence and control of British Parliament. And the word did not appear in most other modern languages until recent times" (1990, p. 11).

Early definitions of leadership focused on the phenomena of group change and process. Leadership was interpreted as having a one-way effect whereby the leader influenced the group. More recent definitions recognize that leadership is a process of influence. These definitions also emphasize the interactive nature of leaders and followers. Leaders influence groups but are simultaneously influenced by the needs and wishes of the group members.

Leadership is comprised of two primary elements. First, leadership is intentional, aiming toward the accomplishment of particular goals and outcomes. Second, leadership is interactional, involving relationships between two or more individuals in a particular situation.

Whether leadership is an act or a behavior, a form of persuasion, an exercise of power, an exercise of influence, an interaction, or an end result, what matters most is that the definitions and meanings of leadership are examined consciously and critically in working toward a broad understanding of leadership theory and practice. As Bass (1990) suggests, "The search for the one and only proper and true definition of leadership seems to be fruitless, since the appropriate choice of definition should depend on the methodological and substantive aspects of leadership in which one is interested" (p. 18). To gain an understanding of this, leadership needs to be regarded through a wide lens that offers some insight into how we see and interpret it.

Leadership also needs to be understood historically. **Hegemony** suggests that as a culture develops, systems of meanings and values are actively created by both groups and individuals (Henderson and Bialeschki 1991). Hegemony explains how dominant meanings and interests, which are inherited from past tradition, explain our present condition and provide an understanding of certain assumptions taken for granted about what makes a good leader, what leadership qualities are valuable, and how we define leadership. An understanding of the role of hegemony contributes to an understanding of some of the limitations of the early theories of leadership. It also helps explain some of the barriers to contemporary leadership and offers a means for critiquing the way that leadership has been viewed in society.

The ideal then in understanding leadership theory and practice is to critically reflect on the historical underpinnings of leadership: how it was defined, who held power, and what traits were considered dominant. As leaders, the challenge is to build upon this knowledge in the development of new paradigms.

Purpose of Leadership Theories

Nothing is supposed to be as practical as a good theory: "Theories of leadership attempt to explain the factors involved either in the emergence of leadership or in the nature of leadership and its consequences" (Bass 1990, p. 37). Toward that end, the focus of leadership training and practical preparation must be grounded in theory and in the concepts, ideals, and conclusions that have been researched and used by leaders across a variety of settings. This section on leadership theory will introduce both early and contemporary theories of leadership. It will highlight the difference between transactional and transformational leadership, noting that many of the early theories of leadership were predominantly transactional in nature, while the contemporary theories focused more on the transformational nature of leadership.

Early Leadership Theories

The earliest literature on leadership is concerned predominantly with theoretical concerns. Early leadership theories were based on hierarchic models from industrial organizations. In this context, leaders oversaw production and employees and were expected to maintain efficiency and discipline. Leaders gave orders and workers were expected to follow them. There was little opportunity within these hierarchical leadership models for workers to think creatively or to have ideas for improving their methods or work. The leaders of these groups were expected to be highly authoritarian and the workers were expected to be passive and obedient.

Most early theories define leadership according to either traits or styles. Trait theories assume that certain physical and psychological characteristics

Courtesy of Ben Lawhon

Leadership style is contingent on the learning environment.

Learning Activity 4.2

What are some of the commonly held assumptions about leaders and leadership in these early theories? What are some of the limitations? Define hegemony. In what way does hegemony provide us with a critique of these early theories?

predispose some people to leadership. Charismatic and heroic leaders often exemplify these characteristics. Style theories assume that particular kinds of behavior underlie leadership ability. Superimposed on these leadership theories are the dimensions of situational dependence and contingency. Situational theory takes into account the leader, the followers, and the situation while contingency theory posits that a leader is motivated from either a task orientation or a relationship orientation. These categories (trait, charismatic, style, situational, and contingency) classify the five broad categories of early leadership theory.

Trait and Great Men Leadership Theories

According to the **trait theory of leadership,** leaders are born, not made: "If the leader is endowed with superior qualities that differentiate him from his followers, it should be possible to identify these qualities" (Bass 1990, p. 38). This assumption forms the basic premise of the trait theory of leadership. Trait theory describes a leader as one who exhibits a certain set of physical, intellectual, and interpersonal characteristics. This traditional leader would show good posture, be attractive, speak firmly, act confidently, be task oriented, and be assertive. These so-called great men were leaders who were endowed with superior qualities from birth.

The **great men theory of leadership** explains leadership by focusing on the greatness of actual leaders. According to this theory, certain men were predestined to be leaders based on factors such as birth order, family background, education, and upbringing. Leadership was predominantly a monopoly of the aristocracy. It was historically understood that the world was shaped by the leadership of great men, including Moses, Winston Churchill, Thomas Jefferson, and Lenin (Bass 1990). This theory assumes that these leaders make history and that the causes of real,

intended social change can be traced back to the purpose and decisions of the most visible actors on the political stage (Burns 1978). It was highly unusual for a female to be considered a leader. In some cultures, however, such as in certain Native American traditions, women were accepted as tribal leaders. In fitting with this theory, these women were tribal chiefs as a result of the characteristics they exhibited, their family lineage, and their training (Jordan 1996).

Until the 1940s, most research about leaders and leadership focused on the traits of leadership in individuals. Leaders were seen as possessing certain attributes that did not belong to nonleaders. Eventually this pure trait theory fell into disfavor, concluding that each individual and each situation had to be considered to better understand both leaders and leadership (Stogdill 1948).

Charismatic and Heroic Leadership Theories

According to **charismatic leadership theory,** charismatic leaders have played a significant role politically, economically, and socially throughout history. A consideration of the influence of Martin Luther King, Jr., Adolf Hitler, or any number of actors, musicians, and politicians helps to illustrate the influence of charismatic leaders. Charismatic leaders do not merely inspire; they generate unusually passionate reactions in their followers: "Charismatic leaders often emerge in times of crises as prospective saviors who, by their magical endowments, will fulfill the unmet emotional needs of their completely trusting, overly dependent, and submissive followers" (Bass 1990, p. 184). Some variance in the charismatic phenomenon is due to the leader and the specific charismatic leadership qualities that the leader possesses; however, the situation, the interaction of the individual with the followers, and the historical moment also play a role.

Burns (1978) prefers to speak about the heroic leader and suggests that "heroic leadership is not

Imagine yourself on a 30-day wilderness trip with an autocratic leader. What kind of behavior would you expect this leader to exhibit? What would the experience be like from a participant's perspective? What would the group experience and learning be like? Under what conditions would this style of leadership be most appropriate?

simply a quality or entity possessed by someone; it is a type of relationship between leaders and led" (p. 244). The result of these efforts is that dormant followers become active, motivating others while furthering the purpose and mission of the leader. According to Bass, "If successful, charismatic leaders bring about radical transformations in their groups, organizations, and societies" (1990, p. 184).

Style Theory of Leadership

Leadership styles are the ways in which leaders express their influence. The historical interpretation of the style theory identifies particular kinds of behavior that underlie leadership ability. According to this theory, a number of factors determine leadership style. These factors are determined predominantly through an individual's personality.

The three main categories of leadership styles are autocratic, democratic, and abdicratic (Bass 1990). An **autocratic or authoritarian leader** is highly directive and does not allow input from group members. The leader rarely reveals reasons behind decision making or actions and believes that participants should do as they are told. Using this style, a leader may in fact make all the decisions for the group. Early models of leadership emphasized the need for a leader to maintain firm control of the group at all times, expressing this through a highly autocratic approach.

A **democratic leadership style** emphasizes the need for group members to be involved in decision making. The group may vote on decisions or may base decisions on the majority opinion. An **abdicratic or laissez-faire leadership style** allows the group to operate on its own. The leader provides information when

asked but otherwise stays out of the group process. The leadership style that a person chooses to express will depend on that person's orientation to the task and relationship. Certain situations will require a leadership style that may be more process-directed (relationship and means) or more product-directed (task and ends).

Most of the early research on leadership styles compared pure examples of each style. However, you are unlikely to find a purely democratic or purely autocratic leader in real-world groups. A more modern interpretation of the style theory of leadership will be presented in chapter 5.

Situational Leadership Theory

Situational theories are models of leadership that take into account the leader, the followers, and the situation and explain leadership as based on the time, place, and circumstance (Bass 1990).

The leadership situation and the group influence decision making.

Situational leadership theory accounts for two ideals: 1) any situation plays a large part in determining leadership qualities and the leader for that situation, and 2) the leadership qualities of an individual are themselves the product of a previous leadership situation that have molded the individual.

In contrast to the great men and trait theories, situational leadership theories suggest that 95% of human progress is unconnected to great individuals. Rather, great leaders like Mahatma Gandhi and Martin Luther King, Jr., appeared at a critical historical moment of socially valued causes, devoted themselves to those causes, and both contributed to those causes and profited greatly from the work of many others (Spiller 1929; Carson 2003). Thus, according to the situational theory, leaders emerged and developed as a result of social, cultural, and economic conditions.

Contingency Leadership Theory

Contingency leadership theory explains leadership in terms of an individual's style of leadership and the response of the group. Fiedler (1967) suggests that a leader is motivated from either a task orientation or a relationship orientation. Different leaders prefer to focus on either the job to be done or the people in the group. The contingency theory is based on the premise that leadership depends on the appropriateness of the leader's style to the task. Three factors—the relationship between the leader and the group, the task structure, and the power of the leader—all contribute to a leader's influence. Group effectiveness will depend on leadership style and the degree to which the group situation is favorable by providing the leader with influence over group members.

Consideration of these five broad categories of leadership (trait, charismatic, style, situational, and contingency) provides a foundation on which to build an understanding of contemporary leadership theory. It is important to avoid fully rejecting one theory and supplanting it with a new theory. Rather, all theories need to be considered in developing contemporary models. As James (1880) states, great individuals need help—their leadership qualities need to fit the situation. Likewise, Stogdill (1948) concludes that leaders' traits bear some relevance to success as a leader and there are certain leadership qualities that a leader must possess, regardless of the situation.

Transactional Versus Transformational Leadership

The early leadership theories presented thus far have focused on the transactional nature of leadership. For Burns (1978), the transactional leader approaches followers with an eye to exchanging one thing for another. These transactions comprise

A balance of both technical and interpersonal skills are integral to outdoor leadership.

Courtesy of Tim O'Connell

the bulk of the relationship between leaders and followers and typify the early theories of leadership. **Transactional leadership** applies to leaders who are task oriented and able to direct their groups in specific ways to accomplish finite goals. Transactional leaders work to gain their group's compliance through various approaches: offering rewards, threatening punishment, appealing to group members' sense of altruism, or appealing to followers' rational judgment. Transactional leaders have little involvement with the group. They intervene in the group process only when the group is getting off track. Bass (1990) notes, "Most experimental research, unfortunately, has focused on transactional leadership, whereas the real movers and shakers of the world are transformational leaders" (p. 23).

By 1960, the dominant paradigm for the study of leadership had evolved from research on the traits and situations that affect leadership to something more dynamic (Bass 1990). This shift in focus coincided with research on transformational leadership. Burns (1978) suggests that while the transactional leader works within the framework of self-interests, the transformational leader moves to change the framework. Contemporary theories began to consider the affective, intellectual, and action traits of the individual as well as the specific conditions under which the individual operates. Leadership was now seen as contingent on traits and situations involving an exchange between the leader and the led.

The transformational leader asks followers to transcend their own self-interests for the good of the group. Transformational leaders must consider the need to develop themselves, the circumstances of the leadership situation, and their followers, transcending the needs of any given moment in time and considering what is important for the present and in the future. The transformational leader must also seek to satisfy the followers' higher needs by engaging the "full person" of the follower. In this sense, transformational leadership results in a mutual interchange between leaders and followers.

Transformational leadership is closer to the prototype of leadership that most people have in mind when they describe their ideal leader. Transformational leaders have a strong sense of mission and an ability to attract a loyal and committed following (Harris and Sherblom 2002). For an example, think back to the opening vignette. If Michio had opted to stick with his original plan and complete his preplanned ropes course sequence, he would have most likely done so to fulfill the preassigned task. His leadership would have reflected the transactional nature of his relationship with the ropes course participants. Because Michio chose to deviate from the prescribed task, opting to focus more on the group's needs and their relationship with one another, Michio was able to offer participants a transformational experience, one that most likely had a greater effect. Transformational leaders have the ability to lead their group from "what is" to "what is describable" to "what ought to be" (Rosenthal and Buchholz 1995).

Transformational leaders produce leadership behaviors that fulfill four main functions. These are sometimes referred to as the four Is (Bass 1990):

- Idealized leadership provides vision and a sense of mission, instills pride, and helps gain trust and respect.
- Inspirational motivation communicates high expectations and expresses important purposes in simple ways.
- Intellectual stimulation promotes intelligence and careful problem solving.
- Individualized consideration gives personal attention, treats people individually, and both coaches and advises.

The discussion that follows will consider early research on transactional leadership and trait theory as seminal to an understanding of contemporary theory. The main emphasis will be on the potential of transformational leadership.

Contemporary Leadership Theories

Today, leadership appears to be more art than science. Contemporary leadership theorists seek to identify different types of leadership and relate them to the practical demands of society. Harris and Sherblom (2002) maintain that it is useful to describe the traits and behaviors that effective leaders share. Although leadership has been broadly researched, no one theory fully explains the subject. For this reason, several perspectives of leadership theory and styles taken together can contribute to a knowledge of leadership practice and in turn, may help respond to Burns' (1978) concern that people understand far too little about leadership. There are too many contemporary leadership theories to fit into this small space, so we will briefly introduce three: feminist, authentic, and servant theories.

Learning Activity 4.4

Imagine that your cabin group has arrived on the first day of summer camp. What tasks do the boys typically dive into upon arrival? What tasks do the girls typically dive into? Are these tasks gender neutral or gender specific? What stereotypes are associated with different tasks? Is this seminal to our discussion of leadership theory? How does this information contribute to a discussion of feminist leadership theory?

Feminist Leadership Theory

In numerous studies of mixed-sex groups, males tend to emerge as leaders more often than females (Aries 1976). Additionally, leadership traditionally is associated with stereotypical male traits and behaviors, such as hierarchy, dominance, competition, authoritarianism, and task orientation, and it is associated less often with stereotypic female values and qualities, such as harmony, concern for people, unity and spirituality, caring, and relationship orientation (Henderson and Bialeschki 1991).

Influential women have been classified in a number of ways throughout the course of history, and many of these descriptions have been unflattering. Stereotypes of women leaders include the earth mother who brings home-baked cookies to meetings and keeps the communal bottle of aspirin in her desk, the mother figure who provides solace and comfort, the sex object who fails to establish herself as professional, and the iron maiden who tries too hard to establish herself as a professional.

It was believed that the 1990s would be the decade of women in leadership because more women would be entering the workforce and because the authoritarian socialization of males would not be as effective in the workplace of the future. However, research suggests that despite the increase in the number of women in leadership roles, merely employing more women does not suffice if women continue to remain powerless within organizations and if a more **feminist model of outdoor leadership** does not receive recognition.

Contemporary models of **feminist leadership** theory have focused on specific aspects of organizational structure change (Henderson 1996). Within such models, attention is paid to both process and product and traditional notions of power are reconsidered, allowing all people to experience the same potential for success. All persons additionally have the same potential to become leaders. A feminist transformative perspective of leadership would regard communication as upward, downward, and lateral. According to Henderson, "The content of that communication would be oriented toward advice, counsel, and collective decision making" (p. 114). Control and safety of the group would be the responsibility of all members of the group. This approach to leadership, which addresses the psychological structures of leadership, is supported by Noddings (1984), who suggests that leaders must develop an ethic of care that supersedes, and in essence transcends, gender differences.

Authentic Leadership Theory

At its deepest level and in consideration of contemporary leadership theories, leadership is authentic self-expression that creates value and meaning. Leadership is then expressed in direct, purposeful action. Terry (1993) has developed a model of leadership (**authentic leadership theory**) that is grounded in this notion of authenticity. He maintains that authenticity is a fundamental condition of being human, and truly authentic leadership is impossible to reach because one can never find absolute truth. Rather, a leader has to explore all perspectives and, in so doing, come as close as possible to authenticity.

Terry has built a foundation for developing authentic leadership based on the principles of dwelling, freedom, justice, participation, love, and responsibility. Dwelling is the process of "showing up" and being present and respecting the diversity of people. Freedom involves the ability to make choices and participate in the social conversation. Justice is based on a principle of fairness that ensures equality, equity, and adequacy among group members. Participation involves taking action. Love is the recognition that people

Learning Activity 4.5

What are ways for you to nurture the development of a more feminist model of leadership? For example, imagine that you are leading a group of high school students on a backpacking trip through the Catskill Mountains in New York. A pattern begins to develop early on during the trip. The two most physically able boys in the group start passing the slower group members simply because they are faster. Your group is 2 hours into the hike when you realize that all of the boys have somehow ended up in the front half of the group and all of the girls have ended up in the back half of the group and the distance between the two groups is growing.

Ask yourself the following questions: Is this okay? Why or why not? If you were to approach this scenario from a feminist perspective, what might you do to bring this incident to the attention of the group? How might you problem solve with the group to try to rectify the situation?

are in relationship to one another. Responsibility impels people to recognize who they are and what they are doing.

Leadership is the courage to call forth authentic action in oneself and others, to increase dwelling, freedom, justice, participation, love, and responsibility. Leaders must live and impel others to live according to these authentic principles. It is through living out these principles that leaders can model an authentic and ethical engagement with the world. This model of leadership has transformative potential for both followers and leaders.

Servant Leadership Theory

Greenleaf (1977) maintains that *serve* and *lead* are words that are overused and are too often associated with negative connotations. He poses the question of whether the ideas of servant and leader can be "fused in one real person, in all levels of status or calling" (p. 7). Greenleaf's *Servant Leadership* (1977) grew out of his interest in Herman Hesse's book, *Journey to the East* (1956). The story tells the tale of a band of men on a mythical journey. The central figure of the story is Leo, who accompanies the group as a servant, doing menial chores. Leo also sustains the group through his spirit and his song and all goes well with the journey until Leo disappears. After some years of wandering, the narrator finds Leo, who is actually the titular head of the order that sponsored the journey, a guiding spirit, and a great and noble leader.

This story confirmed for Greenleaf that the great leader is a servant first. One who acts as a servant first is always searching, listening, and not only

Courtesy of Erin Lotz

A good spot for base camp? Servant leaders put the group's needs first.

believing but expecting that there is hope for the future. In a number of studies on leadership in countries outside of North America, this notion of being of service to others is one of the most important aspects of leadership (Bass 1975). The practice of **servant leadership theory** manifests itself in an ethic of care whereby the leader, who is a servant first, ensures that other people's greatest needs are being met.

Greenleaf argues that perhaps one of the current dilemmas is that far too many people presume to lead but do not see any more clearly than their followers how to lead, in what direction to direct their leadership, and toward what purpose. A leader needs inspiration, needs to provide ideas and structure, and needs to take the risk of failure along with the chance of success. The servant leader needs to say, "I will go; follow me," while knowing that the path is uncertain. Along the way, the leader understands the needs of the group, listens, withdraws at times, is aware and perceptive, shows acceptance and empathy, and is persuasive.

Imagine yourself on an exciting new adventure. You have been asked to lead a sea-kayaking trip to Baja, Mexico. It is the first time that the company that you work for is offering this trip. You are feeling physically fit from a summer of guiding trips and are keen to explore a new area. You meet the group in San Diego and immediately realize that many of the trip participants have chosen Baja as a relaxing vacation destination and are not interested in the same type of extended trip that you are. The first night's camp is on a beautiful island only 1 mile (1.6 kilometers) from the mainland. A couple of individuals within the group are so enamored with the spot that they propose to use the site as a base camp and begin to convince the other group members to stay. You are extremely disappointed to hear this because this does not fulfill your own desires. You are presented with two options. You can try to convince people of the value of spending the trip exploring more of the area or you can approach your leadership role from the perspective of servant first, authentically listening and then leading in such a way that the group's needs are met. Approaching your role of leader from an ethic of care and seeing value in being of service to others offers great transformational potential for both you and your trip participants.

There are many other contemporary theories of leadership, including collaborative, community, and educational theories and theories of followership, to name a few. The study of leadership theory can only enhance our understanding and knowledge of leadership, leaders, and the led. The potential for individual transformation, alongside the potential for systemic transformational change, can be better understood as more contemporary theories of leadership are studied.

Summary

It is important to develop a theoretical understanding of leadership in order to engage in meaningful leadership. This chapter has introduced a variety of possibilities to help you begin to understand and more clearly define leadership. Leadership has been described from a historical perspective, and trait, charismatic, style, situational, and contingency leadership theories have been discussed. The distinction between transactional and transformational leadership has been identified, and a number of significant contemporary leadership theories have been presented, including feminist,

Professional-Development Portfolio Activity

Write a 2-page essay describing your personal philosophy of leadership. What is leadership? How should it be used? What are some of the ways to lead? Knowing some of your personal strengths and limitations, which leadership style or theory is a good fit for you? In what ways do you need to develop yourself as a leader?

authentic, and servant leadership. Perhaps most importantly, it has been noted that none of the theories, ideals, or situations should be wholly disregarded and supplanted with new and unique information. Rather, a historical understanding of leadership theory alongside an understanding of contemporary leadership theory will guide future leaders to a broader understanding of leadership.

Selected References

Aries, C. 1976. Interaction patterns and themes of male, female, and mixed groups. *Small Group Behavior* 7: 7-18.

Aristotle. 2000. *Politics*. Trans. B. Jowett. New York: Dover.

Bass, B.M. 1975. *Exercise life goals*. Scottsville, NY: Transnational Programs.

Bass, B.M. 1990. *Bass and Stogdill's handbook of leadership: Theory, research, and managerial applications*. 3rd ed. New York: Free Press.

Burns, J.M. 1978. *Leadership*. New York: Harper & Row.

Carson, C. 2003. Martin Luther King, Jr.: Charismatic leadership in a mass struggle. Retrieved January 28, 2003, from www.stanford.edu/group/King/additional_resources/articles/charisma.htm.

Fiedler, F.E. 1967. *A theory of leadership effectiveness*. New York: McGraw-Hill.

Greenleaf, R.K. 1977. *Servant leadership: A journey into the nature of legitimate power and greatness*. New York: Paulist Press.

Harris, T.E., and J.C. Sherblom. 2002. *Small group and team communication*. 2nd ed. Boston: Allyn & Bacon.

Henderson, K.A. 1996. Feminist perspectives on outdoor leadership. In *Women's voice in experiential education*, ed. K. Warren, 107-118. Dubuque, IA: Kendall/Hunt.

Henderson, K.A., and M.D. Bialeschki. 1991. Feminist perspectives on women in recreation leadership. *Journal of Applied Recreation Research* 16(4): 281-296.

Hesse, H. 1956. *Journey to the East*. London: P. Owen.

James, W. 1880. Great men, great thoughts, and their environment. *Atlantic Monthly* 46: 441-459.

Jordan, D. 1996. *Leadership in leisure services: Making a difference*. State College, PA: Venture.

Machiavelli, N. 1981. *The Prince*. 3rd ed. New York: Bantam.

Noddings, N. 1984. *Caring: A feminine approach to ethics and moral education*. Berkeley, CA: University of California Press.

Plato. 1986. *The Republic*. Trans. B. Jowett. Buffalo, NY: Prometheus Books.

Rosenthal, S.B., and R.A. Buchholz. 1995. Leadership: Toward new philosophical foundations. *Business and Professional Ethics Journal* 14: 25-41.

Spiller, G. 1929. The dynamics of greatness. *Sociological Review* 21: 218-232.

Stogdill, R.M. 1948. Personal factors associated with leadership: A survey of the literature. *Journal of Psychology* 25: 35-71.

Terry, R. 1993. *Authentic leadership: Courage in action*. San Francisco: Jossey-Bass.

chapter 5

Leadership in Practice

" I focus on what you can put into people rather than what you can get out of them. " —**Leroy H. Kurtz**

- Leadership traits and qualities—This chapter will discuss the traits and qualities of successful outdoor leaders.

- Leadership power—Power comes from a number of sources. It may be reward, coercive, legitimate, referent, or expert (French and Raven 1968).

- Leadership styles—Style of leadership refers to the way in which leaders express their influence.

- Leadership models—A number of models are introduced in this chapter.

- Caring leaders—The caring leader acts out of an ethic of care and service by attending to the group and ensuring that the needs of individuals within the group are met.

The chapter concepts relate to the following core competencies:

- Foundational knowledge (CC-1)—An understanding of outdoor leadership theory is an important aspect of the field's foundational knowledge.

- Self-awareness and professional conduct (CC-2)—Acting mindfully and intentionally as an outdoor leader and developing knowledge and sensitivity about how we affect others are part of self-awareness and professional conduct.

L aird could not believe his good fortune. This was only his second year as a camp counselor and he had been hired as part of the camp's wilderness trip staff. Laird was in his second year of college, studying economics. He had originally been hired as a water-ski instructor and had joined his cabin group on a 5-day wilderness trip on the Flambeau River in Wisconsin the previous summer. He and his group returned from that trip with a sense of accomplishment and community that Laird had never before experienced. He was enthusiastic about the opportunity to do more paddling this summer as an assistant trip leader.

Laird's first trip of the summer was a 3-day Namekagon River trip with eight campers. His coleader on the trip was Ashley. Ashley was in her early 20s and had just graduated from college with a degree in outdoor recreation. The group set off from camp and was on the water by late morning. The trip pace was relaxed and everyone seemed to be getting along. They arrived into camp at 5 in the evening, tired and hungry. Laird hopped out of his boat, grabbed his tent, and headed for a flat, scenic spot along the riverbank to set up his camp. The campers eagerly hopped out of their boats as well and looked around, wondering what to do next.

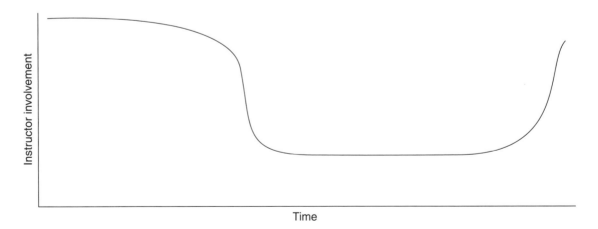

Figure 5.1 A representation of the level of instructor involvement over the course of a wilderness trip.

(continued)

Ashley asked the group to get in a circle and proceeded with a lesson on how to set up camp. With this information, the group sprang into action and in an hour, all tents were up and a pot of water was boiling.

As the group sat down with Ashley for a hot drink, Laird wandered over, noticing that Ashley's tent was not even up yet. "Looks like you missed out on all the good spots, Ashley. Bummer for you," he said. Ashley said that she was sure that she would find a good spot later. The group ate dinner and told ghost stories around the campfire until it was time to go to bed.

Ashley and Laird had a quick meeting around the campfire that night. Ashley told Laird that his sense of humor and enthusiasm benefited the group, but she also expressed her concern that Laird took too much time for himself. She explained to him that at the beginning of a trip, a group typically needs a lot of direction. She would start a trip with a somewhat autocratic approach and as the trip progressed, she would become more abdicratic in her leadership style. She explained how she tried to be flexible with her leadership style and that her style depended a lot upon factors such as the weather, the group, the trip route, and the length of the trip. Ashley took a stick and drew a graph in the sand for Laird, displaying the level of leader involvement over time on a typical trip and how leadership style needed to accommodate the group's changing needs (figure 5.1).

Needless to say, Laird was impressed. Ashley was equally surprised at herself, saying, "You know, I never thought that I would use all that theory I learned in school!"

Chapter 4 introduced leadership models and theories in an attempt to provide a solid foundation of leadership knowledge. The focus of this chapter will be to connect those general theories to the practice of outdoor leadership. Learning outdoor leadership is no small task. Your task as a burgeoning outdoor leader is to take some of what you're learning from your leadership course, this textbook, your peers, and your professors and then practice, practice, practice. Learning about outdoor leadership is only the first step in the process of becoming an outdoor leader.

Ashley and Laird's experiences in the opening narrative highlight the fact that leadership is more art than science. It is more than a set of learned skills and competencies. Your previous experiences, your personality, the group, and other variables all factor into the practice of leadership. There are as many different styles of leadership as there are leaders. Consider your classmates for a moment. Some seem to possess a great deal of natural leadership ability. They volunteer often, use a tone of voice that commands attention, display a high level of self-confidence, and tend to have peers respond to them in a positive way. Other students have a quiet competence that can inspire great confidence in their peers. These leaders are often thoughtful listeners and supportive members of the group and may often lead from the middle or back of the group rather than the front.

Your own leadership development begins with identifying your natural leadership style and then developing an understanding of other styles and approaches as a means to developing your leadership ability. Remember that you can't be everything to everyone. Your leadership style may not always be a perfect fit for every situation and every group member. You must be authentic. Yet, natural inclination and ability alone are also insufficient. You must develop an understanding of your limitations and strive to balance your natural strengths by overcoming your limitations. As a preliminary activity to identifying your leadership style, consider learning activity 5.1 on the next page.

Outdoor leadership preparation is not an exact science; however, this chapter will introduce some of the elements that factor into your development as an outdoor leader. This chapter will first examine outdoor leader qualities and traits alongside leadership competencies and skills. The questions "Who will lead?" and "How will they lead?" will be posited as a means to identify the ways in which we become leaders and express leadership. Leadership styles will be introduced and you will have the opportunity to further examine your own leadership style. A number of outdoor leadership theories and models will be presented, including conditional outdoor leadership theory (COLT), the Outward Bound process model, the change model, and the motivational needs theory. Developing an ethic of service and an ethic of care as an outdoor leader will be emphasized, as well as the ideal of leading with integrity and humility.

Learning Activity 5.1

The concept of yin and yang is the Chinese perspective of balance and continual change.

Yin and yang are dependent opposites that must always be in balance. The opposites flow in a natural cycle, each always replacing the other. Just as the seasons cycle and create a time of heat and cold, yin and yang cycles through active and passive, dark and light, and so on. Yin and yang evolved from a belief of mutually dependent opposites that cannot live without the other. The Eastern view of opposites is, if you will excuse the pun, opposite of a Western view.

The Western perspective tends to look at things as black or white, right or wrong. There is separation and unrelatedness in the Western perspective, whereas the Eastern view sees opposites as evolving and cycling. There is neither right nor wrong. Instead there is balance, transformation, interaction, and dependent opposition. We need both to maintain a balance.

Yin and yang can further be explained as a duality that cannot exist without both parts.

Use the yin and yang symbol to list your individual strengths on one side and limitations on the other, and then share your thoughts with one or two other people. Then list specific actions you could do to try to bring your strengths and weaknesses into better balance.

For example, if your strengths are relationship oriented (you listen well, you solicit frequent participant feedback, you have an ability to "read" a group, you exhibit a flexible leadership style) while your limitations are that you need to improve paddling skills, learn how to light a fire in any weather condition, and get Wilderness First Responder certification, then you can begin to develop a plan to bring these two parts of yourself into balance. You may need to consider specific strategies for how you will begin to improve upon your limitations, for example, by concentrating on developing your technical skills.

Leadership Qualities

Effective leadership begins with an understanding of the traits and qualities and skills and competencies that factor into that process. It also begins by considering the question, "Who will lead?" If you recall, chapter 4 outlined the trait theory of leadership, which maintains that leaders are born, not made. This early theory of leadership described a leader as one who exhibits a certain set of characteristics. Such a leader speaks firmly, acts confidently, is task oriented, and is assertive. Although this theory of leadership is antiquated,

it can help inform this discussion. It has been shown that certain **leadership traits and qualities** as well as skills and competencies are important in outdoor leadership.

Traits and Qualities

A trait is a distinguishing characteristic or quality. In general, people believe that a leader is someone who has many positive qualities. Studies have suggested that those qualities include creativity, positive attitude, high expectations, integrity, sense of responsibility, courage, authenticity, self-awareness, and high ethical standards.

While research has shown that many of these qualities are significant (Bass 1990; Hitt 1990; Jordan 1996), you must possess a variety of traits, qualities, skills, and competencies to be an effective leader. Unfortunately, there is no simple equation to calculate effective leadership. In addition, simply possessing these qualities will not necessarily provide you with the ability to effectively lead. Effective leaders must develop a level of self-awareness that enhances the study and practice of leadership. Each individual's personality contributes to leadership and each person innately possesses many of the aforementioned traits and qualities. Other behaviors are learned with time and experience. Developing your ability as a leader boils down to practice, practice, and more practice.

Skills and Competencies

Kouzes and Posner (2003) are two authorities on leadership. They have categorized the attributes of successful leaders into five practices, including modeling, having a shared vision, challenging the process, enabling others to act, and encouraging the heart.

- Modeling. This practice refers to the adage, "I would never ask anyone to do anything that I was unwilling to do myself." Not only does this apply to physical tasks, it also includes talking about values and beliefs.

- Inspiring a shared vision. This means finding a way to express what could be and allowing others to buy into that goal. Kouzes and Posner maintain that leadership is a dialogue, not a monologue. Knowing other people's visions, fears, and dreams can help formulate a plan.

- Challenging the process. This involves having a goal and figuring out how to accomplish that goal.

- Enabling others to act. Enabling others to act means allowing others to do good work. If individuals within a group never have an

opportunity to practice decision making, for example, they will not improve that skill.

- Encouraging the heart. This involves displaying authentic acts of caring. Voicing appreciation and celebrating success can be ways to encourage the heart.

Recent research on outdoor leadership (Jordan 1996; Priest and Gass 1997) outlines the skills and competencies necessary for outdoor leadership. For the purpose of this text, we have outlined the eight core competencies that we deem necessary for effective outdoor leadership:

- foundational knowledge (CC-1)
- self-awareness and professional conduct (CC-2)
- decision making and judgment (CC-3)
- teaching and facilitation (CC-4)
- environmental stewardship (CC-5)
- program management (CC-6)
- safety and risk management (CC-7)
- technical ability (CC-8)

As an outdoor leader, you need to be attentive to developing each of these competencies as a component of your leadership development.

Part of this development involves understanding leadership theories and how they can be employed. Part of this development also involves understanding your own personal strengths and limitations. Your growth as an outdoor leader will come about experientially, but you can help foster this growth through journal writing and other forms of reflection. You can also help foster personal growth by soliciting and responding to feedback from mentors and participants. These aspects of leadership will be discussed in other chapters.

Who Will Lead?

A leader is either appointed or emerges from the membership to lead. It is important to consider

Learning Activity 5.2

Consider your own outdoor trip experiences. What traits and qualities did the leader possess? How did these factors influence the group? The trip experience?

the question of "Who will lead?" because both the quality of an experience and the outcome of that experience may be in doubt without adequate leadership. Responding to this query may not be as easy as it seems. Some groups may naturally be drawn to the individual who exhibits the most leadership traits. Other groups may naturally defer to the individual with the most experience. Still other groups may feel that no one person needs to be designated as a leader and leadership should be shared among its members. Often groups devote so much time and energy to the leadership question that the productivity of the group suffers.

Designated Leader

A person who is appointed as a leader is generally referred to as a **designated leader.** As an outdoor leader, you will most often find yourself in this role. You may be the leader of the day on a field-based experience for class or you may find yourself leading a group of campers as your paid summer employment. Most often you will assume the role of leader because someone has hired you or appointed you as the designated leader for a particular trip.

Emergent Leader

When leaders are appointed, an interesting problem may occur. On occasion the appointed leader has never led any group and may be unable or unwilling to carry out the role. In such cases, one person from within the group will often emerge

A variety of outdoor leadership skills and competencies contribute to effective leadership.

as the leader. (There may be other circumstances that lead to emergent leaders as well.) Consider some of your previous experiences with your classmates. Do one or two people come to mind when you think of the concept of the emergent leader? Do you know of certain individuals who naturally rise to the occasion in class and field-based experiences? Those individuals may be recognized by the group as leaders because of their previous experience, conflict resolution abilities, or general enthusiasm, without ever having been appointed as the leader. A leader who emerges from a group often has the respect of the group members. Sometimes a group has both a designated leader and an **emergent leader.**

Elected Leader

You may find yourself in the position of being an **elected leader.** For example, as an outdoor recreation student, you may have displayed natural leadership ability by taking initiative, volunteering to lead weekend trips for the outing club, or serving as a peer mentor to incoming freshman. Because of these activities, a student nominates you to be vice president of the outing club and you win the election—you are an elected leader. Elected leaders are often admired by those who follow.

Shared Leadership

Occasionally, no single person takes on the responsibility to lead and several members of the group share the leadership role. For some groups, **shared leadership** may in fact be the ultimate goal. Shared leadership works well when several group members are skilled in the tasks necessary to lead the group. For example, you and a group of friends decide to spend a weekend further honing your rock-climbing skills and you adopt a shared leadership approach. Each student contributes skills and knowledge to the weekend outing based on previous experience and areas of expertise.

Halo Effect

Sometimes a person who emerges as a leader in one group or situation and experiences success is expected to be a leader in other groups and situations. Jordan (1996) calls this the **halo effect,** which refers to "how certain attributes or thoughts about a person are carried over into other situations" (p. 25). For instance, you may be out with your recreation course for an introductory ice-climbing day. During the drive to the site, both your peers and your professor have expressed their expectation that you will rise to the occasion on the cold and windy day ahead based on their observation of you during the introductory rock-climbing day. You are nervous about their high expectations for you because although you are a skilled rock climber, you have never been ice climbing before and have never spent a full day outside in such cold temperatures. This is an example of the halo effect.

There are numerous avenues through which individuals may be identified as leaders. No matter how a person gained the role of leader, that person may not be best suited to meet the needs of the group and the situation. Returning to the definition of leadership that was introduced in chapter 4 highlights this idea. Leadership is intentional, aiming toward the accomplishment of particular goals and outcomes, and it is interactional, involving a relationship between two or more individuals in a particular situation. A peer who is playful and able to motivate the class but also influences the class in a disruptive way may be a leader, but the influence would not qualify as leadership because it is not directed toward the desired purpose. Similarly, a leader who is highly task oriented and skilled at accomplishing the intended outcome but does not include the group members in accomplishing the goal would not qualify as a successful leader. That is why both the group and the leader must be aware of what leadership style and competencies are required to move the group toward an intended purpose or outcome.

Leadership Power

Once a leader has been established through a combination of traits and qualities, skills and competencies, and designation, election, or emergence, the next question to be asked is, "How will that person lead?" This section will address that question, examining leadership power.

It has been established that leadership is a process of influence and influence is a key concept in the definition of power (Wilson 2002). Power has been defined as the ability to influence others. Leadership power comes from a number of sources; it may be reward, coercive, legitimate, referent, or expert (French and Raven 1968). No matter what your natural leadership inclination may be or what leadership styles you choose to express, you possess some bases of power that you employ to influence other people.

Reward and Coercive Power

Reward power is influence that comes from a person's ability to provide a benefit that is valued by another person. In other words, it is achieved by rewarding effort. A leader might provide compliments, special attention, or incentives, such as not having to clean up after dinner, for a job well done. A leader can withhold favors as well. This is often referred to as coercive power and usually follows the failure of reward power.

Legitimate Power

Legitimate power is influence that is granted to those who are elected, appointed, or selected to direct others. This power is inherent in the leader's position. For example, the head of a department holds a degree of legitimate power. The person who holds legitimate power has the power to make assignments related to the group's task. Most group members are likely to follow you if you have been given the responsibility to make certain decisions on their behalf.

Referent Power

Referent power is influence that comes when group members identify with a person or greatly value the person's contributions. This form of charismatic power may impel group members to work harder to please the leader. It may also cause members to want to be like the leader and emulate that person's behavior.

Expert Power

Expert power is influence based on a person's abilities or knowledge. The power comes from the fact that the leader or group member has expertise that is important to the group. For example, a person may exercise influence during a rock-climbing trip because she possesses the most technical skills within the group and is seen as the individual most capable of making decisions.

Just because group members have any or several bases of power does not mean they have influence or control in a group. Members seek help from one another to achieve the group's goal. They also need information to determine strategies for accomplishing the goal. When a group is cooperating and when goals are compatible, the group's power is moving in the same direction and there is little resistance. When competition is present or goals are not compatible, the members' power is going in opposite directions and resistance occurs. Groups need to be mutually dependent and share power. However, power is a perception of a group member's resources. Actual resources may be greater or less than that perception. A person can possess many resources that are unknown or ignored by others and therefore have little power in the group. Conversely, a group member can have few essential resources but be perceived as having many resources and is therefore given a great deal of power by others.

Every person within a group has power. The leader has the most power, at least initially. A leader will almost always express more than one source of power. The more sources of power, the greater the potential influence of the person. Leaders who are self-aware and confident have the best chance of using power to help the group move toward the desired outcome. While all five sources

of power are present within a group, Priest and Gass (1997) argue that coercive power ethically has no part in outdoor leadership, since forcing people to act in a certain manner based on negative incentives ignores challenge by choice (see chapter 8) and has the potential to destroy the adventure experience and create barriers to learning.

Leadership Styles

As mentioned in chapter 4, leadership styles are the ways in which leaders express their influence. The three main categories of leadership styles are autocratic, democratic, and abdicratic (Bass 1990; Jordan 1996).

Recognizing some of the limiting factors of these three leadership styles, Tannebaum and Schmidt (1973) identify six subcategories of leadership that place leadership styles on a continuum (see figure 5.2). These subcategories portray a range of approaches to leadership and influence based on a leader's level of authority and the level of contribution from group members. The subcategories include telling, selling, testing, consulting, joining, and delegating. These orientations help determine what leadership style an individual employs in any given situation.

Leadership Models

This section will introduce you to a number of leadership models. These models build upon the intersection of people's innate abilities, an understanding of leadership power and influence, and an understanding of leadership styles. Situational leadership theory will be introduced first as it is the foundation for the

Groups accomplish goals when they cooperate and share power.

© Jumpfoto

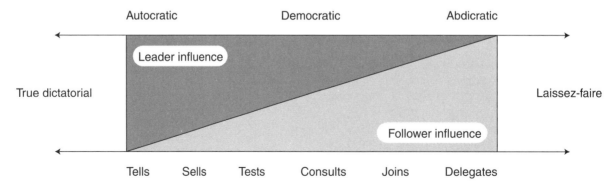

Figure 5.2 A continuum of outdoor leadership styles.

Adapted, by permission, from S. Priest and M.A. Gass, 2005, *Effective leadership in adventure programming*, 2nd ed. (Champaign, IL: Human Kinetics), 245.

outdoor leadership models that follow, including conditional outdoor leadership theory, the Outward Bound process model, a feminist model of outdoor leadership, and motivational needs theory.

Situational Leadership Theory

Hersey and Blanchard's (1982) research of situational leadership is based on the premise that most leadership activities can be classified into either task or relationship dimensions. Task actions involve one-way communication, while relationship or maintenance behaviors involve two-way communication. Hersey and Blanchard's grid of task and relationship actions results in an array of possibilities for how leadership influence is expressed (see figure 5.3). Hersey, Blanchard, and Johnson (1996) built upon this theory by suggesting that leaders must be flexible enough to change their style according to the needs of the group. This model is based on the concept of group readiness. Readiness level is defined in terms of three components: group ability, motivation, and education or experience. Following are the four levels of group readiness:

- R1 (low)—Members are unable and unwilling to do a task or are insecure about it.
- R2 (moderate)—Members are unable to do the task but are willing or confident about it.

- R3 (moderate)—Members are able to do the task but are unwilling or insecure about it.
- R4 (high)—Members are able and willing to do the task and are confident about it.

Leader behavior is thus determined by both the readiness of the group and the group's orientation to the dimensions of task and relationship. Figure 5.4 on page 62 helps illustrate this. The key assumption of the situational model of leadership is that leaders are both able and willing to adapt their leadership approach to the group's situation.

Conditional Outdoor Leadership Theory (COLT)

Priest and Gass (1997) have further developed the situational model and adapted it specifically for outdoor leaders. The **conditional outdoor leadership theory (COLT) model** postulates that outdoor leaders must go beyond the dimensions of relationship, task, and group readiness and look at the level of conditional favorability. This model is illustrated in figure 5.4. Conditional favorability is based on five factors:

1. Environmental dangers: weather, perils, hazards, and objective and subjective risks
2. Individual competence: experience, confidence, skill, attitude, behavior, and knowledge

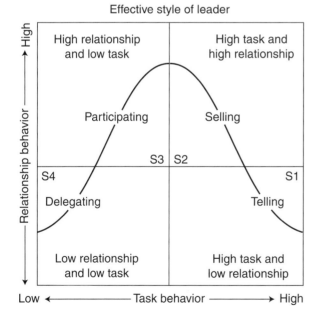

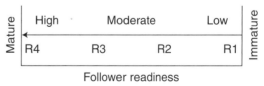

Figure 5.3 Hersey, Blanchard, and Johnson's situational leadership model.

Adapted, by permission, from G. Wilson and M. Hanna, 2002, *Groups in context*, 6th ed. (New York, NY: McGraw-Hill Higher Education), 193.

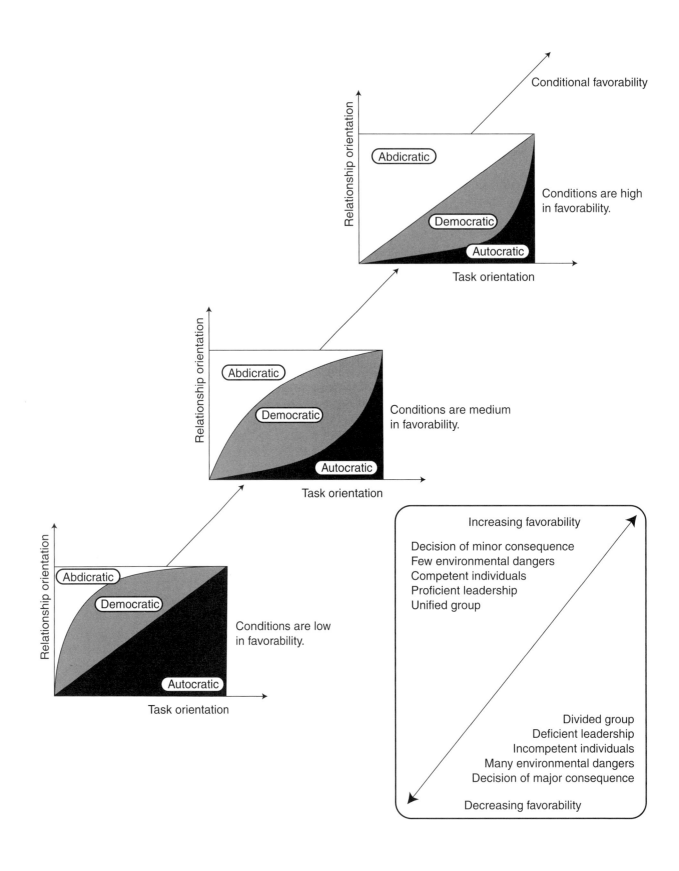

Figure 5.4 Priest and Gass' conditional outdoor leadership theory (COLT).

Adapted, by permission, from S. Priest and M.A. Gass, 2005, *Effective leadership in adventure programming*, 2nd ed. (Champaign, IL: Human Kinetics), 248.

3. Group unity: morale, maturity, cooperation, communication, trust, responsibility, and interest

4. Leader proficiency: credibility, judgment, level of stress, fatigue, and perceived capability

5. Decision consequences: clarity of the problem, sufficient solution time, available resources, expected ramification, and degree of uncertainty or challenge

The COLT model combines leadership styles, leadership orientations of relationship and task, and conditional favorability to help leaders identify whether conditions are low, medium, or high. Conditions of low favorability represent a setting where the dangers may be extreme, the leader lacks certain core competencies, the participants are inexperienced and uncertain, group morale is low, and the consequences of decisions are major. As illustrated in figure 5.4, when conditional favorability is low, the leader may shift toward a task orientation, favoring a more autocratic style. Under these conditions, it is typical for a leader to pay stricter attention to the task to ensure group safety and to retain the majority of the decision-making responsibility (Priest and Gass 1997). Luckily, low favorability is not representative of the more typical outdoor setting. In fact, if conditions of low favorability are routine for you, you need to examine why this is occurring as it may indicate a more systemic problem with the outdoor program or your own leadership ability.

Conditions of medium favorability represent the more typical outdoor setting in which dangers are within acceptable limits and may be more perceived than real, the leader is self-aware and proficient enough, the individuals are responsible, the group gets along relatively well, and the consequences of decisions are reasonable. Under these conditions, if your personal orientation is more focused on relationships, you may prefer to adopt an abdicratic style. If you are more focused on tasks, you may choose a more autocratic style. A democratic style may be most appropriate as a means to balance both tasks and relationships. The aforementioned ideal of a balanced yin and yang style of leadership may be most easily accomplished under conditions of medium favorability.

A trip setting that represents a condition of high favorability is usually desirable because dangers are minimal, the leader is proficient, the individuals are competent and keen, group morale is high, and the consequences of decisions are minor. Under these conditions, the leader may adopt an abdicratic style of leadership that tends to be more oriented toward relationships. This allows the group to have more opportunities for shared leadership and, depending upon the context, may allow for increased group development and opportunities for individual members to grow and learn.

Applying the COLT Model

Let's return to the opening vignette. Use the information in that short narrative to list the level of the five factors of conditional favorability (environmental danger, individual competence, group unity, leader proficiency, and decision consequences). In your opinion, what is the level of conditional favorability? Which leadership style did Laird employ? Which leadership style did Ashley employ? With your increased understanding of COLT, which leadership style was most appropriate and why?

In applying the COLT model to outdoor settings, you must realize that as the situation changes, so must the leadership style. It is also important to realize that the leader's style affects the level of conditional favorability. For example, imagine if Laird had maintained his extreme abdicratic style of leadership as the evening progressed. What would have been the result? Morale would have likely eroded as the group became more confused, tired, and hungry. If Laird adjusted his inclination toward abdicratic leadership to better fit the situation, he most likely would have been able to achieve a result similar to what Ashley

Learning Activity 5.3

Apply the COLT theory to a wilderness trip experience that you have either led or participated in.

achieved. By adopting a more autocratic approach to the group's first night out, Ashley helped maintain a high level of conditional favorability.

Although conditional outdoor leadership theory is one of the best fits as an outdoor leadership model, it would be an oversight to not include some of the other models that inform leadership practice. The model that is employed will be dependent on the leadership situation, the leader, and the group. These models include the Outward Bound process model, the change model, and motivational needs theory.

Outward Bound Process Model

The **Outward Bound process model** (Walsh and Golins 1976) is one of the most influential models in outdoor programming for describing the key elements of an adventure experience. The seven key elements include the learner, prescribed physical environment, prescribed social environment, characteristic problem-solving tasks, state of adaptive dissonance, mastery or competence, and transfer of new learning (see figure 5.5).

This model is one of the earliest efforts at identifying how the process of adventure learning achieves the intended results of a program. Whether the intent of the program is development of technical skills, interpersonal development, or the social and emotional development of each individual, this model has proven effective as a means to accomplish those goals (Priest and Gass 1997). As an outdoor leader, you may wish to consider this model as you develop the sequencing of your own trips and outdoor programs.

Applying the Outward Bound Process Model

Let's return again to the opening vignette for an example of this model in practice. One of the campers, or learners, is Sam. Sam finds himself in a novel and stimulating environment as a group member on the Namekagon River trip. Because Sam is traveling with his cabin group from summer camp and two counselors, his social environment represents a collective effort based on mutual support and trust. The goal is to develop an interdependent peer group that shares a common objective.

The problem-solving tasks that will arise throughout the trip represent all learning domains: cognitive, physical, and affective. Tasks will be sequentially ordered and will increase in difficulty once a base of skills and confidence has been established. Ashley's efforts on the first night represent this progression. Ashley stayed

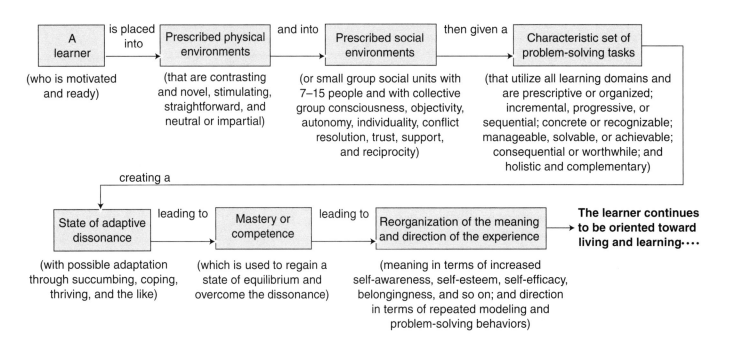

Figure 5.5 Walsh and Golins' Outward Bound process model.

(Walsh & Golins, 1976)

attentive to the group, offering them support when needed so that the group would achieve success with the setup of the first night's camp. If successful, Ashley will need to be less attentive throughout the course of the trip as the campers continue to develop their skills. A state of adaptive dissonance may result as some skills are acquired more quickly than others. Additionally, as the group develops, moments of disquiet may result among certain individuals within the group as behaviors and emotions cause dissonance. Mastery and competence of both technical skills and the affective domain will help regain the equilibrium. This will lead to increased self-awareness and self-efficacy of individuals within the group and the group itself.

Outdoor leaders should bear in mind that their level of involvement throughout this process will vary. Figure 5.1 (page 54) represents instructor involvement over the course of a trip. This graph will change somewhat depending upon the length of the trip and the conditional favorability.

The outdoor setting provides a unique site for personal growth as a result of this process. Mastery alone can provide the motivation for change, but completing such a task in a unique physical and social environment has been shown to have a particularly strong effect. The goal is for this effect to last, which can only be accomplished if individuals are provided with knowledge of how to transfer their newfound learning into other contexts. The importance of this knowledge cannot be overstated. The potential for lasting transformation in people's lives is what makes outdoor leadership such an exciting practice.

Feminist Model of Leadership

While there is no one definition of feminist leadership, there are certain qualities that feminist outdoor leaders may have in common. Warren (1996) identifies some of these commonalities as follows:

1. Many feminist leaders pay attention to relationships, believing that accomplishing tasks and establishing relationships among group members are both central to an outdoor experience.

2. Attention is paid to power relations and authority is often redefined to encompass more egalitarian principles.

3. Risk management becomes a shared concern and consensual decision making is key.

4. Personal experience is validated, particularly the experiences of those individuals who are not privileged by the dominant social structure.

5. The dichotomies of success and failure and right and wrong are eschewed.

While it may be easy to assume that any discussion of feminist leadership is connected to a discussion of women-only wilderness trips, there is value in employing a feminist model of outdoor leadership for coed groups as well (Henderson 1996; Warren 1996). The central concern of any discussion of feminist leadership is that these forms of leadership focus on the correction of invisibility and the inequality, marginalization, and oppression that women have experienced within society; the focus is not on excluding males from the trip experiences (Henderson et al. 1989). A feminist model of outdoor leadership is therefore a more egalitarian approach to outdoor leadership, one in which women have equal rights in outdoor participation and equal opportunities to become outdoor leaders, and in which their "ways of knowing" receive credence alongside more dominant ways of knowing.

Warren and Rheingold (1996) propose one model for educators to consider when implementing a more feminist way of learning and teaching. Warren and Rheingold suggest the following:

1. Work to minimize power differentials. Outdoor leaders need to recognize their power as leaders and seek methods to redistribute that power among group members.

2. Value students' personal experiences. Outdoor leaders need to develop prebriefing, **debriefing,** and reflection sessions that allow students to have a voice in their experiences. Outdoor leaders need to communicate honestly and openly through intent listening and overt action that encourages participant communication and input.

3. Advocate for female learners and use teaching methods that address diverse learning styles. Given that women have distinctly different "ways of knowing" than men, outdoor leaders need to find ways to address these ways of knowing and the learning styles of not only women but of all trip participants. Instructional methods may include consensus decision making, shared responsibility, peer mentoring, and both experiential and more traditional teaching methodologies.

The leader is displaying a feminist style of leadership through collaborative decision making and employing an ethic of care.

4. Create organizational structures that prevent the marginalization of women. Explicit policies need to be established that reinforce parity for women. Pay equity, clear paths for career advancement, skill development, and equal voices in decision making are a start (Warren and Rheingold 1996). Policies for dealing with sexual harassment and for preventing discrimination are also important.

5. Develop a critical consciousness about outdoor leadership. If reducing the marginalization and oppression of not only women but of all people is central to an outdoor trip experience, then consider the ways in which the dominant ideology influences wilderness trip experiences.

This model of feminist leadership provides one framework for outdoor educators to consider if they wish to employ outdoor leadership that actively embraces the egalitarianism that outdoor educators so often profess is central to their practice.

Motivational Needs Theory

American David McClelland is perhaps best known for his development of the needs-based motivation model. In his 1988 book, *Human Moti-* *vation*, McClelland identifies three types of motivation needs: achievement motivation, whereby people seek the attainment of realistic but challenging goals and advancement in their position; the need for authority and power, whereby people have a need to be effective and influential; and the need for affiliation, whereby people have a need for friendly relationships and are motivated toward interaction with other people.

What you should glean from **motivational needs theory** is the ability to identify your motivation and your own needs as an outdoor leader. Far too often, people become outdoor leaders for all the wrong reasons. For some, outdoor leadership provides the opportunity to be in the field and play with the latest and greatest equipment, and these individuals display little regard for their role as leaders and their responsibility to the group. Many outdoor leaders far too often, perhaps subconsciously, use their authority and power to exclude rather than include. Steve Simpson, in a book entitled *The Leader Who Is Hardly Known* (2003), illustrates this with a story (see page 68).

He concludes this story by suggesting that whatever the leaders' motivation or need fulfillment, the result was that the leaders stood out from their students and although the students may have admired the leaders' ability, Simpson

Learning Activity 5.4

Consider some of the following questions that Warren and Rheingold (1996) have encouraged outdoor educators to examine:

- Is using high-tech equipment on wilderness trips and providing trip participants with a detailed list of required personal clothing displaying an ignorance or insensitivity about class issues?
- Are trips scheduled around certain religious holidays and not others?
- Do you believe that you have had equal access to role models, including women and people of color, in your own wilderness experiences and in your training and certification courses?
- Are community service projects meeting the needs of the community, or are they quick-fix trips into disadvantaged communities?

What do these experiences communicate about who is heard and what is valued within the field of outdoor leadership?

---

queries, "Does being admired contribute to effective leadership?" (p. 14). Some understanding of your own motivation and needs as an outdoor leader should help you respond to this question and further develop your self-awareness as an outdoor leader.

Caring Leaders

Chapter 7 will further discuss what it means to develop an ethic of care as it relates to leadership. For the purposes of this chapter, think back to chapter 4 and the central figure of Herman Hesse's *Journey to the East* (page 49). Leo was the group's servant but was also the group member who emerged as the leader, sustaining the group through his spirit and song. At the time, no one knew that Leo was, in fact, the titular head of the Order and a great leader in his own right. Leo exhibited the characteristics of a caring leader and based his leadership on an ethic of service that superseded his own social class. The great leader is servant first. A leader who is a servant first cares for the group by ensuring that other peoples' needs are being met.

There are far too many examples of individuals who exhibit a sanctimonious or know-it-all attitude to cover up their own insecurities or skill deficiencies. There are also numerous examples of individuals similar to the two leaders in Simpson's story, who put their own needs before

the needs of the group. While it may be difficult to teach people how to care and to serve, this ethic must be the foundation of your leadership practice. It may help to ask yourself the following questions: Why did I make the decisions that I made today? Whose interests did they serve? Who benefited from those decisions? Am I truly listening to and understanding the needs of my group? Am I showing acceptance for each individual within the group?

Developing this level of self-awareness is a lifetime commitment and no small task. The results, however, will enhance your abilities as a leader and will grant you the group's respect and admiration. The importance of developing integrity, humility, a caring attitude, and an ethic of service cannot be underscored. Actively working toward the development of this level of self-awareness can be further encouraged through journaling, participant and coinstructor feedback, and peer mentoring, which may help outdoor leaders become more self-aware and develop strategies to turn this awareness into overt action that further encourages their growth and development.

Summary

Leadership in practice involves the influence of leadership traits as well as the necessary skills and competencies required for effective leadership.

Leader Who Is Hardly Known

The paddlers beached their canoes and walked fifty yards downstream to Beaver Rapids. At breakfast earlier that morning, the leaders had forewarned the participants that this stretch of white-water would be the most difficult of the trip and that they would have to scout it out to see whether it was runnable. The group had been paddling for four days, and all the students were now trained both in paddling skills and in treading water. They correctly identified the only possible route through Beaver Rapids. They also, to a person, felt that their skills were not ready for the difficult ferry that would be necessary to position their canoe for the last of three chutes. All of the students decided to portage.

Two of the trip's leaders, however, decided to run the rapids. They asked the Leader Who is Hardly Known and another paddler to go downstream and serve as a rescue boat. They had another student positioned on shore with a throw rope. Fortunately none of the precautions were necessary, as the leaders paddled to perfection the route the students had laid out. All the students cheered as the skilled team shot the last rapid and blasted through the last standing wave.

Later that evening Kathy, one of the two trip leaders who had run Beaver Rapids, waited for the Leader Who is Hardly Known to walk away from the group at the camp-fire. She followed him and said, "I have something to ask you. It is about the rapids Dennis and I ran today. I have seen you canoe many times, and I know your canoe skills are better than mine. You would have enjoyed running the rapids, yet you chose to portage with the rest of the group. I am sure that you portaged for a reason, and I suspect that you did it because you did not want to stand out from the group. Is this true, and do you think that I was showing off when I decided to run the rapids? That was not my intent, but it has been bothering me all day."

The Leader Who is Hardly Known smiled at the leader. "Chuangtze tells a great story about showing off.[1] The story begins with the ancient King of Wu boating on the Yangtze River. The river flows past a place called Monkey Mountain. The king and his entourage leave the river and hike up the mountain. They soon see the monkey for which the mountain is named, and when the monkeys see the king, they drop what they are doing and run off to hide in the deep brush. But one monkey stays. It jumps around and grabs at things to show the king its dexterity. When the king shoots at this monkey, the monkey snatches the arrow out of the air and shakes it at the king. The king then orders his attendants to shoot at the monkey. They bombard the monkey with arrows, and, of course, it is quickly killed.

"The king picks up the dead monkey and hands it to his friend, Yen Pu-i, and says, 'This monkey flaunted its skills and relied on its tricks—and it met with misfortune. Take this as a lesson! Do not exhibit your pride in front of others.'

"Yen Pu-i returns home and goes into training. He rids himself of pride, he learns to wipe any hint of superiority from his face, he always excuses himself from actions that would lead to fame—and at the end of three years he was known throughout his homeland for humility.

"Now you ask me if running the rapids was showing off. That is for you to decide. You are not an arrogant monkey, but neither are you a model of humility. Even if you ran the rapids strictly for fun, you stood out from your students. From what I could tell, the students admired you for it and did not resent your skills. So the question is, does being admired contribute to effective leadership?"

Reprinted, by permission, from S. Simpson, 2003, *The leader who is hardly known: Self-less teaching from the Chinese tradition* (Oklahoma City, OK: Wood 'N' Barnes Publishing & Distribution), 13-14.

However, as noted at the beginning of this chapter, simply possessing such qualities does not necessarily mean that you are an effective outdoor leader. Effective leadership comes with practice. An understanding of leadership traits and the core competencies of outdoor leadership along with a solid base of experience and a high level of self-awareness will contribute to your development as an outdoor leader.

Understanding the context of outdoor leadership is also important. Understanding your own natural inclination and leadership style will help you begin to develop a leadership ability that is balanced and adaptable to different situations. The conditional outdoor leadership theory (COLT) and the Outward Bound process model further confirm the notion that leadership must be context specific. The leadership ideal that above all you must know yourself in order to be an effective leader is emphasized along with the importance of being a caring leader, displaying integrity and humility, and seeing yourself as a servant first.

Professional-Development Portfolio Activity

Complete a leadership inventory to assess your natural inclinations as a leader. *The Student Practices Leadership Inventory* (Kouzes and Posner 1998) is highly recommended.

Selected References

Bass, B.M. 1990. *Bass and Stogdill's handbook of leadership: Theory, research, and managerial applications.* 3rd ed. New York: Free Press.

Burns, J.M. 1978. *Leadership.* New York: Harper & Row.

French, J.R., and B. Raven. 1968. The bases of social power. In *Group dynamics: Research and theory,* ed. D. Cartwright and A. Zander, 259-269. New York: Harper & Row.

Harris, T.E., and J.C. Sherblom. 2002. *Small group and team communication.* 2nd ed. Boston: Allyn & Bacon.

Henderson, K.A. 1996. Feminist perspectives on outdoor leadership. In *Women's voice in experiential education,* ed. K. Warren, 107-118. Dubuque, IA: Kendall/Hunt.

Henderson, K.A., M.D. Bialeschki, S.M. Shaw, and V.J. Freysinger. 1989. *A leisure of one's own.* State College, PA: Venture.

Hersey, P., and K. Blanchard. 1982. *Management of organizational behavior: Utilizing human resources.* 4th ed. Englewood Cliffs, NJ: Prentice Hall.

Hersey, P., K.H. Blanchard, and D.E. Johnson. 1996. *Management of organizational behavior: Utilizing human resources.* 7th ed. Upper Saddle River, NJ: Prentice Hall.

Hitt, W.D. 1990. *Ethics and leadership: Putting theory into practice.* Columbus, OH: Battelle Press.

Jordan, D. 1996. *Leadership in leisure services: Making a difference.* State College, PA: Venture.

Kouzes, J., and B. Posner. 1998. *The student practices leadership inventory.* Indianapolis: Jossey-Bass.

Kouzes, J., and B. Posner. 2003. *The five practices of exemplary leadership: When leaders are at their best.* Indianapolis: Jossey-Bass.

McClelland, D. 1988. *Human motivation.* Cambridge, UK: Cambridge University Press.

Priest, S., and M. Gass. 1997. *Effective leadership in adventure programming.* Champaign, IL: Human Kinetics.

Rich, A. 1996. Leading voices. In *Women's voice in experiential education,* ed. K. Warren, 105-106. Dubuque, IA: Kendall/Hunt.

Simpson, S. 2003. *The leader who is hardly known: Selfless teaching from the Chinese tradition.* Oklahoma City: Wood 'N' Barnes.

Tannebaum, R., and W.H. Schmidt. 1973. How to choose a leadership pattern. *Harvard Business Review* 51(3): 162-175, 178-180.

Walsh, V., and G. Golins. 1976. *The exploration of the Outward Bound process.* Denver: Colorado Outward Bound School.

Warren, K., and A. Rheingold. 1996. Feminist pedagogy and experiential education: A critical look. In *Women's voice in experiential education,* ed. K. Warren, 118-129. Dubuque, IA: Kendall/Hunt.

Wilson, G.L. 2002. *Groups in context: Leadership and participation in small groups.* New York: McGraw-Hill.

chapter 6

Judgment and Decision Making

© Jumpfoto

❝ Talent without discipline is like an octopus on roller skates. There's plenty of movement, but you never know if it's going to be forward, backwards, or sideways. ❞ —H. Jackson Brown, Jr.

Chapter Concepts

- Judgment—Judgment is an informed opinion based on past experiences.
- Good judgment—Good judgment is the ability to arrange experiences, resources, and information in a commonsense way to obtain positive results.
- Decision making—Decision making is the process of choosing the best option.
- Simple decisions—These decisions have fewer variables, limited consequences, and outcomes that are relatively predictable.
- Complex decisions—These decisions are characterized by uncertainty in terms of information, options, or outcome.
- Decision-making models—Models are used to guide the decision-making process and are based on cost–benefit analysis.
- Decision-making methods—The main methods for making decisions are leader's decision, consensus decision, voting decision, arbitration decision, chance decision, compromise decision, and expert decision.

The chapter concepts relate to the following core competency:

- Decision making and judgment (CC-3)—You can develop your judgment and decision-making abilities through an understanding of the decision-making process, models, and methods.

Nate and Meg were on day 2 of a 5-day kayaking trip in the Apostle Islands National Lakeshore on Lake Superior, leading a group of 10 people. They had just visited the sea caves on Sand Island and were preparing for a 1.5-mile (2.4-kilometer) open-water crossing to York Island. It was noon and the wind was just starting to pick up. A few members of the group voiced their need to get out of the boats and stretch their legs. Other members were starting to get hungry. Nate and Meg suggested that the group take a quick snack break while the two of them took a moment to discuss the crossing.

Nate and Meg knew that they only had a couple of minutes to come to a decision. Meg predicted that the wind would only pick up as the day progressed and she suggested that the group make the crossing now, despite their discomfort. If the group was unable to get to York Island that afternoon, they would have to backtrack to the mainland, missing out on the trip to the Raspberry Island lighthouse and the day hike on Oak Island. Nate was concerned about the fact that some of the participants were hungry and uncomfortable in their boats. He wasn't sure they should set off on a breezy, 1.5-mile crossing under those conditions. He understood that the group would be unable to complete the proposed itinerary but reminded Meg that there were still many interesting options for the group if they were unable to complete the full loop. He suggested that the group return to their previous campsite to have lunch and to reassess the group's fitness and the weather conditions.

Although she attentively listened to Nate's concerns, Meg disagreed with his assessment of the situation and his suggestion that the group return to camp. This was her fourth trip in the Apostle Islands and she had not yet made the full loop with any of her groups. No other trip leader seemed to come back from the Apostles having not completed the proposed itinerary except for her. She was concerned about what people would think of her if she returned without completing the intended trip route yet again. She was also questioning her own decision-making ability. She wondered if her overcautious nature had prevented her from completing the loop on past trips. She wanted to push herself mentally and felt that she had the technical skills and stamina to encourage the group members to push themselves physically. She really did believe that the group would be fine with the crossing. It was just a matter of going for it.

In the couple of minutes that Meg and Nate had been discussing the situation, the wind had begun to blow a bit stronger. This further impelled Meg to conclude that the group should make the crossing immediately before the weather worsened. For Nate, this was a clear indicator that the group should stay on Sand Island. In the end, Nate, Meg, and the group decided that the safest course of action would be to stay on Sand Island. The group enjoyed a wonderful day of hiking.

Decision making is the process of choosing the best option from a collection of possible options. Leaders make decisions or facilitate group decision making regularly throughout the course of a trip. For this reason, developing the process of decision making is a critical component of outdoor leadership education. Although this concept may seem somewhat straightforward, developing a process of decision making is no small task, in part because there is no such thing as a perfect decision. Consider, for example, Nate and Meg's situation. What do you think is the best decision concerning this scenario? How did you come to your decision?

Developing a process of decision making should not be confused with the need to develop sound judgment. Judgment is based on past experience and the outcomes of decisions that were made. In essence, judgment is a process of gathering relevant data. These data are then used to inform the decision-making process. Both decision making and judgment are difficult competencies to teach and learn. Developing these competencies requires the ability to see potential outcomes that may result from a decision. Consider the practice of meditation, which involves "opening" the "third eye," the eye that sees and hears everything. The third eye focuses on the sixth chakra in the body, in the middle of the forehead between the eyebrows. It is the center of wisdom and seeing. It is a symbolic representation of intuitive wisdom that helps you to see the big picture more clearly. You will need to adopt this metaphoric third eye as part of the process of developing judgment and decision making as a leader. Your third eye develops with experience; you will begin to see more patterns and your judgment will improve with each experience.

Developing the ability to see the big picture and recognize patterns is integral to decision making and judgment. In many ways, developing a third eye with which to see the big picture is a bit like playing chess. Avid chess players often describe how good players need the ability to make good decisions with the added pressure of time. Perhaps even more importantly, they need to be able to forecast the result of their decisions. Chess players need to be prepared to adjust their next decision if the forecasted result does not happen, which is often the case. In this sense, playing chess is similar to outdoor leadership. Leadership ability depends in part on a person's ability to make timely and quality decisions that anticipate a myriad of outcomes. One study that tested the effects of time pressure on chess players concluded that expert decision making develops over time and is based on an ability to recognize and respond to patterns (Klein 1998). It could be similarly concluded that a leader's judgment and decision-making abilities will improve over time with an increased knowledge of how decisions are made and their effects, knowledge that is gained through personal experience.

The purpose of this chapter is to introduce you to the role of judgment in decision making, to highlight some of the variables in decision making, to identify the differences between simple and complex decisions, to present models for decision making, to introduce methods of decision making, and to integrate ideas of decision making and leadership styles. The goal is for you to use this theoretical knowledge to develop judgment and decision-making abilities that you can apply to your own outdoor leadership experiences.

Judgment

Judgment lies at the heart of any discussion that involves problem solving or decision making. According to Paul Petzoldt, founder of the National Outdoor Leadership School (NOLS), judgment is knowing what you know and what you don't know (1984). It is a requisite skill of leadership, as important as technical skills. Petzoldt concedes that teaching techniques without commensurate judgment can in fact be dangerous.

Judgment is an informed opinion based on past experience. Good judgment is the ability to arrange experiences, resources, and information in a commonsense way to obtain positive results. Judgment is therefore inherent to the decision-making process. Judgment is particularly valuable when a leader is stalled at some point in the decision-making process. The best way to learn judgment is to do the following things (Gookin, Doran, and Green 2001, p. 18):

- Seek knowledge via formal education
- Use mentors and coaches
- Practice, practice, and practice, learning from each experience
- Maintain a self-development plan based on feedback from nature and from others

Priest and Gass (1997) suggest that judgment cannot be taught but it can be developed. They contend that the trick to developing judgment lies in the power of reasoning; experience alone is insufficient to develop judgment. They encourage leaders to engage in a process of evaluation and thoughtful reflection. Judgment is the basis for

Good judgment provides the basis for sound decision making.

Decision-Making Process

Some decisions are simple while others are quite complex. Simple decisions may include when to stop for a snack, what to eat for a meal, and what book to take on a trip. Some of the decisions that you will face as a leader will be simple. For example, you may need to decide whether to choose chili or pasta for dinner on a particular night. But many of the decisions that you will face will be much more complex than this, such as in the opening scenario. You will need to use judgment to gather relevant data before beginning the decision-making process.

You will then need to weigh your options, considering the pros and cons of each option, and then consider a process for decision making. You will need to be aware of the consequences of the decision for the group, for you personally, for safety and risk management, for costs, and for trip quality. You will need to develop a strategy for decision making whereby you balance those concerns along with the need to make timely decisions that sometimes involve group input and sometimes do not.

The decision-making process begins with the process of gathering data, which involves taking a look at the situational variables.

Situational Variables

Before further investigating how to proceed with the decision-making process, it is imperative to first develop an understanding of the variables involved in a decision. The main variables that are involved in decision making focus on the questions who, what, why, when, where, and how:

- For whom is it a problem?
- What is the problem?
- Why is it a problem?
- When is it a problem?
- Where is it a problem?
- How is it a problem?

Let's practice determining variables by using the opening scenario. Nate and Meg would be able to gather the following data by answering the questions just described:

- The decision involves both the participants and the trip leaders.

decision making. The opening narrative provides an example of this. Both Nate and Meg were using judgment to make a decision about whether or not to do the open-water crossing. Meg's past experience, along with her knowledge of the area, provided her with information upon which to judge the weather. Meg knew that as the afternoon wore on, the wind would become stronger. Nate used his past experience and knowledge about people and groups to know that when participants are hungry, tired, and uncomfortable, it is not a good time to attempt an open-water crossing. Nate and Meg took time to evaluate the situation and engage in thoughtful reflection about the potential outcomes. In other words, they were engaged in the judgment process. They were using judgment to gather data relevant to the scenario to inform the decision making that would follow.

- The problem is one of physical safety.
- It is a problem because some participants have expressed discomfort and may not be up to the task.
- It is a problem of immediate concern but the decision could be put off until later.
- The situation is even more problematic because of where it is occurring (the cold water of Lake Superior).
- It is a problem because Meg has a strong interest in completing the crossing and Nate is less certain that the group should proceed.

As you can see, this process of gathering data provides us with a great deal of information that we can use to inform the decision-making process.

Simple Versus Complex Decisions

Through the process of gathering relevant information and brainstorming, a group can identify the relevant variables in the decision-making process. **Simple decisions** have fewer variables, limited consequences, and outcomes that are relatively predictable. **Complex decisions** are characterized by uncertainty in terms of the information, the options, or the outcome. Identifying the level of complexity will allow you to respond to simple decisions relatively effectively and quickly. Be attentive to this continuum of complexity so that you do not find yourself spending undue amounts of time and energy on relatively simple decisions. Simple decisions should not be time consuming; typically, simple decisions do not significantly alter the nature of the experience and group investment in these decisions tends to be low.

However, what may initially appear to be a simple decision may become more and more complex if the decisions do not fully address the issue. For example, let's say you are the leader of a 10-day backpacking trip in Canyonlands National Park. You have a student who tends to complain about every little ache and pain. He approaches you during the late afternoon of the sixth day because he thinks that he has a blister on his heel. It has been hurting more and more as the day has progressed. You are a mile from camp and you and the group members are tired and hungry. You tell the student that the distance to camp is short, asking him if he can hang in there for another 30 minutes. He agrees. When you arrive into camp, the student slips off his boot and discovers an open blister about the size of a quarter. You clean the wound and apply second skin (a gel-like substance used to protect an open blister) to the injury, knowing that you will now need to monitor the wound closely for infection. In this example, what appeared to be a simple decision grew in complexity as a result of the original decision.

Decisions lie along a continuum of complexity as illustrated in figure 6.1. The number of variables involved and the degree of consequences influence the complexity of each decision. Most of the decisions outdoor leaders make will lie somewhere toward the middle of the continuum.

Some of the decisions outdoor leaders must make are complex. Decisions may involve length of route, daily travel distances, how to search for a lost group member, whether or not to evacuate someone with a small burn, and so on. The following discussion will introduce three models for making decisions.

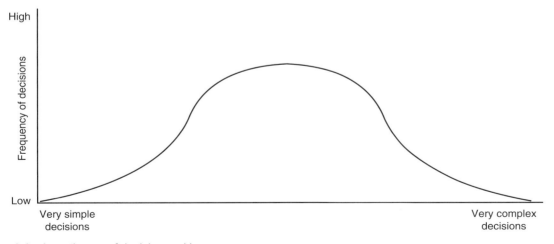

Figure 6.1 A continuum of decision making.

Learning Activity 6.1

Using the sample bell curve from figure 6.1, identify the variables that would contribute to the decision-making process in the following scenarios. Draw a bell curve with "simple" on one end and "complex" on the other. How simple or complex is the decision in each scenario? At what level of complexity would you position each decision on the bell curve?

You are about to leave for an extended backcountry trip leading 10 high school students in the Adirondack Mountains of New York. Two students suddenly realize that they forgot their flashlights. What should you do? What if it was their rain gear that they forgot? What variables would change? How would the level of complexity change?

You work for an outdoor company based in Minneapolis, Minnesota. You are on your way to Lake Powell in Utah to guide a kayaking trip. You are driving past Ames, Iowa, 3-1/2 hours into your trip, with your two coleaders, a van full of equipment, and a trailer with eight sea kayaks on it when you suddenly remember that you forgot to put the stoves in the trailer. The company is a nonprofit organization whose principle tenets include safety, quality, and cost effectiveness. What should you do?

You are guiding a group of three adults on a kayak and fishing trip on Lake Nipigon. You are getting ready to go paddling on the remote north end of the lake. You are camped on an island and are certain that there are no bears on the island. Should you hang your food (which would require you to enter into the dense bush), put the food in the boats' hatches, or "tarp it"? "Tarping it" would require wrapping a tarp around the food and then placing pots and pans over the bundle. If the bundle is disturbed, the sound from the pots and pans will serve as an alarm.

Decision-Making Models

This section will introduce you to three decision-making models that are based on cost–benefit analysis. As the name suggests, the cost–benefit approach to decision making is based on adding up the value of the benefits of a decision and subtracting the costs. For example, the potential benefits of making the open-water crossing in the opening scenario may include increased participant satisfaction, feelings of accomplishment, and the fulfillment of Meg's goal to complete the intended loop. The cost of making the crossing is that one or more boats may flip. Because the trip is on Lake Superior, the cost of a boat flipping may be fairly high due to the cold water. If you subtract the cost of a boat flipping from the potential benefits, you end up with a decision for how best to proceed.

The three decision-making models that follow will expand on this simplistic approach. The **analytic model of decision making** is a linear model that uses an analytic method for making decisions and is most effective in addressing simple decisions. The **natural decision-making model** and the **creative decision-making model** are nonlinear models that are most effective in addressing decisions that are complex and involve many situational variables.

Analytic Model of Decision Making

Numerous decision-making models have been published. The majority of these are linear, analytic models. Most of these models include some or all of the following steps:

- Define the problem
- Gather relevant information
- Consider priorities
- Consider options
- List solutions
- Evaluate solutions and consequences
- Implement a decision
- Reevaluate

For example, consider the following scenario. A trip group is on Jones Island in the San Juan Islands in Washington. They receive a weather forecast indicating that a heavy fog will be rolling in overnight. Some members of the group have to catch the ferry back to the mainland the following day because they have flights to make. With an hour of daylight left, the group has to make a decision about whether to stay on the island or return to the mainland.

Applying the analytic method to the following scenario would provide you with some relevant information upon which to base your decision:

- Define the problem—People need to get back to the mainland and there is the potential for them to get stuck on Jones Island because of a fog advisory.

- Gather relevant information—There is potential fog, more than one person needs to catch a flight, the group is physically able, and the group would be paddling in the dark.

- Consider priorities—Participants do not want to put themselves or the group in any sort of danger and yet they have strongly expressed their need to return home the following day.

- Consider options—Stay on Jones Island and risk being fogged in, attempt to paddle the next day in the fog, or do a night paddle.

- List solutions—The two best solutions are to stay on Jones Island or do the night paddle.

- Evaluate solutions and consequences—The main consequence to staying on Jones is that there is a high potential that the group will be fogged in and participants will not make it home. One consequence for doing the night paddle is danger due to other boat traffic; another danger is not knowing where the group will be able to find a camp once the crossing is made (the group is small so this unknown is less of a concern).

- Implement a decision—The group opts to do the night paddle.

- Reevaluate—Trip leaders check in regularly and the group makes the easy crossing in 30 minutes. The group finds a campsite 15 minutes later and is able to set up a suitable camp in the dark. The next day is completely fogged in and the night crossing becomes the highlight of the trip for the group!

This structured, linear model can be useful as a framework to help a group with the decision-making process. It can also be useful for both group members and group leaders who may lack experience in the decision-making process. The model may be the most useful in helping you to make timely and effective simple decisions and allowing you to evaluate the consequences of those simple decisions, preventing the simple from becoming more complex.

The linear nature of this model provides a framework for people who may lack experience with decision making; it also serves as a reminder for experienced leaders who may need a checklist to help guide the decision-making process. That said, the highly structured nature of the analytic model presents some limitations. It may be cumbersome and time consuming for most decisions that need to be made while on a wilderness trip. Additionally, in a typical wilderness trip environment, information is often lacking at each stage of the model. For example, situational variables, such as weather, may make it impossible to fully gather all relevant information. Information is often incomplete and situations are in flux in a wilderness environment. For this reason, leaders often have to rely on their intuition and past experience when making decisions.

Natural Decision-Making Model

Most experienced outdoor leaders rely on systematic thinking, common sense, intuition, and experience-based judgment in the decision-making process. Kosseff (2003) refers to this process as natural decision making, suggesting that

© Jim West

Some decisions require quick action, while others allow the leader more time to think.

the analytic model of decision making is more conducive to confirming decisions that have already been made. Outdoor leaders are usually called upon to make quick decisions, although far too often leaders feel compelled to make decisions more quickly than they need to. The first step in the decision-making process is to start by stopping. In other words, it may be best to begin with no action and to simply consider the situation. This will help you determine the gravity of the situation. For example, if a sea kayak tips over unexpectedly while a group is paddling on Lake Superior, there is a need to act quickly. This urgency is based predominantly on the cold temperature of the water and the necessity of getting the person out of the water quickly. On the other hand, if a canoe tips over on a Boundary Waters trip on a hot day in August, the result of this scenario may be an everybody-in water fight.

The natural decision-making model is nonlinear. It relies on the ability to think systematically, listen to and apply anecdotal information, and use common sense and natural intuitive ability. Furthermore, this process involves reflecting upon past experiences and applying them to new ones.

For example, you have theoretically mastered the technique of orienteering but have yet to experience it firsthand. You have been told by a number of people that you should combine your knowledge of orienteering with map reading to fully hone your backcountry skills. You decide to apply your newfound knowledge and choose a relatively short walk through the bush to assess your orienteering ability, relying solely on your compass. You take a bearing and then tuck your map into your pack. You progress through the bush, knowing that you should reach an old logging camp if your bearing is accurate. One hour later, you peripherally spot the camp, half a mile (.8 kilometers) off your intended bearing. You take the map out of your pack to determine what went wrong and realize that you unknowingly were walking slightly off your bearing the whole time, trying to avoid a low-lying swampy section in the woods. You now better understand how and why it is important to use a map and a compass when orienteering. Your knowledge of reading bearings, map reading, choosing stoppers along the route, and noting contours as you travel improves with experience. As you gain more experience, your decision-making ability will also develop.

Creative Decision-Making Model

The creative decision-making model is also nonlinear but the level of structure and the approach that is employed will depend upon the situational variables. This model involves the use of inductive and deductive reasoning. Creative decision making is based on pattern recognition, reflective thinking, simulation, and extended brainstorming, as illustrated in figure 6.2.

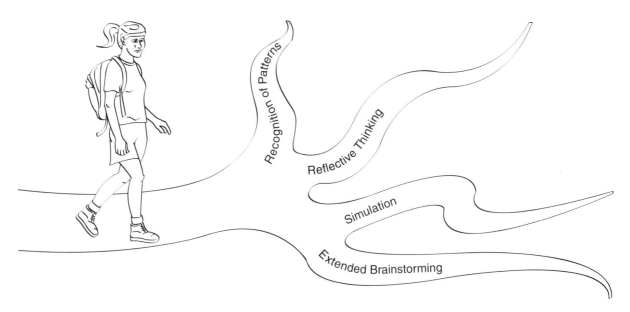

Figure 6.2 The creative decision-making model may require the leader to use any one or all of the following "paths": recognition of patterns, reflective thinking, simulation, or extended brainstorming.

Pattern Recognition

The **recognition of patterns** involves developing a sort of sixth sense. You will begin to recognize certain patterns as you lead more and more wilderness trips. These patterns include weather prediction, participant behavior, the average distance that a group paddles in a day, and how much pasta to pack for a group of 10. The more experience you have, the greater your recognition of these patterns will become. This process is also called inductive reasoning. Inductive reasoning is used to develop general concepts from specific experiences.

For example, you are an experienced sea kayaker and you have been on many personal trips. You know from experience that you and your paddling partner are able to pack up camp in about 1.5 hours and that you paddle an average of 3.5 miles (5.6 kilometers) an hour in calm weather conditions. You receive a call from a friend who is working at a summer camp. The camp is looking for an experienced paddler to help colead a 6-day kayak trip. You agree to colead the trip and suggest a route based on your previous experience. On day 1 of the trip, you are shocked to discover that the group needs 3 hours to pack camp, eat breakfast, load the boats, and get on the water. You quickly discover that a group of 10 people travels at a much different pace than a group of 2. You and your coleader decide to adjust the intended route accordingly. As you continue to lead more and more trips, your accuracy in predicting travel times for groups improves. Your ability to recognize patterns will become more refined and your inductive reasoning will improve with experience.

Reflective Thinking

In a book entitled *How We Think* (1933), John Dewey suggests that decisions should be based on a process of **reflective thinking.** "The Road Not Taken," a Robert Frost poem, helps illustrate this. In the poem, a traveler has finished a journey that involved a decision about which path to choose.

The traveler concludes, "Two roads diverged in a wood, and I— / I took the one less traveled by, / And that has made all the difference." In this scenario, the traveler must either arbitrarily choose which fork to take, trusting to luck for the outcome, or he must discover grounds for the conclusion that a given road is the right path to take. Any attempt to decide the matter through

critical thinking will involve inquiring into other facts, bringing to mind past experiences, or further observation. This process involves reflective thinking and deductive reasoning.

Reflective thinking is aimed at the discovery of facts that will help determine which road to choose. Reflective thinking is employed when a situation is ambiguous, when it presents a dilemma, and when alternatives are available (Dewey 1933). When uncertainty is present and information is missing, you must rely on your memory of general concepts, making specific predictions to fill in for uncertainties. This is the process of deductive reasoning. In this case, the traveler would look for certain signs that the path she chooses will result in the intended outcome. The traveler may wish for her route to be both beautiful and safe. She would then make a prediction of which path to take based on her general understanding of conditions that contribute to beauty and safety.

The Road Not Taken

Two roads diverged in a yellow wood,
And sorry I could not travel both
And be one traveler, long I stood
And looked down one as far as I could
To where it bent in the undergrowth;

Then took the other, as just as fair,
And having perhaps the better claim,
Because it was grassy and wanted wear;
Though as for that the passing there
Had worn them really about the same,

And both that morning equally lay
It leaves no step had trodden black.
Oh, I kept the first for another day!
Yet knowing how way leads on to way,
I doubted if I should ever come back.

I shall be telling this with a sigh
Somewhere ages and ages hence:
Two roads diverged in a wood, and I—
I took the one less traveled by,
And that has made all the difference.

Robert Frost, 1915.

Simulation

If time permits, simulation may be a valuable technique in the decision-making process. Simulation involves step-by-step consideration of each decision and the outcomes of the decisions. Imagine that you and your group are on a mountaineering trip in the Sawtooth Range of Idaho. It is early summer and the rivers are running fast and high. You are on your way to the base camp and you come across a swift-moving river crossing. A wet log crosses the river and it is obvious that many people have used the log to cross this stretch of river. If you were on your own, you would not hesitate to walk across. However, you are responsible for a group of eight teens, some of whom are more agile than others. You suggest that the group stop for lunch. While they are eating, you walk over to the river's edge. You look upstream and downstream. You mentally picture a student on the log and imagine a fall into the river and the swift current. You can visualize that the outcome of a fall may be serious. You quickly decide to set a fixed line and to personally carry the students' packs across the log. Everyone makes it across successfully as a result of your ability to mentally simulate the potentially negative outcomes of a hasty decision.

Extended Brainstorming

Creative decision making may also involve an extended session of brainstorming. When truly difficult decisions present themselves, do not hesitate to take the time, when it is available, to list all ideas. This process will allow you to fully consider unconventional options. Leaders need to learn to develop 360° vision, which involves consciously transferring the focus from the conventional to the unconventional. While the recognition of patterns is important, far too often leaders overlook some of the best options by employing the same techniques over and over again. Be careful to not overstandardize your mental checklist.

The analytic model clearly represents the most structured approach to decision making. However, because the nature of wilderness travel is infused with uncertainty, this model has limitations. Additionally, there are few standard responses to most problems that arise over the course of a trip. For this reason, some combination of these decision-making models may provide the most useful application. The model in figure 6.3 will help to illustrate this.

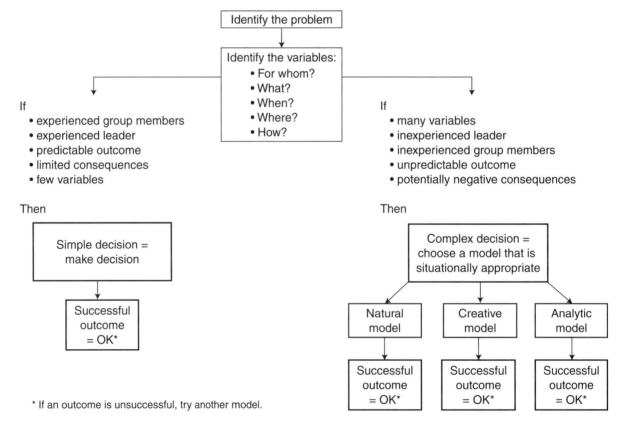

Figure 6.3 Combination of three decision-making models.

Think back to one of your own wilderness trip experiences. It can be a trip that you either led or participated in, or it can be some other leadership-based experience. Write a brief scenario (using some of the examples from this chapter) of a decision that needed to be made on the trip; the more complex the decision, the better. Get into small groups and apply one or a combination of the decision-making models to try to solve the case study. Report back to the class, discussing the decision-making process and the end result. Provide the class with information on what actually happened and how the problem was resolved.

Decision-Making Methods

You may be asking yourself, "Now what?" To review, this chapter has thus far introduced the importance of using judgment to gather relevant data to assist with making decisions. You have been introduced to the difference between simple and complex decisions. Three decision-making models have been described along with examples of how to apply those models in real-life situations. This section will now present different methods that a leader can employ to make decisions, which will lead into a discussion of decision making and leadership styles.

Imagine for a moment what it would be like if you, as a leader, had to gain consensus every time you made a decision. Conversely, imagine if you chose to flip a coin to aid you with decision making, opting to ignore all the situational variables. Just as there is no one decision-making model that works for every situation, there is no one method of decision-making.

The main methods for making decisions are leader decision, consensus decision, voting decision, arbitration, chance decision, compromise decision, and expert decision.

- Leader decision: The leader makes a decision without consulting the group members.

- Consensus decision: The leader would like the group to come to full agreement about a particular decision.

- Voting decision: A voting decision may occur if the leader wants to get input quickly from the group and is not seeking unanimity.

- Arbitration: An outside source, or arbitrator, would listen to and consult with the group and offer a recommendation on how the group should proceed. Arbitration may occur if the leader lacks expertise in a certain area or if the

group is at a standstill and needs an outside source to be involved in the decision-making process.

- Chance decision: Chance decides. For example, if a group needs to decide whether to have chili or pasta for dinner that night, they may make this decision by flipping a coin.

- Compromise decision: If a group is unable to come to consensus on a particular issue, they may choose instead to make a decision based on compromise. In this instance, certain group members may compromise their position to allow the group to move forward.

- Expert decision: On some occasions, the decision may be left to an expert. The group leader may lack the expertise to make a particular decision and there may be an expert in the group who is better informed and able to do this.

Groups can employ any number of methods when making decisions.

Table 6.1

Advantages and Disadvantages of Decision-Making Methods

Decision-making method	Advantages	Disadvantages
Leader decision	• for simple, routine decisions • when time is short • when group has less experience	• lack of group input and "buy in" • the group may have knowledge that would contribute to the decision
Consensus decision	• full input from the group • greater potential for creative solutions to problems • commitment from all involved	• time consuming • requires skilled leader to facilitate
Voting decision	• useful for decisions where you want some level of group input and time is short • quick and straightforward	• usually results in unhappy, minority group members • full commitment and participation are absent
Arbitration	• delegates responsibilities to an outside source • most valuable when the group lacks expertise and experience	• does not utilize knowledge and experience of the group members • no commitment by group
Chance decision	• quick and efficient • good for very simple decisions, involving few variables and no "real" consequences	• highly random • no input or commitment from the group
Compromise decision	• equal input from all group members • everyone has a "voice" in the process	• time consuming • reaching a compromise may not result in the "best" decision • may not have "buy in" from a number of group members
Expert decision	• delegates responsibilities to someone who possesses the most expertise • good when time is short • good when the group lacks expertise	• no input or commitment from the group • decision may alienate either the expert or the group members

Table 6.1 identifies the advantages and disadvantages of each method.

The decision-making method that is employed will depend upon the situation. These categories also are more discreet theoretically than they may appear in practice. For example, a leader decision may involve a process whereby the leader, under a time constraint, makes a decision, communicates that decision to the group, and expects the group members to follow. Under a different set of conditions, however, the leader may ask for group input. Group members may act in a consultative role whereby the ultimate decision is still made by the leader but that decision is made with the input of the group.

The two categories of consensus and compromise highlight the difference between decisions that are made unanimously and decisions that are made based on group unity. The Religious Society of Friends (Quakers) offers an interesting insight into the differences between these two methods of decision making. In a sense, the process of coming to unity involves the 80–20 rule. If 80% of a group can agree with a decision and the decision needs to be made in a timely manner, then it may be wise for that decision to move forward with majority approval. In a sense, the 80–20 rule is one example of a decision based on compromise. Quakers believe in trying to reach unity when making decisions. Unity does not involve a process whereby

Learning Activity 6.3

Under what conditions would you use these methods of decision making? Would you ever "flip a coin" and let chance determine the decision? When? For what kinds of decisions would gaining consensus from the whole group be important?

everyone is in agreement with a particular decision. That is unanimity, or consensus. Unity involves a process whereby each and every person who has something to contribute to the decision-making process does so. As people continue to contribute their ideas, a sense of consensus begins to develop and people proclaim "I agree" or "I can unite with that." Often, some people continue to disagree. They may express this by saying, "I would be uncomfortable with that decision." Discussion continues in an attempt to reach consensus. But true consensus in the form of unanimity is often quite difficult to reach. What typically happens in such an instance is that the group may move forward with a certain decision. The dissenters will withdraw their opposition to the decision so that the meeting may proceed but will ensure that their opinion on the matter is understood, stating, "I will step aside but would like my disagreement to be noted." The process of reaching unity is time consuming but has the advantage of full group participation and commitment (Sheeran 1983).

Decision Making and Leadership Styles

Both the decision-making model and method you choose will intersect with the earlier discussion on leadership styles. If you think back to chapters 4 and 5, your approach to making decisions may depend upon the leadership style you employ, whether you adopt an abdicratic, democratic, or autocratic approach. Your decision will also depend upon the conditional favorability of the situation. In an emergency situation where you are both the leader and the expert, you will be required to use good judgment to make timely decisions. If you are the instructor of a course and the conditions of favorability are high, you may find that you make very few decisions as the formal leader of the group.

The modified model in figure 6.4 uses Hersey and Blanchard's (1982) assessment of group readiness (chapter 5) as an indicator of which

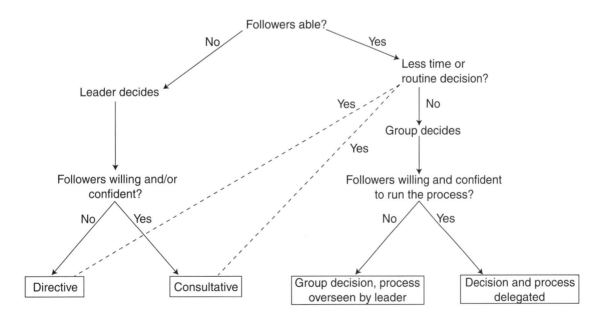

Figure 6.4 A modified form of Hersey and Blanchard's model for choosing a decision-making style.

Adapted from the National Outdoor Leadership School, 2001, *2001 NOLS leadership education toolbox* (Lander, WY: NOLS), 20.

decision-making style is most appropriate for which situation.

This model is based predominantly on factors such as time, the ability of the followers to be involved in the decision-making process, and the complexity of the decision.

Additionally, the methods and models of decision making that you employ will depend upon your past successes and failures with those decisions. Consider this concept as it relates to leadership style. When novice leaders are presented with a challenging wilderness trip environment, they may adopt a very autocratic leadership style in an attempt to gain greater perceived control of the environment. The novice leader needs to be attentive to adopting a leadership style that is appropriate to the situation and the level of conditional favorability, weighing leadership experience as one factor against a backdrop of many factors.

Past successes and failures relate to the decision-making process as well. It is quite common for a leader who made a decision that resulted in a negative outcome to adopt a leadership style and decision-making process that is more conservative than the next situation demands. This is, of course, human nature. But it is important to not overreact by adopting a decision-making style that is overly autocratic.

For example, you have just returned from a sea-kayaking trip in the Rossport Islands on Lake Superior. You had a boat overturn on that trip, in part as a result of your decision to do an open-water crossing in windy conditions. The outcome of that decision was that you had a trip participant with mild hypothermia who declared that she would never take a trip with the agency again. You are scheduled to go out on another trip to Rossport Islands in 2 days. During the posttrip debrief, you were strongly chastised by one of the company's administrators for your poor judgment and decision making. You feel a sense of dread about your upcoming trip. You suggest to your coleader that the group may benefit from doing day trips from a base camp on Wilson Island instead of traveling to some of the outer islands. Now read Learning Activity 6.4 and answer the questions.

Your decision-making ability will mature alongside your overall leadership ability. It is important to be attentive to the outcomes of your previous decisions and to try to recognize any patterns that may be developing as a result of your past successes and failures. It is equally important, however, to not be paralyzed by some of the negative outcomes of your past decisions. This form of experience-based judgment will develop with practice.

Summary

Decision making is about choosing the best option from a collection of possible options. It involves developing judgment and choosing a decision-making model and method to help you determine the best option. While the models and methods of decision making may appear to be discreet theoretically, they will be less so in practice. Your judgment, the situational variables involved, and the level of favorability will all play a role in the method and model that you employ. It is necessary to develop your judgment and decision-making ability through experience and reflection. Use both your successes and your failures to improve your abilities and remember that there is no such thing as a perfect decision. The approach to developing judgment and decision-making skills is the same as that for learning to lead. These skills will develop over time with education, with experience, and as a result of the reflective process.

Learning Activity 6.4

Using the Rossport Islands example on this page, answer the following questions. Is doing day trips from a base camp on Wilson Island the most appropriate decision for the group? Why or why not? What are some of the considerations guiding that decision?

Professional-Development Portfolio Activity

Keep a journal of "A Day in the Life of You," describing decisions that you make during the day. Distinguish between simple and complex decisions. Write a 1-page essay in which you draw conclusions regarding decision making from the day. What did you learn?

Selected References

Dewey, J. 1933. *How we think: A restatement of the relation of reflective thinking to the educative process.* Lexington, MA: D.C. Heath and Company.

Frost, R. 1969. *The poetry of Robert Frost.* 9th ed. Ft. Worth, TX: Holt, Rinehart & Winston.

Gookin, J., M. Doran, and R. Green, eds. 2001. *2001 National Outdoor Leadership School (NOLS) education toolbox.* Lander, WY: NOLS.

Hersey, P., and K.H. Blanchard. 1982. *Management of organizational behavior: Utilizing human resources.* 4th ed. Englewood Cliffs, NJ: Prentice Hall.

Klein, G. 1998. *Sources of power: How people make decisions.* Cambridge, MA: MIT Press.

Kosseff, A. 2003. *Appalachian Mountain Club (AMC) guide to outdoor leadership.* Boston: AMC Books.

Petzoldt, P. 1984. *The new wilderness handbook.* 2nd ed. New York: Norton.

Priest, S., and M. Gass. 1997. *Effective leadership in adventure programming.* Champaign, IL: Human Kinetics.

Sheeran, M.J. 1983. *Beyond majority rule: Voteless decisions in the Religious Society of Friends.* Philadelphia: Philadelphia Yearly Meeting.

chapter 7

Values and Ethics

© Sport the Library

" The worst sin towards our fellow creatures is not to hate them, but to be indifferent to them; that's the essence of inhumanity. " —**George Bernard Shaw**

Chapter Concepts

- Values—Values are beliefs, not facts. They affect how people think, judge, feel, and act.
- Ethics—Ethics is the study of moral values and conduct.
- Kohlberg's model of moral development—This model identifies six stages that can be used to assess moral development.
- Ethic of care versus ethic of justice—An ethic of care is based on relationships. An ethic of justice, on the other hand, operates upon the principles of fairness and reciprocity.
- Profession versus professional—It has been argued that while outdoor leadership may be a profession, it is not yet professional.
- Model for making ethical decisions—This 5-step model relates to professional practice.

The chapter concepts relate to the following core competencies:

- Self-awareness and professional conduct (CC-2)—Acting mindfully and intentionally as an outdoor leader and developing a strong sense of personal and professional ethics are part of this competency.
- Decision making and judgment (CC-3)—Making ethical decisions is an important part of decision making.

It was Hilary's first season leading wilderness trips. She had just completed her degree in outdoor recreation and was keen to apply all that she had learned. Hilary received her contract from a wilderness trip company and was pleased to discover that she would be leading a number of trips with Seth. Seth was a seasoned veteran of the company. She had heard that he displayed great balance as an outdoor leader, possessing superb technical skills alongside exceptional interpersonal skills and leadership ability. Seth and Hilary were scheduled for an 8-day backcountry trip on Yellowstone Lake in Yellowstone National Park.

It was 10 p.m. on the fifth day of the trip and Hilary was thrilled with how well the trip had been going. The group was getting along and the scenery and wildlife were unbelievable. She and Seth were working well together as coleaders. She was particularly impressed by his willingness to share leadership responsibility. She was learning that Seth was a gracious, fair, and caring leader. Hilary was heading toward her tent that night, however, when she heard giggling and whispering coming from Seth's tent. She listened a bit more closely and heard a woman's voice. She wasn't sure what to do, especially since she was uncertain about what was really going on in Seth's tent. What she did know is that the company had emphasized throughout staff training that leaders were not allowed to be romantically involved with participants during the trip. The

company policy was clear about this particular ethic. Hilary did not want to jump to any conclusions so she decided to wait and talk with Seth the next day.

Hilary approached Seth the next morning with her concern. Seth told her to mind her own business and walked off, leaving Hilary confused and somewhat irritated. It was clear that Seth did not want to talk about it and Hilary thought that it was probably best to let it go since the rest of the trip was going so well. During the rest of the trip, though, Hilary continued to notice Seth blatantly flirting with a particular woman and that the two of them would often excuse themselves early from the campfire, claiming that they were tired. Hilary wanted to maintain a good relationship with Seth while on the trip, so she decided to wait and bring the issue up again during their posttrip debriefing.

When the trip was finished and the two of them were meeting for the debriefing, Hilary decided that she would mention to Seth again what she had heard on that night and what she had observed throughout the trip. Again, Seth said that it was none of her business, refusing to talk about it. This behavior confused Hilary a great deal since it was so out of sync with the rest of his behavior on the trip. Hilary did not know what to do. Should she try to talk with Seth again? Should she tell him how much his breach of policy bothered her? Should she talk with the program director about her concern? Hilary was experiencing an ethical dilemma.

Outward Bound was founded in part as a response to an ethical dilemma. In 1932, Kurt Hahn, a German, spoke out publicly against Hitler and the Nazi movement (Richards 1999). Hahn's address was in direct response to Hitler's Beuthen telegram, in which Hitler demanded that five storm troopers be released despite their convictions and death sentences for trampling a young Communist to death in front of his mother. Specifically, Hahn wanted to better understand the motivation behind this killing. He wondered why people stood by and watched this brutal attack. He questioned the values and beliefs of the people who witnessed this attack and the values and beliefs of the attackers. As a result of these questions, Hahn was persecuted by the Nazis and imprisoned for his beliefs. He was later released at the request of the British government and exiled from Germany.

Hahn moved to the United Kingdom, where he turned his attention to solving the problem of the deaths of young sailors on torpedoed merchant ships in the Battle of the Atlantic during World War II. As noted in chapter 2, Hahn developed Outward Bound as a response to this problem. Outward Bound and Hahn's other educational initiatives (Gordonstoun School, United World Colleges, Salem Schule, and Duke of Edinburgh's Award Scheme) were all based on the notion that educating young people for the purpose of building moral character was just as important as training the intellect. Hahn developed these schools as a direct response to some of the questions he had regarding the ethics behind the attack of the young Communist in Germany and from the writings of William James. James (1949) saw that war, while producing a host of immoral actions and destructive consequences, also often produced behaviors that brought out the best in people. James believed that the aims of society would be advanced if some mechanism could be produced that continued to develop these moral qualities in people without the destructive and immoral aspects of war. The principles of Hahn's educational ideals were therefore constructed in part around this provision of a moral equivalent to war (Priest and Gass 1997). Hahn's aim was to use adventure education as a tool to arm young people against the allure of fascism and war.

Hahn was greatly influenced by the writings of Plato. In *The Republic* (360 b.c.e.), Plato suggests that the fundamental goal of education is the development of human character to attain "just" citizens to exist in and rule an ideal state. Plato became devoted to better understanding ethics through an examination of justice and notions of right and wrong. He sought to define and identify good, bad, and virtue, and emphasized the necessity of turning thoughts and beliefs into direct action. Leadership therefore occurs within a practice, or actions. Plato asks "What is the right way to live?" and encourages people to question whether their practice (beliefs and actions) is ethical.

What, then, is the role of values and ethics within the context of outdoor leadership? At the Association for Experiential Education (AEE) Conference in the fall of 2000, speaker Dan Garvey asked the members in attendance, "How many of you think that you do 'good' in your work?" He further posited, "What good do you do and how do you know?" These may not have been his exact words, but the intention behind those questions was to encourage outdoor leaders to thoughtfully examine their professional practice. The basic premise of this chapter is that a person who has thought about ethical matters is better able to handle these matters than someone who has never thought about them.

This chapter introduces ethical theories, helping you clarify your worldview and its influence on your practice. Many discussions on professional ethics focus on the potentially destructive results of certain practices, advising leaders what not to do. Instead, this discussion will center on what leaders should do. We will begin by identifying the role of values and ethics in outdoor leadership. Kohlberg's theory of moral development will be introduced as a means to differentiate between an ethic of care and an ethic of justice. The chapter will end with a discussion of professionalism in outdoor leadership.

Values and Ethics in Outdoor Leadership

Few people would question that a leader ought to be ethical. The difficult part is defining what constitutes ethics. Whose values determine whether a practice is ethical? We may find it hard to describe what it means to be an ethical leader beyond simple words such as honest and fair. Jasper Hunt is an educational philosopher who has contributed enormous insight into ethics in outdoor and experiential education. He provides a good starting point to look at the role of values and ethics in outdoor leadership.

Hunt (1994) argues that the distinction between morals and ethics is historical and the terms may

Learning Activity 7.1

What are your values? Make a list of the 10 things that you value most in life. This list may include family, religion, wilderness, peace, and so on. How might these inform and influence, either directly or indirectly, your own leadership and the decisions that you make?

be used interchangeably. He maintains that "the study of ethics is the study of why one state of affairs is morally better or worse than another state of affairs" (p. 5). He suggests that there is a distinction between values and ethics, however. A set of values guides a person's life, and any description of a person's ethics would be based on an understanding of the person's values. To understand ethics and what influences ethical conduct, leaders need to gain an understanding of values. The next section will take a brief look at values.

Outdoor leaders must prepare to handle different kinds of ethical dilemmas, such as group members breaking branches from live trees.

Sources of Values

We often hear that a person who has strong values makes for a good leader. But, what are values? Where do they come from? What role do they play in leadership? Are they fixed or modifiable? These are some of the questions to ask yourself as you begin to explore the role of values in outdoor leadership. It has been shown that leaders' values influence their decisions and the directions they take; therefore, an exploration of values is a good place to begin an understanding of leadership practice.

Values Defined

Values are beliefs, not facts. They affect how one thinks, judges, feels, and acts. Values are determined and identified by a number of factors. Many of these factors relate to individual upbringing, including home environment, education, religious belief, and socioeconomic class. Leaders communicate what they value through what they say as well as how they act and interact. Leaders communicate their values through the clothes they wear, the questions they ask, the people they respond to, the way they respond to people, and the behaviors that they recognize and reward. Outdoor leaders build trust and respect by behaving ethically and consistently from a solid value base. Developing this base may require some time and attention.

Axiology

The question of values deals with notions of what a person or a society conceives of as "good." **Axiology** is the branch of philosophy that seeks to answer the question, "What is of value?" (Knight 1989). In *The Nature of Human Values*, Rokeach defines a value as "an enduring belief that a specific mode of conduct or end-state of existence is personally or socially preferable to an opposite or converse mode of conduct or end-state of existence" (1973, p. 5). Modes of conduct may include end-values as goals and as standards, such

Learning Activity 7.2

Draw your "lens" (see figure 7.1) considering the sources of your values: religion, education, travel, upbringing, environment, socioeconomic class, gender, sexuality, race, and so on. What is your epistemology or way of knowing (and seeing) the world?

as honor, courage, civility, honesty, and fairness. A value system is the organization of these beliefs along a continuum of relative importance.

Epistemology

Epistemology is the branch of philosophy that studies the nature, sources, and validity of knowledge (Knight 1989). Roughly translated, epistemology means "ways of knowing." It seeks to answer such questions as "What is true?" and "How do we know?" Epistemology is therefore rooted in an understanding of the sources of truth. (Also see figure 7.1.)

All leaders have a set of values that guides them in the selection of objectives and in the decision-making process. Once the sources of values have been identified and understood, attention should be directed toward the sources of ethics.

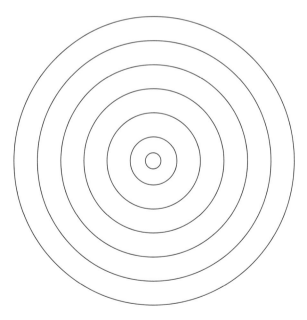

Figure 7.1 In order to better understand values and their influence, people need to develop an understanding of the lens through which they "see" the world and interpret sources of truth.

Sources of Ethics

Leaders who are aware of and consistent in their ethics are generally well-respected and effective. But, what is ethics? What role does it play in leadership? What does it mean to be an ethical person? Ethics is the study of both moral values and conduct. For the most part it is focused on moral reasoning. A study of ethical behavior seeks to provide answers to such questions as "What should I do?" and "What is the good life for all people?" Ethical theory is concerned with providing the "right" values as the foundation for the "right" actions (Knight 1989). It suggests that certain actions are more appropriate than others.

The questions at hand are, "How does a leader go about determining ethical conduct?" and "How does a leader determine the 'right' action in a given situation?" In thinking back to the opening vignette, for example, was Seth's behavior ethical? Why or why not? How should Hilary proceed with her knowledge about Seth's apparent ethical breach? This section will introduce you to ethical principles and theories as a means to understand how to respond to those questions.

Principle Ethics

Principle ethics are guided by a set of rules, often proactively determined by a governing professional organization or by the current professional standards of behavior (Jordan and Meara 1990). Hunt (1994) refers to this as ethical objectivism: "The ethical objectivist maintains that in order for an act to be a good act, it must have been made in accordance with some source of morality that transcends the limitation of a particular person or set of limited circumstances" (p. 10). In other words, a principle ethic is an ethic that is established by a governing body. The governing body, be it a church, government, or company, determines whether or not an act is ethical.

One source of objectivism is the Judeo-Christian religious tradition. Within this tradition, the good

Learning Activity 7.3

Give an example of each kind of ethic below, and list some weaknesses of each ethical stance.

- Principle ethic
- Virtue ethic
- Consequentialist ethic
- Nonconsequentialist ethic

act is action taken in accord with the will of God. One example of a principle ethic within this tradition is the Ten Commandments. Principle ethics and ethical objectivism impel individuals to look outside the situation in order to determine right from wrong. Laws represent another form of principle ethics. If this principle were applied to the ethical dilemma in the opening vignette, Seth's behavior would be determined to be unethical because the company policy clearly states that romantic involvement of any kind is unacceptable.

Virtue Ethics

Virtue ethics are guided by the virtues associated with being a moral outdoor leader rather than the principles of being ethical. Virtue ethics are concerned with professional character traits, focusing on the questions of "Who shall I be?" and "Am I doing the best for my participants?" (Jordan and Meara 1990). According to this ethic, an individual must examine the factors and influences of each act, maintaining that the right decision is defined by each situation and cannot be linked to any decision made in other situations. Hunt (1994) refers to this as ethical subjectivism, whereby a good action is one that any individual holds to be good. The source of ethics for the subjectivist is the individual person: "The ethical subjectivist maintains that if a person claims that an act is a good act, then that claim is a sufficient condition for the act being good" (p. 9). In the opening vignette, for example, Seth may reason that his behavior is ethical, arguing that he knows right from wrong and that his ethical behavior depends on the situation.

Consequentialist Ethics

One of the most common approaches in determining right from wrong is to make judgments in terms of the highest good. The highest good is also called the **summum bonum,** or the supreme good from which all others are derived (Hunt 1994). Ethical consequentialism provides an application for the practice of normative ethics. Normative ethics is not only objective; it is universal: "The consequentalist reasons that the only way to apply the summum bonum to specific cases is in terms of the results of a given act" (Hunt 1994, p. 15). Therefore, if the end result of an act has good consequences in terms of the highest good, then the act itself is judged to be a good act. If the act results in bad consequences, then the act is a bad act. The focus is on the end result of the action.

Utilitarianism is a **consequentialist theory of ethics** that maintains that an act is good only if it brings about the greatest good for the greatest number. There are two fundamental pillars of a utilitarian approach to ethics. "Happiness" is the first pillar and "for the greatest number" is the second pillar (Mill 1962). Imagine yourself on a wilderness trip where the group's main goal is to have a relaxing experience. From a utilitarian perspective, you would most likely not impel this group to paddle long distances every day. Rather, you might set up a base camp and take day trips, providing the option to relax at camp or go on short day paddles.

Nonconsequentialist Ethics

The **nonconsequentalist theory of ethics** is concerned with the acts themselves, or the means. The nonconsequentialist argues that the emphasis for ethical decision making should be the nature of specific acts. The fundamental question asked by the nonconsequentialist is "What did I do?" (Hunt 1994). Acts within this tradition are predetermined to be good or bad based on the standard set by the summum bonum. For example, telling lies is bad, regardless of the end result of the lies.

Learning Activity 7.4

You are the leader of a training trip for outdoor leaders. The trip is 30 days long and designed to address and assess a number of outdoor leadership competencies. One of these competencies is the ability to respond in a first aid scenario. You decide to stage a scenario by asking one member of the group to simulate a broken bone. You ask the student to fake an injury for a sustained period of time, thus allowing you to assess the ability of the group to react to the first aid emergency. You insist that this student maintain the role-play so that other group members don't realize the emergency is staged. Is this ethical? Use some of the terminology and information from the previous section on sources of ethics in your response.

Imagine yourself on a 16-day paddling trip in northern Ontario. This trip is a requirement of an advanced university course. You have been told by the leaders of this trip that smoking is not allowed. According to the leaders, the rationale behind this rule is that smoking is bad for your health; cigarette butts can start fires; and some members of the group may be adversely affected by the smoke. You have been a smoker for 6 years. You are convinced that you will be unable to quit; you have tried to quit before. You make the decision that you will limit yourself to two cigarettes a day. You decide that you will smoke far away from the rest of the group and you will hide the fact that you are smoking from the leaders. You are pretty sure that you will be able to keep this a secret and that no one else will be affected by your decision. Additionally, you will take all of your cigarette butts with you so that there is no environmental damage from your decision. Is this ethical? What ethical principles and theories would best support this type of decision? Use terminology and information from the previous section on sources of ethics in your response.

The previous overview of sources of values and ethics is summarized in table 7.1. This overview is an attempt to provide a foundational understanding of the ethical principles and theories that should be considered before beginning the decision-making process. Consideration of the good, the means, and the end will contribute to the development of a methodology and framework to help guide leaders toward making ethical decisions. There is widespread agreement that moral and ethical decisions need to be made. However, there is great disparity among leaders about *how* these decisions should be made. Garvey (1999) argues that we already teach morals and values either intentionally or unintentionally in our outdoor programs. Developing an understanding of ethical principles and theories will help you transcend a reliance on pure emotion to settle conflicts. The following discussion of the stages of moral development should also help.

Six Stages of Moral Development

Theories of personal development that explain the process of value formation abound. One of the most well-known of these theories is **Kohlberg's six stages of moral development** (1981).

Kohlberg used this model to measure moral development. In the first two stages (the preconventional level), the preadolescent is oriented toward punishment, defers to superior power, and sees proper actions as those that satisfy needs, mainly one's own. In the next two stages (the conventional level), the emphasis is on conformity and gaining approval, which merges into a concern with authority and fixed rules. In the last two stages (the postconventional level), moral orientation is more principled. The focus is on general ethical standards, on principles that are logical, comprehensive, universal, and consistent. It is in the congruence

Table 7.1

Ethical Principles

Ethical principle or theory	Definition	Example
Principle ethics (ethical objectivism)	• guided by a predetermined set of rules • encourages individuals to look beyond the situation in order to determine "right" from "wrong"	• a company's policies and procedures manual • the Ten Commandments
Virtue ethics (ethical subjectivism)	• guided by the individual • concerned with the question of what is moral, virtuous, and "right" • situationally dependent	• in the vignette, Seth was operating under this principle, claiming that his decision to become involved with a trip participant was situationally dependent and superseded the company's policy
Consequentialist theory of ethics (normative ethics) • Utilitarianism	• focused on the end result of the decision • guided by determining the greatest good for the greatest number	• some may justify the necessity for war, arguing that regardless of the means, if the end result serves the intended purpose and outcome and serves the greatest number of people then the act of war is justified
Nonconsequentialist theory of ethics	• focused on the acts themselves (the means)	• a pacifist would argue that regardless of the end result of war, any act of war is "wrong" and unjustified

of the levels of need and other motivations and of the states of moral development that leadership becomes enlivened with moral purpose.

Consider the character Jean Valjean from Victor Hugo's *Les Misérables*. Valjean was caught and imprisoned for stealing a loaf of bread to feed his family. Studies have shown that adolescent boys and girls would address this ethical dilemma in very different ways. In her seminal book, *In a Different Voice*, Gilligan (1982) highlights this disparity. Gilligan suggests that a boy would locate truth in logic. He would most likely derive a solution to this dilemma in the same way he would solve a mathematical problem. The preadolescent boy would reason that laws have mistakes and you can't have laws written for every possible scenario. Therefore, the boy would reason that it is acceptable for Valjean to steal the bread because his family would otherwise go hungry. The boy is scored at the conventional stage of Kohlberg's scale (see figure 7.2), a mixture of stages 3 and 4, for his ability to use deductive logic to solve the dilemma, to differentiate morality from law, and to see how laws can have limitations concerning what is just.

In contrast, Gilligan suggests that a preadolescent girl's response to this dilemma would convey a very different impression of moral development. When asked if Valjean should have taken the bread, her reply would mostly likely seem evasive and unsure. She would most likely consider neither property nor law but rather the effect that the theft would have on the relationship between Valjean and his family and society. A preadolescent girl might reason that if Valjean steals the bread, he may prevent his family from being hungry for the day, but he may also end up in jail and then his family would be in an even worse situation. She would approach this ethical dilemma not as a mathematical problem to be solved but as a dilemma involving humans in a narrative of relationships that extends over a period of time. She would consider other solutions to the dilemma, suggesting that Valjean talk with other people in the community about his problem before taking the bread, concluding that stealing is not right. Her solution lacks moral logic and structure. It is based more on an intuitive feeling or sense of right and wrong. It considers options that supersede laws or rules. She considers both long-term effects and alternative solutions. The preadolescent girl in this example does not quite fit Kohlberg's scale but may be scored somewhere between Kohlberg's preconventional and conventional stages of moral development. She displays an inability to think systematically about the concepts of morality or law and displays a reluctance to challenge authority or examine the logic of "truth." When considered in the light of Kohlberg's definition of the stages of moral development, her moral judgments appear to be a full stage lower in maturity than those of the boy.

These two children see two very different moral problems. Kohlberg's theory of moral development provides a ready response to the boy's logic but seems to be unable to address the girl's approach to solving this dilemma. Her response appears to lie outside the moral domain. Both of these preadolescents are intelligent and are perceptive about life. The disparity lies in the way that they think about conflict and choice and in their different modes of moral understanding. There is something highly limiting about Kohlberg's theory of moral development concerning the girl's ability to develop higher levels of moral judgment.

This disparity lies at the heart of a discussion of an ethic of care versus an ethic of justice. Gilligan argues that the sexes differ in moral reasoning; women focus on care and responsibility while men are preoccupied with rights and justice. Neither method of reasoning is superior to another, but Gilligan suggests that both need to be considered.

Ethic of Care and Ethic of Justice

An **ethic of care** is based on relationships. One person responds to another out of love or natural inclination. An ethic of justice operates upon the principles of fairness and reciprocity, giving credence to the summum bonum, which gives ethics a mathematical and logical appearance and moves the discussion beyond the sphere of actual human activity. It has been argued that Kohlberg's model of moral development overemphasizes a hierarchy of moral reasoning (Noddings 1984).

An ethic of care takes a relationship-oriented approach to moral development. Girls and women tend to choose this ethic more often than boys and men. An ethic of care considers not only relationships but the effects of decisions over a period of time (Mitten 1996). Mitten maintains that while an ethic of care is a feeling mode, it is not necessarily an emotional one: "At the heart of this ethic is the maintenance of the caring relationship" (p. 166). The universal aspect of this ethic is the caring attitude, or being able to be cared for and being able to care about.

Within an **ethic of justice,** decisions are based upon principles of fairness and reciprocity. For the most part, this approach concentrates on a hierarchical structure of moral reasoning. It focuses on the establishment of principles and that which can be logically derived from them. According to this ethic, using principles keeps ethical decision

Preconventional level	**Stage 1.** The focus is on punishment and obedience. **Stage 2.** The focus is on satisfying needs, mainly one's own.
Conventional level	**Stage 3.** The focus is on conformity and gaining approval. **Stage 4.** The focus is on authority and fixed rules.
Postconventional level	**Stage 5.** The focus is on the social contract and public interest. **Stage 6.** The focus is on moral principles.

Figure 7.2 Kohlberg's six stages of moral development.

making rational and objective rather than emotional. This ethic fits well into Kohlberg's theory of moral development.

It has been argued that an ethic of care represents a more feminine ethic and an ethic of justice represents a more masculine ethic. The goal of outdoor leadership should be to embrace an ethic of care that supersedes these gendered prescriptions. The relationship-oriented nature of outdoor leadership impels us to develop an ethic of care within our practice.

Professors often deal with ethical dilemmas that highlight this distinction. For example, it may be clearly stated in a course syllabus that students will receive a 10% reduction for each day that an assignment is late. Inevitably, a few students hand in late assignments throughout the course of a semester. Some students would appear to have a valid reason for turning in their assignment late. If a professor were to operate using an ethic of justice, she may tell students that regardless of their reason, they will receive a 10% reduction per day late because the professor feels the need to maintain the same level of fairness for all students. If a professor were to adopt a more relationship-oriented approach based on an ethic of care, the professor would most likely hear the student out first and then make a decision based on care for that student. In other words, in some cases a student may have a compelling reason as to why an assignment is late. An ethic of care allows a professor to care for that student at that moment in time, regardless of what principle ethic or rule may be in place.

An ethical leader should treat group members consistently rather than cultivate special relationships with individuals.

Professionalism in Outdoor Leadership

It was suggested earlier that leadership as a professional and ethical practice need to be better understood. The question that needs to be answered is "Is outdoor leadership a profession or a set of techniques?" Priest and Gass (1999) suggest that the outdoor leadership profession is becoming more professional. They indicate that one important step toward this professionalism is the development of a unique body of knowledge. They further maintain that a profession follows an ethical code of conduct that cares for client welfare. The ethical issues that are relevant here are the special moral obligations of practitioners of outdoor leadership and the specific set of moral standards that govern outdoor activities. Professional associations often develop a code of ethics to aid individuals in subscribing to a consistent professional ethic.

Code of Ethics

While there is no universal code of ethics or conduct in place for the outdoor leadership profession, Hackman and Johnson (1991) offer the following six criteria that they believe are important to ethical leadership:

- A leader should not intentionally send deceptive or harmful messages.
- A leader should place concern for others above concern for personal gain.
- A leader should respect the opinions and attitudes of group members and allow them the freedom to consider the consequences of their actions.

- A leader should stand behind members when they carry out policies and actions approved by the leader and the group.
- A leader should treat members consistently, regardless of sex, ethnicity, or social background.
- A leader should establish clear policies that all group members are expected to follow.

Refer to chapter 3 for examples of the National Recreation and Park Association (NRPA) and the therapeutic adventure professional group (TAPG) of the Association for Experiential Education (AEE) codes of ethics.

While the general criteria provided by Hackman and Johnson and the more specific criteria found in the NRPA and AEE codes of ethics may serve as a good starting point, it is clear that development of the overall outdoor leadership profession's code of ethics needs continued attention. Consider, for example, the role of psychiatrists, doctors, and nurses. Are there a code of ethics and set of standards that guide their professional practice? Could you say the same for outdoor leaders? If doctors, nurses, and other professional practitioners are operating under an ethical code of conduct, do outdoor leaders need the same kind of code in their own practice? Priest and Gass (1999) impel us to consider that while outdoor leadership may be a profession, it may not yet be professional.

Outdoor Leadership as Professional Practice

Outdoor leadership as professional practice is where the study of ethics begins to merge with the practice of outdoor leadership. A discussion of outdoor leadership as professional practice must begin with a definition of what is meant by practice. McIntyre (1984) describes a practice as any coherent and complex form of socially established cooperative human activity. The "goods" internal to that form of activity are realized in the course of trying to achieve those standards of excellence that are appropriate to the activity. Using this definition, Hunt and Wurdinger (1999)

suggest that coiling a climbing rope is not a practice but teaching rock climbing is. An outdoor leader may have the ability to effectively coil a rope but may be unable to work toward achieving goods internal to the practice. For outdoor leaders to excel, they must be able to do more than simply master a set of technical skills; they must be able to work toward achieving the ideal ends associated with that practice. In the case of an outdoor trip, the ends may include group safety and group satisfaction.

The goods or standards of excellence achieved by an outdoor leader are attainable only by those who practice outdoor education. According to McIntyre (1984), external goods are those that are, in essence, outside the practice. Hunt and Wurdinger (1999) give an example of this. If an outdoor leader takes a job guiding climbing trips in order to finance a personal mountaineering expedition and the instructor does an adequate job, is paid for the job, and goes on the expedition, then the good that the instructor receives is the money. On the other hand, internal goods are attained purely because of the excellence achieved by participating fully in a practice. An outdoor leader will receive satisfaction by being recognized as achieving a high level of excellence in leadership ability.

McIntyre suggests that entering into a practice involves standards of excellence and obedience to rules as well as the achievement of internal goods. In thinking back to Aristotle's view of ethics and virtue that was presented in chapter 4, you may remember that Aristotle believed that the development of ethics and virtue is the development of the right habits expressed through practice. The question then becomes "Which habits are right and virtuous within the practice of outdoor leadership?"

Virtues of Outdoor Leadership Practice

Certain virtues may be common for all outdoor leaders concerning both the technical and moral areas of professional practice (Hunt and

Learning Activity 7.5

List some other virtues that you see as important to outdoor leadership.

Wurdinger 1999). Certifications have provided one means of assessing leaders' qualifications in specific outdoor activities (Ewert 1985). Program accreditation is another indicator that an adventure provider or organization has met certain criteria for safety, ethics, and curriculum. Both certification and accreditation represent one step in the direction of better defining outdoor leadership as a professional practice.

However, if McIntyre (1984) is correct about moral virtues being essential for the achievement of excellence within a practice, then it would follow that a professional outdoor leader is obligated to begin to define what is virtuous within the practice. One precondition for entering a professional practice is that practitioners be honest. Justice is another virtue essential for the practice of outdoor education. And compassion lies at the heart of the aforementioned ethic of care.

While it may be easy for individuals to identify what virtues they believe are important to the practice of outdoor leadership, the fact remains that there are no universal standards that define acceptable practice across the broad range of programs that currently exist. Hunt (1995) argues that

Ethical practice is displayed through ethical decision making and action; ethical campers know to pack out ashes before leaving the area.

while outdoor education is on the way to becoming a practice, it is not quite there yet.

Model for Ethical Decisions

The previous chapter addressed decision making in great detail. This section will present one model for making ethical decisions specifically related to professional practice. The first step in making ethical decisions is to ask, "What is the practice I am engaged in?" and "What is the ideal end of the practice?" If, for example, the goal of a particular trip is to provide opportunities to enhance students' self-esteem through positive peer interactions and one student is consistently putting down others, it may be important for you to act quickly to resolve the problem even though there is no real threat to physical safety. Once you have identified the practice and the ends, the next step is to list your options, considering your obligations to the group and the potential effects of your decision.

The third step is to consider the ethical guidelines under which you are operating. If you are working for an organization or under an association that has an established code of conduct, then apply that code to the decision-making process. For example, NRPA members agree to abide by a code of ethics that includes adhering to the highest standards of integrity and honesty in public and personal activities and striving for personal and professional excellence (Clark 1995). Policy and procedure manuals represent another source of guidelines.

The fourth step in the decision-making process is to employ the ethical principles and theories in this chapter and use them to help determine which factors are relevant. For example, should your decision be based on the greatest good for the greatest number (utilitarianism)? Or are there situations when concern for an individual's safety outweighs your decision to seek the summum bonum? If you are operating under a professional code of conduct, should you employ it even if it does not fit the situation? Are there times when employing a virtue ethic would supersede this principle ethic (code of conduct)?

As outdoor professionals, it is important to make objective ethical decisions. Yet you will most likely have a personal opinion, a personal investment, and a natural inclination that will also contribute to the decision-making process. For this reason, you must consider and recognize your own epistemology, the lens through which

A Model for Ethical Decisions

Step 1—Identify the ideal end or objective of the activity.

Step 2—List options.

Step 3—Identify the ethical guidelines under which you are operating.

Step 4—Employ the ethical principles and theories (see table 7.1).

Step 5—Identify your own bias and how it may affect the decision.

Figure 7.3 Summary of the 5-step model for making ethical decisions.

Learning Activity 7.6

Apply the 5-step model of ethical decision making to the following scenarios:

- You are a recent graduate from an outdoor recreation program. You will be spending your first summer as an Outward Bound instructor. Your first trip is with a group of teenagers from the inner city of Toronto. Your "book" knowledge of this particular group is that these at-risk youths may require an autocratic leadership approach so that you can maintain order. Your coleader has 10 years of experience and you have heard great things about her. However, you finish the first day of the trip a bit shaken up. As previously agreed, your coleader has just introduced the topics of the full-value contract and challenge by choice and presented the information in a manner that offered the participants no real voice in the process. In fact, she repeatedly raised her voice and yelled at the group, telling them to shut up. A number of participants have been acting out and pushing her buttons as a result. It is day 1 of a 28-day trip.

What should you do?

- You are 25 years old and are guiding a Smithsonian-sponsored trip on the Green River in Utah. You are the primary guide of this group of nine, although a paid naturalist is on the trip as well who will provide the group with interpretive talks and walks. Because of the natural environment in which you are traveling, there is a Leave No Trace environmental ethic of "pack it in, pack it out," including human waste. On day 3 of the trip, you overhear a female participant telling her husband that she is squeamish about using the "rocket box" to go to the bathroom. He responds by telling her to just go behind a big rock nearby because no one will know.

How do you respond to this ethical dilemma?

you see the world, and weigh that alongside the other components of the process. Understanding your own bias will only contribute to making the right decision. Neglecting your bias will only detract from that process. This fifth and final step in the decision-making process may be the most challenging. Figure 7.3 illustrates this five-step process.

Summary

Values and ethics define a person. Participants and coleaders look for high standards, clear ethics, and the exercise of appropriate values in leadership. An understanding of some ethical principles and theories will help you develop these high standards and make ethical decisions. There are

Professional-Development Portfolio Activity

Consider how your personal lens (from activity 7.2 on page 91) influences your values and beliefs. What are your personal values and ethics? How might they influence you as a person? As a leader?

Use this information and some of the knowledge that you have been acquiring over the course of the readings to build upon the essay on your philosophy of leadership that you started in chapter 4.

policies and procedures in place to help with this process, but they represent only part of the equation. You will need to examine your own values and beliefs and superimpose those on the principle ethics that are already in place.

Studying values and ethics and thinking about ethical matters will make you a better leader. You must then put your ethics into practice. As an outdoor leader, you are involved in developing not only your own practice but also helping to establish outdoor leadership as a professional practice. Your individual efforts and attention to ethical matters will contribute to developing the profession.

Selected References

Aristotle. 2000. *Politics.* Trans. B. Jowett. New York: Dover.

Clark, D. 1995. A new code of ethics for NRPA. *Parks and Recreation* 30(8): 38-43.

Ewert, A. 1985. Emerging trends in outdoor adventure recreation. In *Proceedings: 1985 national outdoor recreation trends symposium II,* ed. G. McClellan. Atlanta: USDI National Park Service.

Garvey, D. 1999. Outdoor adventure programming and moral development. In *Adventure programming,* ed. J.C. Miles and S. Priest, 133-139. State College, PA: Venture.

Gilligan, C. 1982. *In a different voice: Psychological theory and women's development.* Cambridge, MA: Harvard University Press.

Hackman, M.Z., and C.E. Johnson. 1991. *Leadership: A communication perspective.* Prospect Heights, IL: Waveland Press.

Hunt, J.S., Jr. 1994. *Ethical issues in experiential education.* 2nd ed. Dubuque, IA: Kendall/Hunt.

Hunt, J.S., Jr. 1995. Ethics and experiential education as professional practice. In *The theory of experiential education,* ed. K. Warren, M. Sakofs, and J.S. Hunt, Jr., 331-338. Boulder, CO: AEE.

Hunt, J.S., Jr., and S. Wurdinger. 1999. Ethics and adventure programming. In *Adventure programming,* ed.

J.C. Miles and S. Priest, 123-131. State College, PA: Venture.

James, W. 1949. *Essays on faith and morals.* New York: Longmans, Green.

Jordan, A.E., and N.M. Meara. 1990. Ethics and the professional practices of psychologists: The role of virtues and principles. *Professional Psychology: Research and Practice* 21(2): 107-114.

Knight, G.R. 1989. *Issues and alternatives in educational philosophy.* 2nd ed. Berrien Springs, MI: Andrews University Press.

Kohlberg, L. 1981. *The philosophy of moral development.* San Francisco: Harper & Row.

McIntyre, A. 1984. *After-virtue.* 2nd ed. Notre Dame, IN: University of Notre Dame Press.

Mill, J.S. 1962. *Utilitarianism: On liberty.* New York: New American Library.

Miner, J.L. 1999. The creation of Outward Bound. In *Adventure programming,* ed. J.C. Miles and S. Priest, 55-63. State College, PA: Venture.

Mitten, D. 1996. The value of feminist ethics in experiential education teaching and leadership. In *Women's voices in experiential education,* ed. K. Warren, 159-171. Boulder, CO: AEE.

Noddings, N. 1984. *Caring: A feminine approach to ethics and moral education.* Berkeley, CA: University of California Press.

Plato. 1986. *The Republic.* Trans. B. Jowett. Buffalo, NY: Prometheus Books.

Priest, S., and M. Gass. 1997. *Effective leadership in adventure programming.* Champaign, IL: Human Kinetics.

Priest, S., and M. Gass. 1999. Future trends and issues in adventure programming. In *Adventure programming,* ed. J.C. Miles and S. Priest, 473-478. State College, PA: Venture.

Richards, A. 1999. Kurt Hahn. In *Adventure programming,* ed. J.C. Miles and S. Priest, 65-70. State College, PA: Venture.

Rokeach, M. 1973. *The nature of human values.* New York: Free Press.

Williamson, J., and M.A. Gass. 1993. *Manual of program accreditation standards for adventure programs.* Boulder, CO: AEE.

Teaching and Facilitation

Part III pertains to teaching and facilitating individuals, groups, and activities in the outdoors. Most outdoor leaders feel the most pride when they successfully guide others to learn new skills, discover hidden abilities, appreciate the abilities of other group members, and recognize and celebrate all accomplishments.

Leaders cannot do their job without preparation; attention to the people, place, and activity at hand; or practice. We learn our craft by understanding the foundations of or theories associated with leadership, group development, and facilitation. We learn by being self-aware—knowing our own abilities and limitations—by knowing how we interact with small groups of people and how we affect change in a larger organization.

Chapter 8, Understanding Facilitation, describes the goals of facilitation, the challenges found in the facilitation process, and how to go about developing facilitation skills.

From that starting point, chapter 9, Facilitating Personal Development, describes facilitating personal growth in outdoor contexts. That personal growth belongs to our participants and to us as leaders. Developmental theory and the domains of behavior are central to understanding the ability to foster personal growth.

Chapter 10, Facilitating Group Development, leads to understanding groups, their development, their relationships, and how to observe behaviors that lead to either effective or ineffective groups.

Chapter 11, Challenge Course Leadership, focuses on facilitating groups in a specific setting—the challenge course. Because of the prevalence of challenge courses today, much information is available pertaining to functions and competencies of leaders in this setting.

Finally, chapter 12, Teaching Strategies, provides a broad introduction to teaching in the outdoors. Included are reviews of experiential education theory, outdoor teaching techniques, and lesson planning for outdoor activities.

Learning is a journey and the path is full of pitfalls, mountains, raging rivers, dry deserts, and prickly trees. Stay focused on what you want to be and you will evolve into an excellent outdoor professional. Excellence is the best anyone can be and it is a personal goal. Go for it!

Understanding Facilitation

© DavidSandersphotos.com

" It's what you learn after you know it all that counts. " —John Wooden

Chapter Concepts

- Goals of facilitation—Facilitation is a component of effective teaching and making meaning of outdoor experiences.

- Challenges in the facilitation process—Some participants do not value the meaning of the experience as much as simply doing the activity physically.

- Developing facilitation skills—There are specific ways to gain experience and feel comfortable facilitating others' experiences. Facilitation is a skill like any other and improves with knowledge and experience.

The chapter concepts relate to the following core competencies:

- Foundational knowledge (CC-1)—Understanding and applying theory and purpose of facilitation is part of the profession's foundational knowledge.

- Self-awareness and professional conduct (CC-2)—Awareness of one's abilities and limitations in a professional context is crucial.

- Teaching and facilitation (CC-4)—Leaders need the ability to teach and translate experiences found in an outdoor program context.

Karen arrived at the challenge course 30 minutes early. It was her first "apprenticeship" experience on the course. After her training experience she was positive that she could help a group develop into a cohesive, positive unit and that they would learn to communicate, trust, and support one another. Her instructor in the challenge course leader training had taken 20 beginner leaders and in 4 days had transformed them into a tight group of friends. They had played games, gone through a progression that developed trust, successfully completed many initiatives, and cheered for one another on high elements. They had willingly provided practice time for each other and learned safety and rescue techniques. Working with groups on the challenge course would enhance Karen's leadership abilities and she had demonstrated that she could lead activities in her training. She was on her way to adding more skills to her résumé.

Karen was working with a seasoned veteran on the challenge course. Jim had led many groups through the daylong activities and his reputation as a facilitator was outstanding. He was known for his creativity, his facilitation skills, and his thoroughness. Karen was indeed riding a lucky streak. Karen waited for Jim so that they could review roles and assignments for the day and gather the props for the morning's activities, but the group arrived first. Karen introduced herself and informed them that the lead facilitator would arrive soon. She opened the equipment shed and began gathering the props for the activities she had

participated in during her training. Jim sped into the parking lot, looked at Karen's pile of props, and told her they were not using any of that stuff. "Get the group circled up," he said, "I'll start in a minute." Karen did as she was instructed. Jim came over to the group, said hi, and then looked at Karen and said, "My lovely assistant will start us out with an introduction game while I set up the high course."

Karen was stunned and unprepared. This was a large group of 40 kids. She looked at the group and swallowed, then instructed them to say their name and an item that they would take on a picnic that started with the same letter as their name. The second person would say her name, add a picnic item, and then repeat the first person's name and item. After a handful of people had introduced themselves it was clear that the group was bored and the game was taking too long. Karen had no idea what to do to fix the problem so she kept smiling and encouraging the group. A couple of times she even stopped the game to scold the group about paying attention and learning names and that they would not get to do the fun stuff until they completed the activity.

Karen was hoping that Jim would return before the game finished so he could help out, but he didn't. After the game was finished Karen tried to debrief the exercise. She got very little response and the answers she did get were not what she anticipated. One boy stated he was bored, a girl said she already knew everyone's name, and another boy asked her if she would go out

(continued)

(continued)

with him! This was not anything like Karen's training group. In that group everyone loved getting to know one another. They had actually played several versions of the name game, and each one brought new information into the group. The instructor had elicited wonderful responses during every debriefing. This day was turning out to be horrible and it had just begun!

Jim returned, quickly gathered the group around him, and had them talk about what they wanted out of the day, what the day would entail, and where the water and restroom facilities were. He had reviewed their assumption of risk forms and asked a few questions for clarification. He explained challenge by choice and got the group excited. They couldn't wait to hear what he had to say next. He ran them through an activity and Karen watched. At the end of the day, Karen was asked to debrief every game, initiative, and element. She asked what the participants learned, how they felt about it, and how they would use the activity in the future, and she got little or no response each time. Karen vowed to go to the coordinator of outdoor adventure, Scott, the next morning and quit. Clearly, she was not good at facilitating the challenge course!

The next morning Karen still felt confused and frustrated. She went to Scott's office and relayed her experience to him. He asked how she set the tone for the day. She hadn't because Jim had told her to start a name game. Only when he came back after the game had he determined what the group wanted from the day and how it would be structured. Scott also asked about the group's response to the name game. Karen said she didn't think they liked it because they were in the sun, it took a long time, and they wanted to do something more active.

"Did you think about changing the game?" Scott asked.

"No, I thought we were supposed to complete an activity and debrief it before we moved on. That's what we learned in training," she answered.

"Was learning occurring if they were bored? Is there another way to learn names and to be active?"

"Probably," mumbled Karen. "But I think I'm not cut out to facilitate at the challenge course."

"Karen, I watched you throughout training. You were an outstanding student, and I don't want you to give up. Let's look at what it means to facilitate a group. You need a clear beginning, middle, and end to your activity. You need to observe the group and respond to their abilities and at the same time lay the groundwork for future activities. Not every debriefing is exactly the same. Sometimes it doesn't require anything from you, only impressions from the students. I want you to work with me this coming weekend. There are 15 participants and they want to work on the following things. . . ."

Over time, Karen learned how to set up herself and the group for success. She became the most requested challenge course facilitator because she always knew what to do and how to get the most from a group. She learned that every group is different even if they have the same goals as another group. The size of the group matters. The composition of the group matters. The motivation of the group matters. Karen learned that with care she could make a difference for everyone. Now Karen can laugh about her first experience. She allowed another facilitator to bully her and she was not prepared for the group. Never again did she depend on someone else to carry the day. She had activities ready to go and others in the wings in case a group did not respond to something. She learned to ask for responses in the debriefing that related to the goal of the activity. Karen became an effective facilitator!

This chapter will begin with the goals of **facilitation** and then move to the theory behind it. Facilitation and teaching do not have the same purposes but many elements are present in both. An effective facilitator makes a simple activity meaningful and many positive and negative behaviors can be brought to light. To be effective, facilitators must understand the experiential learning cycle and believe in its value. Everyone will develop their own style of facilitation that fits with their personality. Many types of facilitation require changes in style, however. Just as Karen had to learn what worked for her, you will have to try many methods to effectively reach a group or individual. The chapter concludes with ways to help participants transfer learning from an outdoor context to the home environment. Making meaning of an experience takes guidance and effective communication, but a successful facilitation experience is satisfying beyond imagination.

Goals of Facilitation

Leading others in the outdoors does not guarantee that learning will occur. An outdoor experience can bring joy and wonder and can help people develop new relationships and make discoveries.

An outdoor experience encourages people to learn things about themselves, others, and the natural world. However, it is possible to be outdoors and miss these opportunities or not enjoy the experience. Some participants do not want to learn in the outdoors—it feels unsafe in its newness, they have had previous negative experiences, or they are not interested in being an active learner. An effective facilitator can shift the outdoor experience from a mere excursion in the outdoors to a dynamic learning experience.

Like any process, the goals of facilitation depend on many factors. Foundational factors include the philosophy of the sponsoring organization, the intentions participants have for success in the experience, the style of the leader, and the physical environment. All of these factors and more should be considered before meeting a specific group. Then the question becomes, what are you going to facilitate? Is it a meeting, activity, group development, support, cooperation, self-awareness, or another possible outcome? Karen knew some questions to ask groups but she was unclear about what she was trying to facilitate. The result was a poor first attempt at facilitating a group.

Facilitation is the process of moving a group or individual toward a desired outcome. The dictionary defines facilitation as making something easier. A facilitator, therefore, is a catalyst for making experiences possible. In this chapter we will explore styles and techniques for facilitation. Facilitation styles include leadership styles but change more often to adapt to the needs of the group at a particular moment. Some people confuse facilitation and teaching. There is much overlap in style and substance, but often facilitation is viewed as less directive than teaching. Greenaway (2004) poses a useful distinction between facilitation and teaching. He states, "In facilitation the goal is usually for people to learn something that nobody knows at the beginning, whereas in teaching the goal is to learn what the teacher already knows." There is some latitude in styles when facilitating because the leader is doing whatever is necessary to move a person or a group toward the agreed-upon outcome.

Facilitation Styles

Facilitation has been described as making things easier for others. However, making something too easy can bore learners and limit learning to only what the leader wants students to know. Facilitation is an enabling role that keeps the learner, rather than the facilitator, central to what is happening. A leader's facilitation style is based on many variables, some of which are internal and some of which are external. Internal factors include beliefs, communication ability, and valuing others. Personal belief systems are strong perceptual filters that affect expectations and behavior. For example, the Pygmalion effect means that what we expect or believe about someone is what we get. If we think someone is smart, we view them that way and they perform to our expectations. If we view someone as ineffective they most likely will live up to our expectations. Our perceptual filters can limit ourselves, too. A frog only perceives things that move as food and therefore will starve in a box of dead flies. If we understand how others perceive the world, we can work to establish a rapport with them.

External preparations for a group start with a plan based on variables before a group arrives.

Facilitation occurs in many places.

- The first variable is the age and maturity of the group. Usually the younger the group the more they depend on the leader and require coaching. The maturity of any group changes as the group interacts. In the beginning a group is more dependent on the leader and therefore requires more direct leadership and coaching.

- The length of the program is another variable. Generally groups build skills over time so a short course or a single-day event encourages direct leadership. The longer a group is together the greater the opportunity to use more indirect methods.

- The expressed goals of the program are the third variable when planning for success. The outcome will dictate the style of presenting a challenge and debriefing it. Sometimes a group has no agenda except to have fun and to get acquainted, which would create more opportunities for multiple activities with little transfer necessary. However, if a group is working on communication or improving problem solving, the choices might be limited with more translation of the experience occurring.

- Finally, the readiness of the group must be assessed. Some groups can manage safety and conflict because of their experiences together. They are ready for more complicated challenges. Other groups take longer to develop the trust necessary to leave the ground or move independently.

Facilitation styles are either direct, meaning they are telling or selling, or indirect, meaning they are coaching and encouraging while staying focused on the students. Evidence supports the effectiveness of direct facilitation styles, especially with motivated students. Such a style keeps the leader focused, pacing the group through activities and processing when necessary. It requires the leader to stay on task and allow little downtime, to be able to recognize changes in the group's climate, and to have a repertoire of activities that are appropriate for the situation. A new facilitator must practice a variety of behaviors and styles to learn what works with different groups.

Nondirective Facilitation

Nondirective facilitation uses a laissez-faire style that allows participants to determine which way they will go. The facilitator creates an opportunity that allows participants to follow that path. While this style is not comfortable or appropriate all of the time, it can be effective. When you believe the students can find their own solution to a problem and find that solution rewarding, a nondirective stance can be effective.

Appreciative Facilitation

Appreciative facilitation emphasizes what works well and concentrates on success and achievement. Identifying moments when the group is working at its best helps you identify desired behaviors and emphasize them. Sometimes asking what is going well focuses the attention on what is working rather than what is not working. This style is based on research related to the Pygmalion effect—the students become what the teacher believes them to be.

Activity Facilitation

Activity facilitation occurs during a group activity. Sometimes the facilitator enables a group to achieve a task in the time available. To make experiences more meaningful, the facilitator interjects during the activity to influence what is experienced. Most of the time such influence involves changing the rules in some way. There should always be a clear beginning, middle, and end in activity facilitation. Discussing the goal of the activity in the beginning sets a target that groups can shoot for. The middle portion of the activity is the actual participation in a game, initiative, or other activity. When it has run its course the end is called. Some sort of summary, debriefing, or conclusion increases the value of the experience.

Group Facilitation

Group facilitation can apply to groups in any context. Group dynamics in the outdoors can have a greater effect on a person than the outdoors alone. Even if group development is not a priority, group facilitation skills are necessary to keep the group on task. If a primary goal is team building, then group facilitation is absolutely necessary. At a minimum, outdoor leaders want to build a climate for learning.

Directive Facilitation

Adventure programming is a more directive style of facilitation and leaves little to chance. Priest and Gass (1997) have developed categories of facilitation techniques commonly used in outdoor settings. The first two occur before and during the experience: frontloading and framing the experience.

Frontloading is prebriefing or setting the stage before an activity. The facilitator tells the group what they should learn from the experience in order to create focus and a reference point for the group. **Framing** the experience helps a group make sense of the experience. Stories or **metaphors** help the group understand how a particular activity relates to their lives outside of the experience. Taking an activity and making it meaningful by relating it to the needs of students can be powerful. Instead of climbing a rock, students may be learning to stay focused on life goals. Instead of jumping off a power pole to catch a trapeze, we can reach for our dreams.

Other facilitation methods proposed by Priest and Gass typically occur after the experience. One is letting the experience speak for itself. Often it is assumed that by simply taking part in an experience, learning has taken place. Accomplishing a summit climb rarely needs an explanation, for example. After the difficulty of ascending a peak, just being there is enough for most people. Speaking for the experience, on the other hand, allows the facilitator to interpret the experience for the group. By telling the group what they have learned and how they might apply that new knowledge in the future, the facilitator can emphasize desired outcomes or learning.

On a recent expedition a student leader commented that she wished she had pushed her group more before arriving at the destination. When asked if she had brought the group in safely and feeling good she readily admitted that she had. "Then you did your job!" commented the supervising instructor. Sometimes we lose sight of the most important part of outdoor leadership. Leading others into the backcountry safely and enjoyably is a worthy goal always.

Debriefing can occur during or after an experience. The facilitator asks the group to reflect on their experience and to identify points of learning. Levels of questions are used to extract different information from the group. Facilitators must be clear about what types of information they want and the group's ability to respond.

There are many ways to debrief an experience. Leaders use journaling, photography, and drawing, to mention a few techniques. Getting thoughtful responses from participants is the key element. Later in this chapter we will discuss processing experiences.

Without the meaning elicited during facilitation, this is just a jump of trust.

Luckner and Nadler

Luckner and Nadler (1997) describe essential processing skills:

1. Preparation—Allow time for processing; encourage setting personal and group goals; address the most important concerns that have evolved during an activity; process immediately after major events; balance prac-

tical considerations of discomfort, fatigue, hunger, time, and group type; assess the participants; position the group so everyone can be seen and heard and no one is excluded.

2. Fostering a caring environment—Use appropriate tone of voice; allow participants to speak freely; show empathy; respond to feeling and content; personalize meaning; create an atmosphere for caring, sharing, and trusting by encouraging everyone to belong; listen and be involved; be genuine; use consistent behavior with all participants; give praise and words of encouragement; respect everyone's personal limits.

3. Communication skills—Use appropriate nonverbal communication such as eye contact, facial expression, and body posture; observe nonverbal behavior and draw from it; ask for feelings about specific events; be an active listener; ask more open-ended questions than closed; use directed questions to highlight issues, roles, and behaviors; provide sufficient time for individuals to think of a response.

4. Feedback—Redirect destructive, manipulative, or dominating behaviors; allow only one person to speak at a time; give everyone a chance to speak; keep the group focused; focus on behavior that can be changed; reframe negative experiences into positive learning; use humor; vary length and intensity of debriefing sessions; use a variety of methods for debriefing; use rules of feedback.

5. Sequencing—Provide gentle and small opportunities to disclose; highlight process by moving from content to process; address all types of learning, including physical, cognitive, and affective; provide closure.

There are many processing techniques, and each leader will use several types of processing with any group.

Choosing a Facilitation Style

Choosing a style of facilitation is not an easy task. Several styles have been described, and they all have advantages and disadvantages. Facilitators have their own style based on their values, experience, and personality. Mixing techniques and styles that are different from your personal style serves the students at a moment in time. Knowing when to take charge, when to back off, and when to negotiate has to do with the situation, the group, the task at hand, and the facilitator's personal style. Over time facilitators learn when and where to apply a variety of techniques.

Transfer of Learning

Transfer of learning refers to taking an experience and applying that learning elsewhere. It represents the integration of learning from the participant's experience with life back home. Learning can be direct when the participant actually experiences and understands something new. It can also be indirect, meaning one person can learn from another person's experience. This vicarious learning is just as powerful and important as direct learning. Transfer of learning should be considered an essential element of learning. Transfer of learning can be couched in the phrase **future pace**—any learning that occurs needs to be seen as something that will be used sometime in the future. Some learning is used immediately in the outdoors and other learning is transferred to a time in the future. We pace our future learning in the same ways that we pace the present.

Gass (1985) identified three types of learning transfer. First is specific transfer, which involves learning particular skills for use in closely related situations. For example, a knot you learn may be used later to tie into a climbing harness. Second is nonspecific transfer. This refers to learning more general principles, behaviors, or ideas and applying them to a different situation. An example would be learning Leave No Trace principles in the backcountry and teaching them to friends or family on a subsequent trip. Finally, metaphoric transfer refers to learning principles, behaviors, and ideas and generalizing those ideas to a new situation. They are not the same ideas or behaviors or principles, but are similar, analogous, or metaphorical. There must be parallels between two learning environments for a metaphor to occur. For example, expedition behavior is a way for people to learn about relationships used in resident-assistant training back at the university. Of course it is not called expedition behavior in that context, but it might be called citizenship behavior.

Facilitating Change

Change can happen if we believe that all genuine knowledge originates in direct experience (Lin 1967). In the outdoors we have a unique opportunity to teach under optimal conditions for learning. Learning requires several elements. We are taking participants from a safe and comfortable place and asking them to try new activities that will move them toward an unknown, uncomfortable, unexpected, or unpredictable outcome (Luckner and Nadler 1997). Change requires disequilibrium to be complete. Processing these changes makes meaning out of the effort and creates a new comfort zone. Luckner and Nadler developed an adventure-based learning process model from the work of Walsh and Golins, Piaget, and Yalom. The model attempts to explain why adventure-based learning is effective (figure 8.1).

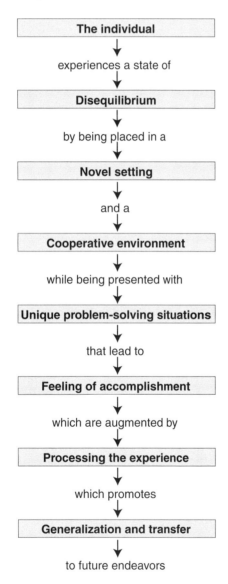

Figure 8.1 Components of the adventure-based learning process.

Adapted, by permission, from J. Luckner and R. Nadler, 1997, *Processing the experience: Strategies to enhance and generalize learning* (Dubuque, IA: Kendall/Hunt), 258.

Facilitation Techniques

Transferring an experience from one context to another requires directing the attention of the participant to possible similarities, differences, uses of lessons learned, or effective behaviors. Following are some ways to spotlight an experience so participants can use it in other situations.

- Reviewing the experience: Literally "re-viewing" the experience from new points of view allows participants to appreciate different approaches to solve a problem, recognize how others contributed to success, or learn new strategies.

- Adding value to the experience: When experiences are reviewed often, participants pay attention to what is happening because they know that a review is coming.

- Making sense of the experience: Simply talking about the experience and listening to what others experienced makes sense of it.

- Making connections with other experiences: Reviewing or processing allows people to make connections to other events or activities.

- Developing learning skills: Processing enhances the ability to learn from individual and group experiences. Participants therefore begin to take responsibility for their own learning.

Many times questioning or discussion are the transference methods leaders use. Questions and comments force the student to be attentive and active in the learning process. Many people rely on Bloom's (1956) taxonomy of cognitive processing or thinking to frame questions. Bloom suggested that cognitive learning occurs at a variety of levels, with each level requiring increasingly complex thinking. He developed six levels of questions that move from a basic to a complex ability to think.

1. Knowledge—Memory or recall of information (e.g., Can you see and name 10 flowers in this area?).

2. Comprehension—Understanding; interpreting or explaining knowledge in a descriptive way (e.g., Explain the legend on a topographic map).

3. Application—Correct use of knowledge; solving rote problems or answering rote questions (e.g., Can you determine the elevation gain from point A to point B?).

4. Analysis—Relationship level; breaking knowledge down into parts and detecting

Learning Activity 8.1

Find a reading that describes your feelings of the outdoors. Share the reading with others in the class.

relationships between them (e.g., If a group walks 1 mile [1.6 kilometers] in 60 minutes over flat terrain, what effect will climbing 50 feet [15 meters] have on their pace?).

5. Synthesis—Creative level; putting together pieces to form a whole or to formulate a solution (e.g., Can you develop an accurate time plan for hiking 5 miles [8 kilometers] with 1,500 feet [457 meters] elevation gain for a group of 10 hikers?).

6. Evaluation—Opinion level; making judgments about the value of ideas, solutions, or events (e.g., How accurate was your prediction and what variables caused you to miss your goal time?).

It is difficult for people to evaluate something before they have knowledge of it and can apply that knowledge. The levels of questions provide a way to evaluate what participants are learning and their eventual ability to apply knowledge. The taxonomy progression helps us plan a sequence of events from simple to complex.

One method that is useful for questioning is using objects as metaphors. Coming from the adage, "A penny for your thoughts," facilitators have found that using an object that allows the participants to focus their thinking is less threatening for participants and yields more participation in the debriefing process. Even talking through a stick eliminates the stress of speaking in front of the group by allowing someone to hold the power of the talking stick and speak through it. By holding an object, attention is focused on the speaker and the habit of one person speaking at a time is reinforced.

As we'll see in the following sections, there are other ways to process an experience.

Readings

Readings can help frame an activity or can help articulate a reflection. A collection of readings is helpful for addressing feelings and experiences. Sometimes a person in the group writes a poignant piece that can be shared.

Journal Writing

Journal writing is a strong tool for processing an experience. Providing enough time for writing is often the challenge for the leader. A leader may assign a free-write period before or after an activity that will elicit thoughts and feelings. A specific question may be assigned to focus responses.

Dyads

Another tool is using dyads (pairs) or small groups for discussion. Dyads encourage more personal

Focusing on an object generates thoughtful reactions to events.

Learning Activity 8.2

Develop a full-value contract for your class. Check commitment with thumbs-up.

interaction and encourage discussion about topics that might not be brought up in a larger group. Dyads are particularly effective early in a program or after a crisis situation such as a close call or conflict. Small group discussions of three or four people also encourage interaction with a group size that is comfortable yet large enough to have a variety of perspectives.

Activity Sheets

Some leaders use written activity sheets that have blanks in statements for participants to fill in or guide participants to make a list or answer questions. They provide immediate responses and are a starting point for a follow-up discussion.

Isolation

Isolation or solo experiences are used in a variety of programs, including Outward Bound. In long expedition-style experiences they provide time alone for reflection and self-evaluation. Solo experiences can be sprinkled throughout a course as well.

Drawing

Drawing or sketching encourages people to get in touch with what they are experiencing. For some people drawing is their outlet of choice and provides a vivid reminder of experiences and places.

Challenge by Choice

Choosing challenge as a learning method, or **challenge by choice,** is a philosophy that has emerged over the years. If individuals are not ready to move out of their comfort zone because of physical, psychological, or emotional reasons, the activity will not affect the participant in a desirable way. Challenge by choice allows participants to choose their level and type of challenge and even to say no to an activity. It permits the participants to look at themselves from the perspective of a supportive group. Supporting choice is part of developing a trusting group. Finding an important role in the group for a person who opts out of an activity keeps the participant engaged and often uncovers

new abilities or fills a needed role for the group's task accomplishment.

Outdoor leaders should ask everyone to challenge themselves. It is a thin line between honoring self-assessment and nudging students forward because we know they can succeed. One approach is to have each student try a challenge based on the current resources available. Those resources include the group members, the leader, the safety equipment, the preparation or lead-up to an activity, and of course the individual. Having students watch, asking them to assist in preparation, and noting the lead-up activities that have prepared the group for success are all tools we can use.

Full-Value Contracts

Full-value contracts are used to gauge the level of commitment for a single activity or for a whole experience. They make group members aware that the group's success will take everyone's cooperation. Many programs have developed their own form of a full-value contract. Usually the contract involves three elements (Rohnke 1989):

- Agreement to work together as a group and to work toward individual and group goals. This means being responsible for yourself in the learning community.

- Agreement to adhere to certain safety and group behavior guidelines. These guidelines help ensure psychological safety as well as physical safety.

- Agreement to give and receive feedback, both positive and negative, and to work toward changing behavior when appropriate. This means using feedback in ways that assist an individual or group in reaching desired outcomes.

The emphasis of the full-value contract is up to the facilitator and may depend on the abilities of the group (for example, to give and receive feedback) or the complexity of an activity.

The use of thumbs-up, thumbs-down, or thumbs-sideways allows for a quick check of commitment as time passes. Thumbs-up means,

"You can count on me, I am totally on board with the idea and the process." Thumbs-sideways can be interpreted as, "You can count on me, I don't agree totally with the idea or the process, but I am willing to go along with the plan." Thumbs-down indicates an unwillingness to move forward, as in, "You cannot count on me to fully participate" or "I am uneasy with the plan." It is worth taking the time to clarify goals and intentions whenever someone gives a thumbs-down.

Challenges in Facilitation

Facilitation contains many elements, including theories, techniques, and styles, which we have already discussed. The following section discusses how we present ourselves to others, articulate what we want, and communicate our observations. The challenge for each leader is to be aware of one's own strengths and weaknesses and to develop an individual style of effective communication.

Elements of Communication

Facilitation is about effective communication. Sending and receiving an intended message is much easier said than done! Communication is used to share information, to command others, to resolve conflict, to persuade or influence others, and to express oneself. Striving to be an effective communicator is an important facilitator goal. First, a leader wants to speak at the appropriate level of the audience. Speaking clearly, concisely, and without jargon makes the message easy to interpret and understand. Keeping the message content focused is also important. Many people like to relate stories about themselves when communicating to others. That is a fine method as long as all discussion is not centered on one person's experiences, which gives a feeling of self-importance to the speaker but does little to enhance the communication process.

Communication, like other facilitation skills, must convey not only fact but feeling as well. Using a dull, flat voice in telling people that they are going to have fun will not be convincing. Likewise, laughing off a dangerous situation makes you seem foolish. Keeping verbal and nonverbal cues congruent punctuates the message.

Nonverbal communication can have as much of an effect or more than verbal communication. Albert Mehrabian of UCLA was the first to put percentages on the relationships between verbal and nonverbal communication. Neurolinguistic practitioners have found that words alone are only 7% effective, but when a certain tone of voice is added they become 23% effective. If we add actions of body and face, our words become 70% effective, and when we add emotions, which are a combination of tone and actions, our words become 93% effective (Mehrabian 1971). That is a powerful message.

We also know that there is a gap between speaking and listening. We can listen to about 650 words per minute but can only speak at 125 to 155 words per minute. Therefore, as facilitators we try to avoid physical distractions for participants. We are aware that boredom can occur because the listener's brain is searching for more than we can speak. Communication is a loop—it requires a sender and a receiver.

The sender must try to anticipate how a message will be heard or interpreted. Messages are best heard when the sender is credible and can make the message clear and complete. Miscommunication occurs when messages are ambiguous, timed wrong, or sent when there are distractions. The receiver of the message may encode the message incorrectly by focusing on part of the message instead of the whole story. Therefore, feedback to check communication effectiveness is essential. Obstacles to effective communication occur at both the sending and receiving ends. For the sender, the barriers are having disorganized thoughts, trying to communicate too much, using improper language, prejudging the receiver, letting strong emotions get in the way, and avoiding the real concerns of the receiver. For the receiver, barriers to effective communication include prejudging the sender, having poor listening skills, being defensive, letting strong emotions get in the way, making incorrect assumptions, and having a mismatched communication style with the sender.

Communication within the group can cause problems as well. Lack of cohesiveness, bias, ineffective leadership, unwillingness to participate fully, and a lack of openness to opposing viewpoints will limit communication. Assumptions about what people are thinking or trying to communicate is dangerous. We can observe behavior and even count the consistency of that behavior, but that is all we know for a fact in a group. Who speaks, who does not speak, who begins every conversation, and who disengages part way through a task are all examples indicating a group's communication patterns. To assume anything other than observable behavior leads to gossip in the group. The only one who can tell us why a particular behavior is occurring is the

Listening is an essential communication skill.

person displaying the behavior, and even that kind of self-awareness would be extraordinary.

Listening as a Communication Skill

Listening is an important communication skill. We listen with our ears and with our eyes. As we hear another person speak we are constantly looking for nonverbal clues that will verify or devalue the message. Words sometimes get in the way of effective communication, so clarifying what is heard is essential.

Feedback is a form of message clarification. It is information asked for or given in order to make another person more aware of personal behaviors. Effective feedback is behavior oriented. The person speaking or providing feedback must take personal responsibility for what is said. The information should be specific, timely, and given with the receiver's feelings in mind. It can only be given for behaviors that can be changed. Ideally feedback is sought. Providing feedback should be seen as a service to others that helps make them more self-aware or participate more fully in the group. There should also be enough time for the receiver to question the feedback or ask for confirmation from others.

For facilitators, one of the most interesting challenges is to accurately assess our own feelings, intuition, and conceptual frameworks. With experience and attention the three eventually become integrated. But as Johnson and Johnson (1987) state, "Among poorly trained and inexperienced facilitators, feelings and intuition may be given a 'mystical' sense of rightness and followed blindly as a form of emotional anarchy" (p. 393).

Feelings in Communication

Feelings are a source of information about the relationships in a group. Feelings are, however, prone to misunderstanding or bias, especially when the authority of the leader is being questioned or when the leader feels anxious.

Additionally, because of personal fears and anxieties, everyone has blind spots that distort what is actually taking place in the group. If leaders are too emotional, they should use caution when relying on their feelings for information. Self-understanding leads to a more accurate reading from your feelings.

Intuition—That Gut Feeling

Intuition is a process where a person is not exactly sure how their conclusions were made. It seems to be a combination of awareness of your feelings and the ability to trust those feelings to make a judgment about how or when to intervene in a situation. An intuitive leader is attentive, observant, and empathetic to the group process and has previous experience from which to select a behavior. Intuition presents itself as a fleeting feeling or comfort or discomfort with the present situation. Attending to those feelings helps make any intervention timely and appropriate.

Feelings and intuition create risk for the facilitator. A conceptual framework allows leaders to piece together bits of information to gauge the group's progress in building relationships or in staying focused on the goal. The conceptual framework cannot rely on a one-time occurrence as fact. Sometimes noting behaviors at least three times gives the leader confidence that something is truly happening in the group. The first time something occurs it can be considered a *happening.* The second time the same behavior occurs it is forming a *pattern.* The third time the behavior happens it can be considered a *habit* and can be addressed with confidence. Conceptualizing what is occurring assists in decision making and keeps interventions on a rational level. However, like intuition, using only conceptualization limits a leader's effectiveness in facilitating behavior.

Participant Motivation

Facilitation and motivation are related concepts. It is difficult to facilitate anything if a person or group is not motivated. Teaching others to be motivated involves helping participants identify self-regulation skills so they can set their own goals and manage their own learning and performance. There are many motivation theories that we can use in this process. For example, the ideas of Maslow, Herzberg, McClelland, and others are used heavily in businesses and organizations, while Keller proposes a theory that may be more applicable to outdoor leadership. The theory provides clues about how to create motivation. It is called the ARCS theory (1979).

- A = Attention. Arouse the attention of students by using novel, surprising, or uncertain events. This aspect is automatic in outdoor settings, but you can also vary instructional methods.

- R = Relevance. People enjoy learning about things they already believe in or are more interested in. Relate what the students will be doing to their frame of reference (use of metaphor). Have students express their own goals for participating.

- C = Confidence. Confidence in one's abilities is heightened when the tasks are challenging. However, having multiple achievement levels keeps students motivated and limits anxiety about completing a high-skill activity. Feedback specific to how a student can improve performance is essential. Even failure can build confidence if the student attributes failure to poor strategy rather than a total inability to accomplish the task.

- S = Satisfaction. Students base satisfaction on the comparison of personal achievements related to the achievements of others in the same learning environment. Positive reinforcement and meeting standards lead to satisfaction.

Motivating participants can sometimes be challenging. If participants did not have a choice in the experience they may resist joining in the group's activities. Once a group is established members may also resist if they feel they are being changed by the leader. Determining why resistance is occurring is a good place to begin. Some leaders ignore resistance and press on, but carrying a group for any length of time is exhaust-ing. Resistance is not necessarily opposition; it may merely indicate that the group's needs have not been considered. Clarifying the goals of individuals and the group is a useful technique. It also shows who has bought into the goals and the process. Being genuine in your concern is helpful for eliciting this needed information.

Reframing the situation means taking a look at the intention of the group and pointing out observed behavior. There will be a gap between the two if the group is resisting. Both the content (goal) and context (procedures and relationships) can be examined. Sometimes writing a contract and referring to it when a group resists is a helpful technique.

Interpersonal Conflict

Conflicts can occur for a variety of reasons. Some conflicts occur because resources are unevenly distributed in a group. For example, some people seem to always have more information than others about upcoming activities. Participants may become concerned that the leader is favoring

Assuring that conflicts are encouraged and supported builds effective groups.

someone or they may feel cheated because they don't also know that information. Interpersonal conflicts come from personalities, styles, values, or habits. Conflict can worsen when it is not addressed in a meaningful way for those involved. If someone who is experiencing conflict is told to forget about it, the conflict may shift to frustration with the process and it will take longer to find the main problem.

Regardless of the source of conflict, people choose to address conflict in different ways. Avoidance is one method—"Forget it, try to live with it, the trip will be over soon and then I never have to see the person again" is commonly heard when conflict arises. Others will deny a conflict is occurring and make noncommittal statements about wanting to resolve any differences. For example, in her book *Leadership in Leisure Services: Making a Difference* (2001), Jordan describes many methods that people use to deal with conflict.

A very practical behavior to use when conflict comes up and you are unsure about what to do next is to adopt a cowlike attitude. This means stay in the neutral zone and do not let your emotions or stress go way up or way down.

Avoidance

Avoidance is a nonassertive method of dealing with problems. Lack of respect for self or others or a fear of reaction from others fosters this approach. No one wins with avoidance and it blocks group development.

Accommodation

Accommodation is also a low-assertiveness technique but involves some cooperation. With little regard for personal needs, others' requests are fulfilled in an attempt to preserve harmony.

Competition

Competition is a high-assertiveness, low-cooperation approach to conflict. It means taking care of your own needs in the situation with little regard for others. Dominance is the desired outcome. This method can cause many other problems in the group.

Compromise

Compromise is something we are taught to do to make everyone happy about an outcome. However, it often leads to everyone being unhappy because everyone has had to give up something.

Collaboration

Collaboration is a problem-solving approach where each person works to meet the goals of the other. Everyone tries to find satisfactory solutions and accept responsibility for those outcomes. Neither the person nor the situation is lost in this process. Collaboration requires skill, however, because each person must be aware of her own needs and be willing to look at the problem from another point of view to develop a workable outcome.

Developing Facilitation Skills

A leader is expected to be skilled and knowledgeable. This is true your first day of work and carries forward from there. The responsibilities of maintaining a safe learning experience, assessing individual and group needs, providing instruction, facilitating personal development, and evaluating experience are all skills a leader needs to have. It is a huge responsibility and the skills are learned over time in no particular order. There is no substitute for experience, so working with groups in a variety of situations will enhance your abilities. Concrete tasks can also provide an edge for a developing leader, including the following:

1. Manage time well. Be prepared ahead of time so the group does not have to wait for you to get ready. This includes setting up an activity, having the equipment checked and prepared, and leaving time for transitions between activities.

2. Plan more activities than needed. This means having a contingency plan in case you need to switch directions in the middle of a sequence or in case a group completes tasks quickly.

3. Be clear about when a group can provide input. Some decisions will be the leader's, some can be the group's, and some will be jointly made.

4. Be clear about the responsibilities of the leader. Safety, instruction, observation, facilitation, raising issues in the group, and clarifying statements and issues are the responsibility of the leader.

5. Know what is inappropriate or what inhibits a group's progress. Talking only about yourself and your accomplishments does not focus

the group on their experience at the moment. Also, judging, preaching, and allowing others to do so usually isn't useful.

6. Maintain balance. The leader is the motivator for a group to reach its potential. Your belief in them and their abilities will dictate their success to a large degree. Balancing action and discussion, experience and learning is desirable and based on the ability of the group.

7. Practice timing and pacing. Making well-placed observations and changing rules to allow forward progress are based on observation. Most teachers in a classroom allow a couple of seconds for a response after asking a question, but most people are not that quick, especially when faced with a novel situation. Being quiet so others can think and respond is a needed skill.

Summary

Developing facilitation skills requires practice. Then it requires practice and after that more practice! Other than that, knowing your group and what they want out of an experience; setting a clear outcome; asking for feedback from others; speaking in front of groups; and paying attention to what works all the time, what works some of the time, and what does not work at all are important in developing a repertoire of facilitation skills. Have fun with it!

The ultimate goal of an adventure experience is to help individuals make connections to what they are learning so they can combine their own insights and desired behavior with their own style during the experience and when they return home. With practice, Karen eventually became skilled at making meaning from experiences at the challenge course and helping her participants think about how they would apply that learning when they left the site.

Selected References

Association of Research Libraries. 1996. Facts about learning. Washington, DC. Association of Research Libraries Web site: www.arl.org/training/ilcso/learnfacts.html.

Bloom, B.S. 1956. *Taxonomy of educational objectives.* London: Longman.

Cornell, J. 1989. *Sharing the joy of nature.* Nevada City, CA: Dawn.

Dewey, J. 1938. *Experience and education.* New York: Collier.

Fosnot, C.T. 1989. *Enquiring teachers, enquiring learners: A constructivist approach for teaching.* New York: Teacher's College Press.

Gass, M. 1985. Programming the transfer of learning in adventure education. *Journal of Experiential Education* 8(3): 18-24.

Greenaway, R. 2004. Facilitation and reviewing in outdoor education. Retrieved July 8, 2005, from the *Active Reviewing Guide,* http://reviewing.co.uk.

Heron, J. 1999. *The complete facilitator's handbook.* London: Kogan Page.

Professional-Development Portfolio Activity

Facilitate an activity. Write a 1-page reflection paper about the following:

- What went well?
- What improvements could be made to enhance your facilitation (i.e., voice, posture, preparedness, giving directions, appropriateness, debriefing technique, how much coaching was needed for the group's success, and so on)?
- What would you do differently (i.e., with this group, with a group of participants who are younger or older, with a group that includes a person with a physical disability, and so on)?

Overall evaluation if 0 is the worst possible presentation and 10 is the best:

0-------1-------2--------3--------4-------5--------6-------7--------8--------9--------10

Johnson, D.W., and F.P. Johnson. 1987. *Joining together: Group theory and group skills.* 3rd ed. Englewood Cliffs, NJ: Prentice Hall.

Jordan, D.J. 2001. *Leadership in leisure services: Making a difference.* 2nd ed. State College, PA: Venture.

Keller, J. 1979. ARCS model of motivational design. Retrieved July 8, 2005, from www.ittheory.com/keller1.htm.

Knapp, C. 1992. *Lasting lessons: A teacher's guide to reflecting on experience.* Charleston, SC: ERIC/CRESS.

Kolb, D.A. 1984. *Experiential learning: experience as a source of development.* Englewood Cliffs, NJ: Prentice Hall.

Kouzes, J.M., and B.Z. Posner. 2002. *The leadership challenge.* 3rd ed. San Francisco: Jossey-Bass.

Lin, P. 1967. Quotation from Chairman Mao Tse-Tung. Peking, China.

Luckner, J.L., and R.S. Nadler. 1997. *Processing the experience: Strategies to enhance and generalize learning.* Dubuque, IA: Kendall/Hunt.

Mehrabrian, A. 1971. *Silent messages.* Florence, KY: Wadsworth.

Priest, S., and M.A. Gass. 1997. *Effective leadership in adventure programming.* Champaign, IL: Human Kinetics.

Rohnke, K. 1989. *Cowtails and cobras II.* Dubuque, IA: Kendall/Hunt.

Schoel, J., D. Prouty, and P. Radcliffe. 1988. *Islands of healing: A guide to adventure based counseling.* Hamilton, MA: Project Adventure.

Smith, T.E., C.C. Roland, M.D. Havens, and J.A. Hoyt. 1992. *The theory and practice of challenge education.* Dubuque, IA: Kendall/Hunt.

Wickes, S. 2000. *The facilitator's stories: What's it like to facilitate at your very best?* Brathay Journal, Organisation Development: Topical Papers. Issue No. 2 (August). Cumbria, UK.

chapter 9

Facilitating Personal Development

" If there is no struggle, there is no progress. " —Frederick Douglass

Chapter Concepts

- Human development—Not all activities are appropriate for all ages or stages of human development. Knowledge of human development assists in making good decisions related to outdoor programming.

- Developmental domains—Program goals are directed toward specific developmental domains. The domains are physical (psychomotor), cognitive (intellectual), and socioemotional (affective).

- Theories of development—There are numerous theories and empirical research that help us to better understand the nature of human development.

The chapter concepts relate to the following core competencies:

- Foundational knowledge (CC-1)—Understanding and applying developmental theory to successful outdoor activities is part of foundational knowledge.

- Self-awareness and professional conduct (CC-2)—Professionals should be able to relate to various populations, regardless of where they are in the life span. This ability begins with self-awareness—knowing where you are developmentally in relation to others.

- Teaching and facilitation (CC-4)—Choosing appropriate activities for all people and recognizing the importance of being inclusive is important in facilitating personal growth and development.

With the confidence he gained from his first outdoor leadership course 5 years ago, Peter decided to enroll in an adventure trip to Nepal. The instructors were apparently experienced and skilled so the trip seemed safe. The participants were from all over the country. They all had enjoyed previous outdoor experiences. Everyone looked fit and ready for a fun adventure. The group met their instructors in Katmandu. They were whisked away to their hotel and were given a quick briefing. The next day they explored the city and surrounding areas. Bicycles were rented and with bells clanging they joined the traffic around Katmandu. They visited various shrines and temples. There were monkeys, monks, and fun-loving children wherever they went. They took many pictures and then scanned the market for souvenirs.

The next day the group boarded a bus to travel toward the mountains. They were met by a group of Sherpas and porters who would cook, guide, and carry their clothing and equipment. Peter was psyched—this was going to be great! They hiked through river beds and mountains, gaining and losing enormous amounts of elevation each day. Since it was fall, the weather was clear and cool. The group practiced the Nepali language each evening by playing volleyball with the porters and singing songs with them.

One day the instructors offered the group the chance to hike over a pass at 17,700 feet (5,395 meters). There was some discussion about the route since the group had been advised to bring light hiking clothes. If anyone had extra warm sweaters or jackets they shared them with the porters. Peter thought it was a great idea to have such a challenge and get to a high elevation. He had total faith in the instructors and the program. It was snowing when they left camp at 3 in the morning. Up they climbed in two groups.

After 10 hours of hiking, the group was in trouble. One girl was suffering from hypothermia and a Sherpa carried her back down the mountain. Others were lying in the snow, vomiting, or just sitting, exhausted. The two hiking groups had lost sight of each other, and none of the participants really cared. They would keep going as long as they were told to. Finally, the head Sherpa ran up to the lead group and said the group would return to camp. The group turned around and stumbled down the trail. Exhausted, cold, and sick, they finally made it to camp. The next day the experience was debriefed. The instructors informed the group that the porters had turned back well before the group had and refused to carry the groups' belongings to the next camp. It was also revealed that the next camp, a communal hut, had no firewood. The last group over

(continued)

(continued)

the pass had used all of it the previous night. With the condition of the group they thought four or five people could have suffered severe hypothermia or death if they had not turned back.

The group was quiet. Peter thought he would have been one of the unlucky ones since he had wanted to lie down and go to sleep in the snow, a sure death sentence. He had strained a leg falling down the trail and was really scared. Mostly he had lost faith in the leaders and their ability to make safe decisions. He doubted his own abilities and swore that he would never participate in another organized trip unless he had all the details first. What had he been thinking, trying to go to over 17,000 feet in sneakers and cotton pants! He had known better but trusted the leaders completely to make good decisions. The more he thought about it, the angrier he got, mostly at himself for doing something that was so unsafe. The experience also made Peter want to become an outdoor leader so that others could have safe and enjoyable experiences. He would get the training necessary to work with participants at their ability level. He also learned that life is fragile and it would be easy to die in the outdoors!

Peter's overconfidence after his first course was misplaced. He knew that outdoor experiences could change someone for the better, but now he had learned that poor decisions by leaders could lead to potential disaster. Peter understood and could reframe his scary experience so that he became determined to do better and to share what he had learned with others. He sought out further training and opportunities to learn technical skills. His teaching experience helped him work with groups effectively and be sensitive to needs of participants at different age and experience levels. He returned to graduate school and studied experiential education and leadership.

Peter had been forced to look at himself critically. He learned not to take nature for granted. He became much more self-aware, which helped him develop into an excellent outdoor leader. Peter has now led hundreds of students through the mountains. In retrospect, he is glad that he had experiences that made him pay attention to what people can tolerate in outdoor situations. He makes conservative decisions and routinely leads safe trips. Peter was lucky to be able to derive the positive from a negative experience. He became a more complete human and a successful, mature outdoor leader.

Understanding human development is important to outdoor leaders because knowing what is typical for an age group or a developmental stage in life helps us plan appropriate activities that combine the right amount of challenge with the participant's ability. Human development is a well-documented and complex phenomenon. Researchers have studied how humans develop physically, emotionally, and intellectually across the life span. Outdoor leaders need a foundation of knowledge that makes programs physically and psychologically safe for the participant. Taking people beyond their abilities stresses their coping abilities and may harm them. That is not what the outdoor leadership profession is about. Instead, challenging a person within their abilities supports growth and learning.

At the beginning of this book, we noted that one of the primary goals of outdoor leadership is to facilitate opportunities for personal growth and development among program participants. Outdoor education and outdoor recreation both aim to provide individuals with opportunities for growth and development, or self-actualization. This chapter focuses on this aspect of our roles as outdoor leaders.

Rules for Being Human

1. You will receive a body. You may like it or hate it, but it will be yours for the entire period this time around.

2. You will learn lessons. You are enrolled in a full-time informal school called life. Every day in this school you will have the opportunity to learn lessons. You may like the lessons or think them irrelevant and stupid.

3. There are no mistakes, only lessons. Growth is a process of trial and error experimentation. The "failed" experiments are as much a part of the process as the experiment that ultimately "works."

4. A lesson is repeated until it is learned. A lesson will be presented to you in various forms until you have learned it. When you have learned it, you can then go on to the next lesson.

5. Learning lessons does not end. There is no part of life that does not contain its lessons. If you are alive, there are lessons to be learned.

6. "There" is no better than "here." When your "there" has become "here" you will simply obtain another "there" that will, again, look better than "here."

7. Others are merely mirrors of you. You cannot love or hate something about another person unless it reflects something you love or hate about yourself.

8. What you make of your life is up to you. You have all the tools and resources you need. What you do with them is up to you. The choice is always yours.

9. Your answers lie inside you. The answers to life's questions lie inside. All you need to do is look, listen, and trust.

10. You will forget all of this!

Cherie Carter-Scott in *Chicken Soup for the Soul.*

Nature of Human Development

"Development is the pattern of change that begins at conception and continues through the life span" (Santrock 1998, p. 16). Development involves growth as well as decay. It is the product of three general processes: biological (psychomotor), cognitive, and socioemotional (affective) (Santrock 1998). These separate processes are often referred to as developmental domains. Some people divide socioemotional processes into separate categories, one focusing on emotional processes and another focusing on social processes. In this text, we will treat these as a single category or developmental domain.

Biological processes refer to physical growth, including such things as height and weight, strength, endurance, agility, speed, and so forth. Biological processes are an important concern to outdoor leaders when it comes to facilitating motor skill development among program participants. This occurs whenever you teach a program participant a new skill (kayaking skills, rock climbing skills, etc.).

Cognitive processes refer to intellectual growth, including language acquisition, memory, intellectual abstraction, and so forth. Cognitive processes are a concern to outdoor leaders whenever you attempt to facilitate intellectual development among program participants. This occurs when you attempt to convey new information to program participants (principles of river dynamics, principles of top rope anchor systems, etc.). Cognitive development is easy to measure. Can someone identify 10 common flowers in a region? Can someone accurately take a bearing from a map?

Socioemotional processes refer to an individual's relationship with others as well as an individual's relationship with him- or herself. This developmental domain is perhaps the most elusive of all in terms of measuring personal growth. We can take clues about emotions from observed behaviors such as smiling, laughing, and crying; however, not all observations are totally accurate or relate directly to the activity at hand. The attitudes, moods, and feelings of people during an event are important, although you have to be careful not to read too much into your observations. Many leaders do not pay attention to the socioemotional domain at all, which is a mistake in the outdoors.

Socioemotional processes also involve how a person gets along with others in a group. It is important to consider how a person interacts with others, especially in a self-contained group in the outdoors. As leaders, it is important to note who is interacting with whom and how. Chapter 10 focuses more extensively on the nature of group interaction and development.

Development in each of these domains does not occur in isolation from development in other domains. Development that occurs in each of these domains is interconnected with development that occurs in the other domains. Development in one domain is often integral to development in the other domains. For instance, language acquisition, which falls within the realm of cognitive development, is dependent on the ability to interact socially, which falls within the realm of socioemotional development. Indeed, communication is the basis of all social interaction. Language acquisition, furthermore, is dependent on motor skill development, especially in using sign language to communicate with others. In the case of language acquisition, cognitive, socioemotional, and biological development all occur in conjunction with one another.

This text considers human development in terms of these three different developmental domains. It presents various theories that provide the basis of our understanding of human development in each of these domains.

Theories of Human Development

There are many theories associated with human development. The study of human development is filled with volumes about the complexities of the developmental process. People experience certain common abilities during the various stages of life where physically we hone our motor skills, cognitively we develop intellectual abilities, and socioemotionally we develop values, beliefs, and attitudes about ourselves as well as the world around us.

This section will describe several theories of human development, including psychoanalytic theory, cognitive theory, behavioral theory, social theory, and sociocultural theory. The goal for you is to gain a general understanding of how humans become unique individuals. This information does not give us license to predict behavior, but it does set certain parameters or expectations of what individuals will be like.

Psychoanalytic Theory

Development has been viewed from many perspectives, one of which is the psychoanalytical perspective. Freud (1856-1939) was one of the first to describe development in psychoanalytic terms, interpreting human development in terms of intrinsic drives and motivations (Freud 1935). According to Freud, most of these drives are irrational and unconscious but they influence every aspect of a person's thinking and behaving. Today, many theorists find Freud's work inadequate or wrong, but his work serves as the foundation of psychoanalytic theories of human development.

Erikson (1902-1994) acknowledged the influence of the unconscious and the irrational urges of early childhood (Erikson 1963). He proposed eight stages of human development. Each stage has a central challenge or developmental crisis that must be resolved. While outdoor leaders generally do not work with people until upper elementary school grades, the early stages set up individuals for later challenges and should be learned. Erikson's views have fared better than Freud's because his theory is more comprehensive and applies to a wider range of behavior.

Birth to Age 3: Trust Versus Mistrust

Babies and toddlers either learn to trust that others will care for their basic needs including feeding, warmth, cleanliness, and physical contact, or they learn to lack confidence in others. Trust leads to a tolerance for frustration and increased ability to delay gratification. Mistrust leads to anxiety and emotional distress in response to frustration.

Positive behavior toward infants and toddlers includes holding them, assuring them, providing positive experiences for success, and providing positive feedback.

Ages 1 to 3: Autonomy Versus Doubt

One either learns to be self-sufficient in many activities including eating, walking, and exploring, or to doubt one's abilities. Children try to control their behavior but have poor judgment about their capabilities.

Positive behavior toward toddlers includes cheering success and redirecting failure. Consistent corrections will improve decisions.

Ages 3 to 6: Initiative Versus Guilt

Children want to undertake many adultlike activities, sometimes overstepping the limits set by parents and feeling guilty. Conscience is developed in this stage.

Positive behavior for preschoolers includes giving concrete rewards and punishments, giving positive feedback, and having tolerance

Human development is enhanced by experiences with others.

for playing games over and over. These children want to repeat success and will play the same game often if they have mastery of it.

Ages 7 to 11: Industry Versus Inferiority

Children learn to be competent and productive in mastering new skills. However, when mastery eludes them they experience feelings of inferiority and the fear that they are unable to do anything well. Erikson views this stage as the decisive one in preparation to assume adult roles.

If leaders want to feel loved they should work with this age group! The children will try anything and will want an adult to witness their accomplishments—"Watch me, watch me!" They will imitate your walk, talk, and slang. When they are overwhelmed, think about how to help them by breaking complicated tasks into smaller steps. This is the stage when feedback is heard louder—when children learn they are clumsy, not artistic, lack singing ability, and so on. Many will carry those ideas with them throughout life. The idea is to program success and trying. This age group is very group or team oriented and they like it when everyone wins!

Adolescence: Identity Versus Role Confusion

During this stage a conscious effort to find out "who I am" occurs and sexual, political, and career identities are established. Role confusion may occur when a child is confused about what roles to play. Earlier conflicts in identity may be revisited.

Positive behavior toward adolescents: The boys will taunt each other with gender-laden putdowns (e.g., Are you scared like a girl?). It is a time when the girls might outplay the boys. They are physically stronger in the early part of this stage but are aware that they might not be heard in the group. Girls may give up or not show their abilities so that they do not intimidate the boys. Make sure that groups buy into group success and celebrating everyone's efforts. How you frame an experience to measure success is very important. For example, "We are going to hike until we need to stop" is different from "We are going to hike until we get to a destination," and "We have to get to a destination" is different from "We are going to get everyone into camp feeling energetic and safe."

The concept of everyone having a job is an important one. Everyone must learn every job in camp. If that does not happen the group will be in trouble if the "stove lighter," for example, gets hurt or sick. Make those with abilities accountable for teaching someone else. Their ability to teach one another is important to the group, and they share in one another's success.

Early Adulthood: Intimacy Versus Isolation

Young adults seek companionship and love with one another. The alternative is to become isolated from others through fear of rejection and disappointment.

Everyone should have a job and role in the group. Understanding group process and identifying when someone does something for the good of the group supports this stage of life. Young adults love adventure and are ready to do almost anything leaders ask them to do.

Middle Adulthood: Productivity Versus Stagnation

A feeling of contributing to the next generation through meaningful work, creative activities, and raising a family is a primary task. Otherwise people in this age group stagnate, feel self-absorbed, or feel a sense of going nowhere and doing nothing important.

Later Adulthood: Integrity Versus Despair

Older adults try to make sense out of their lives by seeing life as meaningful, or they despair about goals that were never reached. While this is not an age group that we see often in outdoor activities, more and more older people are seeking experiences that eluded them earlier in life.

Psychoanalytic theories help to explain developmental processes that occur in the socioemotional domain of human development. They help to explain such things as identity development, self-concept, social deviance, and so forth.

Cognitive Theory

Cognitive theory focuses on the development and structure of individuals' thought processes. The Swiss philosopher Jean Piaget (1896-1980) is the leading proponent of cognitive theories of human development. Piaget is interested in the construction of knowledge or how a person builds knowledge over time. His theory emphasizes the role of individuals in constructing their own cognitive realities. Rather than being conditioned by one's environment (as behavioral theorists propose), individuals assimilate new knowledge into existing knowledge and adjust to this knowledge through an intellectual process of symbol processing.

Learning Activity 9.1

Develop an appropriate outdoor activity for people in one of the following age groups: 6 to 8, 9 to 12, 13 to 15, 16 to 18, or 18 to 25. Can you defend why the activity is appropriate based on your knowledge of human development?

Piaget examined how individuals learn throughout the life span. Like Erikson, he proposes a model of development in which individuals progress through a series of stages to higher levels of cognition. He argues that cognitive development occurs in four distinct stages:

- Birth to age 2 (sensorimotor stage)—A person uses senses and motor abilities to understand the world. This is why young children put things in their mouth, need colors and lights for stimulation, and respond to sounds.

- Ages 2 to 6 (preoperational stage)—Children use symbolic thinking to understand the world, including language. Usually the thinking is egocentric; children understand the world only from their perspective.

- Ages 7 to 11 (concrete operational stage)—Children understand and can apply logical operations or principles to help interpret experiences objectively or rationally rather than intuitively.

- Ages 12 and up (formal operational stage)—Adolescents and adults are able to understand abstractions and hypothetical concepts.

Another important concept in cognitive theory is the idea of cognitive equilibrium. People seek to make sense of experience by reconciling it with existing understanding. When existing understanding does not fit the present experience, people fall into disequilibrium, or cognitive dissonance, an imbalance that initially produces confusion and then leads to growth as a person modifies old understandings and constructs new ones to fit the new experience. This is a key basis for teaching and learning—new learning comes from disequilibrium. Attempts to regain equilibrium—balance—typically result in personal growth and development.

Piaget has been criticized for overgeneralizing the nature of cognitive development, because intellectual development involves many factors. Nonetheless, his theory helps us to understand how development occurs in the cognitive domain.

A novel experience creates an opportunity to learn about oneself and others.

Behavioral Theory

Behavioral theorists posit that human development can be understood best by observing human behavior and the environmental determinants of that behavior (Santrock 1998). Two of the most notable behavioral theorists include Ivan Pavlov and B.F. Skinner.

Pavlov developed the idea of classical conditioning. By using stimulus and response, he found that an organism comes to associate a neutral response with a meaningful one and then responds to the former in the same way as the latter. You have probably heard of his experiment with dogs where he would ring a bell at feeding time to condition the dogs to associate the sound of the bell with food. Eventually, the dogs would salivate at the sound of the bell in anticipation of feeding time, whether food was present or not. Have you ever responded that way when called to dinner by the sound of a bell or your mother's voice? This experiment led to the development of what is known as conditioned response.

Skinner extended Pavlov's work, developing a behavioral theory known as operant conditioning. This theory posits that a person is conditioned to associate a particular behavior with a particular consequence and behaves accordingly. Individuals will avoid behaviors that result in negative consequences and engage in behaviors that result in positive consequences. We now call such consequences negative and positive reinforcements and use this theory often when teaching or facilitating programs. Many special education programs are grounded in the behavioral approach to learning and development.

Reinforcers can be intrinsic or extrinsic in nature. Examples of intrinsic reinforcers are feelings of satisfaction, pride, or a sense of accomplishment. Extrinsic reinforcers come from outside of us and are typically physical symbols of completion like a T-shirt, pin, or certificate.

The difference between behavioral theory and cognitive theory is that behavioral theory considers the mind to be shaped by environmental conditions or determinants, whereas cognitive theory considers the mind a construction of mental process. A cognitive theorist would suggest that the mind is shaped primarily through abstract thought. A behavioral theorist would suggest that the mind is shaped primarily through experience.

Social Theory

According to **social learning theory,** people learn new behaviors from observing others and patterning behavior after that of others. This is called modeling. A person may pay attention to a modeled behavior, store information about it, and later retrieve that information from memory (Bandura 1977, 1986, 1989). These cognitive and motivational processes help explain why susceptibility to modeling changes as people mature. With age,

children are more discriminating observers. Also, social learning is affected by self-understanding because the standards we set for ourselves and our confidence in our ability to meet them influence our motivation to learn from various sources, whether they be peers, mentors, or media stars.

Self-efficacy comes from social learning theory. In essence, self-efficacy is our perception of what we can or cannot do. It is developed from direct and indirect experience. It can also be transferred—if someone you perceive as having high ability cannot do a particular task, you may feel that you will fail too. On the other hand, if someone you perceive as having low ability completes a task, you may feel confident in your own abilities. Having attainable goals helps a student develop self-efficacy. Once one skill is mastered the next is easier.

Sociocultural Theory

Urie Bronfenbrenner (1995a, 1995b, 2005) is the leading proponent of this theory. Sometimes referred to as ecological theories of human development, the sociocultural view posits that all people must acquire the skills and knowledge essential for living in their culture. In traditional societies where there is little social change, the lessons learned in childhood are good for a lifetime. In modern technological societies, tools, skills, customs, and values are constantly under pressure to change. Sociocultural theory seeks to explain the growth of individual knowledge and competencies in terms of guidance, support, and structure provided by a broader cultural context. Human development is the result of the dynamic interaction between people and their surrounding culture.

Considerations for Outdoor Leadership

The theories that we have just discussed in part provide the basis for our understanding of human development. How do these theories inform what we actually do as outdoor leaders? In this section we will discuss several issues that give us a sense of why this information matters to us in our practice as outdoor leaders. These issues include emotional intelligence, diversity and leadership, moral development, and effects of human development on program design.

Emotional Intelligence

People are born and grow differently. In 370 b.c.e. Hippocrates noted that people are born with fundamentally different temperaments or are predispositioned to act in certain ways. Perhaps you have noticed children who need a lot of attention and those who do not, some who get anxious and some who accept whatever comes their way. In the early 20th century it was argued that people are born without dispositions and are very impressionable. For example, Pavlov saw behavior as mechanical responses to stimulation. A person could be conditioned to learn anything.

In the 1920s Carl Jung theorized that people are different in fundamental ways (1921). He posed that a person's instincts are "archetypes" that drive them from within. There is no hierarchy of instincts; they are all equally important.

Each of us has an inclination toward introversion or extroversion, which Jung describes as either being worn out by other people (introvert) or gaining energy from being around other people (extrovert). He combines introversion and extroversion with four basic psychological functions: thinking, feeling, sensation, and intuition. According to Jung our preference for a given function is characteristic and we can be typed by this preference. Thus, he advanced the concept of function or psychological types. His ideas were forgotten until Isabel Myers and her mother Kathryn Briggs developed a questionnaire based on his ideas that identifies 16 patterns of action and attitude (1975). The Myers-Briggs Type Indicator is used extensively as a research tool and a training tool. It is designed to determine personality types of individuals. This is a useful instrument to outdoor leaders because it can help us to develop a greater awareness of our own personalities. Consequently, it can help us to develop a greater awareness of how we interact with others and the effects that our personalities are likely to have within a group.

People who love the outdoors share common values—the shirt reads, "People who play in nature."

Our awareness of our own personality types is often referred to as emotional intelligence. The concept of emotional intelligence was initially popularized by Goleman (1995), who suggests that emotional intelligence consists of a variety of competencies: self-awareness, self-control, and empathy. Combined with the abilities of listening, resolving conflicts, and cooperating with others, a person with these competencies would be considered emotionally intelligent. Sounds like a lot of skills to become an effective outdoor leader, doesn't it? These skills relate specifically to CC-2 (self-awareness and professional conduct).

This issue of emotional intelligence is also important to outdoor leaders in understanding the motivations, attitudes, and behaviors of program participants. A participant's personality (motivation level, persistence, responsibility, need for structure or flexibility, rules for completion, etc.) has a significant effect on the dynamics of a

Learning Activity 9.2

Role-play how a cognitivist, a behavorialist, and a social theorist would teach someone how to build a fire. Which teaching methods are easier? Which are more satisfying for the participant?

Learning Activity 9.3

You can take an emotional IQ test on www.queendom.com. Discuss your results in small groups.

group. Such factors as the need for peer approval, reactions to discipline, fear of failure, and so forth can all impact the character of a person's participation in a group and consequently impact how a group gets along together.

Diversity and Leadership

The powerful benefits of outdoor programming should be available to everyone. It becomes an ethical issue when outdoor leaders exclude participants. The fundamental premise for providing outdoor adventure services is the fact that participants grow and become better people as a result of participation. Outdoor leaders are committing an ethical blunder when programs are not designed to be inclusive and leaders end up limiting who receives the powerful benefits of outdoor programming. Outdoor leaders have a duty to make accommodations for all who seek our services. In addition to a moral obligation, laws are in place to protect the public's civil rights. Three laws dictate an outdoor leader's programming decisions:

- Americans with Disabilities Act (ADA)—The ADA ensures access to public services for individuals with disabilities. Outdoor experiences available to the public fall under ADA guidelines. Programs and services must be made accessible to everyone or reasonable accommodations must be made to include people with disabilities. This would include challenge course programs in settings such as camps, YMCAs, schools, and parks and recreation departments, to name just one example.

- Rehabilitation Act (Section 504)— This act ensures that individuals with disabilities are not discriminated against when participating in programs that receive federal assistance. Schools and federally funded youth programs are two common examples of programs that fall under the juris-

diction of the Rehabilitation Act where challenge course programming might be found.

- Individuals with Disabilities Education Act (IDEA)—IDEA requires that all children be afforded appropriate public education without discrimination. This includes nonacademic and extracurricular activities such as challenge course experiences.

Inclusion means allowing anyone who wants to be involved to be involved. Despite all that we have in common as humans, people are different in many ways. Figure 9.1 illustrates various characteristics that distinguish us from one another. Despite differences in gender, age, ability, religion, and so on, outdoor leaders are morally obligated to cater to all populations. As noted previously, there is legislation, the ADA, that requires reasonable steps to be taken to ensure inclusion. Does that mean that anyone can participate in outdoor activities? The answer is no! Reasonable accommodation is just that—reasonable. If the accommodation requires major changes in the activity or affects other group members' experiences dramatically a person may be excluded from participation. An example would be the need to provide a nurse for a participant on an expedition-type

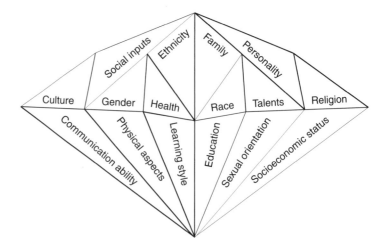

Figure 9.1 Everyone has many sides or facets. Uniqueness comes from the size of a facet.

course. The nurse adds a person to the permit and might prevent another person from participating. Additionally, the nurse may not have the skills or inclination to be on an expedition and would need extra supervision that would limit the amount of time the leaders spend with participants. A more suitable program for the person with disabilities and the nurse could be located instead.

Inclusion means we have to investigate how to make outdoor programs accessible so all can challenge themselves by choice.

Moral Development

As we saw in chapters 2 and 7, many of the outdoor programs that emerged during the 20th century, including the Scouts and Outward Bound, were developed to address concerns about perceived moral declines in society. Moral development is one of the primary goals of many traditional outdoor programs. As such, it is a concern to the aspiring outdoor leader. Even if facilitating moral development among individuals is not a source of motivation for you, as a professional outdoor leader, it is an issue with which you should be familiar.

Moral development is often discussed in terms of character education. It falls within the realm of socioemotional development and is addressed specifically by such theorists as Laurence Kohlberg (1981) and Carol Gilligan (1982), theorists who were discussed in chapter 7. Character education strives to provide a "moral compass" for students by guiding choices in behavior and attitudes. The Center for Character Development (2000) cites six areas for inclusion in a curriculum. They are trustworthiness, respect, responsibility, fairness, caring, and citizenship. Immediately these words conjure up what occurs on an extended outdoor trip. Upon further delineation they provide a basis for developing individuals and groups.

- Trustworthiness relies on integrity, honesty, reliability, and loyalty.
- Respect is self-explanatory, but it develops as a result of being reliable, honest, and loyal and having integrity.
- Responsibility infers a sense of duty to self and others, accountability, excellence, and self-control.
- Fairness includes treating people equally and impartially, being fair, and being open to different viewpoints. Listening is a useful skill for being fair.

Including all participants strengthens a group's experience.

- Caring is being emotionally engaged with yourself and others.
- Citizenship requires you to contribute to your community and to respect authority.

Effects of Human Development on Program Design

One of the more significant ways in which human development affects our practice as outdoor leaders is the impact that it has on program design. How you structure an experience for a group of teenagers is going to differ greatly from how you structure a similar experience for a group of elderly adults.

This is particularly true when it comes to the role of physical challenge in an experience. Of all the areas of human development, we have the most knowledge about physical development because it can be measured in terms of height and weight. Norms for growth exist from birth to old age. Gender influences growth patterns at certain times in our lives. We are used to ranges of height and weight that are considered normal. Insurance companies predict life span on such norms. There is rapid growth after birth, followed by a steady increase in height and weight, another rapid growth period during adolescence, and then a leveling-off. Full physical growth is completed by the late teens. Growth ends in the late teens or early 20s. However, the shape and size of the body often change during adulthood. These changes reflect the aging of tissues as well as external factors like diet and exercise. A loss of height due to osteoporosis occurs when there is a lack of weight-bearing exercise and calcium.

Why is this information important? Physical characteristics affect motor skill development. Body shape, height and weight, and other physical traits affect the development of such motor skills as balance, speed, and agility. Teenagers typically are not as coordinated as young adults because of constant physical growth. Outdoor leaders typically worry about young teenagers tripping over growing feet that their minds have yet to accommodate in terms of physical coordination. Outdoor leaders also worry about physical limitations of older adults, whether those limitations are a result of worn-out joints or faulty hearts. Outdoor leaders also recognize that physical disabilities can affect an individual's ability to participate in an activity.

Outdoor leaders must also take socioemotional development into consideration when structuring a program. It is common practice among whitewater rafting companies, for instance, to enforce a minimum age requirement for many of the more extreme sections of whitewater that they run. The concern is that younger participants are not equipped to handle the emotional stress (not to mention physical and intellectual challenge) that a crisis or emergency situation on the river might present.

Outdoor leaders treat cognitive development similarly, structuring intellectual aspects of activities and lessons according to participants' level of cognitive development. All of these considerations come into play as outdoor leaders design and structure programs for course participants.

Summary

The outdoors provides many opportunities for humans to grow and develop. By hiking, paddling, or just exploring, people develop stronger muscles, bones, and cardiovascular systems. People learn new things about the environment that add to their intellectual knowledge and may stimulate curiosity that fosters new learning. And it is easy to think of examples of how emotions are tapped through an outdoor experience. Feelings like joy, doubt, pride, compassion, fear, and satisfaction can occur in short time periods. For the outdoor leader, meeting the needs of participants in the different domains of behavior requires judgment and planning. What is appropriate for an 8-year-old is not appropriate for a young adult.

Outdoor leaders have an opportunity to facilitate development in individuals. By planning and implementing age-appropriate activities, people can begin to learn about themselves, their effectiveness in a small group, and their effectiveness in the larger community. Members of the group need opportunities to perform well and not so well so that they receive feedback in response to behaviors. Once feedback is received a person can choose to use that information or reject it. Calling attention to behaviors is just that—bringing an awareness to participants that they may not have had before. Most people are grateful for the information and are particularly pleased when their attempts to change their behavior are recognized.

Each outdoor leader and program has gimmicks for helping participants develop as individuals, such as providing personal introductions to the group. Encouraging members to share poetry, prose, or songs that they have developed on the trip provides insight. Keeping journals, doing peer evaluations, and taking time to get to know every other person in the group either formally or informally are all tried and true methods of encouraging participants to share themselves with the group and to support others who are sharing themselves. Everyone is a multifaceted being, and viewing others and ourselves through different facets offers a trusting and intimate view that we rarely see among everyday acquaintances. Perhaps this is the real benefit of leading others in the outdoors. Group members see each other as whole people rather than seeing only one attribute. Often the intimacy experienced in an outdoor group is what is remembered and valued, even beyond the scenery!

At the same time, working as an outdoor leader helps each of us to develop in new ways. We become more self-aware, develop a high level of self-efficacy, and become physically, mentally, and emotionally stronger. Every time an outdoor leader travels with others in the backcountry the potential for self-learning and self-awareness is enormous. A well-led and well-designed program has benefits for all who are involved. Leaders are put into positions where self-discovery opportunities abound. We are able to take what we learn from one group and reinforce or try a different behavior with another group. What to share with groups and what not to share needs to be explored so that the integrity and role of leader are maintained.

Professional-Development Portfolio Activity

Imagine that you are leading a group of students on a weeklong canoeing trip. How would you structure the experience differently for a group of 12- to 14-year-old students than you would for a group of 21- to 25-year-old students? In a short essay, describe how each group is different developmentally, and describe how these differences would affect your leadership of each group. Refer to the three developmental domains when discussing developmental differences, and refer to the conditional outdoor leadership theory model presented in chapter 5 when discussing the effect of these differences on your leadership of each group.

Selected References

Bandura, A. 1977. *Social learning theory.* Englewood Cliffs, NJ: Prentice Hall.

Bandura, A. 1986. *Social foundations of thought and action: A social cognitive theory.* Englewood Cliffs, NJ: Prentice Hall.

Bandura, A. 1989. Social cognitive theory. In *Annals of child development,* vol. 6, ed. R. Vasta. Greewich, CT: JAI Press.

Berger, K.S., and R.A. Thompson. 1998. *The developing person through the life span.* 4th ed. New York: Worth.

Bronfenbrenner, U. 1995a. The bioecological model from a life course perspective: Reflections of a participant observer. In P. Moen, G.H. Elder, and K. Luscher (eds.), *Examining lives in context: Perspectives on the ecology of human development,* pp. 599-618. Washington, DC: American Psychological Association.

Bronfenbrenner, U. 1995b. Developmental ecology through space and time: A future perspective. In P. Moen, G.H. Elder, and K. Luscher (eds.), *Examining lives in context: Perspectives on the ecology of human development,* pp. 619-647. Washington, DC: American Psychological Association.

Bronfenbrenner, U., ed. 2005. *Making human beings human: Bioecological perspectives on human development.* Thousand Oaks, CA: Sage.

Center for Character Development. 2000. Josephson Institute of Ethics, Los Angeles, CA. www.charactercenter.com.

Campbell, L., B. Campbell, and D. Dickinson. 2004. *Teaching and learning through multiple intelligences.* 3rd ed. Boston: Allyn & Bacon.

Erikson, E.H. 1963. *Childhood and society.* 2nd ed. New York: Norton.

Erikson, E.H. 1968. *Identity: Youth and crisis.* New York: Norton.

Freud, S. 1935. *A general introduction to psychoanalysis.* Trans. J. Riviare. New York: Modern Library.

Gilligan, C. 1982. *In a different voice: Psychological theory and women's development.* Cambridge, MA: Harvard University Press.

Goleman, D. 1995. *Emotional intelligence.* New York: Bantam Books.

Haywood, K.M., and N. Getchell. 2001. *Lifespan motor development.* 3rd ed. Champaign, IL: Human Kinetics.

Jung, C.G. 1921. *Psychological types: Chapter 10.* Trans. H.G. Bayes. Internet resource developed by Christopher Green, York University, Toronto.

Kohlberg, L. 1981. *The philosophy of moral development.* San Francisco: Harper & Row.

Lewin, K. 1935. *A dynamic theory of personality.* New York: McGraw-Hill.

Myers, I., and K. Briggs. 1975. *Myers-Briggs Type Indicator.* Mountain View, CA: CPP.

Piaget, J. 1952. *The origins of intelligence in children.* Trans. M. Cook. New York: International Universities Press.

Santrock, J.W. 1998. *Child development.* 8th ed. Boston: McGraw-Hill.

Skinner, B.F. 1953. *Science and human behavior.* New York: Macmillan.

chapter 10

Facilitating Group Development

> The most human thing we can do is comfort the afflicted and afflict the comfortable.
> —Clarence Darrow

© Jumpfoto

Chapter Concepts

- Group development theory—Groups develop in predictable ways as they move toward a goal and take care of each other emotionally.

- Group development process—Stages of group development require a variety of leader behaviors to maximize the resources in a group.

- Expedition behavior—Expedition behavior refers to relationships encountered when working with groups in outdoor settings.

- Observing groups—Effective leadership depends on timing and accuracy. Methods of observation assist in pinpointing useful and nonuseful behaviors in groups.

The chapter concepts relate to the following core competencies:

- Foundational knowledge (CC-1)—Leaders need to be able to understand and apply group theory in outdoor contexts.

- Decision making and judgment (CC-3)—Leaders must use judgment to minimize risk in decision making.

- Program management (CC-6)—Management skills help ensure safe and enjoyable experiences in the outdoors.

The group was getting along great. Kate, Mike, and Jordan were happy with themselves as instructors and with the group. The group was practicing lessons that they had been taught during their 2-week outdoor leadership course. The course was on the west slope of the Teton Mountains and the setting fit the course plan and the group. Every day someone commented on the beauty of the place and the wonderful group of people. As the days went on, the instructors watched and waited for the group to clash over something. It had rained and they had walked some hard, long days but the group kept smiling.

"This is such a good group. When will we see some conflict so we can move forward?" asked Mike. "Will we stay in the forming stage the whole time?"

"It's possible," answered Jordan, "and if we don't have a little eruption soon, when it does happen we'll have to suppress it because there won't be time to work through the conflict."

"I like the fact that we have an easy group. Isn't it fun not to have to deal with emotions and contrary opinions?" added Kate. "Let's just sit back and go with it. I don't think we should push them into conflict."

The instructor team kept a close watch over the group and were ready for any ripple. The group had performed well and they were planning independent hikes for the last 2 days of the course. The night before the instructors would leave the group there were final introductions by group members and a debriefing. They seemed ready to go. It was just past dark and the group had little inclination to leave the circle and head for their tents. All of a sudden one member of the group started to cry. In a matter of moments it seemed like everyone was crying. What was happening? It wasn't any mishap or hurt feelings. The group had identified with one last sad story during the introductions. It moved them to tears and now they could not seem to stop. After quite a while the group calmed down and everyone seemed to be OK.

Kate, Mike, and Jordan got to their tent and wondered what that was about. "Kate, do you cause groups to cry every time?" asked Mike.

"No way!" responded Kate. "I've never experienced anything like that before."

Jordan identified the episode as the conflict phase of the group. This group was full of people that did anything and everything to keep the group happy. They accommodated everyone else and so it had seemed that all was fine within the group. In reality, emotions were building and the thought of losing the support of the instructors and of the imminent end of the course pushed some group members to emote. They needed the release to accomplish the next phase of the course—the independent hike. Mike questioned this analysis and thought the hike should be cancelled and the instructors stay with the group.

(continued)

"If they're off balance they might make some poor decisions," he argued. "Tonight might only be the preamble to a larger conflict in the group, and what if we're not there to help them through it?"

Kate suggested that they see how the group was doing in the morning and decide then about what to do. "If they're tentative and not talking to one another, we'll cancel their hike out or one of us will go with each group. If they're ready to go and seem together emotionally, we'll let them go independently. We can take our time before we have to make a decision. We may need the day to work through the emotions in the group and see if it's possible for them to perform together."

Mike reluctantly said, "OK, but it makes me nervous about what will happen if we guess wrong."

Kate replied, "We won't guess—all of us have to be sure. We need to trust what we have seen in this group. Let's review who is in which group and make sure we have some stability in each. We will help them recommit to each other and get everyone in safely."

The instructors in this group were experienced and had talked through all kinds of scenarios before they started the course. They knew that an independent hike out was always rewarding for students, but it was optional in a course. The instructors had been looking forward to a day in the campground to finish evaluations. Tempering their needs and desires with the needs of the group tested each of them. They continued to talk about options until each of the instructors was comfortable with the goals for the next day and committed to doing whatever was best for the whole group.

As it turned out the group was anxious to complete their independent hikes. They were reviewing their plans when the instructors called for a meeting. All the members were exchanging information freely, were aware of possible problems, and were committed to demonstrating their leadership abilities over the next 2 days. The instructors questioned the whole group and individuals as well. It was clear that they were feeling good and performing well. The instructors reviewed all plans and left the group in early afternoon. When the groups came back into the campground they were all smiling and anxious to relate their experiences to the instructors. They cheered each other and themselves.

The instructors were well aware of stages of group development. They monitored the group without pushing them. They supported a "blip" of emotion, which was all this group needed. They had several plans for helping the group resolve any conflicts before releasing them for an independent hike. They were also aware of their own needs as instructors and how their desired outcome might bias their decision making. Through careful problem solving, their outcomes were successful. While they discussed previous experiences with groups, each instructor recalled huge arguments and anger for multiple days. Jordan had even had a fistfight break out in one of his previous groups! This group, on the other hand, had a subtle shift. It was all they needed to move them into a performing unit. Not all groups behave the same and it takes practice to "read" a group and their movement toward an interdependent, functioning unit. This is a challenge for leaders and participants alike!

In this chapter the ideas of how groups relate and develop over time will be covered. Additionally the role of the leader when facilitating groups as they develop will be explained. **Expedition behavior** is a convenient way to identify key relationships within a group as well as group relationships with other groups and outside agencies. Expedition behavior is a term regularly used in outdoor adventure programs. You may find that the concepts of expedition behavior are applicable in everyday life!

Group Development Theory

Each of us is born into a group. Most people could quickly name dozens of groups with which they are affiliated. Family, friends, neighborhoods, clubs, school, and religious affiliations all provide us with group experiences. While there are many definitions of what makes a group, most social scientists define a group as two or more individuals who interact with each other, are interdependent, define themselves and are defined by others as a group, share norms, influence each other, find the group rewarding, and pursue common goals (Johnson and Johnson 2001). Johnson and Johnson simplify this convoluted set of concepts with the following definition: A group is two or more individuals in face-to-face interaction, each aware of his or her membership in the group, each aware of the others who belong to the group, and each aware of their positive interdependence as they strive to achieve mutual goals.

This definition provides us with some important clues about what a group is. At the very least it is a changing or dynamic cluster. Some groups are more effective than other groups.

Core Group Functions

An effective group has three core functions: accomplishing goals, maintaining itself internally, and changing in ways that improve its effectiveness. Group members need certain skills or behaviors to accomplish the goals that create an effective group (Jordan 2001; Russell 2001; Alcorn 1985; Johnson and Johnson 2001). Behaviors that move a group toward accomplishing goals are often called **task behaviors.** Such behaviors include

- asking for information,
- giving information,
- defining directions,
- summarizing what others have said, and
- energizing the group.

Maintenance behaviors keep group relationships positive. They require paying attention to the feelings of others as action is occurring. Such behaviors include

- encouraging participation,
- facilitating or directing communication patterns,
- releasing tension or comic relief, and
- interpersonal problem solving.

Group members take on a variety of behaviors in the group. The following is a checklist to make everyone aware of when they added task or maintenance behaviors to the group. It is called the "Good on Me Checklist" (Summers 1997).

- Asked for help
- Received feedback openly
- Gave developmental feedback
- Identified a problem
- Provided solutions
- Increased my skill level
- Supported a group member
- Accepted leadership
- Gave up leadership
- Praised a team member
- Contributed my ideas
- Looked for value in every experience

Reprinted with permission of Scout Cloud Lee, VisionUs, Inc.

A group's goal dictates the balance between task and maintenance behaviors. The overall goal of a group should stay relatively constant; however, the small steps necessary to achieve the main goal are constantly reviewed and revamped as a group develops. Sometimes the task is so urgent that no maintenance behaviors are needed. An example might be a first aid situation. In other cases the relationships between group members may be so tenuous that taking time to make and strengthen relationships is exactly what a group needs. It may be dangerous to allow a group to physically move forward if they feel psychologically or emotionally unsafe. Group members need to understand what an effective group is and how individual behavior promotes or blocks this effectiveness.

Group Structure

When attempting to achieve a goal, a group structure develops. The structure consists of role definitions and group norms that regulate interaction among group members.

Effective group members help each other.

Roles and Norms

A **role** is a set of expected behaviors associated with a position in a group. A **norm** is a parameter that defines acceptable behavior in the group. Once a structure is formed, the group becomes something separate from the individuals that make up the group. It moves from "I" to "We." The structure also orders ways that members influence each other while trying to reach group goals. When members influence each other leadership emerges. Leadership is one aspect of a group's structure. "Followership" is another. There cannot be leaders without followers and vice versa.

Decision Making

Another aspect of the group structure is decision making. A decision implies that some agreement has been achieved about how a group will go about accomplishing its goals. A decision is just one step in the overall problem-solving process, but it is a crucial one. An effective decision has five main characteristics: 1) the resources of the group are fully utilized; 2) time is well used; 3) the decision is of high quality; 4) the decision is fully implemented by all group members; and 5) the group's problem-solving ability is enhanced.

Decisions can be hampered by many factors such as lack of group maturity, conflicting goals of group members, failure to communicate and use information, egocentrism of group members, unwillingness to hear disagreement with ideas, inappropriate group size, letting others make the decision, power differences and distrust, premature conclusions, lack of time, and inability to get an idea into the discussion. For more on decision making, see chapter 6.

Communication

Communication is another essential part of group structure. Setting and reaching group goals, making decisions, and resolving conflict all rely on communication ability. Since words sometimes get in the way of communication, this aspect of relating to others is a critical skill for leaders and group members alike. As leaders we accept responsibility for the effectiveness of communication. If communication is not occurring or is not going well, the problem belongs to the leader!

Communication involves sending messages effectively. This means phrasing the message so it can be understood, having credibility as a sender, and asking for feedback about what the receiver heard. The second part of communication is receiving messages effectively. The receiver must want to understand the ideas and feelings of the sender and must interpret the sender's ideas and feelings correctly. The idea is to achieve understanding so that people can move toward a goal. Opposition or disagreement may be seen as obstructions but are actually helpful in the long run if new and better ways of achieving goals are established. There can be many barriers to communication, including physical barriers like competing noise, how long group members have been sitting, temperature, lighting, and time of day. Physical barriers can usually be changed or compensated for. Other barriers are more difficult to adjust. Examples include attitudes, personal distractions (e.g., worrying about home), and not feeling a sense of belonging within the group because of age differences, gender, or experience.

To improve communication in a group, communication behavior must first be observed. This allows you to notice any problem sources. Sometimes basic skills of giving and receiving feedback need to be introduced. Sometimes a group needs to use a talking stick so that interruptions are minimized. Sometimes quiet group members are overlooked and need some attention.

Communication is interpersonal and whatever interferes with the relationships among group members interferes with their communication. Cooperation helps a group's effectiveness, while competitiveness, either in setting goals or in member relationships, can hamper communication and relationships and hence the group's effectiveness.

Conflict

Conflict is an essential component of a group's development. Without disagreement, new ideas are minimized and the full abilities of group members are not used. The key aspect of disagreement is to simply disagree with an idea, not to minimize a person's competence. Resolving conflict is like resolving any problem. The essential information is presented and examined from several points of view. Differences are clarified, ideas are integrated, and each person is validated for individual contributions.

Effective Groups

Some groups are effective and others are not. Because we work in groups in the outdoors, knowing what makes a group effective or ineffective is important. In effective groups individuals' talents and skills are recognized and utilized, as demonstrated in the following ways:

- Goals are cooperatively structured, clarified, and changed so there is a match between individual and group goals.
- Communication is an open and accurate expression of both ideas and feelings.
- Leadership is distributed among all group members to accomplish goals.
- Ability and information determines influence and power. Therefore, power is shared.
- Decision-making procedures are matched to the situation.
- Controversy and conflict are seen as positive for members' involvement in the group, quality of decisions, and maintenance of positive relations in the group.
- Interpersonal and group behaviors are stressed and cohesion is built through inclusion, affection, acceptance, support, and trust.
- Members evaluate the effectiveness of the group and decide how to improve its functioning.

Ineffective Groups

In ineffective groups individuals' skills or ideas are overlooked, ignored, or hidden. Such a group would have the following attributes:

- Members accept imposed goals; goals are competitively structured.
- Communication is one-way and only ideas are expressed; feelings are suppressed.
- Leadership is delegated by authority—membership participation is unequal and only goal accomplishment is emphasized.
- Position determines influence and power—obedience to authority is the rule.
- The highest authority always makes decisions.
- Controversy and conflict are ignored, denied, avoided, or suppressed.
- Members are controlled by force and rigid conformity is promoted.
- The highest authority evaluates the group's effectiveness and decides how goal accomplishment may be improved.
- Persons who desire order, stability, and structure are encouraged.

Process of Group Development

It has been established that groups have certain structures and members of groups have roles and norms that they fulfill. Groups seek to achieve goals, or forward movement. Unlike a machine, a group does not perform at its best when it is brand new. It takes time, skill, and patience for a group to develop into a fully functioning, interdependent unit.

Group development has been described in many ways. Essentially, a group has a life span and therefore has a beginning, middle, and end. What happens during its development is fairly constant and predictable. Not all groups move forward to become highly functional. Many of the groups that we work with in the outdoors never get beyond the beginning stage of development. Short amounts of time together, accomplishing the group's goal quickly, and being transient are all factors. Some people think they can ignore problems in the group because the course is only a certain number of days long.

Tuckman's Theory of Group Development

Tuckman's theory of group development is a commonly used model. He notes that groups develop through forming, storming, norming, performing, and transforming stages (Tuckman and Jensen 1977).

Forming
The forming stage is when people first come together as a group. They begin to get to know other people by asking safe questions and they begin to find their place in the group. Most people are excited about the possibilities for the group or they would not be present, so there is a lot of agreement and general socializing in this stage. A group can stay in this stage for a long period of time.

Storming
Storming occurs when there is conflict within the group. Conflict is essential for group growth and it allows differences and frustrations to be aired. Conflicts can occur with assigned authority figures, other participants, or progress or lack thereof toward the goal. This frustration can be small or large.

Norming

What emerges from conflict is a norming stage where participants are valued for who they are and not how they conform. The group moves from a group of individuals to a unique community of learners who respect each other and are grateful for the diversity offered. Often in-jokes, group slang, and group behavior emerge at this point.

Performing

The group can begin to perform at higher levels once norming is complete. They recognize the skills and contributions of one another and are willing to share leadership and responsibility for moving the group toward its goals. Task and maintenance roles are also distributed. There is true interdependence at this point.

The forming stage can be fun.

Transforming

Finally, groups transform when they have met their goals and either decide to disperse or to reset new goals and move forward even more. A group also transforms when a member is added or leaves. Just changing one member forces the group to start over and form again.

While the development of groups looks linear, it is really more like a spring. Group development is circular and as the group completes a cycle it can either go around again in the same stage or move on to the next stage. Any change in the group, like the addition or deletion of a group member, forces the group back to the beginning. The group will not take as long to get through the forming stage but it will have to repeat it and every other stage it has experienced. Changes also include goal achievement, a new or more challenging activity, and any barrier to success that forces a group to start over.

This is how groups form. Groups also have sub-groupings that go through the same developmental stages. They include tentmates, cooking groups, friendship groups, and leader groups.

Role of Leaders in Group Development

The leader has roles to play in each stage of group development. During the forming stage, participants often feel some uncertainty related to acceptance, inclusion, and safety. The leader needs to provide essential information to assuage those concerns. Knowing a schedule of events, where the bathroom is, and assisting with par-ticipant interactions is important to participants. Remember, information is power in a group, so anything related to upcoming plans should be communicated to everyone in the group at the same time. In the forming stage often an explanation of roles and responsibilities are laid out for both leaders and participants, early goal setting is accomplished through an exploration of participant expectations, and time is spent to reduce anxiety. The tone of the course is set early and how a leader approaches and interacts with the group in an initial meeting is critical to success. There is dependency on the leaders; the group wants the leader to be great and the group wants a clear plan for the near future.

During the storming phase of group development the group may resent leaders or feel let down for some reason. Leaders may be viewed as good or bad, strong or weak. They may not live up to the idealized being some group members see. Conflict can be among group members as well. Trying to accommodate individual differences in the group causes strain because the harmony is crumbling within the group. Leaders should allow conflict to occur and, if there is time, encourage confrontation of issues. This is when communication skills must be accurate and leaders must keep their own defensiveness in check. A good question to ask is, Whose problem is it? Is it a problem between two people, does the problem affect the whole group, will the problem affect the group's likelihood of reaching its goals? Meet the issue at the lowest possible level in the group;

in other words, involve only the people who are directly affected by the conflict. The leader does not always have to solve the problem. However, the leader may have to encourage confrontation or pose as a mediator.

As the group moves toward norming, attention to maintenance is important. Some members of the group may be feeling out of place in the group after conflict and are trying to find a niche. With a functional group the leader can help facilitate activities that help the group bond together, such as taking some time away from the group (allowing group members to have some alone time), organizing a potluck dinner, or having each participant give a gift to someone else. The leader is becoming more of a member of the group and members of the group are taking on leadership. This is a satisfying time for all involved and there is real camaraderie.

Following closely is the performing stage. Group norms and roles are well established and the focus is on goal achievement. The group relies on the leader for technical support and as a safety check but is not totally reliant on the leader. Leaders can be more spontaneous in their relationship with members of the group. The leader should be pleased with progress toward group goals. Despite the quality of the group, though, assigned lead-

ers can never give up their responsibility to the group.

In the transforming stage, the leader's role becomes important again in terms of asserting leadership. The participants are trying to make sense of their experience and may be responding to the end of the group in a variety of ways. Some people withdraw, while others want to assure themselves of a future with the group by arranging for activities after the group is dissolved. The group is in disarray again and the leader can assist by recognizing dependency issues, assuring the group that what happened during their experience is important, and fostering transference of the experience. Some sort of celebration or ritual helps accentuate accomplishments and the end of a group.

Coleadership

Little research has examined the dynamics of two or more outdoor leaders working together. Most research on coleadership has been conducted in social work or psychoanalytic settings. Winter (1976) theorized about the coleader relationship and its influence on the development and behavior of a group. She states, "When the group is led by two individuals—a co-leading pair—the fluctuating expectations and demands, and the interplay between members and leaders over time, become especially complex and interesting. The dyad can be viewed as a small group in its own right—developing over time with its own internal issues, linked to the phases and preoccupations of the larger group at the time" (p. 349). She divides group development into four phases as proposed by Mills (1964): 1) encounter; 2) differentiation, conflict, and norm building; 3) production; and 4) separation. She also adds categories about the group's concerns, members' feelings toward coleaders, tendencies of coleaders, and backstage concerns of the coleaders during each stage of group development (see table 10.1).

In a subsequent study about coleaders, Stempler (1993) described how to build successful coleader relationships. Before actual group work begins, task equity between

Coleaders need to communicate with one another often.

Table 10.1

Stages in Coleader Roles and Concerns

Phase	Group members' general concerns	Members' feelings toward coleaders	Tendencies in coleader roles in group	Coleader backstage concerns
Encounter	Initial uncertainty, fear Concerns with safety, acceptance, inclusion	Dependency on and idealization of leaders Group wants leaders in harmony Group wants clear plan	Unity, unified front Uniformity of role Close monitoring of each other's actions and reactions	Desire to agree, focus on similarities Promote uniformity to policy
Differentiation, conflict, and norm building	Intermember leadership struggles Concerns with accommodating differences	Resentment of leaders and leader solidarity Differentiation of leaders (good-bad) Attempts to divide and conquer leaders	Beginning of differentiation along stereotyped roles Strain and conflict	Disagreement, competition, power struggles, criticism Development of methods to handle problems
Production	Group norms and roles well established Focus on task	Group looks to leader for realistic help, direction of task	Role differentiation based on abilities Interaction more spontaneous	Respect for and acceptance of differences Coleader relationship less important than group task
Separation	Trying to make sense of experience Solidarity concerns	Members more dependent again Group wants interpretation of what happened Exploration of relationships with coleaders after trip	Roles in group more uniform again	Mutual support as group disbands Concern about meaning of group and coleading experience Separation from group and each other

Reprinted, by permission, from S. Winter, 1976, *Stages of co-leader roles and concerns.*

leaders is created. Some suggested ways to create equity are to determine roles, set parameters, and establish opportunities for each leader to contribute to the group. Flexibility among leaders with their leadership style is important to support the growth of the coleader relationship. Other studies have also stated that attempting to equalize power, responsibility, and use of skills and developing competence and comfort in assuming various facilitating roles and styles are essential.

Keeping the group's goals in sight is of utmost importance and can be accomplished through awareness of relevant concerns, careful planning, and evaluation of coleader and group processes. Coleader dynamics can make or break an outdoor adventure experience. Positive coleader dynamics will add to the learning of the group, whereas negative relationships can be disastrous. Taking time to develop trusting, supportive, and respectful relationships among coleaders may be the most important job leaders have.

While coleadership has been examined in other fields more than in outdoor leadership, there is much evidence to suggest that certain methods of matching abilities and styles is an important aspect of trip leading. Furthermore, the dynamics of multiple leaders are magnified when more than two leaders are working with a group.

Pretrip Considerations

Courses actually begin well before meeting participants in the field. This pretrip portion of a course can begin several years or months before the arrival of participants. The planning and preparation part of the trip is marked with visualization and anticipation of what will happen on the course. The leaders discuss their perceptions of the course and develop a tangible product to market. Anticipation is used as a tool to gain interest in the course. The leaders communicate details about the course to potential participants, hoping to create a realistic perception of the field experience. Problems can occur in the field if leaders are not in agreement about the course.

Leaders should meet at the trip location before the arrival of participants. They should spend time together before the trip to get a feel for one another's tendencies, preferences, and style. Like the participants, the leaders will experience the group process. The leaders will be more useful in assisting the group with their dynamics if they are not in the midst of the same stages of group development themselves. This time should also be spent acclimating to the trip environment. Altitude, humidity, air quality, and temperature differences can affect anyone. Adjusting to the environment before participants arrive will enable leaders to assist participants through the acclimatization process.

It is also important for the leaders to gain as much firsthand knowledge of the course location as possible. For the student, surprises can provide a learning experience, but for the leader, these surprises indicate a logistical failure and can become a safety concern. Precourse time also should include discussing the purpose, priorities, participants, place, and plan for the first 48 to 72 hours of the course, which helps to get the team aligned.

Program Implementation

Once in the field, one leader should be designated as lead instructor. Telling the group who the lead instructor is may or may not occur. The group usually figures out who the ultimate decision maker is. In order to share some of the responsibilities, different instructors may have primary responsibility for certain aspects of the course, such as emergency coordination, logistics, or technical skills. Many societies, including Western societies, are made up of such hierarchical systems and a newly forming group gains comfort from this type of system. Who does what, when, and where is worked out during the planning sessions. Some of this may be detailed in an organization's policies and procedures. If not, the instructors must agree on roles and responsibilities. Communication from the leader group to the student group is planned—how to share information, when to share information, how to answer questions from participants, and which information to share.

Once in the field the leaders need to debrief each day and sometimes more than once during the day to maintain their subgroup, provide feedback, and work through any problems. This is done separate from the group and allows the leaders to vent, question, and receive other perspectives of what is happening in the group. The daily leader debriefing and exchange encourages a strong group of leaders who are pursuing excellence in their own development. It keeps the instructor group centered and cohesive. When in the storming stage of development, groups will tend to "divide and conquer" and the instructor team can become a target. A united front is critical, yet the instructors must pursue their own issues within the instructor group. Competition is the most likely problem. The group can sense disquiet and will take sides. This is called triangulation.

In a way the instructors are on a different trip than the participants. While they are part of the larger group, they too must have time to enjoy each other's company. Otherwise, leading is very lonely!

Postprogram Considerations

After the course it is important to become removed from the students, physically and psychologically. The group has ended and while it may come together again in another way, there needs to be a time for reflection and rest. Rather than formally reviewing the course, this is a time for leaders to check in with other leaders' immediate needs.

The instructors will debrief the course and share feedback with each other, especially if there have been difficult situations or people in the group. There is no hurry to do this; however, it is best completed in a timely way before a leader begins another trip. Time away from the other leaders is also needed. If you treat yourselves as a group, as recommended, then there is a need to disconnect from the experience before the analysis phase.

Individually, instructors should review their personal journals and pictures, write up a course summary, complete evaluations, and review the students' evaluations of the course. After gathering a fresh perception of the course, leaders should debrief the course. Sometimes this is done with a supervisor. If the debriefing process is formalized, leaders can feel more comfortable in a critical analysis of the course.

Reunions

Reconnecting with the group may bring closure through opportunities to recall moments of the experience and the people. This is an enjoyable part of the experience and can reinforce what was gained from the expedition. Picture parties and group presentations are effective ways of accomplishing closure. If participants on the course are spread across a large geographic expanse, they can exchange e-mail information, and a Web page can be developed for participants to visit and reminisce about their course.

Expedition Behavior

In the 1930s Paul Petzoldt was part of the American expedition attempting to summit K2, one of the most difficult mountains to climb in the world. After spending months together on a ship to India and then hiking from Darjeeling to start their ascent, the group was well acquainted with each other and their habits. No one made it to the summit of the mountain on that expedition but an outcome of that trip was the development of a term that has served groups in the outdoors well. This term, *expedition behavior,* suggests how an effective group behaves when in an isolated community. It can be used as a blueprint for a community's success or for its failure to meet its goals. The term is neutral in and of itself. We can place adjectives of effective, ineffective, good, or poor in front of it to define the relationships that exist within an outdoor adventure group.

The following subcategories of expedition behavior provide a convenient way to set up a community in the outdoors and also provide a reference point for feedback and evaluation. Expedition behavior is about relationships in the group. It is also about taking responsibility for one's behavior in those relationships. It builds a communication and trust system in the group. Clearly this is an important component for facilitating group growth in the outdoors.

Individual to Individual

The relationships between individuals, or individual-to-individual expedition behavior, is the first dynamic everyone faces. In one-on-one situations we will like some people more than others, have something in common with the other person, and note differences easily. In an expedition format individuals must navigate their relationships with each and every member of the group. Primarily we must take responsibility for our own behavior. When interacting with another person we must become sensitive to the needs and behaviors of others. If one person is an early riser and has coffee and breakfast cooked by the time the tentmate appears, that is fine as long as it is understood that other camp chores will be shared. When a person feels pressured to complete a task so it will get done, resentment can build. This is the point when the two individuals must talk about the tasks at hand and the system they will use to complete those tasks. Individual-to-individual behavior is the first and potentially most important relationship on an expedition. This other person hears about your fears and joys as you share a tent space.

The bottom line: Negotiate relationships.

Individual to Group

The individual-to-group relationship is how each person relates to the whole group. Individuals need to take responsibility for their own safety and well-being and ask for assistance from the group from time to time. This might mean stopping to fix a hot spot on the foot. It might mean asking for a helping hand during a river crossing. It might mean admitting that you don't feel well. No one likes to bring attention to a perceived weakness. However, a hot spot that goes unattended turns into a blister. A person who doesn't ask for a needed helping hand could create a rescue situation. A person who feels ill can stop a group cold. Responsible individuals stop before a situation becomes a hazard to themselves or to the group finishing its goal. Of course, this can only occur if a person feels that the group will support and actually praise this behavior.

The bottom line: Ask for what you need.

Group to Individual

Once an individual has alerted the group to a problem, the group needs to support that effort

When connected by a rope, the members of the team are responsible to each other. This is an example of group-to-individual expedition behavior.

Group to Group

Group-to-group behavior is how one group behaves when they encounter another group in the backcountry. Respecting another group's experience and goals is the key to such encounters. Certainly it is fine to speak with others but conversations should be short and concise. It is disappointing to find out that a destination lake is not much to look at according another group. It is frustrating to hear that the ridge is 10 minutes away and half an hour later you are still struggling uphill. It is rude to comment on another group's gear, clothing, or cleanliness. We only know what our group is like and the culture that we build. Judging others is not a useful way to relate, nor is taking away the fun of discovery. Other groups have rights to enter the backcountry and are neither better nor worse than our group. Being noisy or obvious distracts from an outdoor experience and we must monitor our behavior to not inflict our group's culture on others. As for the etiquette of the trail, in most cases when hiking, the group moving uphill has the right of way. Ask your group to step off the trail and wait until they pass. In the case of horses on the trail, hikers should ask the lead rider where they should be. Most of the time the group will be asked to stand on the downhill side of the trail so that if a horse shies it will shy uphill and be safer for the rider and the horse. Saying hello is fine, but wait for the other person to start a conversation.

Even the clothes we wear and the equipment we use affect others. While neon orange is handy in a rescue situation, for general purposes a more muted shade blends into the background better and makes your group less obvious.

The bottom line: Think of courtesy and you have it made in all aspects of expedition behavior.

by stopping and handling the problem. Even thanking a person for calling for a rest begins to foster a group's camaraderie. Many times others in the group have been waiting for someone else to ask for a break or to fix sore feet. Often when one person needs a snack others do as well and when a person has a hot spot so do several others. The more this behavior is practiced the easier it gets to ask for what you need. Group-to-individual behavior might also mean that the group makes a decision for an individual. If a person is lagging behind and having trouble with the weight of a pack, the group may take some extra weight to share the load until that individual gains some fitness. This can be explained by stating on any given day anyone in the group can feel weak, tired, or ill—even the instructors! The group does not succeed if every individual does not take responsibility for self and others. Safer and more enjoyable trips are a result of positive expedition behavior.

The bottom line: Support others gratefully.

Individual to individual, individual to group, and group to individual are the internal aspects of expedition behavior. The question is often posed, How many members of the group are there? The obvious answer is to count the number of people, including leaders. However, if you count each person and add one more for the group, you have a much more accurate count. Think about it. There is a myriad of potential relationships in every group—that is what makes groups fun!

Group and Individual to Local Populace

Many trailheads and exit points are near small rural communities. Imagine what it is like to see a new person or group fresh from the trail invade the local restaurant, ice cream store, or grocery! Suffice it to say it has an effect. Noise, vocabulary,

Learning Activity 10.1

Act out different scenarios of good and bad expedition behavior. Talk about how each situation could result in good and bad relationships.

and odors can be offensive to others. We have group jokes and may even be proud of our burly look. However, being aware of the effect that we have as a group and being respectful and knowledgeable about the area will help avert conflict and bad feelings. Once again, good expedition behavior allows the local population to welcome us to their community rather than prevent us from returning in the future.

The bottom line: Respect the culture you are in.

Group and Individual to Managing Agencies

As outdoor leaders you will have to be knowledgeable about the land managers in the area where you are going. They may be government employees or private landowners. Each has different access rules and regulations to allow access, and each land agency has different regulations allowing or preventing certain activities. For example, on U.S. Forest Service land you might have cows grazing in your campsite. You may hear loggers cutting trees. You may have ATVs, motorcycles, horses, or snowmobiles sharing trails with you. In terms of expedition behavior we face the challenge of knowing and understanding the rules and regulations and adhering to them. If you feel strongly about how the land should be used, write your senator or representative or choose another area for your trip.

The bottom line: Be good citizens on the land.

Observing Groups

A leader watches with a purpose. A beginning step is simply noting who arrives first, who arrives last, who engages enthusiastically in activities, who speaks, and who does not speak. Watch interactions. Watch how a group handles a problem. Watch for reactions, smiles, nodding heads, or laughter. Watch for signs of fatigue, stress, or discomfort. One way to keep track of such occurrences is to count. The first time a behavior happens it is considered a happening. It may indicate something or may not. The second time a behavior occurs it is a pattern, and the third time you can be sure the behavior is a habit. Individuals show us their habits, such as being on time or being late.

Once behaviors are determined to be habits, the leader can comment about them. For example, it has been noted that the group shows up for meetings about 5 minutes late. Is this a behavior that the program and the group want to support? What is happening in the group that leads to this behavior? Leaders are safe in commenting as long as they focus on the behavior and can give specific examples of stated behaviors. What this method of observation allows is nonbiased comments. The leader is not saying something is good or bad, just what is!

In instructional sessions it is difficult to teach and watch at the same time. A simple strategy is to have one leader watch the group while another is teaching. The second leader may lead the debriefing because she has identified patterns and habits. Switching back and forth will develop the skills of observation, feedback, and team teaching.

Another exercise that is helpful for leaders and students is to track their own behavior. Each day we go through many experiences. If you push the pause button and reflect on personal performance during the day you can answer the following questions (Summers 1997):

- What did I do really well?
- What was challenging for me?
- What can I improve on?
- What have I seen in others that I really like?
- What have I seen in others that I would like to see less of?
- What questions do I have?

Learning Activity 10.2

Push your pause button and review your day. Answer the six questions on page 145 about your personal performance. Think about what you can do to make tomorrow better.

Summary

Conscious experience in groups is important for leaders. Understanding the fundamental goals of the experience and herding the group toward those goals is a giant task. Leaders must be comfortable and aware of their own abilities and limitations. A leader must always be observant, and a leader must put group needs over personal needs in the outdoors. Making a plan that is achievable and challenging both physically and emotionally is critical. Learning to lead and to follow is imperative. Noting when you have a reaction to a person or a behavior will help you learn about interaction. Working on communication skills, conflict resolution skills, and task and maintenance behaviors and allowing a group to develop is a rewarding experience for everyone. Some experiences are short in length and an instructor will worry more about reaching goals than the feelings of participants. As you gain experience you will gain confidence about what you can and can't handle in a group. Opening a person emotionally and not being able to put them together again or not having time to let a person regain balance is dangerous and can have negative effects. Lead within your abilities, whether it is with the skills for group process or with technical abilities.

Expedition behavior provides parameters for acceptable relationships in the outdoors. It also provides a way to monitor how people interact within the group and with outsiders. Each of these relationships helps build a group.

Groups develop over time and many groups never move beyond the forming stage. There might not be time enough to develop further or there might be resistance to becoming a highly functional group. Groups often overestimate their development and believe that one episode of conflict pushes them to norming and performing. Remember the spring? Groups cycle and can stretch for long periods of time in one phase.

Working in and with groups will provide many opportunities for self-reflection as a leader. Note the moments when you reach your maximum tolerance or when you need to back off. A coleader is helpful in the learning process. Groups will teach each of us many things about ourselves. We should be grateful for every opportunity to learn from them.

Selected References

Alcorn, S. 1985. What makes groups tick? *Personnel* (Sept.) 63: 52-58.

Galanes, G.J., and J.K. Brilhart. 1997. *Communicating in groups: Applications and skills.* 3rd ed. Reading, MA: McGraw-Hill.

Johnson, D.W., and F.P. Johnson. 2001. *Joining together.* 8th ed. Englewood Cliffs, NJ: Prentice Hall.

Jordan, D.J. 2001. *Leadership in leisure services: Making a difference.* State College, PA: Venture.

Mills, T.M. 1964. *Group transformation: An analysis of a learning group.* Englewood Cliffs, NJ: Prentice Hall.

Professional-Development Portfolio Activity

1. Observe a group in which you are a member.

   • Can you describe the subgroups within it?

   • What stage of development is this group in (forming, storming, norming, performing, transforming)?

   • What are the key relationships in the group? Who is in charge? Who keeps the group on task? Who monitors or maintains the group with relational skill?

2. In the group, choose a behavior to observe. For example, chart who talks to whom, who can get others to buy into an idea, who speaks but is not heard, who asks for feedback, who is the first to arrive, who is the last to arrive, and how much dead time there is. Chart your findings. If a behavior occurs at least three times, share your findings with the group.

Petzoldt, P. 1984. *The new wilderness handbook.* New York: Norton.

Russell, R.V. 2001. *Leadership in recreation.* 2nd ed. Boston: McGraw-Hill.

Stempler, B.L. 1993. Supervisory co-leadership: An innovative model for teaching the use of social group work in clinical social work training. *Social Work with Groups* 16(3): 97-110.

Summers, J. 1997. *Content manual: Train the trainer.* Stillwater, OK: Vision Us.

Tuckman, B.W., and M.A. Jensen. 1977. Stages of small group development revisited. *Group and Organization Studies* 2(4): 419-427.

Winter, S.K. 1976. Developmental stages in the roles and concerns of group co-leaders. *Small Group Behavior* 7: 349-363.

chapter 11

Challenge Course Leadership

" There is only one thing more painful than learning from experience and that is not learning from experience. " —Archibald MacLeish

Chapter Concepts

- Challenge course programming—Outdoor leaders must be able to design and implement programs based on a body of knowledge and skills specific to challenge courses.
- Challenge course leadership—Outdoor leaders must be able to apply experiential learning theory, adventure education theory, and leisure theory to lead purposeful challenge course experiences.
- Challenge course facilitation—Outdoor leaders must be competent in facilitating challenge course experiences for all populations based on a specific set of technical skills and knowledge.

The chapter concepts relate to the following core competencies:

- Foundational knowledge (CC-1)—Challenge course leadership involves applying knowledge of theories and concepts related to education, recreation, and therapy.
- Self-awareness and professional conduct (CC-2)—Leaders can provide effective challenge course experiences by being self-aware and following a standard of professional behavior.
- Teaching and facilitation (CC-4)—Challenge courses require specific technical skills.
- Program management (CC-6)—Part of program management is planning and implementing challenge course programs.

Stacey appeared to be the strongest member of her group. She had successfully completed the white-water kayaking section of the Hudson River. Rock climbing presented no obstacles that pushed her beyond her comfort zone. She breezed through the grueling backpacking portion of the trip through the high-peak region. Yet, she seemed distant from the group. Stacey rarely shared in group discussions at the end of the day. She kept to herself and spoke only when approached by others. When talking among themselves, most group members commented that they did not know or understand Stacey. The purpose of the trip was to develop the participants' leadership skills. The group represented the student leadership team from a high school in northern New Jersey. The school administration sponsored this adventure-based experience to New York's Adirondacks in order to improve their effectiveness as peer leaders. Each year, the student leadership team relished the task of choosing their destination. This year posed no exception when the group enthusiastically picked New York's Adirondack State Park.

Stacey was new to the school and felt different from her peers. She voted for a trip to the Adirondacks simply to avoid conflict. She secretly wished to head farther north to the Canadian wilderness, a place she had always dreamed of visiting. Even when the trip started, she went along with the others but purposefully kept a low profile. She used her physical strength, as opposed to teamwork, to successfully deal with most challenges. Stacey's instructors were concerned that she was holding her true self back. They sensed that she was stifling her leadership potential. Fortunately, the challenge course portion of the course was the next scheduled activity after the backpacking trip. The itinerary called for the group to spend 2 days at a local conference center.

Other group members were on track and displayed significant personal growth. For example, Rory, the school vice president, tended to speak first and take charge in group meetings. Through group feedback, he began to understand that he needed to sit back and become a better listener. Justine, one of the sophomore senators, tended to be intimidated by the older students. The rock-climbing portion of the trip allowed her to develop genuine trust with older members of the group. All group members were slowly becoming an effective team, with the exception of Stacey. The instructors put their heads together in order to design an experience that would benefit the group with a special twist for Stacey. A full day was designated for challenge course activities. Stacey's instructors carefully organized a progression of activities that would further facilitate group growth.

Initial team-building activities were crafted to move Stacey into a meaningful leadership position. Stacey

(continued)

(continued)

was put in a position to make leadership decisions and use interpersonal skills beyond anything she had experienced thus far on the trip. When the group made it to the end of the day, the culminating problem-solving activity required total group commitment. Stacey was reeling with excitement. The group completed the final activity with genuine group spirit signi-

fied by loud cheers and hugs. Stacey finally felt like part of the group. Stacey made significant progress as a result of her challenge course experience. She left the program with feelings of connection and respect for her team members, and she became a prominent leader in her school.

The power of a **challenge course** experience is dependent upon effective leadership. Activity design, thoughtful progression, attention to risk management, and the ability to apply adventure education theory make up challenge course leadership skills. Stacey's instructors were properly trained and experienced in the art of challenge course facilitation.

Challenge course leadership is now an integral part of outdoor leadership in North America. Many outdoor organizations in Canada and the United States integrate challenge course activities into their programming services. There are over 15,000 challenge courses in the United States today (Attarian 2001). Outdoor education centers, camps, youth programs, schools, private businesses, and a myriad of other agencies offer challenge course experiences. Traditional adventure sports such as backpacking, kayaking, rafting, climbing, and caving are commonly partnered with the challenge course experience. Aspiring outdoor leaders must seriously consider developing their challenge course leadership skills in order to be competitive in the job market. Challenge course experience serves as an excellent tool to improve overall outdoor leadership effectiveness.

Challenge courses are commonly referred to as high ropes courses, low ropes courses, team-building courses, and group initiatives, among others. Individuals who lead challenge course experiences are commonly referred to as challenge course leaders or challenge course facilitators. It is beyond the scope of this chapter to outline all leadership functions and technical skills associated with challenge course leadership. This chapter provides the foundation of knowledge and skills necessary to be an effective challenge course leader. We will first look at the challenge course profession from a historical standpoint and discusses various challenge course environments. Next we will venture into programming concerns from a leadership perspective. Finally, we will finish with further discussion on chal-

lenge course leadership and associated leadership competencies.

Challenge Course Profession

Early challenge courses were constructed in-house based on the creativity and the ingenuity of staff members. No universal standards existed to govern programming practices. Risk management reflected no uniformity among programs. Professionals estimate somewhere between 700 to 800 courses existed in the 1980s (Attarian 2001). The steady growth of programs pushed the outdoor leaders running these programs to express concern regarding safety and acceptable practices. The first formal gathering of challenge course professionals occurred in 1988 at the North Carolina Outward Bound school. This meeting gave birth to the first professional challenge course organization in the United States, which later became known as the Association for Challenge Course Technology (ACCT). The ACCT developed universal challenge course installation standards as their first formal task during their 1991 symposium. The ACCT emerged the summer of 1993 (ACCT 2004).

The ACCT has evolved into a respected professional trade association that advances challenge course technology. The organization provides membership services such as conferences, newsletters, industry updates, standards, and access to insurance coverage for challenge course programmers. Beyond their original installation standards, ACCT also developed standards in the following areas: inspection standards (includes safety inspections); technical standards for challenge course operations (includes management and operation standards as well as staff competencies); and ethical standards (ACCT 2004). In 2003, another professional association officially formed to support the profession. The Professional Ropes Course Association (PRCA) mission states, "The mission of the PRCA is to develop user friendly standards, ropes challenge course documents, and to define, document and outline the construction/ operational practices for the ropes challenge course industry. The documents of the PRCA will be used for course evaluations, insurance criteria, and professional development" (PRCA 2003, p. 1). The PRCA has created a manual of standards and provides professional services for challenge course professionals.

At this time, no universal certifications exist for challenge course leaders. The certifications that do exist are specific to organizations and programs. Facilitator training models and curricula are also specific to programs. Basic facilitator training tends to be a minimum of 40 hours in length (Rohnke et al. 2003; Carlson 2003). Advanced facilitators and course directors require about 80 training hours. The ACCT (2004) standards list approximately 81 staff competencies or facilitator standards. Forty hours of training would not ensure complete competency in all areas, so many programs require newly trained facilitators to apprentice or shadow experienced leaders in order to hone their skills under a watchful eye. As new courses are built, many builders offer training as part of their overall service. It is important for leaders to facilitate based on the specifics of course design. The universal installation standards developed by the ACCT have limitations, as builders may exercise varying degrees

of flexibility in a course design. Challenge course managers have additional flexibility as local policies and procedures are established. Challenge course leaders must be aware of this fact and be willing to participate in recertifications, in-house staff trainings, and updates each time work is obtained on a different course.

Origin of Challenge Courses

In order to gain a deeper appreciation of challenge course leadership, the history of challenge course programming must be understood. As described in previous chapters, the Outward Bound movement played a significant role in the birth of outdoor leadership as we know it today. The British Outward Bound schools borrowed the original concept from their military, and the majority of British Outward Bound instructors possessed military backgrounds. The first British course was built sometime in the 1940s. It was believed to simulate working high in the rigs of sailing ships. British Outward Bound students underwent rigorous training on the challenge course to prepare for sailing expeditions in the rough seas off the English coast.

Challenge course programming was an important curricular component when the first U.S. Outward Bound school formed in 1962 (Miner and Bolt 2002; Wagstaff 2003). Ernest "Tap" Tapley designed and built the first U.S. Outward

A typical high-element course built on telephone poles.

Bound challenge course when he was charged with the task of creating the first U.S. Outward Bound base camp in Marble Canyon, Colorado. The founders of Outward Bound sought Tapley based on his mythical reputation as a gifted outdoorsman. There were few outdoorsmen who could climb mountains, ski steep terrain, climb steep faces, backpack great distances, and mentor young people like Tap Tapley. Part of Tapley's preparation to establish a U.S. Outward Bound school entailed traveling overseas to visit the British Outward Bound Eskdale school. The British Outward Bound instructors knew of Tapley and were eager to share their knowledge. They made sure that Tapley experienced the Eskdale challenge course as part of his training. In addition, Tapley had U.S. military experience with the 10th Mountain Division and was well acquainted with military obstacle courses. Tapley's inspirational design for the Marble Canyon course stemmed from these experiences and his own creativity.

Challenge Courses in the Beginning

The course at Outward Bound's Marble Canyon base camp began with a 35-foot (11-meter) rope ladder. This element produced as much apprehension and nervousness as did rock climbing and rappelling. Students were taught to **belay** one another. Falls were encouraged in order for students to experience the full effects of belaying. After a session, students sat around Tapley for a question-and-answer session. Tapley would ask a question related to the experience and students would reply. This form of debriefing was exercised to maximize the educational value of the Outward Bound experience (Wagstaff 2003). The Outward Bound movement began to flourish in the late 1960s and early 1970s, and as a result, Outward Bound produced a number of competent instructors. These instructors learned the art of challenge course programming and carried this knowledge to other settings.

In addition to the Outward Bound movement, another movement known as hébertisme used challenge course activities to educate young people. George Hébert served as a French Navy officer. His focus was the physical conditioning and training of the French navy. In 1913, he gave a demonstration of his training methods before the French Physical Education Congress: "Hébert's view on education was a return-to-nature approach with emphasis on development of 'moral values and virile character'" (Cousineau 1976, p. 3). Hébert designed his obstacle courses

An indoor course located in a gym.

to foster physical movements such as jumping, climbing, running, walking, crawling, balancing, throwing, lifting, and carrying. Hébertisme created opportunity to discover personal potential and limitations while moving in a natural environment (Wagstaff 2003). Two Canadian army officers who served in France during World War II were exposed to hébertisme as an educational tool. As a result, they implemented a program in 1949 at Camp Ecole Trois-Saumons located near Québec City, Canada.

Movement Into Mainstream Education

Project Adventure holds the distinction of being one of the first organizations to integrate challenge course programming into mainstream education (Prouty 1999). Project Adventure founders and early instructors were former Outward Bound staff who were significantly influenced by Outward Bound philosophy. The U.S. Department of Education funded a grant that enabled the establishment of Project Adventure in 1971 as a nonprofit educational organization. Project Adventure found its way into school settings as this exciting brand of experiential education proved to be engaging and motivating for students. Outward Bound instructors continued spreading

Learning Activity 11.1

In small groups, create a historical time line of important dates, events, people, and organizations that have influenced challenge course leadership and programming.

their influence by constructing challenge courses in other settings such as college campuses and summer camps.

Course Environments

Challenge courses can be found in diverse settings. Agencies that construct challenge course facilities can be creative with their physical space. Lack of open space does limit the number and type of low and high elements, but professional builders have the opportunity to exercise creativity when building elements. Following are diverse settings and environments where high and low courses have been constructed:

- Forested areas with large trees are a popular setting for challenge courses. The first courses built in Canada and the United States were located in groves of trees that would support the use of ropes and cables.

- Planted telephone poles in open spaces later became an alternative to tree courses. Many organizations did not have access to forest resources to construct a tree course. Planted telephone poles became a popular alternative. Strategically planted poles allowed for a tremendous amount of flexibility in course design.

- The first generation of pole courses gave way to an innovative, free-standing design. Three large telephone poles are arranged to form a giant tripod. Low and high elements are then strung between the poles. This design is a good choice when open space is limited.

- The rafters and walls of gymnasiums or ceiling space above indoor swimming pools are also used to construct high elements. Agencies such as schools that wish to provide indoor programming use what is typically considered wasted or unusable space.

- Conference centers support challenge course programming as a team-building tool for conventions and meetings. Contracted builders construct a temporary course in large open spaces (indoors or outdoors) to be dismantled after the event.

Challenge Course Programs

To understand the art of challenge course leadership, we must address challenge courses in a programming context. Effective challenge course leadership is the ability to provide successful programs that accomplish predetermined goals. One of the major barriers in challenge course programming is the lack of understanding by the public as well as the novice outdoor leader. Challenge course programming is an intentional process that is facilitated by a trained leader. For most, the term *challenge course* conjures visions of individuals balancing on ropes, logs, and cables 50 feet (15 meters) above the ground. The uninformed tend to stereotype this vision as a large jungle gym with little purpose other than to have fun or provoke fear. Challenge courses are actually much more complex than the stereotypical vision of "high wire acts." Rohnke et al. define a challenge course as, "An experiential adventure program which offers groups and individuals the opportunity to participate in a series of activities involving mental, physical and emotional risk taking" (2003, p. 3). Professionals facilitate challenge course experiences based on goals and objectives intended to produce specific outcomes. The activities that make up the challenge course experience must be sequenced and facilitated to meet program goals. Challenge course environments are diverse in physical makeup. Whether the facilities are indoors or outdoors, the overall outcomes will remain the same if fundamental programming goals are kept at the forefront of a leader's priorities.

Program Goals

Not all challenge course experiences are intended to have the same outcome. Outcomes vary depending on the program's goal orientation.

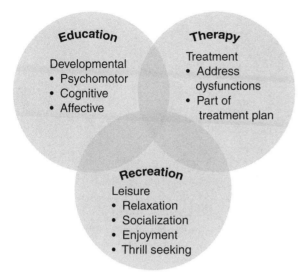

Figure 11.1 Goal orientations of challenge courses.

Challenge course outcomes can be viewed in the context of three global goal orientations (figure 11.1): recreation, education, and therapy. These goal orientations may stand alone or be combined to produce a variety of outcomes. Novice leaders must first understand the differences and similarities between these three program goals. They must also know what is necessary to effectively facilitate each experience. As you might suspect, these global goals can be applied to many adventure activities beyond challenge courses. For example, canoeing, rock-climbing, and backpacking programs can be designed with these goals in mind. The following sections describe each goal orientation.

Recreation

Challenge course experiences that focus on recreation occur during a participant's leisure time or time free of obligation. Motivations to participate in recreation are as diverse as the individuals who participate. Relaxation, socialization, enjoyment, thrill seeking, skill development, and self-improvement are just a few examples of motivating factors. These motivations may be conscious or unconscious reasons for participation. Skilled leaders provide an opportunity for these personal goals to occur. Leaders ensure safety and use facilitation strategies to maximize the leisure experience. A leisure experience occurs when an intrinsically motivated participant has freedom of choice and has perceived control over the activity. It is up to the participants to pull what they wish from the experience. Recreational experiences can

foster educational or therapeutic outcomes, but they occur within the leisure context.

For a better understanding of a recreational goal-oriented experience, consider the new sport of zip-line touring. For example, an ecotourism company in Hawaii constructs a series of zip lines as part of a jungle trek for tourists. Guides facilitate technical tasks such as fitting harnesses and connecting to the system. The goal is to have fun by spicing up the day hike with adventure. Along a traditional hike through a tropical forest, tourists are hooked up to cables and sent sailing through the tree canopy and over ravines and rivers, sometimes hundreds of feet off the ground. Participants are primarily tourists on vacation who seek the thrills, enjoyment, and relaxation of recreational activities during their leisure time.

Education

Challenge course programs geared toward educational experiences are intentional and developmental in nature. Formal goal setting and assessment occurs. Facilitators intentionally design experiences to foster educational outcomes. Participant psychomotor, cognitive, and affective domains are specific development targets. Leaders guide participants through a sequenced process based on educational theory, and outdoor leaders use experiential learning theory as the basis for their teaching methods. Direct experience, reflection, generalization, and application are the four phases of experiential learning theory that are used in teaching process. (See chapter 12 to learn more about the experiential learning cycle.) Outcomes are assessed throughout the educational experience. A final evaluation occurs to determine if goals have been accomplished. The ultimate goal is to facilitate change within the participant.

Stacey's story at the beginning of this chapter describes a challenge course program with educational goals. Program goals focus on developing personal and group attributes such as self-confidence, communication skills, and teamwork. Leaders facilitate reflection activities and weave discussion into overall goals and objectives. Another example is corporate experiences. Individual departments, leadership teams, and other intact groups found within a corporate structure participate in challenge course activities. Participation is based on specific educational intents. For example, the intent may be to increase productivity through team building. Facilitators take coworkers through a series of team-building experiences to address and resolve concerns in the workplace.

Learning Activity 11.2

Identify and research agencies that provide challenge course services. Through individual presentations and discussions, have the class categorize the programs based on the three goal orientations.

Therapy

Recreational and educational challenge course experiences in general can be therapeutic. Participants may walk away with a sense of renewal and personal growth. Challenge course programming used as therapy, however, is specific in focus and methodology. A medical model serves as the foundation for challenge course programming used as therapy. If considered therapy, licensed or certified health care professionals are involved. Therapists construct individual treatment plans based on medical diagnoses. Comprehensive assessments are completed to determine therapeutic effectiveness. Therapeutic goals might consist of correcting dysfunctional behavior or improving an individual's quality of life. For example, a regional substance abuse center uses challenge course activities as part of the patients' rehabilitation program. Doctors, counselors, and therapeutic recreation specialists all work together to design individual treatment plans. Challenge course programming serves as a tool within a larger treatment process.

Program Components

Challenge course programs typically include a series of activities that can be adapted to meet any program goal. New professionals must take great care to be well versed in all aspects of challenge course programming. Activities that occur on the ground and high in the air serve different but equally important purposes. Four fundamental program components must be mastered in order to effectively facilitate a challenge course experience. The components are games and icebreakers, group initiatives and trust activities, **low elements,** and **high elements.** Each component serves a specific function within the larger programming process. The four program components must be carefully sequenced based on individual and group needs.

Challenge course facilitators guide groups through a process to achieve predetermined goals. Outcomes are then assessed to determine levels of success. What makes challenge course programming part of the outdoor leader's venue is the need for both technical and leadership competencies to facilitate this adventure-based activity. For example, leaders must know belay systems, knots, spotting techniques, and rescue skills as well as the physics of falls in relation to breaking strengths of equipment. Each of the four program components requires specific technical skills.

In addition to technical skills the leader must understand adventure education theory and be able to apply it effectively. The challenge course leader should be able to match the level of challenge with the participants' ability and readiness. An untrained challenge course leader endangers participants physically and psychologically when the challenge is facilitated inappropriately. A properly facilitated challenge course experience based on sound adventure pedagogy offers unique developmental opportunities, as displayed by Stacey after her adventure experience. The following sections provide an overview of the four program components and skills necessary to facilitate each.

Games and Icebreakers

Games, icebreakers, warm-ups, and deinhibitizers are synonymous terms to describe initial activities to warm up a group physically and socially. The leader purposefully uses these activities to foster group development during the early stages of group dynamics. Activities might include name games, tag games, or stretching exercises. Program tone and initial group norms are established. Setting a positive tone and productive group norms allows the group to successfully navigate through the remainder of the process.

Group Initiatives and Trust Activities

Group initiatives are problem-solving, team-based activities that require no specialized safety systems. For example, facilitators present the group with a challenge to move a bucket of water from point A to point B without spilling the water. They must remain 10 feet (3 meters) from the can at all times and they have the use of six 15-foot (5-meter) ropes to move the bucket. Group initiatives serve as the perfect instrument to develop interpersonal skills and teamwork. Leaders must facilitate these activities in such a way that the group is empowered to solve problems without interference or reliance on the leader.

Trust activities are designed to foster a sense of trust among group members. They may or may not involve problem solving. They vary in design but the intended outcome is deepened interpersonal relationships. One of the most classic trust activities is the trust fall. A group member falls from height into the arms of group members. Leaders must carefully facilitate trust exercises based on an awareness of group readiness. If the group is not ready for a particular activity, it could backfire and undermine trust, causing a breakdown in interpersonal dynamics.

An outdoor group attempts the fidget ladder, a low element.

Low Elements

Low elements may be stationary, permanent structures or they may be portable. Specific safety systems must be put into place. Low elements usually don't require a belay system but do require that group members spot to ensure participant safety. Low elements may be individual or team activities. For example, the group may be challenged to transport all members through a giant spider's web made of string. In order to complete the activity, participants must be lifted off the ground by other group members and passed through the web's holes. Some holes are low while other holes may be 6 feet (2 meters) or more above the ground. Great care must be taken not to disturb the web. Participants must protect each other by lifting properly and spotting, which is required to prevent a serious injury from a fall. Low elements also foster interpersonal skills and teamwork. In addition, low elements are used to develop trust, group cohesion, communication skills, and intrapersonal skills. Leaders must be aware of safety

concerns as well as limitations of the activities. Care must be taken to properly brief and debrief these dynamic activities to accomplish program goals. Leaders must be competent facilitators and possess technical knowledge specific to each activity.

High Elements

High elements are individual and team activities that require a belay system for safety. Participants are required to climb or be lifted a significant distance from the ground. Belay systems typically consist of a rope that is connected to the climber. The rope is rigged to prevent the climber from a dangerous fall. High elements share many of the same benefits as group initiatives and low elements. They are particularly effective at bolstering self-confidence, self-efficacy, and other intrapersonal attributes. Specific technical skills are required of the leaders. Belaying, equipment use, course setup and inspection, and other tasks must be mastered. Leaders must also be able to facilitate the psychological and emotional effects of perceptions of risk. This is where competency in adventure-based leadership comes into play. A leader's ability to properly facilitate a high element will influence participant outcomes.

A group engaged in the spider's web.

A participant crossing the Burma Bridge high element.

Key Leadership Functions

Numerous leadership concepts discussed throughout this text apply to challenge course leaders. Challenge course leaders must apply leadership styles appropriately, and they must exhibit traits and behaviors that characterize effective leadership. Following are four key functions specific to the challenge course process. While these functions have application in other adventure contexts, they represent common practices within the challenge course industry. These practices enable leaders to facilitate recreational, educational, or therapeutic experiences. They help define the facilitation practices of a true professional.

Full-Value Contract

A full-value contract is a traditional tool in adventure-based programming (Schoel, Prouty, and Radcliffe 1988). Due to the experiential nature of challenge course activities, a mechanism is needed to provide behavioral and attitudinal guidance for groups. Creating a full-value contract is an effective solution, and challenge course leaders must be able to facilitate the development of the contract. The full-value contract allows the group to be more self-directive and self-monitoring. A leader uses this technique to make the experience more developmental as opposed to recreational. Project Adventure provides guidelines for the development of a full-value contract when working with different age groups as seen in table 11.1. Of course more sophisticated models can be created depending on the nature and goals of a group. The majority of professional challenge course leaders integrate the contract at the start of a program. See chapter 5 for more information on the full-value contract.

Challenge by Choice

Challenge by choice is another tool commonly used by challenge course leaders. The nature of adventure-based programming requires that participants have a choice in the level of challenge they take on. Challenge course activities are no exception. Participants typically experience many perceived emotional, psychological, and physical risks during programs. It is an accepted practice for leaders to give their participants a choice when risk is involved (Wurdinger 1997). Providing a choice promotes an atmosphere of self-control and personal freedom, and therefore participant motivation comes from within rather than from an outside force, resulting in personal empowerment. Empowerment creates a positive environment for learning and growing. Challenge by choice is not a license for participants to opt out of participation, though. Challenge course leaders must have the ability to exercise challenge by choice without

Table 11.1

Examples of Full-Value Contracts

Elementary (grades 3-5)	Middle school (grades 6-8)	High school (grades 9-12)
Play hard	Be here	Be present
Play safe	Be safe	Pay attention
Play fair	Set goals	Speak your truth
	Be honest	Be open to outcomes
	Let go and move on	Create a safe environment

Panicucci 2002, p. 9

compromising program effectiveness. See chapter 8 for more information on challenge by choice.

Sequencing

Challenge course experiences may last from an hour to several days. They can also be part of a curriculum that occurs over the course of a school year. Therapeutic programs may integrate challenge courses into long- and short-term treatment plans. Sequencing is the art of choosing appropriate activities and organizing them into an intentional progression to accomplish goals and group needs. Leaders create a draft progression of activities when developing the initial activity plan. Competent leaders create sequences that are appropriate for the group according to group skills, abilities, goals, program objectives, and social and cultural needs (ACCT 2004). Sequencing changes occur during the event as leaders evaluate the process. No secret formula exists for proper sequencing. Leaders must be able to plan, observe, react, and adjust based on their own instincts and experience (Rohnke and Butler 1995). The following represents a generic sequence for a full day of challenge course activities:

1. Orientation: Leader gives a general overview and safety briefing that includes challenge by choice.

2. Full-value contract: Leader helps establish healthy group norms from the beginning.

3. Warm-up activities and icebreakers: Group does activities that stretch the body and allow for initial assessment of group norms and function. They help facilitate initial stages of group development. Debriefing is typically not used at this point.

4. Initiatives: Leaders use a progression of problem-solving activities from simple to complex. Debriefings can be integrated into the process at this point.

5. Low elements: Low elements are higher-level initiatives that facilitate further group work and trust building. Low elements also are used to assess and prepare groups for high elements. Belaying is not required but may be an option. Debriefing is encouraged on a deeper level.

6. High elements: High elements require belaying and are designed to promote personal or group growth. Debriefing is also a part of this aspect.

7. Closing activities: Final activities are designed to bring the entire experience together as educational lessons from the day are reviewed. Reflection as a group and as individuals is encouraged.

Processing

Processing, debriefing, and reflection are synonymous terms that describe the method used to facilitate a meaningful experience. Processing theory and techniques are discussed in detail in chapter 8. Novice leaders tend to struggle most with this function. Training and experience in the art of processing is required to create learning environments that facilitate self-actualization, self-discovery, and self-awareness. The goal is to have the group analyze their own process and provide solutions for improvement. Ultimately, lessons learned will be carried beyond the program into real-life situations. It has been established that challenge course programs are a series of activities. How does the leader connect and build upon these activities through processing? Beginning leaders may fall into the trap of systematically debriefing every activity before

Plan a half-day challenge course program for an athletic team. The season has just begun. The coach seeks guidance in establishing healthy team norms that will promote a sense of team spirit and identity. In small groups or as an individual, (1) create a rough draft of a sequenced program, (2) create the process for developing a full-value contract, (3) create an introduction for challenge by choice, and (4) identify potential processing strategies.

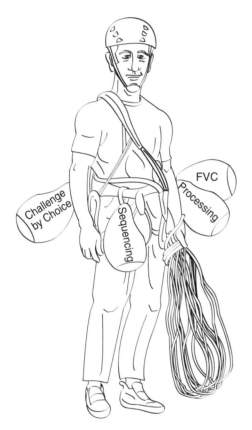

Figure 11.2 Skilled challenge course leaders possess key knowledge and abilities to facilitate challenge course experiences.

moving on to the next. The debriefing typically consists of a question–answer session led by the facilitator. However, veterans know the process is dynamic and they have a large "bag of tricks" (figure 11.2). Knowing at what point to process and the appropriate processing tool to apply is a skill developed through experience.

Leader Competencies

Along with the general leadership functions, challenge course leaders must possess specific competencies to provide safe, enjoyable, goal-driven experiences. Competencies relate to the leadership and technical skills necessary to facilitate challenge course activities. No universal competencies exist for challenge course leaders at this time. The ACCT includes competencies in their handbook of challenge course standards (2004), and others have outlined basic facilitator functions and training requirements (Carlson 2003; Rohnke and Butler 1995; Rohnke et al. 2003). It is difficult for the novice leader to know where to start. Following is a summary of common themes found in challenge course literature. The novice should use it as a starting point to assess abilities and knowledge. The competencies listed in this section provide only a broad overview of what a challenge course facilitator should know and be able to do. For a more detailed understanding of competencies, refer to the established professional standards mentioned throughout this chapter.

General Competencies

Basic leadership skills are needed to effectively facilitate challenge course experiences. Challenge course leaders guide participants through diverse activities that require strict attention to safety. Professional leaders must also focus on program quality throughout the process. Leaders must be able to critically analyze a dynamic process and make numerous decisions to ensure goal attainment. All groups and experiences will be different, which requires the use of judgment. Exercising sound judgment based on experience and training is a critical skill for all challenge course leaders. Professional leaders must be able to apply theory and properly manage the adventure experience.

The following checklist represents general leadership competencies that serve as the foundation for professional challenge course leadership. Challenge course leaders must possess the knowledge and have the ability to do the following:

- Exercise sound judgment based on an acute self-awareness of one's abilities and limitations.
- Exercise decision-making skills congruent with an agency's policies and procedures to ensure a safe, enjoyable, goal-oriented experience.
- Conduct oneself in an ethical manner consistent with a program's philosophy and mission.
- Create a safe environment to protect and nurture a client's physical, emotional, psychological, and spiritual domains.
- Apply experiential and adventure education theory in a challenge course context.
- Apply sound risk management principles associated with the body of knowledge of challenge course programming.

Facilitation Competencies

Certain leadership skills are required in a challenge course context. These facilitation competencies represent specific, technical knowledge beyond the required general competencies. Safety and program quality remain primary facilitation goals. Challenge course leaders who possess the following skills will properly manage participant safety and enhance program quality. Therefore, challenge course leaders must be able to do the following:

- Properly sequence activities to meet individual and group goals. For example, if the group wishes to work on communication skills, the leader would select initiatives that promote the use of communication skills. Debriefing would focus on the group's communication process.
- Assess participants' readiness as activity demands increase. Leaders must be able to monitor a group's physical condition, emotional state, and ability to focus. Lack of attention or fatigue could result in a serious accident if the activity is inappropriate.
- Assess appropriate situations for spotting. This means knowing when to have group members implement spotting protocol by assessing the potential for a dangerous fall. Safety for all must be taken into consideration in addition to the climber's safety.
- Teach appropriate spotting techniques and monitor a group's application of these techniques. A leader must have strategies

to effectively teach spotting techniques. A leader's ability to teach and monitor progress is important so that participants are able to master this crucial skill.

- Determine when belays are needed in conjunction with spotting or to replace spotting as a safety mechanism. Under some conditions a group cannot effectively spot a member, for example, when the climber is too high off the ground. In such cases a belay must be set up to ensure participant safety.
- Assess the physical environment and adapt programming based on environmental hazards such as weather. For example, if lightning were a possible threat, the leader would not expose the group by putting them on high elements.
- Apply group development theory. Leaders must know how to sequence activities and exercise appropriate leadership styles depending on the developmental level of a group. For example, when the group is forming, the leader should be more directive and facilitate activities to break the ice.
- Exercise conflict resolution skills. If the group enters the conflict stage of group dynamics, a leader must be able to guide the group. Otherwise, the group could get stuck and not bypass the problem. The result would be a negative, unproductive experience.
- Brief and debrief activities. As part of the experiential learning cycle, leaders must be able to use briefing and debriefing to help groups reflect on the experience to reach their goals.
- Properly orient a group for a challenge course program. A leader must be able to set the proper tone in the beginning. Setting tone helps establish mutual expectations and sets the stage for appropriate behavior.
- Design and implement inclusive activities so that all group members are included.

Technical Competencies

Along with facilitation skills, a challenge course leader's skills would not be complete without fundamental technical knowledge and skills. Technical skills are acquired through training and extensive practice. One incorrect knot or improper belay could seriously injure a participant or the leader. Periodic updates and skill checks are common practices among professional program providers. As the industry evolves, techniques and knowledge associated with technical operations also change. Challenge course leaders must

Students take a facilitator knot-tying test.

possess knowledge and abilities as represented in the following checklist:

- Safely facilitate belaying using a variety of static and dynamic belays. Static belays involve proper use of climbing lanyards and other situations where the climber does not depend on assistance from others. For example, a leader climbs a telephone pole using a lanyard, sometimes known as rattails or lobster or crab claws, under her own power. The lanyard will prevent a long fall if used properly. Dynamic belays involve the belayer and climber on the same system. For example, the participant is tied into a climbing rope and the belayer is on the other end using some type of mechanical breaking device. The climber depends on the belayer to catch a fall.

- Be competent when climbing in a leading-edge environment. This is a situation where a conventional fall-protection system or overhead belay system is not available.

- Possess special skills such as setting up and facilitating specialty elements such as zip lines, climbing towers, and the pamper pole.

- Identify, tie, and assess a variety of knots. Leaders should be able to tie their own knots and to assess the quality of a knot tied by someone else. At a glance, the leader should identify a faulty or improper knot.

- Exercise appropriate equipment use, care, and inspection. Many types of technical equipment exist for challenge course use. Leaders should know how to use equipment and ensure that it functions properly. For example, a leader must be able to inspect a climbing harness and know when to retire a potentially dangerous harness.

- Inspect course hardware. Leaders must be able to apply general knowledge of challenge course construction. Bolts, cables, wood, and other materials should be monitored each time the challenge course is used. Leaders must be able to identify faulty equipment to prevent an accident.

- Setup and takedown of events. Many elements require leaders to rig pulleys, ropes, and cables in order to facilitate the activity. Knowledge of proper setup ensures safety and enjoyment for all involved.

- Manage safety issues associated with each activity. All games, initiatives, low elements, and high elements are different and therefore have their own safety concerns. Challenge course leaders must understand the limitations of the activity and the physical facilities of that activity.

Risk Management Competencies

General competencies, leadership skills, and technical skills all relate to overall safety and risk management. However, there are certain risk management skills that all challenge course leaders must master. Challenge course programming has existed long enough now that the profession holds a clear understanding of problem areas. Professionals know from accident data and formal networking when systems or procedures need alteration. Challenge course programming involves inherent risks that cannot be underestimated. Attention to sound risk management ensures that professionals are managing risks to the best of their abilities. Challenge course leaders must be able to do the following:

- Manage participant behavior. Participants who stray from a leader's realm of control could easily hurt themselves and others. A leader must be able to foresee inappropriate behavior before putting the participant in a dangerous position. For example, if a participant cannot focus on simple game directions, the leader should assume that more complicated elements requiring complex directions would not be appropriate.

- Institute an agency's risk management policies. Risk management policies vary among agencies. Leaders must know protocol specific to the program they are working for.

- Interpret participant medical information. Leaders must be able to understand medical conditions and their relationship to challenge course activities. Leaders must attempt to be inclusive without putting participants at risk. For example, a leader might have to assess how a knee condition would affect participation.

- Administer appropriate agency forms. Medical forms, waiver forms, assumption of risk forms, photo releases, and other forms are all part of administering a challenge course program. Leaders have a responsibility to follow agency protocol when administering paperwork.

- Communicate effectively the inherent risks and hazards associated with challenge course programming. Leaders are trained to manage the risks associated with challenge course programming. Sound risk management dictates that leaders articulate the inherent risks to the participant. Leaders typically do this in the beginning as part of an orientation.

- Implement an agency's emergency-response plan. In an emergency, a leader must take

An instructor belays a participant up the climbing tower.

action based on a formal emergency-response plan. Protecting others, calling for help, administering first aid, and other critical actions are expected of a leader.

- Perform rescues and lowers as outlined by agency protocol. Challenge course activities necessitate that leaders be able to lower participants to the ground from high places. The ability to rescue and lower participants is a critical skill needed to prevent injury.

Inclusion

Challenge courses are readily accessible to the general population. Ropes course activities do not require specialized environments (e.g., cliffs, white water, steep mountain trails) as do other outdoor adventure activities. Challenge courses

Learning Activity 11.4

Create a personal competency checklist based on the categories just discussed: risk management, technical skills, facilitation skills, and general abilities. Compare your list to the previous checklists. Discuss the results to ensure an accurate understanding of each competency. Discuss ways to improve competency deficits.

are abundant, affordable, and in some cases even portable. A challenge course is the perfect adventure activity available to all populations. Professional outdoor leaders have an ethical and legal duty to include individuals of all abilities in challenge course activities. The untrained and inexperienced cannot visualize people with disabilities 40 feet off the ground traversing an element or solving a complex group initiative. Most people stereotype adventure activities as an exclusive domain for the physically and mentally able. Professional outdoor leaders, however, possess a very different vision. Professional associations have embraced inclusion as a professional obligation. ACCT standards require that service providers "practice in a manner that is non-discriminatory on the basis of race, gender, sexual orientation, political affiliation, age, physical or cognitive ability, religion or socio-economic status" (2004, p. 30). The Association for Experiential Education (AEE) has also dedicated a section of their accreditation standards to universal access (1995).

The group transfers a participant from a wheelchair to an accessible low element.

Leader's Duty

The powerful benefits of challenge course programming should be available to everyone. It is unethical for outdoor leaders to exclude participants. The fundamental premise for providing outdoor adventure services is the fact that participants grow and become better people as a result of participation. Outdoor leaders have a duty to make accommodations for all who seek their services. In addition to a moral obligation, laws are in place to protect the public's civil rights.

How to Facilitate Inclusion

Challenge course activities can be modified and adapted with minimal effort. Creativity based on sound programming principles creates a foundation for inclusion. From a technical standpoint, resources exist such as ACCT vendors who design and build accessible challenge course programs. Haul-system designs, adaptive equipment, and technical modifications are examples of ACCT vendor services. From a leadership perspective, Rogers (2003) urges leaders to focus on the team-building nature of challenge courses by remembering the four Cs. The four Cs are natural outcomes associated with team-building activities:

- Cooperation—Social integration on a meaningful level
- Communication—Development of interpersonal communication skills
- Caring—Relationship formation such as trust, respect, understanding, and openness
- Consequences—Natural consequences inherent in experiential activities; participants learn from their decisions and actions

The four Cs reflect the typical needs of all individuals, including those with disabilities (Rogers 2003). A challenge course leader must match individual needs with program outcomes. Activities are then designed to promote specific aspects of the four Cs based on assessed needs.

Activity Example Using the Four Cs

Twenty teenagers are scheduled for a day at the challenge course. Preactivity interviews with group leaders indicate that people are not getting along and tend to be self-centered. These teens seem to be intolerant of one another. Two of the teens have wheelchairs and one is legally blind. The challenge course leaders decide to focus the day on relationship formation. They carefully sequence activities that will facilitate trust and understanding. Problem-solving activities are designed that require the resources of all group members. The full-value contract specifically addresses levels of participation and behavioral norms. The leaders purposefully guide debriefing activities so that the teens learn from their behaviors and decisions. The group begins to realize that they can accomplish amazing things if people are allowed to be themselves. They begin to realize that each person has distinct gifts that they bring to the group. Respect and a celebration of differences result from the day's activities. Follow-up evaluations 6 months later reveal that tolerance and respect are now the group norms.

Activity Design

Another component of successful inclusive programs is the leader's ability to modify and adapt activities. The following basic guidelines are suggestions found from several sources (Rogers 2003; Rohnke et al. 2003; Schleien et al. 1993; Havens 1992). Refer to table 11.2 as a guide to facilitating inclusive programs.

Table 11.2

Inclusive Programming Techniques

General
Focus on abilities rather than disabilities. Stress collaborative participation.
Avoid starting at a lower level. Start at the highest level exhibited by individuals.
Modify or change only what is necessary. Keep the normalization principle in mind by providing what the public would normally experience.
Design programs based on skills progression. As skills and confidence increase so should the level of challenge.
Allow participants to have a voice in modifications or changes when appropriate. Many will have accurate understandings of personal abilities.
Communication
Never pretend to understand someone if the message is unclear. Ask people to repeat themselves until you understand. Bring pencil and paper when interpreters are not present. When appropriate rephrase questions in a yes-or-no format or devise another mode of communication such as tapping or blinking if speaking is a problem.
Use inclusive language that is not negative, judgmental, or paternalistic. Paternalistic could mean referring to adults as kids or overemphasizing routine achievements. To be positive and nonjudgmental use objective terms to emphasize each individual's abilities such as referring to a person in a wheelchair as a "person with a physical disability" as opposed to "crippled." Avoid using "normal"; rather use the phrase "people without disabilities."
Open communication and feedback between leaders and participants are critical. A participant should be empowered to create and articulate the best options for any given situation.
Equipment
Maintain equipment inventory that includes gear that fits all sizes, especially full-body harnesses and helmets.
Be sure to have balls and objects on hand that make noises, but always attempt to stay as close to the standard version as possible.
Retrofit elements so that leaders can adjust height and size and control level of difficulty. It is important to adapt elements on an individual level.
Have mats, boards, and other portable flat, hard surfaces available to improve accessibility.
Elements
Provide challenge course elements that encourage participants to crawl, climb, scoot, or roll so that wheelchairs and crutches can be left behind.
Provide infrastructure for belays if additional safety is needed.
Provide haul systems so that participants can access high elements.
Haul systems should be designed so that they can either be self-hauling or used as a group initiative.

Learning Activity 11.5

Divide into groups. Each group's task is to design and facilitate an inclusive activity for the rest of the class. Designate observers to take notes and assess the level of inclusion.

Summary

Since the advent of modern adventure programs, challenge course programming has established itself firmly in the adventure curriculum. The success of Outward Bound played a huge role in the evolution of challenge course programming, and Project Adventure and the ACCT represent key players in the birth of the profession.

It is not uncommon for outdoor leaders to gain their initial training within a challenge course context. Facilitators learn technical and leadership skills that are transferable to other adventure settings. For example, novice leaders gain valuable experience guiding groups through the stages of group development. It is the perfect lab to develop group management skills that are transferable to other adventure activities.

As discovered by Stacey and her group at the beginning of this chapter, the benefits of challenge course participation can be profound. Challenge course programming is a versatile tool to produce a variety of outcomes. Stacey experienced a renewed sense of self. Her self-confidence and leadership abilities soared. She ultimately became a vital member of an effective team.

Outcomes are associated with three global goal orientations: recreation, education, and therapy. In order to intentionally direct experiences toward specific, desired outcomes, challenge course facilitators must be competent in a variety of areas. Challenge course leaders must exercise judgment and decision-making skills required of all outdoor leaders. Competencies in leadership and facilitation, technical skills, and risk management skills must be mastered. Challenge course leaders must also be able to involve people of all abilities and backgrounds. Successful challenge course experiences are inclusive, and people of all abilities and backgrounds benefit.

It should be clear at this point that challenge courses have become synonymous with outdoor adventure experiences, and outdoor professionals would do well to become familiar with this dynamic program venue. Skilled challenge course facilitators also have the opportunity to transfer their craft to a variety of adventure settings. Challenge course facilitation plays an important role in the professional life of the modern outdoor leader.

Selected References

Association for Challenge Course Technology (ACCT). 2004. *ACCT challenge course standards.* 6th ed. Martin, MI: ACCT.

Association for Experiential Education (AEE). 1995. *Manual of accreditation standards for adventure programs.* 2nd ed. Boulder, CO: AEE.

Attarian, A. 2001. Trends in outdoor adventure education. *Journal of Experiential Education* 24(3): 141.

Carlson, J. 2003. Considerations when training facilitators. In *Developing challenge course programs for schools,* ed. S. Wurdinger and J. Steffen, 87-101. Dubuque, IA: Kendall/Hunt.

Cousineau, C. 1976. *Hébertisme.* Ontario: Ministry of Culture and Recreation.

Havens, M.D. 1992. *Bridges to accessibility: A primer for including persons with disabilities in adventure curricula.* Beverly, MA: Project Adventure.

Miner, J., and J. Bolt. 2002. *Outward Bound USA: Crew not passengers.* 2nd ed. Seattle: Mountaineers Books.

Panicucci, J. 2002. *Adventure curriculum for physical education: Middle school.* Beverly, MA: Project Adventure.

Professional Ropes Course Association (PRCA). About the PRCA. 2003. Retrieved April 26, 2004 from www.prcainfo.org/about_the_prca.

Prouty, D. 1999. Project Adventure: A brief history. In *Adventure programming,* ed. J.C. Miles and S. Priest, 93-101. State College, PA: Venture.

Rogers, D. 2003. Teaching for accessibility. In *Developing challenge course programs for schools,* ed. S.

Professional-Development Portfolio Activities

1 As a class, dedicate a full day engaged in a challenge course program in order to experience an entire program progression as represented in this chapter. It is recommended that students gain the experience before reading and discussing this chapter.

2 If available in your area, participate in a 30- to 40-hour class on challenge course facilitation so that you are able to facilitate challenge course experiences on a regular basis.

Wurdinger and J. Steffen, 189-228. Dubuque, IA: Kendall/Hunt.

Rohnke, K., and S. Butler. 1995. *Quicksilver: Adventure games, initiative problems, trust activities and a guide to effective leadership.* Dubuque, IA: Kendall/Hunt.

Rohnke, K., J. Wall, C. Tait, and D. Rogers. 2003. *The complete ropes course manual.* 3rd ed. Dubuque, IA: Kendall/Hunt.

Schleien, S.J., L.H McAvoy, G.J. Lais, and J.E. Rynders. 1993. *Integrated outdoor education and adventure programs.* Champaign, IL: Sagamore.

Schoel, J., D. Prouty, and P. Radcliffe. 1988. *Islands of healing: A guide to adventure based counseling.* Beverly, MA: Project Adventure.

Wagstaff, M. 2003. History and philosophy of challenge courses. In *Developing challenge course programs for schools,* ed. S. Wurdinger and J. Steffen, 3-16. Dubuque, IA: Kendall/Hunt.

Wurdinger, S.D. 1997. *Philosophical issues in adventure education.* 3rd ed. Dubuque, IA: Kendall/Hunt.

chapter 12

Teaching Strategies

"What I hear, I forget. . . . What I see, I remember. . . . What I do, I learn." —Chinese proverb

Chapter Concepts

- Teaching outdoors—Teaching is discussed primarily in the context of instruction during extended, overnight trips, including expeditions. However, the contents of this chapter may be applied to other situations such as workshops, seminars, guided trips, and academic classes.

- Teaching effectiveness—Specific technical skills are needed to be an effective outdoor leader, including outdoor teaching techniques and lesson planning.

- Experiential education—The foundation of outdoor teaching is the experiential process. This process is a hands-on learning experience that is supported by guided reflection, generalizations, and direct application.

The chapter concepts relate to the following core competencies:

- Foundational knowledge (CC-1)—Outdoor leaders should be able to understand and apply experiential learning theory and learning styles theory.

- Self-awareness and professional conduct (CC-2)—Outdoor leaders must be aware of their abilities and limitations in a teaching context. This also includes monitoring personal teaching style and adjusting it to ensure participant learning.

- Teaching and facilitation (CC-4)—Teaching is a vital part of outdoor leadership.

Alicia waited patiently for the group to arrive. She was both excited and nervous as she anticipated the 7-day backpacking trip in New Mexico's Pecos Wilderness. A local summer camp had hired Alicia to teach older campers wilderness skills through an expedition format. Alicia felt prepared after recently completing her Wilderness First Responder course and the in-house staff training. She contemplated whether the campers would like her but then laughed quietly at her nervousness. She assumed her fleeting doubts were a symptom of first-course jitters. Alicia forced herself to focus on the positives. Her confidence soared as she reflected on her training and past experience as a junior counselor. Alicia knew that she could make a difference in her campers' lives. She would mentor six young women in the art of wilderness living just as she had been mentored many years ago as a camper. Monica, Alicia's junior counselor, rustled around in the gear as they waited. Monica possessed minimal outdoor experience but was very familiar with the camp's operations.

Campers stepped off the bus loaded with duffel bags and millions of questions. Alicia and Monica gathered them in the staging area for a brief orientation and team-building exercises. After polling the group, Alicia discovered they were a highly motivated group and had diverse experience levels. The plan was to equip the group and hike a short distance to their first night's

camp. Alicia gathered the young women into a half-circle with their duffel bags as seats. Standing in front of the group, Alicia began a 45-minute lecture on proper packing technique. Alicia's experience allowed her to detail an effective method to pack the food, group gear, and personal gear into the pack. Properly distributing weight was described in depth. Alicia made sure that she described a system for packing that would ensure convenient access to needed items during the hike. Her lecture also included a comparison of internal- and external-framed packs. Upon completion of the lecture, Alicia felt confident the girls would pack effectively and efficiently. Alicia and Monica left the group to pack so they could complete final details.

When they returned after 30 minutes, the staging resembled the aftermath of a large explosion. Equipment and clothing blanketed the ground. The campers appeared frustrated as they discussed what should go in their packs first. Alicia moved in quickly and began stuffing a pack with the appropriate items. After demonstrating how to pack, the girls immediately understood and began packing with occasional questions. Now an hour behind schedule, Alicia sat them down once again to teach them proper trail technique. This 40-minute lecture enlightened the campers on energy conservation, hiking roles, and trail safety. Again, Alicia felt she needed to cover the subject in depth; after all, an important trip goal was to teach wilderness living

(continued)

skills. Alicia noticed that the girls seemed restless and bored. This behavior did not parallel their earlier, more motivated behavior.

The girls seemed to perk up once they were on the trail. The physical exercise and beauty of the trail raised their spirits and motivation once again. As the group moved down the trail, Alicia visualized the lessons to be covered once the group hit camp. Campsite selection, kitchen setup, cooking, health and sanitation, and shelter building were the critical topics on her list. This long list of topics made Alicia uneasy. She could not see how she was going to cover all of this valuable information before dark. She felt her teaching plan reflected a logical progression of topics to foster skill development and she did not want to rob the campers of valuable information by cutting her lessons short. She would just have to buckle down and get the campers to focus!

The group filed into a beautiful campsite on the edge of a meadow. The crew immediately dropped their packs and danced around to celebrate their first night in the woods, but Alicia quickly rounded up the group for a lesson on campsite selection. The girls' demeanors changed immediately. Under her breath, one camper whispered, "Oh, no, not another lecture." Alicia could not believe what she overheard. Confused and frus-trated, Alicia knew she had heard each girl state during orientation that they signed up for this particular trip to learn wilderness skills. Alicia had taken great pains to plan an optimal experience for skill development.

At this point, Alicia knew enough from her prior leadership experience to back off and let go of her plan. She quickly asked who possessed the skills to erect the tents. Three members raised their hands. Alicia then asked if anyone had any advice for the group. One young woman spoke up and reminded others to look overhead for dead trees and limbs and be sure to find level ground. The others nodded in agreement and turned to Alicia for direction. Alicia sent them off in pairs to erect shelters. The group appeared genuinely pleased with the power to be self-directed.

As the campers erected their tents and organized gear, Alicia sat in frustration. She began to realize that she needed to alter her teaching techniques. She remembered discussions of the grasshopper method, teachable moments, and other instructional strategies during staff training. Before the trip began she had felt the information was not applicable to her situation. Maybe she was wrong, though. It was obviously time to reconsider her approach and try to find more effective methods.

A competent outdoor leader also holds the distinction of being a competent teacher. All outdoor leaders face the challenge of teaching as a daily activity. For example, a raft guide must convey safety information and teach basic strokes to safely navigate white water. A climbing instructor teaches the participant proper climbing technique to improve skill level. A camp counselor teaches Leave No Trace ethics to protect the environment from uneducated campers. A youth leader teaches cooking skills to ensure that campers prepare delicious, healthy meals. Outdoor leaders must effectively convey knowledge, skills, and attitudes to initiate change within participants. The big challenge for many novice outdoor leaders is developing themselves as effective teachers. Understanding the experiential learning process is the first step to effective teaching in outdoor settings.

Most outdoor organizations use experiential education as the primary process to institute change within the participant. Instilling knowledge, developing skills, influencing behavior, and changing attitudes are all possible targets of change. Most organizations promote student-centered learning versus teacher-centered learning. Participants are empowered learners rather than relying on an authority figure to control the entire process.

This chapter discusses teaching in the context of experiential learning. Outdoor adventures lend themselves to an experiential or hands-on learning process. Adventure experiences such as expeditions and trips serve as a perfect medium for experiential education. The grasshopper method and teachable moments are discussed as tools for experiential education in the outdoors. Outdoor leaders must also acknowledge the participant diversity in relation to learning. Learning styles are addressed to enhance the leader's sensitivity to how and why people learn.

This chapter also discusses tips and techniques for outdoor teaching. Most outdoor leaders do not have the luxury of electronic media, chalkboards, and controlled laboratories in the wilderness classroom. Outdoor leaders rely on creativity and ingenuity to teach various subjects. Finally, a quality lesson is based on a well-prepared lesson plan. Lesson plans serve as a critical guide when leaders wish to effectively convey an educational message. Formal lesson plans that consist of goals, objectives, teaching content, teaching strategies, and assessment procedures will be discussed. The ideal outdoor lesson plan would be based on experiential learning methods that meet the needs of diverse learners. Outcomes should reflect intended changes in targeted learning domains such as knowledge acquisition, skill development, attitude change, and behavior modification. As a result of applying learning theory, acknowledging learning styles, developing quality lesson plans, and exercising effective teaching techniques, outdoor leaders possess the power to be effective teachers.

Experiential Education

People learn in a variety of ways such as direct experience, lectures, books, experiments, and personal relationships, to name just a few. Humans learn in order to adapt to their surrounding world. Experiential learning forms the theoretical cornerstone used by most outdoor leaders. Outdoor leaders embrace experiential education as the means to apply experiential learning theory. The Association for Experiential Education (AEE) defines experiential education as "a philosophy and methodology in which educators purposefully engage the learners in direct experience and focused reflection in order to increase knowledge, develop skills, and clarify values" (AEE 2004). John Dewey (1938), a great educator and educational reformer, was one of the first to stress the importance of experience as a meaningful form of education. Dewey perceived experiential learning as a cyclical process of observing a specific situation and surrounding conditions, then recalling past knowledge related to the situation, followed by making judgments based on observations and past knowledge to determine significance.

Dewey's work inspired a number of other models and perspectives that apply to adventure programs (Gibbons and Hopkins 1980; Pfeiffer and Jones 1980; Joplin 1981; Kolb 1984; Priest 1990). Each model provides a unique perspective into learning experientially. This chapter focuses on the work of David A. Kolb, who first began to publish work in the early 1970s. A strength of Kolb's experiential learning model is the concept of learning styles. His work provides an effective way to understand the experiential learning process in combination with learning styles. It is beyond the scope of this text to detail all experiential learning theories and learning style models. The goal of this chapter is to instill an understanding of and appreciation for experiential learning theory and learning styles in the context of teaching in the outdoors. Kolb's experiential learning model is discussed to reach this end, and to further demonstrate the nature of learning, Howard Gardner's theory of multiple intelligences is shared. Gardner provides another perspective that enforces the need to consider diverse learning styles. Armed with the knowledge of learning preferences, the outdoor leader can purposefully compose lessons to meet the needs of diverse learners.

Experiential Learning Cycle

Kolb's (1984) experiential learning cycle consists of four phases: concrete experience, reflective observation, abstract conceptualization, and active experimentation. According to Kolb, learning is maximized when the learner moves through all four phases during the learning process (see figure 12.1). The following discussion defines each phase

Students learn to mountain-bike on moderate terrain.

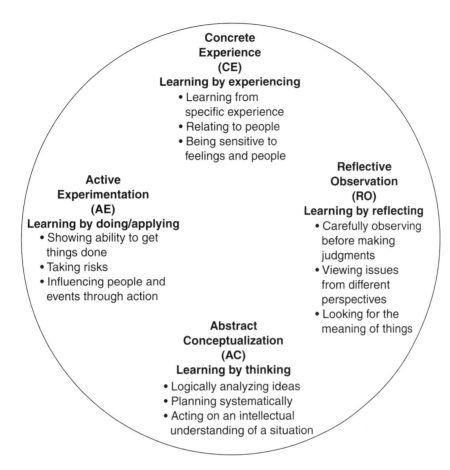

Figure 12.1 Kolb's experiential learning cycle: the four phases.

© 1999, Experience-Based Learning Systems, Inc. Developed by David A. Kolb. Adapted with permission from the HayGroup, Inc.

and includes an outdoor leadership example to clarify meaning.

Concrete experience directly involves the learner in a new activity to gain understanding. The learner has a hands-on experience. For example, a white-water canoeing instructor puts the participants in a canoe on moving water in order to teach the importance of leaning downstream. The participants experience the lesson through all senses in an immediate way. There is no time to stop and think about it. If they do not lean correctly, the boat capsizes.

Reflective observation entails participants reflecting on their thoughts and feelings about an experience. Participants view the experience from many perspectives. The white-water instructor schedules time for students to watch the instructor demonstrate a proper boat lean. Time is also taken to discuss as a group what the participants are seeing and experiencing. The instructor takes the group to a beach and uses a toy canoe to demonstrate boat lean.

Abstract conceptualization is a process to integrate the experience into theories and to generalize in order to formulate explanations or hypotheses. The white-water instructor facilitates a discussion on a nearby beach to enforce the significance of boat lean. Participants conceptualize the lean to understand the dynamics of the water in relation to the boat for facilitating different maneuvers.

Active experimentation involves testing theories and concepts through problem solving and testing in different situations. The white-water instructor facilities an exercise for practicing leans in a variety of situations to test the participants' understanding.

In these descriptions of the learning phases, the white-water instructor moves the students through each phase by integrating a different teaching method or situation to convey information and skills. This model is cyclical and no formal starting or stopping place exists in the learning process. Teachers must mix up their methods and provide a variety of outlets to maximize learning experientially. This was the mistake Alicia made in the opening scenario. She was stuck in the lecture format. To facilitate learning in each of the phases, the following suggestions are offered (Svinicki and Dixon 1987; Kolb 2000):

- Concrete experience: Provide new learning experiences such as games, films, role-playing, lab work, or field work. Peer feedback and discussion during the experience are helpful techniques to implement. Outdoor leaders serve as coaches or helpers in this phase.

- Reflective observation: Have participants take on the role of observer in order to see from different perspectives. Lectures, journaling, group discussions, and questioning are effective teaching techniques in this phase. Outdoor leaders serve as guides and task masters in order to foster the reflective process.

- Abstract conceptualization: Study time alone, reading about theories, building models, creating analogies, and writing papers are examples of teaching methods that enhance this phase. Outdoor leaders serve as communicators of information in this phase.

- Active experimentation: Provide opportunities to practice self-paced learning activities, case studies, and simulations in this phase. Outdoor leaders serve as role models to foster learning during active experimentation.

Learning Styles

In conjunction with the four phases of experiential learning, Kolb's research delineates four distinct **learning styles.** According to Davis, "the term *learning styles* refers to individuals' characteristics and preferred ways of gathering, interpreting, organizing and thinking about information" (1993, p. 185). People are diverse learners. Some participants prefer to watch and listen, while others need to participate and get feedback, and still others need to experiment and apply information. Outdoor leaders who teach to only one learning style make it difficult and frustrating for others to learn. In the opening scenario, Alicia relied solely on the lecture format to convey information and skills. Her campers experienced much frustration because of her limited repertoire.

The challenge for leaders is to develop teaching situations or lessons that address various learning styles. This strategy has many ben-

efits. Outdoor leaders capitalize on individual strengths when learning diversity is addressed. Participants experience satisfaction, fun, and a sense of accomplishment when successful learning occurs. Knowledge of learning styles helps the leader understand differences among students. Behaviors such as inattention, boredom, and restlessness may be symptoms of ineffective teaching techniques. Instead of blaming the participants, the outdoor leader can take a critical look at personal teaching effectiveness and adapt to improve. Outdoor leaders also need to possess an anchor of understanding in order to patiently assist participants when observing difficulties. Outdoor leaders have the opportunity to help participants develop other styles and become more effective learners. Finally, the probability of meeting program goals will increase if leaders pay attention to learning styles.

Kolb's (2000) research narrowed learning styles to four preferred methods: diverging, assimilating, converging, and accommodating (see figure 12.2). Note that learning styles are referred to as preferences. People maintain the capacity to learn in many different ways; it's just that we tend to prefer one style over others in many situations. Outdoor leaders should not typecast or categorize participants based on learning styles. Learning styles vary according to the situation and environment. They shift as individuals grow, develop, and experience life. Kolb stresses that individuals must continually choose which learning abilities to exercise in any given situation. Each learning style can be identified by characteristics and behaviors exhibited in learning situations. Observing behavioral preferences gives the outdoor leader much insight into the participants' learning abilities. The following are generalized characteristics associated with each learning style. Note how each style connects to the phases of the experiential learning cycle.

- Accomodating: Accommodators rely on active experimentation and concrete experience; they like getting things done, leading, taking risks, and initiating activities. They are adaptable and practical, carry out plans, may be perceived by others as impatient, and solve problems intuitively.

- Diverging: Divergers rely on concrete experience and reflective observation; they are imaginative, understand people, recognize problems, and are open-minded and emotional. They like brainstorming to generate ideas and have broad cultural interests.

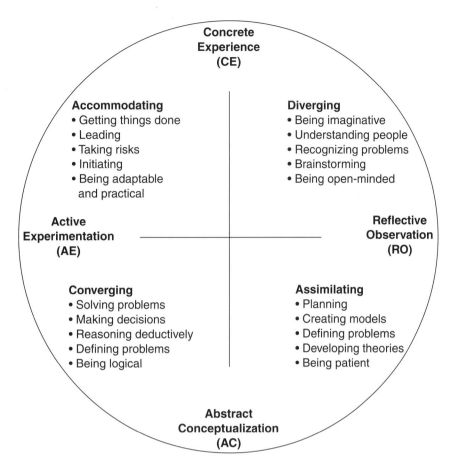

Figure 12.2 Kolb's experiential learning cycle.

© 1999, Experience-Based Learning Systems, Inc. Developed by David A. Kolb. Adapted with permission from the HayGroup, Inc.

- Assimilating: Assimilators rely on reflective observation and abstract conceptualization; they like planning, creating models, defining problems, and developing theories. They are patient and are more interested in concepts than in people and relationships.

- Converging: Convergers rely on abstract conceptualization and active experimentation; they like solving problems, making decisions, reasoning deductively, and defining problems. They tend to be logical and unemotional, and they prefer to deal with things as opposed to people.

To further explain learning styles in the context of outdoor learning, let's look at the following typical scenario. A group of 12 is somewhere in the middle of a 30-day expedition. Basic map and compass skills were covered by the leaders during several previous lessons. The leaders have handed over the navigational responsibilities to the hiking group with the educational inten-

tion of further developing navigational skills. The instructors plan to sit back and observe the group apply past learning. The group finds itself at a trail junction with much confusion over their current location and which way to continue. As the instructors observe, the divergers in the group brainstorm ideas and check in with all members of the group to ensure everyone is happy. The accommodators display impatience. They just want to make a decision and deal with the consequences later. The assimilators attempt to define the problem and are more interested in creating an action plan to get out of the situation. The convergers are unemotional to the chaos erupting in the group and focus only on the map and compass to come up with a plan. As you might imagine, the diversity of approaches creates conflict and frustration within the group. The leaders calmly observe, realizing that diverse learning styles are at work. They are able to intervene and facilitate a solution by working with the different learning styles. They choose to stop the action and encourage the group to process the situation. With new information provided by the instructors, the group devises a plan that can be carried out.

The concepts of experiential learning and learning styles form the basis for effective teaching in the outdoors. In order to maximize learning, outdoor leaders must be aware of the experiential learning process. Leaders make sure instructional design addresses all four phases of the learning cycle. To facilitate this process and meet diverse learning needs, outdoor leaders should carry a large teaching "toolbox." As discussed, leaders must adjust their teaching styles by guiding, acting as task master, coaching, or role modeling to fit each phase of the learning cycle. Leaders must also integrate a variety of teaching methods or tools into their repertoire in order to be effective teachers. Guided discussions, demonstrations, group projects, lectures, role-playing, simulations, stories, self-directed activities, experimentation, and other tools make up the outdoor leader's teaching toolbox.

Theory of Multiple Intelligences

To further enrich the outdoor leader's teaching toolbox, a brief discussion of Howard Gardner's theory of **multiple intelligences** is in order. His work provides another perspective to support the notion that outdoor leaders must be aware of diverse learning styles. Gardner explains that we all demonstrate intellectual abilities in a variety of ways (Gardner 1983, 1993). Gardner defines eight different intelligences that are autonomous and defined by specific characteristics and abilities. The eight intelligences are: (1) verbal–linguistic, (2) visual–spatial, (3) bodily–kinesthetic, (4) naturalistic, (5) musical–rhythmic, (6) mathematical–logical, (7) interpersonal, and (8) intrapersonal (Mitchell and Kernodle 2004). Tra-

ditional education systems typically focus only on mathematical–logical and verbal–linguistic intelligences when teaching content and assessing ability. The challenge for outdoor leaders is to diversify their instructional strategies to capitalize on the diverse intelligences outlined by Gardner. For example, students who tend to be naturalistic in intelligence flourish in an outdoor setting. These students enjoy learning outdoors and exploring and learning about the natural environment. Bodily–kinesthetic learners need to have hands-on experiences and thrive in learning situations that require movement. For a deeper appreciation of the eight intelligences, refer to table 12.1 for a description of each along with corresponding behaviors and suggested teaching activities.

Experienced outdoor leaders naturally mix their teaching strategies to meet the needs of diverse learners. Effective teachers play on the strengths of learners to enhance the learning process for each individual. Take a moment and reflect on a facilitated, positive learning experience you have had recently. You may recall that the teaching methods coincided with your learning preference. You probably had fun and felt focused, immersed in the experience, confident, aware of knowledge obtained, and aware of skills developed—you felt an overall sense of satisfaction. All outdoor leaders should aspire to create learning experiences with these positive outcomes. Outdoor leaders are in the business of making learning a challenging and fun endeavor. As a result, participants experience the numerous benefits associated with outdoor programming. Using Kolb's and Gardner's concepts of learning styles, outdoor leaders can intentionally design powerful learning experiences. The next section of this chapter outlines specific teaching techniques to further assist novice outdoor leaders in the instructional process.

Learning Activity 12.1

Working in small groups, choose one of Kolb's learning styles or one of Gardner's intelligences. Design a teaching technique to meet the needs of that particular style. Use a camp knot such as a bowline or square knot as the teaching subject.

Table 12.1

Gardner's Multiple Intelligences

Intelligences	Characteristics	Behaviors	Instructional activities
Verbal–linguistic	Uses words effectively; learns by reading, writing, discussing, and listening to explanations. Prefers to hear or read instructions.	Enjoys reading, writing, talking, and public speaking. Uses precise language and enjoys plays on words.	Facilitate learning experiences that include journaling, discussions, debates, storytelling, lectures, writing activities, and reading.
Visual–spatial	Able to perceive spatial relationships. Accurately perceives three-dimensional world. Thinks in pictures and images.	Enjoys visuals like drawing and painting. Often doodles. Good sense of direction; understands maps and creates mental images easily.	Facilitate learning experiences that include drawing, painting, puzzles, videos, photography, mapping, and product design.
Bodily–kinesthetic	Able to use a variety of physical skills and easily manipulates objects. Exhibits movement control, balance, coordination, strength, and agility.	Enjoys being physically involved. Uses gestures when talking, is coordinated physically, likes to take things apart, builds things, and may find it hard to sit still.	Facilitate learning experiences that incorporate demonstrations, experiments, role-playing, building, performances, and tactile experiences in general.
Naturalistic	Able to relate to surroundings; sensitive to environment. Able to discriminate among natural things such as animals, plants, and rocks. Recognizes patterns in nature and can group according to features.	Enjoys exploring and discovering. Likes collecting natural materials and is fascinated by natural objects. Aware of natural processes and cycles such as tides, moon phases, and constellations. Likes to identify objects.	Facilitate learning experiences that require observing, exploring, identifying, and categorizing. Time for reflection in nature and metaphors related to nature are effective teaching tools.
Musical–rhythmic	Able to communicate and understand through music. Thinks in rhythms, melodies, and lyrics.	Enjoys humming while working. Taps with foot, hands, or objects. Can remember songs and rhymes. Likes to make up songs. Senses musical elements in nonmusical situations.	Facilitate learning experiences that include singing, performing, or poetry. Challenge learners to create songs, dances, or plays around subject matter.
Mathematical–logical	Able to think in a mathematical context. Effectively uses numbers and reasoning skills to determine patterns and relationships and to predict outcomes, classify, generalize, and test hypotheses.	Enjoys determining cause-and-effect relationships, solving problems, and quantifying outcomes. Follows complex reasoning processes and likes mind puzzles. Can remember thinking strategies and formulas.	Facilitate learning experiences that include problem solving, experimentation, inductive reasoning, deductive reasoning, comparing and contrasting, and finding patterns.

(continued)

Table 12.1 *(continued)*

Intelligences	Characteristics	Behaviors	Instructional activities
Interpersonal	Able to successfully interact with others. Understands people and body language in order to respond and interact appropriately. Accurately perceives others' intents and motivations.	Enjoys discussions with others. Likes team sports and games. Exhibits good listening skills and communicates well. Enjoys caring for others and is empathetic.	Facilitate learning activities that include group work, active listening, leading, giving and receiving feedback, simulations, peer assessments, organizing, and collaborative projects.
Intrapersonal	Able to understand and interpret internal stimuli. Accurately understands self including personal strengths and weaknesses. Aware of own methods of thinking and responding with the ability to modify own behavior.	Enjoys time alone. Tends to be quiet and self-reflective. Always asks questions and tends to operate independently. Does not usually worry about others' feelings or opinions. May daydream and express inner feelings in many ways.	Facilitate learning experiences that include personal inventories, personal reflections, journaling, individual projects, goal setting, and creative games.

Outdoor Teaching Techniques

Two methods specific to outdoor learning require in-depth discussion so that these valuable techniques find their way into the aspiring outdoor leader's teaching toolbox. These methods, referred to as the **grasshopper method** and **teachable moments,** are worthy of discussion due to the unique nature of the outdoor classroom. Outdoor leaders typically spend intense, extended amounts of time with participants. On trips and expeditions, leaders maintain close contact 24 hours per day and have numerous opportunities to teach. Group members share in a series of dynamic experiences as an extended trip unfolds. In addition to program activities such as climbing, hiking, biking, paddling, and so on, life-sustaining activities such as eating, bathing, and sleeping become part of the learning experience. When faced with the challenge of teaching within this dynamic process of expedition living, the outdoor leader has many choices.

Remember the challenges that confronted Alicia? She did not know how to manage her teaching responsibility within the larger context of the trip. She attempted to force the lessons into discrete blocks of time, which affected the flow of activities and the group's morale. Upon reflection, Alicia realized that teaching methods discussed in her staff training had merit after all. The grasshopper method and teachable moments are two teaching techniques or methods that could resolve Alicia's problems.

Expedition Teaching Methods

Paul Petzoldt (1984) coined the term *grasshopper method* as a colorful analogy to explain the expedition teaching process. Small grasshoppers navigate through dense grass, brush, and other obstacles by hopping from one point to the next in search of food or cover. Outdoor leaders also "hop" from one subject to the next during an expedition in order to reach a final destination. In other words, outdoor leaders break topics into small parts throughout a trip and teach content and skills in a systematic manner so that an entire curriculum is covered. Petzoldt expresses concern when novice outdoor leaders attempt to use the grasshopper method. Most outdoor leaders come from traditional education systems where information is given by one source, the teacher, for memorization and then is regurgitated for a grade. This type of education does not lend itself to effective learning in the outdoors. Outdoor leaders are unknowingly conditioned in traditional settings to teach in limited ways. Petzoldt believes that the grasshopper method should be carefully presented to the outdoor leader so that teaching does not occur haphazardly (Wagstaff and Cashel 2001).

To effectively execute the grasshopper method, the situation requires leaders to think and plan ahead. Remember, the fundamental concept of grasshopper teaching is to systematically link a series of topics to cover an entire curriculum. The outdoor leader must hop from topic to topic as opportunities present themselves. At this point, teachable moments merit discussion. While different from the grasshopper method, teachable moments play an important role in the overall process. Teachable moments are lessons taught spontaneously, stimulated by a specific situation or event (Drury and Bonney 1992). Teachable moments surface constantly during an outdoor experience. As groups encounter unknown situations, outdoor leaders have the opportunity to relay information and skills related to the situation. For example, participants hike down the trail and discover a snake. While participant interests are heightened, the leader takes the opportunity to make a brief presentation on snakes by identifying the snake, its characteristics, and its habitat and discussing the snake's place in the ecosystem. Another teachable moment finds a participant struggling with a rain tarp. A knot has been cinched so tight that it is impossible to untie. Frustrated, the participant asks for the leader's help. The leader takes the opportunity to teach a more appropriate knot that requires minimal effort to untie.

As you might suspect, teachable moments are numerous during an outdoor experience. The leader must carefully select appropriate situations to address as *formal teachable moments.* Leaders who address every situation as a formal teachable moment are asking for trouble. Participants tend to disengage if the action is constantly halted for a lesson. If the lesson requires the entire group's attention, time must be taken to round up and organize the group to ensure the message is conveyed to everyone. *Informal teachable moments*

A student gives peers a weather lesson.

include those situations when individuals or small groups within the larger group encounter an opportunity to learn (Drury and Bonney 1992). The leader may choose to informally present a message or skill as part of a casual discussion. This provides powerful learning opportunities for individuals because the timing is immediate and pertinent to the situation. In other words, formal and informal teachable moments take advantage of the participant's desire and motivation to learn.

With an understanding of teachable moments, the outdoor leader is now armed with vital information to understand the grasshopper method. As discussed, teaching opportunities naturally arise during an outdoor experience. The seasoned outdoor leader exercises the ability to predict that certain opportunities will naturally arise, whereas the teachable moment is unpredictable. Knowledge of future situations allows the leader to systematically cover a topic in fragments. By the end of an experience, the fragments add up to form a complete topic. Grasshopper teaching has many advantages. Topics can be covered in small pieces so that information and skills are easily introduced, processed, and practiced before more content is introduced. Grasshopper teaching also allows leaders to manage time effectively during

Learning Activity 12.2

Choose an outdoor topic such as cooking, land navigation, or rock climbing and outline a tentative plan to break this large topic into smaller topics so that it can be taught using the grasshopper method.

a trip. Flexibility and control over the length of a lesson allows leaders to schedule other, necessary activities into a daily routine. A larger curriculum tends to be much more manageable during extended trips if it is broken down into smaller topics.

The grasshopper method is conducive to the overall experiential learning process. Leaders can easily implement a variety of teaching tools so that all phases of the cycle are experienced. Of course, the danger of the grasshopper approach is that you might not meet curriculum goals. There is a possibility that topic fragments will not be covered due to oversight or time constraints. This is why outdoor leaders must be systematic in their approach. Overall trip and program planning plays a huge role in this process. The following example portrays the planning and thought process an outdoor leader uses to facilitate the grasshopper method when on a tentative teaching schedule.

Some leaders are faced with the task of teaching land navigation among many other skills on a 6-day wilderness trip. As they review the schedule before the trip, they tentatively plan their method of covering the entire topic. They discuss the following:

- Day 1—Schedule is full; there is no appropriate opportunity to address navigation.
- Day 2—Only map-reading skills will be taught; the potential campsite is conducive to viewing the surrounding topography so that map-reading skills can be taught using the actual terrain (no more than 30 minutes).
- Day 3—No particular setting or environment is needed to teach basic compass reading skills at some point during the day (no more than 20 minutes). During hiking, encourage participants to use map-reading skills to find the route with instructor assistance.
- Day 4—Many dramatic overlooks of mountainous terrain exist along the hiking trail; use a break during the hike to teach use of map and compass in combination (no more than 30 minutes).

- Day 5—Schedule an off-trail hike and empower the group to find a route to the next campsite.
- Day 6—Facilitate a short activity to test and reinforce participants' knowledge and skills.

This example represents the formal thought process a novice leader may undergo to systematically plan the coverage of a topic based on anticipated situations. As outdoor leaders mature, this process becomes intuitive. Seasoned outdoor leaders with knowledge of terrain, environmental conditions, group abilities, and so on can predict when, where, and how topic fragments will be covered using the grasshopper approach. The need to make formal plans lessens as leadership experience increases. Imagine the amount of work and time it would take to create a tentative schedule for 30 days that covers more than 20 topics in depth. Even if this monstrous schedule could be planned, unforeseen problems and changes would make the plan obsolete in the first few days. Aspiring outdoor leaders are encouraged to obtain field experience under the mentorship of seasoned instructors to develop this teaching technique. In the beginning, novice leaders should at least attempt to outline an overall teaching plan, realizing that flexibility is the key. At the very least, a tentative teaching plan serves as a guide to ensure topic coverage.

Outdoor Teaching Tips

The grasshopper method of backcountry teaching serves as an important tool to manage teaching responsibilities during extended experiences. Also, appropriately managing teachable moments enhances the outdoor leader's teaching effectiveness. Seasoned outdoor leaders acknowledge that many participants simply respond better in an outdoor setting compared to the traditional classroom. In many ways, the outdoor leader possesses a unique opportunity to teach resistant learners through the magic of an outdoor experience. Participants do not view the outdoors as they do the familiar four-walled classroom. Some participants perceive the outdoor classroom as being free from rules and daily responsibilities. Others perceive the outdoor classroom as an unfamiliar environment that requires focus and attention to guard from the unknown. The outdoor leader takes advantage of these perceptions by capitalizing on participants' higher motivation levels and focus.

Even with this advantage, outdoor leaders can negatively affect the learning process or at least not maximize learning potential. Certain outdoor teaching techniques exist that outdoor leaders should practice. Simple teaching practices that address safety, comfort, and fun during the learning process can make a huge difference for the learners. The teaching tips discussed in this section are important considerations when instructing outdoors. These tips address a variety of strategies and techniques to maximize learning. The categories of environmental considerations, teaching props, and timing encompass vital teaching tips unique to the outdoors.

Environmental Considerations

Environmental considerations obviously influence overall learning. Participants become distracted, lose concentration, and disengage when environmental conditions cause discomfort or concern. Outdoor leaders must pay close attention to the immediate environment as they try to create the ideal outdoor learning situation. If outdoor instructors remember to meet the student's basic needs such as food, water, shelter, warmth, and comfort, learning comes much more easily. Cognizance of basic needs is particularly important when living outdoors. Leaders should use the following tips in order to foster the ideal learning environment.

Sun If conducting a formal class, situate participants so their backs are to the sun. Participants should not fight the sun's glare while trying to learn. Leaders should position themselves to face the sun. If you need sunglasses, occasionally lower the glasses for eye contact when making critical points. Whenever possible, form group circles in the shade to protect the group from the sun's harmful effects. Participants who seek the sun always have the option to slide out of a shaded border into the sunlight.

Foul Weather In general, attempting to teach subjects in rain, falling snow, or blowing wind usually results in a mixed participant reaction. While some may be able to focus on the lesson, others are too preoccupied with getting wet or cold to pay attention. Consider other activities according to weather conditions. Before a lesson starts make sure that participants have extra clothing and water handy to minimize disruptions. Building a classroom shelter out of rain tarps or other covers can create a comfortable atmosphere.

Noise Most people would assume that the outdoors is a serene, quiet environment. On the contrary, outdoor leaders compete with streams, rivers, wind, insects, and other environmental factors. Leaders must be able to project their voices so that all can hear. This must be a conscious act at all times.

Terrain Outdoor classrooms can be found on large rocks, forest floors, mountainsides, and beaches. Before launching into a lesson, leaders must choose their location carefully. It is typical for the novice leader to choose a slanted part of the campsite when gathering a group. If the group circles up, some end up downhill, others end up sideways on the slope, and the few comfortable seats are found uphill. Leaders should try to find comfortable spots for sitting and standing for everyone when appropriate. Also, be aware of environmentally sensitive areas when gathering a group of people. Follow Leave No Trace practices and search for durable surfaces such as large rocks or sand (see chapter 14 for more on Leave No Trace practices).

Teaching Props

Outdoor leaders need instructional aids just as traditional teachers do. Instructional aids allow outdoor leaders to mix up teaching strategies to meet the needs of all learners. It is important for outdoor leaders to provide visual examples, graphic demonstrations, and written information to supplement lectures and direct experience. The following teaching tips address creative aids that leaders can use in the field.

Library Many outdoor leaders carry a library. Books on natural history, first aid, cultural history, technical information, and so on go far in supplementing formal outdoor lessons. Books allow participants to digest information through reading and pictures, either as a group or during personal time. A good expedition library enhances the learning process by meeting specific learning styles. With a group of 6 to 10 participants, it is a simple task to divide the library among group members so that one person is not loaded down with too much bulk and weight.

Chalkboard While chalkboards do not exist in the outdoor classroom, variations do. Many times a large diagram drawn in sequence helps make a point. Finding a nice patch of sand or dirt to draw in can be effective. Props such as sticks and rocks become boats, people, boundaries, and so on to help illustrate a point. Some outdoor leaders carry markers to draw on sleeping pads or pieces of clear ground plastic. Dry-erase markers allow leaders to erase and reuse these portable chalkboards.

Concrete Examples The power of an appropriate, realistic example in an outdoor setting cannot be underestimated. In the traditional classroom, teachers often describe situations under the assumption that the student will experience the situations later. The outdoor leader, on the other hand, must take advantage of the rich resources available. For example, when teaching the art of digging a cat hole for human waste disposal, the leader should consider digging an actual hole as a demonstration. For many learners it is not enough to describe the proper way to dig a hole and the environmental rationale behind it. Certain learners will process and apply the skill better if provided a good demonstration or model.

Timing

Timing is an important consideration when teaching outdoors. The timing of a lesson greatly affects the level of learning. The following three teaching tips provide the outdoor leader with advice related to timing.

Creating the Need to Know One of the most powerful outdoor teaching strategies involves motivating the participant to learn by creating the "need to know." Outdoor leaders can facilitate situations that motivate participants to seek knowledge and skills. The leader does this by placing the participants in a situation where they seek knowledge and skills in order to accomplish a task. This is a timing concern that requires careful consideration; using this technique inappropriately can be a safety factor and negatively affect participant attitudes. For example, an outdoor leader attempts to teach a group of teenagers map-reading skills. The group is unruly and has no desire or need to focus on the lesson. The leader empowers the group to self-navigate for the day, and the group becomes hopelessly lost and struggles to interpret the map. At this point, the leader intervenes with an offer to teach map interpretation. The group eagerly agrees and provides their undivided attention for the 30-minute lesson. This strategy backfires when participants perceive they were set up to fail due to lack of information. The leader's choice

undermines the group's trust and the experience becomes negative.

Appropriate Timing The grasshopper method addresses the overall question of when to broach a topic. Beyond this consideration, group readiness comes into play. Leaders must assess energy levels before presenting a lesson. If energy levels are low after a long hike, most participants will revolt if forced to participate in a full-blown lesson. For example, after many hours of hiking, the group may not be able to focus on a 20-minute lesson on campsite selection. Maybe after a rest period, food, and water, the group will be able to focus. The outdoor leader's judgment is crucial in these situations. Many times group energy is highest in the morning and lower at night. Leaders should plan lessons around these peak hours and plan alternative activities for downtime. Leaders should heed the pitfalls of night activities. While some activities are quite appropriate at night, forcing participants to focus in the dark with only candles and flashlights takes away from many topics.

Time Management The final teaching tip involves planning. Participants deserve to be told of activities to come. During a trip, participants must learn to manage time. Rest, food, bathroom breaks, leisure time, camp setup, and other important activities must be calculated into the overall schedule. Competent outdoor leaders adequately inform participants of upcoming events. Materials needed, proper clothing, and estimated start and ending times are shared upfront. This allows participants to be appropriately prepared. Learning is maximized when formal learning activities are balanced with all other activities.

Finally, a warning for aspiring outdoor leaders who excessively push themselves mentally and physically: Leaders must also be rested, nourished, hydrated, and properly clothed in order to meet the rigorous demands of teaching outdoors. Teaching fanatics tend to overextend and exhaust themselves. As a result, teaching effectiveness decreases. Professional outdoor leaders ensure time to meet personal needs so that their teaching truly achieves the desired results.

Lesson Planning

Teachers in all disciplines use lesson plans as a tool for effective teaching. The same holds true for outdoor leaders. With an understanding of experiential learning, learning styles, and outdoor teaching techniques and tips, the foundation exists for a quality lesson plan. Lesson plans serve as formal guides during the instructional process. Outdoor leaders teach in a variety of formats such as expeditions, weekend trips, daylong workshops, clinics, hour-long classes, and more. Program formats vary but the formal lesson plan is applicable in most teaching situations. The remainder of this chapter guides the aspiring outdoor leader in the development of quality lesson planning.

A sample lesson plan is provided to help guide the novice leader in developing lesson plans (see figure 12.3). Note that this sample lesson plan is written so that it can be taught using the grasshopper method or can be taught in one block of time. Keep in mind that this is only one format out of many possible choices. Numerous formats exist for creating an effective lesson plan and vary depending on personal preference, agency protocol, and leader abilities. However, certain fundamental elements of a quality lesson plan should be included in an outdoor context. Competent outdoor leaders write lesson plans down and keep the plan handy as a reference while teaching. An effective teacher would never read a lesson plan to participants word for word. A lesson plan serves as a tool to organize subject matter so that information and skills can be taught in a systematic way. Your lesson plan should be written in such a way that a coleader could pick up the plan and teach with ease. The following sections outline the elements of a quality lesson plan.

Students use a map to navigate.

Goals and Objectives

The first and most important phase of developing a lesson plan is the creation of goals and objectives. Goals and objectives form the foundation for the remainder of the lesson plan. Outdoor leaders must carefully consider intended outcomes and articulate those outcomes in the form of goals and objectives. Goals and objectives can be viewed as a hierarchy. Lesson plan goals form the educational intent behind larger program goals. Objectives are developed once lesson plan goals are formulated. Objectives are specific, measurable outcomes to determine goal success. Most novice leaders are able to create appropriate goals, but developing objectives typically presents a tougher challenge. The **SMART system**—specific, measurable, achievable, realistic, and time-bound—is an effective framework for developing goal-congruent objectives. The following checklist serves as a guide for developing lesson objectives based on the SMART system:

- Specific—Leaders must distill intents and state outcomes as precisely as possible. Objectives should not be written in general terms.

- Measurable—Leaders must create measurable objectives so that outcomes are easily recognizable.

- Achievable—Leaders must create objectives that are possible to achieve. Leaders must assess resources and participant abilities in order to create achievable objectives. Unachievable objectives set participants up for failure.

- Realistic—Depending on the context of the learning environment, leaders must carefully assess whether objectives are realistic based on the nature of a lesson. For example, if participants are learning mountaineering skills in a classroom, it would be unrealistic to expect complete development of mountaineering skills.

- Time-bound—Leaders must create objectives that can be accomplished within a specific time frame. Within the specified amount of instructional time, what is achievable and realistic? If a short amount of time is designated and the objectives are too complex for the amount of time, participants can become frustrated and dismayed. On the other hand, having no time limit could deflate the participants' desire to complete the learning process.

Basic Camping Knots

GOAL

To develop the participants' ability to properly tie and apply basic camping knots

OBJECTIVES

Participants will

1. be able to tie seven basic camp knots,
2. be able to apply knots in appropriate contexts,
3. understand the purpose of each camp knot, and
4. know appropriate terminology.

LESSON CONTENT

1. Three basic concepts to remember when tying camp knots:
   - A good knot should be relatively easy to tie.
   - A good knot should serve the purpose for which it is designed and used.
   - A good knot should be relatively easy to untie.
2. Knot terminology. The following terms establish a common language to assist in knot construction. As knots are tied, they can be described by using these terms.
   - Standing end—The part of the rope that you do not work with while tying a knot. The standing end could be several inches or many feet in length.
   - Working end—The part of the rope that you work with, usually one end.
   - Loop—When the rope crosses under or over itself to form a loop.
   - Bight—A bend in the rope. The rope does not cross to form a loop.
3. Common knots used in an outdoor setting:
   - Bowline—The bowline is a strong knot that forms a loop that will not slip under force. It serves as an excellent knot to anchor the rope to almost any object.
   - Figure 8 on a bight—Another knot used to form a loop. It is very strong knot, but more difficult to untie compared to the bowline once the knot is weighted.
   - Square knot—An excellent camp knot for tying two ends of a rope together. This knot works best with ropes of equal size.
   - Clove hitch—An excellent knot to place over a tent stake, around a tree or pole, or around the top of a nylon food bag to hang in a tree. A clove hitch tightens as force is applied. There are two different methods to tie this knot depending on the application. Excellent for tent stakes or tarp construction.
   - Taut-line hitch—This knot is a handy camp knot because it is easily adjustable. You can tighten or loosen a line by simply sliding the knot up or down the standing end of the rope. The taut-line hitch works by applying friction when it is under tension. Excellent for tarp and tent construction.
   - Trucker's hitch—The trucker's hitch is an excellent knot when a lot of tension is needed in the rope. This knot is easily adjustable and can be untied very quickly. It can be used in many different applications such as tarp construction, tying a canoe on a trailer, or creating a tight clothesline.
   - Slippery hitch or quick-release feature—The trucker's hitch final wrap is with a bight through a loop. This makes the knot a quick-release knot. For example, the quick release could also be used to tie off the taut-line hitch.

TIMING

1. Break this lesson into smaller parts to accommodate the grasshopper method. Instruction will occur over approximately three sessions as follows.
   - When establishing first campsite, demonstrate the bowline and taut-line hitch using tent guy lines.
   - The second or third night, teach tarp construction and demonstrate trucker's hitch with slippery hitch tie-off, clove hitch, and square knot.
   - Teach figure-8 knot during rock-climbing portion of the trip.
2. Lesson may also be taught in one large block of time. Allow at least 2 hours to cover all seven knots using outlined instructional strategies.

INSTRUCTIONAL STRATEGIES

1. Review basic concepts for properly tied knots by describing each one to the group. Provide example of poorly tied knot in a scrap piece of cord that must be cut with a knife. Make point to avoid "knife knots." (8 minutes)
2. Review basic knot-construction terminology by describing and demonstrating each term with a piece of rope. Once demonstrated, review by creating each and asking the group to identify using correct term. (5 minutes)
3. When teaching each knot, carefully describe and demonstrate as group observes. Pass out cords next and have group follow step by step as the knot is demonstrated again. Next, pair group members up and have each team coach one another and practice. Monitor each group and assist as needed. Provide pictures of knots for each group. (5 to 10 minutes per knot)

(continued)

Figure 12.3 Sample lesson plan on basic camping knots.

Figure 12.3 Sample lesson plan on basic camping knots. *(continued)*

4. Break participants into groups to apply knots for each situation as defined by the timing of this lesson. For example, after teaching the bowline and taut-line have the group erect tents by applying appropriate knots. If teaching all knots during one class, allow at least one hour to apply by erecting tarps in small groups. (30 minutes or so—will vary depending on context)

5. Hold a knot relay race by dividing the group into smaller groups once all knots have been covered. Review any inconsistencies or problems with the entire group at the conclusion of the race. Allow time at end for participants to make journal entries by stating the purpose for each knot and other pertinent information. (40 minutes)

MATERIALS AND SUPPLIES

1. 45 pieces of parachute cord (10 feet [3 meters] in length)—enough to construct 5 tarps

2. 5 tarps

3. 5 tents

4. 1 large piece of rope (demonstration rope—easier for whole group to see from a distance)

5. 3 sets of diagrams for each knot—resource for learners who prefer step-by-step diagrams

6. Scrap piece of cord for poor knot demonstration

7. 1 knife

RISK MANAGEMENT CONSIDERATIONS

1. Check outdoor teaching area for environmental hazards such as dead tree limbs, bee's nests, extended exposure to sun, and so on and take precautions.

2. Knot-tying relay race involves running. Check area for tripping hazards. Warn participants to be careful while running.

3. Ensure that participants remain hydrated during extended periods of instruction.

4. Be sure to emphasize proper care of equipment such as tents and tarps.

ASSESSMENT

Evaluation is based on assessment of lesson objectives. The participants wil be able to do the following:

1. Be able to tie seven basic camp knots. Assess by observing participants during final activity, the relay race.

2. Be able to apply knots in appropriate contexts. Assess by observing participants as they erect tents and tarps.

3. Understand the purpose of each camp knot. Assess by having participants describe purpose for each knot in their journals.

4. Know appropriate terminology. Observe participants in teams as they instruct and support one another. Observe whether proper terminology is being used.

REFERENCES

www.climbing.ie
www.netknots.com

Following is a sample goal and corresponding objectives designed to teach basic cooking skills. This class focuses specifically on yeast baking in a backpacking context. The class is 2 hours in duration and will happen during an extended expedition.

- Goal: Participants will learn fundamental yeast bread-baking skills.

- Objective 1: Participants will be able to describe how yeast acts as a leavening agent.

- Objective 2: Participants will develop a quick recipe for yeast bread.

- Objective 3: Participants will demonstrate the six steps to make quick yeast bread.

- Objective 4: Participants will bake one loaf of quick yeast bread using a white-gas backpacking stove and twiggy fire within a 2-hour period.

- Objective 5: Participants will appreciate the flavor and freshness of hot, homemade bread in an outdoor setting.

Note that the objectives are targeted to promote the development of yeast bread-baking skills. The objectives are specific because the participant will be able to describe, develop, or demonstrate knowledge and skills. The objectives are measurable because the participant will demonstrate six steps and bake one loaf of bread. The objectives are achievable because ingredients, cookware, and all resources are available to prepare the bread. The objectives are realistic because the expedition context is appropriate for cooking over a backpacking stove while using a twiggy fire. Finally, the lesson is time-bound within a 2-hour period, and it is feasible to accomplish objectives within the time frame. For another example of goal and objective development, see figure 12.3 on page 184, a sample plan for teaching basic camping knots.

Content Outline

The content outline allows leaders to organize the actual content, or specific information they wish to convey. This section of the lesson plan differs in format and length depending on many factors. Novice outdoor leaders may find themselves outlining detailed content notes, especially when they are unfamiliar with the content or do not have an expert's grasp of the subject. Detailed notes, diagrams, definitions, and explanations may be necessary in this section to support the novice. Experts may only need to create a short outline of key concepts and terms in a sequential order as a simple reminder. Creating a content outline allows leaders to visualize the material in advance, and the outline serves as a tool to review information that is central to the lesson. One of the biggest traps for novice leaders is the "cookbook" approach to teaching, in which the leader ends up using the lesson as a crutch and reads directly off the plan without engaging the class. The lesson quickly becomes a boring lecture as opposed to a dynamic, experiential process. See figure 12.3 for a sample content outline.

Timing and Instructional Strategies

Once goals and objectives are established and the specific lesson content is determined, the outdoor leader must contemplate the best way to convey information and teach skills. Determining appropriate instructional strategies plays a huge role in teaching effectiveness. In order to meet the needs of diverse learning styles, a mix of instructional strategies should be implemented. Also, to effectively implement the experiential learning cycle, instructional strategies must be varied. Professional outdoor leaders find themselves teaching a multitude of topics, and they are required to teach theory as well as skill-based content. Therefore, instructional methods will vary. The outdoor classroom is conducive to a wide range of instructional techniques, many of which have already been mentioned in this chapter. The following list outlines various instructional techniques available to the outdoor leader.

- Lecture—The leader delivers information verbally in a lecture format.
- Directed questions—The leader directs specific questions to the group or individuals based on lesson content. The leader typically is attempting to assess a participant's level of knowledge and understanding.
- Directed discussions—The leader facilitates group discussion based on lesson content. Directed discussions may be focused on the leader's or participants' questions or observations.
- Demonstrations—The leader or participant demonstrates a skill or process to foster the learning process. A good demonstration is done in a deliberate, sequential way and allows time for the participants to practice key skills.
- Stories—The leader or participant shares stories to accomplish lesson objectives. Stories can be based on personal experience or can be told in the third person. A well-told story creates a colorful context and engaging forum for portraying a specific message.
- Role-playing or simulations—Leaders provide participants with a realistic situation that can be acted out. Participants engage in the mock scenarios to apply skills and concepts. Acting out situations in a realistic manner allows participants to experience the learning situation in a controlled environment.
- Case studies—The leader provides real-life problems to stimulate thoughtful discussions. Case studies involve a realistic situation based on relevant background, facts, sequence of events, and issues. The situation described culminates in a point where a decision is required.
- Group exercises—The leader implements group exercises in various forms. The objective of this technique is to engage participants in collaborative learning. Participants work as a team to solve a problem, discuss an issue, or produce a product related to the educational objective.
- Journaling—The leader implements journaling as a reflective tool to promote learning.
- Field application—In outdoor education, field application is one of the most common instructional strategies. Participants actually apply knowledge and skills under field conditions. Leaders facilitate this process based on the ability level of the participants. Participants who require more direction and assistance require more attention from the leader.

Materials and Supplies

A list of materials and supplies needed for the lesson is a critical component of a lesson plan. Outdoor leaders rely on this portion of the plan to ensure that they are prepared to support a lesson with the necessary equipment. Items should be listed along with appropriate quantities. Imagine teaching navigation with a map and compass and forgetting the compasses and not having enough maps. A lesson without proper equipment quickly becomes an ineffective learning situation. The materials and supplies list aids the outdoor leader in lesson logistics. Outdoor leaders should use this section of the lesson plan as a checklist to ensure that appropriate equipment is acquired. See figure 12.3 for an example of a materials and supplies list.

Risk Management

An effective lesson plan for the outdoors includes risk management. Competent outdoor leaders visualize in advance potential hazards associated with the lesson. An awareness of potential hazards is the leader's first line of defense in preventing accidents. Listing potential risks allows the leader to plan with safety in mind. During the actual lesson, the leader has a written reminder so that proper briefing occurs. The leader takes time throughout the lesson to remind and warn students of potential hazards. For example, during a basic rock-climbing lesson, the leader spends a designated amount of time orienting students to the rock site. Safety information regarding helmet use, rock fall, environmental hazards, and equipment use becomes part of the safety briefing. Outdoor leaders need to weave risk management considerations throughout the lesson. As seen in figure 12.3, risk management is given a separate section in the overall lesson plan.

Assessment

Evaluation should be a simple process if sound goals and objectives are created from the start. Evaluation criteria should be based on the established goals and objectives. The outcomes are identifiable and measurable.

Let's go back to the example of the yeast bread-baking lesson to demonstrate how a leader assesses lesson effectiveness through goals and objectives. Each objective is written so that a specific outcome can be identified.

- Objective 1: The first objective states that participants will be able to describe their understanding of yeast as a leavening agent. The leader could easily ask participants for this description through direct questioning during the lesson or by implementing a quick quiz or test of some type.

- Objective 2: The second objective intends for the participants to develop a recipe. The leader could have the participants create a recipe during the lesson using their journals. This is a concrete product that can be assessed by reviewing journals.

- Objective 3: The leader can assess the next objective, to exercise the six baking steps, by observing participants while they make a loaf of bread.

- Objective 4: The fourth objective states that participants will bake a loaf of bread. This is an outcome that can be assessed on many levels. In addition to product creation, taste and presentation could be evaluated through a cooking competition based on fun and teamwork.

- Objective 5: The final objective, that participants will appreciate outdoor bread baking, could be assessed through instructor observation or journal reflections. Participants can demonstrate appreciation if the leader has a bread-eating party at the end of the lesson. Eating hot bread with a variety of toppings can become a great outdoor social event. Participants can be encouraged to document their experience by journaling about the experience or reflecting on it during debriefing.

For another example and more ideas regarding assessment procedures, refer to figure 12.3.

The yeast bread-baking lesson attempts to develop participant knowledge, skills, and attitudes. Each of these domains can be assessed through a variety of methods such as direct questioning, quizzes, instructor observations, group discussions, skill demonstrations, group initiatives such as a cooking contest, and journaling. Note that many of these assessment techniques parallel instructional strategies. All components of the lesson plan must act in concert to promote effective teaching and learning. Don't shy away from the evaluation process. Begin by developing sound goals and objectives so that the rest of the

Learning Activity 12.3

Develop the foundation of a lesson plan and assessment strategies by creating at least one goal and corresponding objectives for the topic of your choice. Then briefly outline how you would evaluate each objective to ensure that the goal is accomplished.

plan will fall into place. Competent leaders are able to assess teaching effectiveness through a conscious evaluation process that is outlined in a quality lesson plan.

References

Quality lesson plans include a reference section. Many times other resources are used to gather information to enhance the teaching process. Outdoor leaders must strive to share current information as outdoor education evolves. Documenting resources provides a record so that leaders can go back to original works with ease. Many times leaders must go back to original resources to review and refresh their understanding of lesson content. It is also a handy tool for others who may teach from the same lesson plan.

Summary

Teaching is one of the core outdoor leadership competencies. Competent outdoor leaders must also be competent teachers. The nature of outdoor leadership requires leaders to convey information, skills, and values in order to optimize the participant's outdoor experience. Outdoor leaders must acquire foundational knowledge of learning theory as well as develop teaching techniques specific to the outdoors. Experiential education forms the basis for outdoor teaching. Knowledge of the experiential learning cycle as well as an understanding of learning styles enables outdoor leaders to become effective teachers. Outdoor leaders can expect participants to exercise a variety of learning preferences, so leaders must implement a variety of teaching methods to ensure a productive learning environment.

Competent outdoor leaders are also able to implement teaching techniques specific to

extended trips. The grasshopper method and teachable moments are two such methods used by outdoor leaders during expeditions. The grasshopper method allows leaders to break topics into smaller, more manageable pieces. Lessons are taught in sequence as foreseeable teaching opportunities arise over the course of a trip. By the end of an expedition, an entire curriculum has been presented using this technique. Leaders use teachable moments when an unexpected opportunity presents itself during the course of a trip. Leaders also increase teaching effectiveness by remembering basic teaching tips. Addressing environmental conditions, timing concerns, and teaching aids helps the leader enrich the outdoor learning environment.

An important teaching tool for outdoor leaders is lesson planning. Competent outdoor leaders create a formal lesson plan to serve as a teaching guide. Lesson plans vary in design and format. No formula exists for the perfect lesson plan. However, certain major components should be included in the outdoor lesson plan. These components consist of goals and objectives, content outlines, instructional strategies, materials and supplies, risk management considerations, and evaluation procedures. If outdoor leaders include these core ingredients, the probability of creating an effective teaching guide increases significantly.

Outdoor leaders must integrate knowledge and skills specific to teaching into their competency regime. No matter the professional position, the outdoor leader will face the challenge of teaching. A clear awareness of one's abilities and limitations coupled with an understanding of experiential learning and outdoor teaching techniques will help ensure successful learning in the outdoors. Upon reflection, it is obvious why Alicia's teaching strategy failed. If she learned from her experience, next time she will consider the concepts outlined in this chapter.

Professional-Development Portfolio Activities

1 Many different learning style inventories are available for you to assess your own learning style. Obtain and complete a learning style inventory of your choice and document the results. Write a short paragraph explaining your personal learning style preference. Include the inventory and results as a component of your portfolio. Search the Internet under "learning style inventories" or "learning styles." One specific resource for obtaining learning style inventories can be found at www.learning-styles-online.com/inventory.

2 Develop a comprehensive lesson plan based on the outdoor topic of your choice. Use the lesson-plan components found in this chapter as your template. Your challenge is to develop a lesson plan that could also be used to facilitate the grasshopper method of expedition teaching.

Selected References

Association for Experiential Education (AEE). 2004. AEE Web site. www.aee2.org/customer/pages.php?pageid=47.

Davis, B.G. 1993. *Tools for teaching.* San Francisco: Jossey-Bass.

Dewey, J. 1938. *Experience and education.* New York: Collier Books.

Drury, J.K., and B.F. Bonney. 1992. *The backcountry classroom: Lesson plans for teaching in the wilderness.* Merrillville, IN: ICS Books.

Gardner, H. 1983. *Frames of mind: The theory of multiple intelligences.* New York: Basic Books.

Gardner, H. 1993. *Multiple intelligences: The theory and practice.* New York: Basic Books.

Gibbons, M., and D. Hopkins. 1980. How experiential is your experience-based program? *Journal of Experiential Education* 4(1): 32-37.

Joplin, L. 1981. On defining experiential education. *Journal of Experiential Education* 4(1): 17-20.

Kolb, D.A. 1984. *Experiential learning.* Englewood Cliffs, NJ: Prentice Hall.

Kolb, D.A. 2000. *Facilitator's guide to learning.* Boston: Hay/McBer.

Mitchell, M., and M. Kernodle. 2004. Using multiple intelligences to teach tennis. *Journal of Physical Education, Recreation and Dance* 75(8): 27-32.

Petzoldt, P.K. 1984. *The new wilderness handbook.* New York: Norton.

Pfeiffer, J.W., and J.E. Jones. 1980. *The 1980 annual handbook for group facilitators.* San Diego: University Associates.

Priest, S. 1990. Everything you always wanted to know about judgment, but were afraid to ask. *Journal of Adventure Education and Outdoor Leadership* 7(3): 5-12.

Priest, S., and M. Gass. 1997. *Effective leadership in adventure programming.* Champaign, IL: Human Kinetics.

Svinicki, M.D., and N.M. Dixon. 1987. Kolb model modified for classroom activities. *College Teaching* 35(4): 141-146.

Wagstaff, M., and C. Cashel. 2001. Paul Petzoldt's perspective: The final 20 years. *Journal of Experiential Education* 24(3): 160-165.

PART IV

Resource and Program Management

This portion of the text addresses resource and program management. Most novice outdoor leaders envision themselves climbing tall mountains, paddling raging rivers, and exploring remote wilderness areas with their clients. The reality for professional outdoor leaders also includes important administrative tasks that ensure safe, enjoyable, and environmentally sound outdoor adventures. In addition, it includes an awareness of the areas into which you are traveling to engage in such adventurous activities.

Chapter 13, Parks and Protected Areas Management, introduces the various governmental agencies that are responsible for managing the United States' parks and protected areas. This information is important because outdoor leaders rely heavily on these areas to conduct programs, and agencies are the gatekeepers to our program sites. We must know the rules and regulations under which areas are managed before we venture into them.

Chapter 14, Environmental Stewardship, addresses our responsibility as outdoor leaders to promote an ethic of environmental stewardship. This chapter considers environmental interpretation and education as tools in promoting a sense of ecological responsibility. Environmental preservation is one of the three primary goals of outdoor leadership.

Chapter 15, Program Management, focuses on broad program management such as goal development, program design, administrative tasks, and program evaluation. Many important administrative tasks occur before and after field-based programs. This chapter challenges the novice leader to view outdoor programming from an organizational perspective.

Chapter 16, Safety and Risk Management, focuses on one of the greatest concerns of any outdoor leader: safety. Risk is analyzed as an important part of the adventure experience, and legal aspects of risk management are discussed. The chapter closes by looking at emergency management procedures. Ensuring participant safety is one of the three primary goals of outdoor leadership.

Chapter 17, Expedition Planning, outlines the process of trip planning. The GO PREPARE system introduces a systematic way for outdoor leaders to plan quality outdoor experiences. This chapter emphasizes the value of proper planning to prevent misadventures. This chapter represents the culmination of this text. As a competent outdoor leader, you should be able to plan and implement single-day and multiday expeditions.

chapter 13

Parks and Protected Areas Management

" Brought into right relationship with the wilderness, man would see that he was not a separate entity endowed with a divine right to subdue his fellow creatures and destroy the common heritage but rather is an integral part of a harmonious whole. He would see that his appropriation of earth's resources beyond his personal needs would only bring unbalance and beget ultimate loss and poverty for all. " —John Muir

Chapter Concepts

- Recreation ecology—Land, water, and living resources provide the context for outdoor education and recreation activities. Our use of these resources is discussed in terms of recreation ecology.

- Resource management agencies—A variety of natural resource management agencies serve as gatekeepers to our parks and protected areas. It is our job as outdoor leaders to assist the agencies in taking care of these areas.

- Resource management principles and practices—The United States' natural resources are managed under an extensive history of legislation. The resource management principles and practices that are derived from this legislation are a central concern to users of these resources, especially outdoor leaders. They dictate how we can use the resources.

The chapter concepts relate to the following core competencies:

- Foundational knowledge (CC-1)—One of the primary contexts in which outdoor leadership is practiced is parks and protected areas, which are under the management of different agencies. These agencies are included within the breadth of the profession. Outdoor leaders often work within the context of these management agencies as rangers, naturalists, and so forth.

- Environmental stewardship (CC-5)—One of the primary goals of outdoor leadership is the preservation of natural resources.

- Program management (CC-6)—A central consideration in program management is the physical context in which programs are conducted. Program managers are concerned with agencies responsible for areas in which programs are conducted, the philosophy under which these areas are managed, and the rules and regulations governing the areas.

Gabriela was serving as the leader of a 2-week expedition in the Colorado Rockies. She was leading a group of 12 students from Briar College, a small college located in the Midwest. Gabriela had begun to plan the trip nearly 12 months before the trip departure. This entailed choosing a general location for the expedition, expedition activities, specific activity sites and routes, an itinerary, and so on. One of the many tasks in the planning process included obtaining permission to use the site that she had chosen for the expedition. The expedition would be conducted on land managed by a federal agency. Gabriela contacted the agency office that was responsible for the area to discover the process for obtaining a permit as well as general rules and regulations for using the area. The agency representative with whom she spoke informed her that no permission was required to use the area unless she was working for a commercial outfitter. Because Gabriela's expedition was sponsored by a nonprofit educational institution, the representative indicated, Gabriela would not need to obtain a permit. The issue of permits and land-use rules and regulations

taken care of, Gabriela proceeded with other aspects of her planning.

The trip was sponsored as an outdoor leadership practicum. The students would receive academic credit for successfully completing the course. Along with paying tuition for the course, each of the students paid an $850 activity fee to cover the cost of food, transportation, and other expenses associated with the expedition. The group loaded into a van early on the day of departure and drove 15 hours to the foothills of the Colorado Rockies. They spent their first night in a state park. On the second day of the expedition, the group drove to the area in which they would be spending the next 2 weeks. As they pulled into the parking lot of the trailhead that represented the start of their expedition route, the group was greeted by a ranger.

Gabriela introduced herself and her group to the ranger. She told him of their nearly 2-day journey from Briar College to Colorado, and she shared details of their long-planned 2-week expedition. After hearing the group's plans, the ranger asked if they had obtained a permit to use the area. Surprised by the question,

(continued)

(continued)

Gabriela informed him of her conversation with the agency representative nearly a year earlier in which she was told that her group did not need a permit to use the area. The ranger indicated that the group did indeed need a permit to use the area. Gabriela's heart sank, and she began to feel sick. She immediately began to plead with the ranger, explaining all that she and the students had invested in the expedition and even offering the name of the representative with whom she had spoken. The ranger refused to yield. Despite the misinformation offered by the agency representative, the ranger indicated that, without a permit, Gabriela's group would not be allowed to use the area. He told Gabriela that if she and her group proceeded with their plans, he would be compelled to cite the group. Such a citation would result in a fine of $1,600. Gabriela and her group left the parking lot in frustration, not sure what to do.

One of the primary aspects of outdoor education and recreation that distinguishes it from other forms of education and recreation is its reliance on natural resources as a context for education and recreation activity. Natural resources are divided into three basic categories: land resources, water resources, and living resources. **Land resources** include forests, grasslands, deserts, snow and ice areas, and tundra. **Water resources** include rivers, bays and estuaries, wetlands, coastal areas, and lakes and reservoirs. **Living resources** include all forms of plant and animal life. Jensen (1995) notes that approximately 58% of all land in the United States is privately held, while approximately 40% is publicly held and approximately 2% is held by Native Americans. Because outdoor leaders rely primarily on public lands and waterways as a context for conducting programs, these areas are the primary focus of this chapter.

This chapter describes governmental agencies that are responsible for managing the United States' natural resources. It offers a history of congressional legislation that affects resource management in the United States. This history of legislation is important because the policies under which resource management agencies operate are derived directly from this legislation. Because most of public lands and waterways are held in some sort of protective or proprietary status, this chapter will discuss resource management specifically in terms of parks and protected areas.

General Concepts in Natural Resource Management

Before discussing the various governmental agencies that are responsible for managing parks and protected areas, it is important to discuss some of the central concepts under which these areas are managed. These concepts are important because they provide resource managers with a framework for deciding how parks and protected areas should be used. They also help to inform the outdoor leader in making decisions about how to interact with the natural environment. Among these concepts are recreation ecology, carrying capacity, dispersed use, sustainable use, and preservation. Another important concept that will be addressed toward the end of the chapter is multiple use.

Recreation Ecology

One of the greatest concerns to outdoor leaders is the effects of outdoor education and recreation activities on the resources used for those activities. In the field of outdoor education and recreation, environmental impact is considered in terms of **recreation ecology.** Hammitt and Cole (1998) note that *impact* is a neutral term. It simply refers to change. They note that ecological impact refers to the environmental effects of the use of our natural resources. Impact can be either positive or negative. The role of the resource manager, accepting the public's demand to use our nation's parks and protected areas, is to ensure minimal impact on these areas through good management practices. "Of concern to the recreation manager are the type, amount, rate, and duration of undesirable change occurring to the resource base as a result of recreational use. We define undesirable change to the resource base to mean degradation to the soil, vegetation, wildlife and water resources" (p. 5).

As Hammit and Cole note, primary environmental impacts include those on soil, vegetation, water, and wildlife. Examples include the following:

- Soil—The introduction of organic matter (e.g., feces, food waste) into the environment and compaction of soil, which leads to increased runoff and consequently increased erosion

- Vegetation—The destruction of ground cover (e.g., grasses and shrubs) and damage to trees
- Water—The introduction of nutrients, pathogens, and other pollutants into water sources
- Wildlife—Disturbance (e.g., interrupting feeding or breeding habits of whales during a whale-watching excursion), alteration of habitats, and killing

One prominent aspect of recreation ecology is the idea that environmental impacts do not occur in isolation from one another. Impact on land, for instance, also often affects water, as the example of soil compaction resulting in increased runoff and soil erosion indicates. The reliance of outdoor education and recreation on the natural resource base presents a dilemma. Increased use of natural settings for recreational and educational purposes has had a detrimental effect on those settings. As the field of outdoor education and recreation continues to grow, we must strive to minimize our impact on these natural areas.

Carrying Capacity

One of the ways in which resource management agencies work to minimize the environmental impact of recreation and other uses of parks and protected areas is by determining the **carrying capacity** of those areas. Carrying capacity refers to the amount of human traffic that an area can withstand before being adversely affected by that traffic. It can be characterized in terms of **biological carrying capacity** and **psychological carrying capacity** (Jensen 1995). Biological carrying capacity refers to effects on the actual resource, whereas psychological carrying capacity refers to the effect of visitors on one another. For example, a common complaint among visitors to mountain summits that are close to urban areas is the proliferation of cell phones on those summits. Some visitors feel the compulsion to call everyone and their uncle to announce that they have reached the mountaintop. This behavior is an imposition on those seeking the solitude that tall mountain summits represent.

Dispersed Use

Management agencies attempt to ensure that an area's carrying capacity is not exceeded through the principle of **dispersed use.** A common statement among environmentalists and resource managers during the past 30 to 40 years is, "They're loving it to death!" This statement refers to the excessive use of some of the United States' most popular parks and protected areas. The principle of dispersed use encourages visitors to explore less popular and less used areas for the sake of dispersing the effects of visitation and use on these areas. Permits, certifications, and licenses are mechanisms used by parks and protected areas managers to ensure that the principle of dispersed use is adhered to in their management practices and that the carrying capacity of an area is not exceeded. National parks, for instance, allow a limited number of individuals to camp in designated backcountry campsites and by permit only.

Preservation

The concept of **preservation** applies to non-renewable resources or those resources that take a long time to regenerate. Fragile environments such as deserts require extended time to recover from visitor effects. Soil surfaces in desert environments—cryptobiotic soil, for instance—are especially vulnerable to negative impacts and require decades to return to their natural state. Our national parks and wilderness areas are managed primarily under the principle of preservation.

Sustainable Use

The concept of **sustainable use** applies to renewable resources such as forests, wildlife, and water. Historically referred to as conservation, sustainable use aims to balance use with replenishment. For example, in the case of the timber industry, this means balancing the harvest of timber with growth of new forests. Used in an efficient and reasonable manner, renewable resources can continually regenerate themselves.

Federal Parks and Protected Areas Management

The executive branch of the federal government is responsible for management of all federally owned natural resources in the United States. There are two primary federal departments that share responsibility for America's natural resources:

Young trees are protected in pine reforestation.

the Department of the Interior and the Department of Agriculture. The legislative branch of the federal government exercises oversight of these two departments and enacts legislation under which these departments are governed.

The Department of Agriculture and the Department of the Interior both consider themselves to be the nation's principal conservation agencies. The primary land management agency in the Department of Agriculture is the United States Forest Service (USFS). The primary land management agencies in the Department of the Interior include the Bureau of Land Management (BLM), the National Park Service (NPS), the Bureau of Reclamation (BOR), and the Fish and Wildlife Service. The Department of the Interior manages approximately 20% of all land in the United States (507 million acres) through its many bureaus and divisions. The Department of the Interior also manages 68% of the country's oil and gas reserves and protects endangered or threatened species. The Department of Agriculture manages 192 million acres of forests and range lands in the United States through the USFS.

Bureau of Land Management

The Bureau of Land Management (BLM) was formed when the United States Grazing Service was merged with the General Land Office in 1946. The organization traces its roots to the Land Ordinance of 1785 and the Northwest Ordinance of 1787, as figure 13.1 shows. Following the American Revolution, the original 13 colonies ceded their western lands to the new national government. Congress created the General Land Office in 1812 to oversee these lands. As the doctrine of Manifest Destiny led the country ever westward and the territory of the United States continued to increase, numerous laws were enacted to encourage the settlement and development of the western territories. Two of the most prominent of these laws were the Homesteading Act of 1872 and the Mining Act of 1872. The Homesteading Act authorized the General Land Office to grant parcels of land to families who were willing to settle on them. This act laid the foundation for the agricultural economy that developed in the West in the late 19th and early 20th centuries. The Mining Act authorized the General Land Office to sell land and mineral rights to companies willing to establish mining ventures throughout the West. These lands were sold at minimal cost to mining companies.

The Mining Act is still in effect today, and it is the subject of considerable controversy. The Department of the Interior continues to sell land and mineral rights to companies today at rates that were established in the 19th century ($5.00 per acre). An example of one such sale occurred on April 2, 2004, when the BLM sold 155 acres near the summit of 12,392-foot Mt. Emmons, which is located a few miles northwest of Crested Butte, Colorado, to the Phelps Dodge Mining Company for only $875.00. The area had served as a backcountry skiing area for decades, and local residents and environmentalists had been trying to prevent such a sale for 30 years. The sale elicited a great deal of outrage and criticism from local residents and environmentalists. The mayor of Crested Butte criticized the sale, saying, "For less than $1,000, Phelps Dodge has acquired 150 acres of federal property next to a resort town where a tenth-of-an-acre lot is selling for $100,000" (Lipsher 2004). Under the Mining Act of 1872, Phelps Dodge is now entitled to open the land to mining as well as a wide range of other kinds of development. Local officials worry about the effect that development on the mountain will have on the tourism industry in the area.

1785 Land Ordinance—Provided for the survey and settlement of western lands.

1787 Northwest Ordinance—Dictated how new states would be created out of the western lands.

1872 Homesteading Act—Successor to the Land Ordinance and the Northwest Ordinance. This act provided parcels of land to settlers moving west who were willing to settle on and develop that land.

1872 Mining Act—Provided for the sale of land and mineral rights to individuals and companies willing to establish mining ventures in the West.

1872 Yellowstone Act—Established Yellowstone National Park as the country's first national park.

1891 Forest Reserve Act—Authorized the president to establish national forest reserves.

1902 Reclamation Act—Established the Bureau of Reclamation, which is responsible for water resource projects in the West.

1905 Transfer Act—Authorized the transfer of forest reserves being managed by the General Land Office to the National Forest Service (NFS).

1906 Antiquities Act—Authorized the president to establish national monuments by proclamation, which made it easier to preserve natural treasures.

1907 Organic Administration Act—Specified that the NFS would be primarily responsible for timber production and watershed protection.

1916 Organic Act—Established the National Park Service (NPS).

1960 Multiple-Use Sustained-Yield Act—Required the NFS to adhere to sustainable-use principles in its management of natural resources.

1964 Wilderness Act—Established the National Wilderness Preservation System (NWPS).

1965 Federal Water Projects Recreation Act—Stipulates that recreation and fish and wildlife enhancement will be given full consideration as purposes in federal water resource management projects.

1966 National Wildlife Refuge System Administration Act—Incorporated existing game preserves, bird sanctuaries, and other areas designated specifically for the conservation of fish and wildlife into one management system.

1968 National Wild and Scenic Rivers System Act—Authorized the protection of designated free-flowing water from uses that would drastically alter the character of the rivers.

1968 National Trails System Act—Established a system of trails nationwide that hold historic or scenic significance.

1975 Eastern States Wilderness Act—Established an additional system of 16 wilderness areas in the eastern United States.

1976 Federal Land Policy and Management Act—Established a unified, congruent set of laws under which the Bureau of Land Management (BLM) currently governs its lands.

1980 Alaska National Interest Lands Conservation Act—Added nine new refuges to the National Wildlife Refuge System (NWRS), increased the size of seven existing refuges, and created numerous wilderness areas within the NWRS.

Figure 13.1 Legislative time line.

Until the passage of the Federal Land Policy and Management Act of 1976, the BLM was governed under nearly 2,000 different land management laws dating to the 19th century. The act has helped to establish a unified, congruent set of laws under which the BLM currently governs its lands.

The BLM currently manages approximately 261 million acres of public land in 12 western states, nearly one-eighth of the land in the United States. The BLM also manages approximately 300 million acres of subsurface mineral resources.

The BLM manages grasslands, forests, mountain areas, deserts, and arctic tundra. The resources that the BLM manages include energy and mineral resources, timber, forage, fish and wildlife habitat, wilderness areas, and historic sites. The mission of the BLM is "to sustain the health, diversity and productivity of the public lands for the use and enjoyment of present and future generations" (BLM 2004).

An example of the areas that the BLM governs that are of interest to outdoor educators is the Colorado Canyons National Conservation Area near Grand Junction, Colorado. There are numerous canyons in this conservation area that are ideal for hiking, backpacking, mountain biking, horseback riding, and rock climbing. The BLM also manages a section of the Colorado River that passes through the area, a section that is popular for rafting, canoeing, and kayaking. Much of the Colorado Canyons National Conservation Area has been designated as the Black Ridge Canyons Wilderness, and there are special rules and regulations for using this area, which we will discuss later in the chapter.

United States Forest Service

The United States Forest Service (USFS) traces its roots to the creation of the Division of Forestry in the Department of Agriculture in 1881. The Division of Forestry was later renamed the Bureau of Forestry in 1901 and the National Forest Service in 1905. Jensen (1995) attributes the creation of the USFS to the Forest Reserve Act of 1891, which authorized the president to establish forest reserves. President Benjamin Harrison immediately set aside 13 million acres in 15 different reserves. Rather than placing the reserves under the jurisdiction of the Division of Forestry, however, he placed them under the jurisdiction of the General Land Office in the Department of the Interior. Under the Transfer Act of 1905, the forest reserves being managed by the General Land Office were transferred to the USFS. The USFS renamed its forest reserves national forests in 1907.

One of the most significant pieces of legislation in the history of the USFS is the Organic Administration Act of 1907. The act specified that the USFS would be primarily responsible for timber production and watershed protection. Another significant piece of legislation in the history of the USFS is the Multiple-Use Sustained-Yield Act of 1960. This act required the USFS to adhere to sustainable-use principles in its management of natural resources. It also expanded the mission of the USFS to include habitat management for fish and wildlife and management of lands for recreational purposes. The forest service motto "Land of many uses" is derived from this law.

The USFS currently manages 192 million acres of land in 155 national forests and 20 national grasslands throughout the United States—an area the size of Texas. The USFS is organized into nine regions, each of which is managed by a Regional Forester. These nine regions are comprised of a

The Buffalo Gap National Grassland, which surrounds Badlands National Park in South Dakota, is managed by the USFS.

collection of forests and grasslands, each of which is managed by a Forest Supervisor. Each forest is divided into districts, each of which is managed by a District Ranger. There are more than 600 districts in the forest service, each employing from 10 to 100 people and each ranging in size from 50,000 to 1 million acres. Ranger districts are where the boot meets the trail in the implementation of forest service policies and functions. District staff members are responsible for the operation of campgrounds, maintenance of wildlife habitats, construction and maintenance of trails, policing of USFS lands, issuance of land-use permits, and so forth. There are currently about 30,000 employees in the USFS. The top official in the USFS is called the Chief. Regional Foresters answer to the Chief, who answers to the Undersecretary for Natural Resources and the Environment, who answers to the Secretary of the Department of Agriculture. The average citizen's first point of interaction with the forest service begins at the ranger-district level.

Dale Bosworth, chief of the USFS in 2005, identifies unmanaged recreation as one of four primary threats to America's national forests (USFS 2005). The other three include forest fires, invasive species, and loss of open space due to development. According to the USFS, damage to

Learning Activity 13.1

Get into a group of three or four. Outside of class, search the local, regional, national, and international press for controversial issues in resource management (such as drilling for oil in ANWR, water rights in the Rocky Mountains, and so on). In class, present your issue. Presentations should include a brief overview of the issue, followed by a class discussion of the issue. You should be compelled to take sides and justify your stance.

forests from unmanaged recreation is the result of off-road vehicles in the forests. The USFS reports that off-road vehicle ownership has risen in the United States from 5 million in 1972 to 36 million in 2002. These vehicles have had a devastating effect in some areas. The primary effects of off-road vehicles include severe soil erosion, spread of invasive species, and damage to wetlands and wetland species.

Bureau of Reclamation and Army Corps of Engineers

Four governmental agencies manage the nation's water resources: the Bureau of Reclamation, the Army Corps of Engineers, the Tennessee Valley Authority, and the National Oceanic and Atmospheric Administration. We focus on two of these agencies here: the Bureau of Reclamation and the Army Corps of Engineers.

The Bureau of Reclamation (BOR), originally called the Reclamation Service, was created in 1902 under the Reclamation Act. The BOR's original mission, as its name implies, was to reclaim (or simply to claim, depending on your point of view) the arid lands of the western United States for development through the construction of dams, power plants, and canals. The BOR oversees approximately 9 million acres of land. It provides water for irrigation to 20% of Western farmers and water for residential use to 31 million citizens in the western United States. The BOR manages approximately 9 million acres of land, 476 dams, 58 hydroelectric power plants, 348 reservoirs, 350 campgrounds, and 308 recreational sites. The BOR employed nearly 6,000 people in 2003 (BOR 2004). The western United States is now dependent on the BOR's many water projects to a degree that most citizens do not realize.

The Army Corps of Engineers traces its roots to the American Revolution when the Continental Congress of 1775 commissioned a group of engineers to construct military fortifications at Bunker Hill near Boston, Massachusetts, to fend off the British. The Corps of Engineers was later stationed at West Point in 1802 where it established the United States Military Academy as an engineering school. Much of the Corps' work historically has been dedicated to the military, but the Corps is also responsible for numerous civil engineering projects. The Corps' civil responsibilities include the maintenance of navigational channels in the United States' waterways (i.e., dredging channels to maintain the depth and width of channels, clearing impediments to navigation, and so on). They also include the construction of dams around the nation for the purpose of flood control. The Corps manages over 12,000 miles of inland waterways, including rivers, lakes, bays, and canals. The Corps also maintains nearly 1,000 harbors and ports around the country. It manages almost 12 million acres (surface area) of water.

Recreation was not initially considered as a potential benefit of the many water projects that the BOR and the Army Corps of Engineers undertook. After their creation, however, the recreational value of these projects became obvious, and Congress acted to take advantage of their recreational value. The 1965 Federal Water Projects Recreation Act in particular stipulates, "Full consideration shall be given to recreation and fish and wildlife enhancement as purposes in federal water resource projects" (Jensen 1995, p. 102). Most of the projects undertaken by these two agencies have a direct and significant impact on the environment. They also consequently have a direct and significant impact, sometimes positive, sometimes negative, on the use of the environment for recreational and educational purposes.

One example of the many projects undertaken by the Army Corps of Engineers that illustrates the recreational value of its work is the Summersville Dam in Summersville, West Virginia. Summersville Dam was constructed in 1965 primarily for the purpose of flood control along the Gauley River. It was initially thought that the primary source of recreation associated with the construction of the dam would be the lake created behind the dam, Summersville Lake. White-water rafting was a burgeoning industry in the eastern United States at the time, however, and it soon became a viable enterprise on the Gauley River below the Summersville Dam. Recognizing both the recreational and economic value of the rafting industry in West Virginia, specifically on the Gauley River, Congress included recreation as an official part of the mission of the Summersville Dam in 1985. This allowed rafting companies to maximize the number of days available for rafting on the river through controlled releases of water from the dam in what is known as the fall draw-down of Summersville Lake. Below Summersville Dam, the Gauley River flows through what is now the Gauley River National Recreation Area. Managed by the NPS, this recreation area encompasses nearly 11,500 acres of land and 25 miles of the Gauley River. While the NPS manages the recreation area, the Army Corps of Engineers continues to regulate the flow of water from the dam. The Corps of Engineers also operates a visitor's center and a campground near the dam. The Corps' facilities at the dam are administered by a resource manager.

National Park Service

While exploring the Yellowstone region with a group in 1870, Cornelius Hedges became the first person to suggest that Yellowstone should be preserved as a national park (Jensen 1995, p. 82). His suggestion came to fruition 2 years later. The United States government dispatched the first scientific expedition to the Yellowstone region a year later under the leadership of Ferdinand Hayden. Little was known about the Yellowstone region before this time. The Lewis and Clark expedition had come close in the early 1800s but did not enter the area that is now Yellowstone National Park. John Colter, one of the members of the Lewis and Clark expedition, is believed to be the first English-speaking person to enter the region. But few believed the wild tales that he and others who followed told of the region. It was the 1871 Geological and Geographical Survey of the Territories led by Hayden that first documented through photographs and written descriptions the unique geological wonders of the place. Widely publicized, the findings of this expedition provided Congress with the impetus to protect the Yellowstone region. The Yellowstone Act of 1872 was passed by Congress and signed by President Ulysses S. Grant to protect the region as "a public park or pleasuring ground for the benefit and enjoyment of the people" (Magoc 1999, p. 19).

The establishment of national parks requires congressional action, and it was nearly 20 years before another national park was established in the United States. Opposition to restricting the commercial exploitation of natural resources was strong during this period. In addition, the country's natural resources seemed to be endless. As the American frontier began to close, momentum gained for the establishment of new parks in order to protect the country's natural treasures. Sequoia, Yosemite, General Grant Grove, and Mount Rainier national parks eventually joined Yellowstone among the country's national parks. Under the Antiquities Act of 1906, the president was given the authority to establish national monuments by proclamation, which made it easier to preserve natural treasures. Several presidents have exercised this authority to set aside public lands from development.

The national parks came under the management of a single agency for the first time in 1916. The Organic Act of 1916 authorized the establishment of the National Park Service (NPS). This act states that the mission of the NPS is "to conserve the scenery and the natural and historic objects and wildlife therein and to provide for the enjoyment of the same in such manner and by such means as will leave them unimpaired for the enjoyment of future generations" (Wright and Mattson 1996, p. 10). This mission created a dilemma for the NPS. On the one hand, the service is required to protect natural treasures. On the other hand, it is required to make these natural treasures accessible to the public for pleasure and enjoyment. National parks emphasize recreation as the sole use of their lands, whereas the USFS and BLM allow recreation but emphasize timber and agricultural production as well as other forms of resource extraction as the primary uses of their lands. The NPS managed 37 different units, or areas, when it was first created. It now manages over 84 million acres of land in almost 400 national parks, monuments, recreation areas, seashores, battlefields, historic sites, and other designated sites around the country.

U.S. Fish and Wildlife Service

The U.S. Fish and Wildlife Service (USFWS) oversees 96 million acres. It is managed under the Department of the Interior. It was created in 1940 with the merger of the Bureau of Fisheries and the Bureau of Biological Surveys, but it traces its origins to the creation of the U.S. Commission on Fish and Fisheries in 1871 and the U.S. Division of Economic Ornithology and Mammology in 1885. The agency historically has been concerned with conservation of living resources and their habitats. The mission of this agency is to conserve, protect, and enhance fish, wildlife, plants, and their habitats for the continuing benefit of the American people.

Most of the lands and waterways under the Fish and Wildlife Service's jurisdiction are part of the National Wildlife Refuge System. President Theodore Roosevelt created the Pelican Island National Wildlife Refuge, the first official national wildlife refuge, along Florida's Atlantic coast in 1902, and the National Wildlife Refuge System was created in 1966. Numerous game preserves, bird sanctuaries, and other areas designated specifically for the conservation of fish and wildlife had been created throughout the United States before 1966, and the National Wildlife Refuge System Act of 1966 incorporated all of these areas into one management system. Numerous other wildlife refuges have been added to this system since its creation. For example, the Alaska National Interest Lands Conservation Act of 1980 added nine new refuges to the National Wildlife Refuge System, increased the size of seven existing refuges, and created numerous wilderness areas within the National Wildlife Refuge System. Over 53 million acres of land were added to the system under this act. The National Wildlife Refuge System now includes over 520 units and over 93 million acres of land and waterways that serve as wildlife habitat. Over 20 million of these acres are designated as wilderness areas.

One of the Fish and Wildlife Service's more notable employees was Rachel Carson, who worked as a marine biologist for the service. Carson's book *Silent Spring* (1962) helped to establish a new ethic regarding the way people perceive and treat the natural environment. The Fish and Wildlife Service currently employs approximately 7,500 individuals in 700 offices and field stations around the country.

Bureau of Indian Affairs

The Bureau of Indian Affairs (BIA) was created in 1824 to serve as the U.S. government's primary agency for interacting with America's numerous tribal governments. The BIA is the successor of the Committee on Indian Affairs, which was created in 1775 by the Continental Congress and originally led by Benjamin Franklin. The BIA's mission initially was to subjugate and assimilate natives into Western society. After a long and tragic relationship between the federal government and America's native peoples, this mission has changed to one that is intended to foster partnerships and to provide service to native peoples. The BIA currently oversees approximately 55 million acres of land. Along with managing these lands, the BIA is responsible for providing educational services to nearly 50,000 American Indian and Alaska Native children. The BIA is important to the field of outdoor education and recreation because, as with other lands managed by the federal government, these lands are a resource for educational and recreational programming.

Wilderness and Backcountry Areas

Among the United States' resources, none capture the imagination as fervently as its wilderness areas.

Back Bay National Wildlife Refuge, Sandbridge Beach, Virginia.

Roderick Nash's *Wilderness and the American Mind* (1967) notes the shift that occurred in humanity's perception of wilderness in the 19th and 20th centuries. Wilderness as the great unknown, something to be conquered, represents the traditional view of wilderness in Western society. However, with the writings of Henry David Thoreau, John Muir, and others, we have come to view wilderness in a new light. As the country became more and more urbanized during the 19th and 20th centuries, cities came to be viewed as centers of chaos and moral decay while wilderness came to be viewed as a place of calm and serenity, moral purity and spiritual rejuvenation. As the American wilderness receded with the encroachment of civilization, cities were no longer viewed as islands of security amid the vastness of the wild and savage landscape. Wilderness came to be viewed as the refuge, and the need to protect it quickly became apparent.

National Wilderness Preservation System

Established under the authority of the Wilderness Act of 1964, the National Wilderness Preservation System (NWPS) has its roots in a preservation system that was established by the USFS in 1924 (Jensen 1995). That year, the USFS established Gila National Forest in New Mexico protecting approximately 500,000 acres of land. The NWPS includes this and all other forest service lands previously designated as Wilderness. It also requires all management agencies of federal parks and protected areas to evaluate areas under their jurisdiction for possible inclusion in the system. *Wilderness* (with a capital "W") refers to areas specifically designated as such under the Wilderness Act of 1964 (Hammitt and Cole 1998; Hendee, Stankey, and Lucas 1990). *Backcountry* (or *wilderness* with a lower-case "w") is a more generic term commonly used to describe wild, remote roadless areas not necessarily included in the NWPS (Hammitt and Cole 1998). Most Wilderness areas are located in the western United States and Alaska; however, the Eastern States Wilderness Act of 1975 established an additional system of 16 Wilderness areas in 13 eastern states (Cordell and Overdevest 2001; Hendee, Stankey, and Lucas 1990). The nation's Wilderness areas are managed by four federal agencies: the BLM, USFS, NPS, and U.S. Fish and Wildlife Service. Management agencies often share responsibility for the same Wilderness area. The Indian Peaks Wilderness

Mountain-biking along the edge of the Indian Peaks Wilderness Area.

Area in Colorado, for instance, is located in both the Roosevelt National Forest and the Rocky Mountain National Park. Both of these agencies are thus responsible for the management of this Wilderness area. The NWPS currently includes 102 million acres.

National Wild and Scenic Rivers System

The National Wild and Scenic Rivers System Act of 1968 authorized the development of the National Wild and Scenic Rivers System (NWSRS). Unlike the NWPS, the NWSRS is not intended to necessarily preserve rivers from commercial use and development. The system is intended only to preserve the character of rivers in the system. It is intended to ensure that these rivers remain free flowing and protected from uses that would cause drastic alterations in the rivers.

The NWSRS includes only 11,300 miles (18,186 kilometers) of river, less than 1% of the total length of rivers in the United States. Typically, only short sections of rivers in the system are protected. Examples of rivers in the system are the Red River in Kentucky (nearly 20 miles or 32 kilometers), the Allegheny River in Pennsylvania (87 miles or 140 kilometers), the White Salmon River in Washington (9 miles or 14 kilometers), and Clark's Fork of the Yellowstone River in Wyoming (nearly 20 miles or 32 kilometers). The system currently includes approximately 175 sections of river.

Agencies that are responsible for managing the rivers under the NWSRS include the USFS, the BLM, the Army Corps of Engineers, the NPS, the U.S. Fish and Wildlife Service, and various state agencies. Permits are typically required for organized groups hoping to use sections of river in the NWSRS. These should be sought from the agency under whose jurisdiction the section of river falls.

National Trails System

The National Trails System Act of 1968, later amended in 1978, established a system of trails nationwide that hold historic or scenic significance. The first two trails designated as national trails were the Appalachian National Scenic Trail, which covers approximately 2,175 miles (3,500 kilometers) from Maine to Georgia, and the Pacific Crest National Scenic Trail, which covers 2,313 miles (3,722 kilometers) from Canada to Mexico. There are now 23 national trails, 15 of which are historic trails and 8 of which are scenic trails. Historic trails include the Iditarod National Historic Trail in Alaska, site of the annual Iditarod Dog Sled Race; the Lewis and Clark National Historic Trail, which traverses the continent from St. Louis, Missouri, to the Oregon coast; and the Trail of Tears National Historic Trail, which traverses sections of nine states over a course of nearly 2,200 miles (3,541 kilometers). Scenic trails include the Appalachian Trail, the Pacific Crest Trail, the Continental Divide National Scenic Trail, and the Natchez Trace National Scenic Trail.

Agencies that are responsible for managing the National Trail System include the NPS, the BLM, the USFS, and the Federal Highway Administration. The trails that are most useful in outdoor education and recreation programming are the scenic trails. They serve as a resource primarily for hiking and backpacking. Organized groups are typically required to have permits to use these trails and should contact the trails' managing agencies to seek permission to use the trails.

State and Municipal Parks and Protected Areas Management

Most of the United States' best-known parks and protected areas, those that receive the most public attention, are under the jurisdiction of the federal government. The Arctic National Wildlife Refuge, Grand Canyon National Park, and Glacier National Park are a few that readily come to mind. For most Americans, these parks and protected areas are far away, and for many, visiting them is a once-in-a-lifetime experience. There are numerous parks and protected areas that receive less attention and are not so remote. Some of the best parks and protected areas available to the public and outdoor leaders are those areas located in our neighborhoods, our own proverbial backyards. Parks and protected areas that people typically take for granted are those that are managed at the state and municipal levels.

State Parks

Natural resource management is typically conducted at the state level by departments of natural resources. The names of these agencies vary. The Department of Conservation and Natural Resources and the Department of Conservation and Recreation are examples of different names used for these agencies. These departments are typically responsible for forest management, fish and wildlife management, land and mineral resource management, water resource management, trails and waterway management, and park and recreation management. Many of the responsibilities of these state agencies are carried out in collaboration with their federal counterparts. The U.S. Fish and Wildlife Service, for instance, relies on state departments to issue licenses for hunting and fishing on all public and private lands and waterways.

State parks are one of the most useful resources at the state level to the field of outdoor education and recreation. Each state park system has its own history of development. State parks generally began to develop in the late 1800s as a part of the broader environmental movement that was taking root at the time. Most states initially established individual parks, later incorporating them into park systems. State parks are typically more accommodating to organized groups than federal land management agencies, particularly in areas of the country where demand for use of federal lands is greatest. Many state parks offer backcountry camping; multiple-use trails for hiking, biking, and horseback riding; and single-use trails designated solely for hiking. Many state parks include lakes that are a great resource for kayaking, canoeing, and other water sports. All organized groups should contact parks in advance to seek permission to use the parks and to discover park rules and regulations.

Municipal Parks

As noted, outdoor recreation and education need not be confined to rural areas or remote backcountry settings (Williams 1995). Urban areas often provide natural settings that are ideal locations for outdoor education and recreation activities. Many of these natural settings are maintained as municipal parks or open spaces. The James River Park System in Richmond, Virginia, provides an excellent example.

The City of Richmond developed along the fall line of the James River during the Colonial period as a natural point of commerce. Oceangoing vessels could travel no farther up the river than the falls of the James to trade for goods. Bateaus, long narrow wooden boats, were navigated down the James River carrying loads of tobacco, corn, and other goods. Once they reached Richmond, the goods were sold to merchants who then sold the goods for export to England and other countries around the world. Modes of transportation have long since changed and the river no longer holds the importance to commerce that it once did, but the river is still considered one of the city's greatest resources. One of the primary reasons for this is the opportunities it offers for outdoor education and recreation.

There is a wide array of activities available to outdoor enthusiasts along the river. The river is famous for its smallmouth bass population. Numerous fishing championships have been held along the river. In addition, the river is touted for its white-water rapids, offering kayakers, canoeists, rafters, and other river enthusiasts a great stretch of beginner and intermediate white water right in the heart of the city. Along the shores of the James River are old bridge trestles that serve as popular sport climbing sites. There are numerous trails along both shores for walking, jogging, or biking. There is also an abundance of greenery and wildlife along the river. Osprey and eagles can occasionally be seen competing for fish. Great blue herons, mallards, and a variety of other birds and animals inhabit the river and its shores. One of the river's bygone modes of travel has been celebrated in recent years in an annual bateau festival along the upper stretches of the river. This festival is one of the primary recreational and educational events along the river each year.

The city has shown remarkable foresight in its management of the river as an outdoor recreation resource under the auspices of the James River Parks System, which is a part of the broader park and recreation system in the city. Numerous community organizations and groups have also contributed to the development and maintenance of the James River Parks, such as the James River Outdoor Coalition and the James River Association.

Using Parks and Protected Areas

When choosing a location for a program, outdoor leaders must consider the following questions. Who manages the area? What are the principles under which the area is managed? Are these principles congruent with the goals of the program? What are the rules and regulations for using the area? Are permits needed to use the area? Where you conduct a program may not depend so much on where you would like to go as on answers to these questions.

Taking Resource Management Principles Into Account

One of the central debates in resource management is the commodity versus preservation debate that arises when competing interests attempt to lay claim to the same resources for different purposes (Agee 1996, p. 34). The concept of **multiple use** is aimed at drawing a balance among the interests competing for the same resource. The USFS, BLM, Army Corps of Engineers, and BOR are all examples of agencies that employ the concept of multiple use in their management practices. These agencies are constantly weighing the interests of different groups vying for the same resource. The USFS, for instance, must satisfy the demands of the timber industry to exploit the commercial value of the nation's forests while also satisfying the demands of those wishing to protect the forests for recreational use. Even among recreationists, the forest service must balance the demands of different kinds of recreational uses. Competition between individuals who prefer to travel into backcountry areas on snowmobiles and other off-road vehicles and individuals who prefer to travel into backcountry areas by nonmotorized means is an example. If you wish to avoid encounters with snowmobiles and other off-road vehicles while in the backcountry, for instance, you should consider using land whose managing agency prohibits off-road vehicles.

Where you travel or choose to conduct a program will depend to a large degree on the extent to which the principles under which different areas are managed are consistent with the values and goals of your program. Some would argue, for instance, that Wilderness areas are inappropriate settings for groups, especially groups whose members are just learning to live and travel in the backcountry. Such groups need nothing more than a generic natural setting that might be found in national forests, BLM lands, or state parks. The clumsiness of beginners in a Wilderness area might result in undue damage to the area.

Permits

One of the primary considerations for anyone planning to use parks or protected areas for recreational or educational purposes is whether permits are required to use those areas. Rules and regulations pertaining to permits are typically different for individuals or small private groups planning excursions into a park or protected area than they are for organized groups. Rules and regulations are also typically different for nonprofit groups than they are for commercial outfitters or guide services. Whether or not you need a permit, however, is determined by whether or not you are being paid to lead a group. If you are being paid, then it is safe to assume that a permit is required. If you are not being paid, you may still need a permit. The answer depends on the agency and its local rules and regulations. Outdoor leaders should always inquire with the agency managing the area into which they plan to travel to determine whether or not a permit is

required. Even if there is no formal permitting process for a particular area, outdoor leaders should seek permission in writing from the individual or agency responsible for the particular area.

To obtain a permit to conduct programs in a particular park or protected area, contact the headquarters of the agency responsible for managing the area. If you hope to lead a group into Rocky Mountain National Park, for instance, you should contact the Rocky Mountain National Park headquarters or visit the park's Web site to obtain information about getting a permit. In highly populated areas, such as the Front Range of the Colorado Rockies, it can be difficult to obtain permits to operate in federally managed parks and protected areas because of carrying capacity and other management issues. Outdoor leaders may be compelled to seek areas that are not as heavily used as those in such densely populated regions of the country. Once you have chosen your site and obtained information on the permitting process, it is a matter of completing and submitting the proper paperwork far in advance. A permit may or may not be awarded. Outdoor programs are typically required to obtain special-use permits to operate in federally managed parks in protected areas.

In the case of Gabriela and her group, after being turned away by the ranger, Gabriela attempted to contact the agency office responsible for the area in which they had planned to conduct their expedition. It was a Saturday, however, and the office was closed for the weekend. She called an agency office in a neighboring area, hoping to find someone that might give her an explanation. This office happened to be open on weekends. The permit officer was not on duty that day, but the representative with whom she spoke indicated that there had been a change in management in the area in which the group had planned to conduct their expedition. The new supervisor for that area held a different interpretation of the rules and regulations regarding permits than the previous supervisor. Unlike the previous supervisor, the current supervisor placed colleges and other nonprofit groups in the same category as commercial outfitters, which are required to obtain permits when leading groups onto federally managed lands.

Gabriela discovered that there are inconsistencies in the interpretation of rules and regulations pertaining to permits for using public lands. A land manager in one region may interpret rules and regulations differently than a land manager in another region. The representative informed Gabriela that even within individual regions and areas, there is sometimes inconsistency in the interpretation and enforcement of rules and regulations. The best advice for outdoor leaders who are told that they do not need a permit to operate in an area is to get that statement in writing from the agency representative or permit officer managing the area. Outdoor leaders should also keep track of personnel changes in the agency offices that are responsible for the areas they plan to use.

If you intend to travel from one management area to another as a part of a single expedition, you must seek permission from the agencies managing each of the different areas in which you plan to travel. The Colorado Trail, for instance, traverses different forests, Wilderness areas, and so on from start to finish.

General Rules and Regulations

Other rules and regulations under which public lands and waterways are governed vary from place to place depending on the character of the agency under whose jurisdiction the land or waterway falls. Even among Wilderness areas the rules and regulations vary. The maximum group size for some Wilderness areas is 12, including livestock such as horses or pack animals. For others Wilderness areas, the maximum group size is 18. Camping is generally prohibited within 100 feet (30 meters) of lakes, streams, and trails in many Wilderness areas, while this distance may be greater in other Wilderness areas. Campfires are allowed in some Wilderness areas but not in others. Though specific rules and regulations vary in governing the use of different public lands and waterways, as outdoor leaders we

adhere to practices that are aimed at the protection and preservation of these resources. Methods for doing so will be discussed in the following chapter.

Summary

One of the primary distinguishing characteristics of outdoor education and outdoor recreation is reliance on natural settings as a context for programming. Most of the land and waterways used for outdoor education and recreation programming are in the public domain. These lands and waterways are managed as parks and protected areas by a variety of federal, state, and municipal agencies. Rules and regulations governing use of parks and protected areas vary from agency to agency. They are generally based on underlying resource management concepts such as carrying capacity, dispersed use, and multiple use. These areas are also governed under the congressional, state, or municipal legislation through which they were created. As outdoor leaders, we must be aware of the agencies that are responsible for managing areas in which we plan to conduct programs. We must also be aware of their rules and regulations for these areas, particularly with regard to permits. One of the primary goals of outdoor leadership is protecting the areas into which we travel for outdoor education and recreation.

Selected References

Agee, J.K. 1996. Ecosystem management: An appropriate concept for parks. In *National parks and protected areas: Their role in environmental protection,* ed. R.G. Wright. Cambridge, MA: Blackwell Science.

Bureau of Land Management (BLM). 2004. BLM facts page. www.blm.gov.

Professional-Development Portfolio Activity

Select a particular public land management agency (such as the National Forest Service, the Bureau of Land Management, the National Park Service, and so on), identify the conservation principles under which the agency operates, and identify the requirements for using land under the agency's jurisdiction. What do you need to do to take a group of people onto the agency's lands for single-day and multiday trips? Contact the local office managing the area to discover the nature of the permitting process. Write a short report describing this process. Include permit application materials in your report.

Bureau of Reclamation (BOR). 2004. About us—fact sheet. www.usbr.gov.

Carson, R. 1962. *Silent spring.* Boston: Houghton Mifflin.

Cordell, H.K. 1999. *Outdoor recreation in American life: A national assessment of demand and supply trends.* Champaign, IL: Sagamore.

Cordell, H.K., and C. Overdevest. 2001. *Footprints on the land: An assessment of demographic trends and the future of natural lands in the United States.* Champaign, IL: Sagamore.

Douglass, R.W. 1999. History of outdoor recreation and nature-based tourism in the United States. In *Outdoor recreation in American life: A national assessment of demand and supply trends,* principal investigator H.K. Cordell. Champaign, IL: Sagamore.

Farina, A. 1997. Landscape ecology as a basis for protecting threatened landscapes. In *National parks and protected areas: Keystones to conservation and sustainable development,* ed. J.G. Nelson and R. Serafin. Berlin: Springer.

Hammitt, W.E., and D.N. Cole. 1998. *Wildland recreation: Ecology and management.* 2nd ed. New York: Wiley.

Hendee, J.C., G.H. Stankey, and R.C. Lucas. 1990. *Wilderness management.* 2nd ed. Golden, CO: North American Press.

Jensen, C.R. 1995. *Outdoor recreation in America.* 5th ed. Champaign, IL: Human Kinetics.

Lipsher, S. 2004, April 6. Feds' sale of mining rights roils locals: BLM's motives, quiet decision on deal draw fire in Crested Butte. *Denver Post,* section A, page 1.

Locke, H. 1997. The role of Banff National Park as a protected area in the Yellowstone to Yukon Mountain Corridor of western North America. In *National parks and protected areas: Keystones to conservation and sustainable development,* ed. J.G. Nelson and R. Serafin. Berlin: Springer.

Magoc, C.J. 1999. *Yellowstone: The creation and selling of an American landscape, 1870-1903.* Albuquerque: University of New Mexico Press.

Nash, R. 1967. *Wilderness and the American mind.* New Haven, CT: Yale University Press.

Phillips, A. 1997. Landscape approaches to national parks and protected areas. In *National parks and protected areas: Keystones to conservation and sustainable development,* ed. J.G. Nelson and R. Serafin. Berlin: Springer.

United States Forest Service (USFS). 2005. Four major threats. USFS Web site, www.fs.fed.us.

Williams, S. 1995. *Outdoor recreation and the urban environment.* London: Routledge.

Wright, R.G., and D.J. Mattson. 1996. The origin and purpose of national parks and protected areas. In *National parks and protected areas: Their role in environmental protection,* ed. R.G. Wright. Cambridge, MA: Blackwell Science.

chapter 14

Environmental
Stewardship

© Mark Radel and Wildwater Expeditions

" Wilderness
management is 80 to
90 percent education
and information and 10
percent regulation. "
—**Max Peterson, former
chief of the U.S. Forest
Service**

Chapter Concepts

- Environmental ethics—Environmental ethics serves as a foundation for environmental stewardship and as a framework for how we treat and interact with our environment.

- Ecological literacy—Ecological literacy is a form of critical literacy that is essential to making good decisions about the environment.

- Environmental preservation through education—One of the primary goals of outdoor leadership is environmental stewardship, which is accomplished primarily through education.

- Leave No Trace—Leave No Trace is a set of principles and practices that guide use of the outdoors. It provides a specific ethical framework for minimizing our impact on the natural environment.

The chapter concepts relate to the following core competencies:

- Self-awareness and professional conduct (CC-2)—Outdoor leaders need an awareness of their relationship with the natural environment and their impact on the environment.

- Decision making and judgment (CC-3)—Ecological literacy is essential to making sound judgments about interactions with the natural environment.

- Teaching and facilitation (CC-4)—Outdoor leaders strive to protect the environment by educating users about how to minimize their impact on the environment, specifically through the principles and practices of Leave No Trace.

- Environmental stewardship (CC-5)—Every facet of this core competency is discussed in this chapter.

Jake works as a professional raft guide on the New River in West Virginia. Jake's primary responsibility as a raft guide is to ensure the safety of his guests while navigating the raft down the river. A secondary responsibility is to entertain his guests along the way. The river provides much of the entertainment, but Jake tries to enhance that entertainment by telling jokes and stories along the way. Jake has developed an extensive knowledge of the New River Gorge that allows him to entertain his guests by sharing information about the cultural and natural history of the gorge. The New River Gorge contains approximately 14 ghost towns. The history of these towns is based on coal mining. In sharing the history of these towns with his guests, Jake weaves together a tale that brings the gorge to life in the minds of his guests.

Jake focuses on several different aspects of the history of the New River Gorge. He first focuses on the geological history of the gorge. Sure to point to the irony in the name of the river, Jake notes that the New River is the second oldest river in the world, second only to the Nile. The New River is so old that it actually predates the Appalachian Mountains, considered the oldest mountain range in the world. Before the rise of the Appalachian Mountains, the river flowed through a low-lying, marshy, swampy area filled with peat bogs. Over the years, as the mountains rose and the peat bogs became compressed by the weight of the mountains, coal began to form, filling the Appalachian Mountains with some of the richest deposits of coal in the world.

Jake also shares the history of the old ghost towns that he and his guests pass as they raft down the river. One of these is the town of Beury, named for Colonel Joseph Beury. No one knows whether Colonel Beury was an actual colonel or not. Folks assume that he assigned himself the title because of the distinction that it offered. Joseph Beury came to the New River Gorge from Pittsburgh in the early 1870s in search of coal. He shipped the first railroad car of coal from the gorge in 1873. The Industrial Revolution was in full swing at the time, and there was a great demand for coal to fire the steel and iron mills of Pittsburgh and other cities in the Northeast. The coal from the New River Gorge was a high-quality coal that, once refined into coke, an even more energy-efficient form of coal, helped to generate the production of some of the best steel and iron in the world. The 14 towns that eventu-

(continued)

(continued)

ally grew up in the gorge each has a unique history. Countless people spent their lives in these towns, lives filled with the drama of the lives of people everywhere. The common element in each story, however, is coal, and the drama of these towns died with the demise of the mining industry in the New River Gorge in the 1950s.

Finally, Jake also focuses on the ecological impact of the mining industry on the gorge. Today, little remains of the 14 mining towns that once existed in the gorge, just the ruins of old mining operations and the remnants of old town buildings. In most cases, they are shrouded in vegetation. Someone once commented during the heyday of coal mining in the gorge that looking down into the New River Gorge was like looking into the depths of hell; the only difference was that the gorge has a river running through it. Black smoke billowed from the coke ovens that refined the coal, leaving a dark haze lingering at the rim of the gorge. With the fires of the coke ovens dotting the landscape below, looking down into the New River Gorge through this haze conjured images of Dante's *Inferno*.

The gorge has recovered remarkably well from the environmental degradation caused by the mining industry. The rafting industry began to develop in the gorge in the 1960s, supplanting mining as the primary base of economic activity in the gorge. Today, because the primary industry in the gorge is adventure-based tourism and recreation, the federal government, private companies, and others are working to keep the gorge in a pristine state. To this end, the gorge was designated as the New River Gorge National River under the National Park Service in 1978. The gorge now enjoys the same federal protection and management that other national parks and protected areas enjoy. The National Park Service has dedicated millions of dollars to preserving the natural and cultural history of the gorge.

Jake's mastery of guiding a raft, his ability to tell a good joke, and, more importantly, his ability to bring the New River Gorge to life through his storytelling makes him stand out as a raft guide. This is evidenced in the substantial tips he receives from guests at the end of each day.

The previous chapter focused on the role of parks and protected areas in outdoor education and recreation. It introduced the various federal, state, and municipal agencies that are responsible for governing these areas. The principles and practices under which these areas are governed are particularly important to outdoor leaders because they greatly affect the welfare of the resources on which we depend to conduct recreational and educational activities.

One of the primary concerns of the management agencies discussed in the previous chapter is protection of the environment. One of the most effective tools available to these agencies in protecting the environment is education. Education is an essential tool in helping the public to become good stewards of the natural environment. Outdoor leaders, whether working as river guides, hunting guides, or park rangers, are in a unique position to help fulfill the goal of environmental preservation through education. This chapter focuses on **environmental interpretation** and environmental education as two means for accomplishing the goal of environmental preservation through education. It focuses on the role of education in fostering responsible stewardship of our natural environment.

Environmental Ethics

Matre (1990) indicates that there are two prevailing views of the world. One is the cornucopian view of the world as a horn of plenty that will always yield resources to satisfy human needs. Continual technological advancements in such fields as agriculture during the past 200 years affirm this view. This view is based on the classical liberal, progressive ideology on which the United States was founded. The other view is of the world as a finite vessel with limited resources. The idea is that humans must learn to temper their appetite for the earth's resources in order to ensure the existence of an environment that can sustain the life of humans and all other species on earth for generations to come.

When exploration and settlement of the American West began in the early 1800s, the continent was seen as a vast expanse that would take centuries to populate. Settlers exceeded those expectations in less than a century, and in 1893, famous historian Frederick Jackson Turner declared the western frontier closed. No longer was the West seen as an endless frontier with an endless supply of resources. The frontier was disappearing. Americans were becoming aware of the limitations of the North American continent during this time. Individuals like John Muir became champions of environmental preservation, and groups like the Appalachian Mountain Club (est. 1876), the American Canoe Association (est. 1880), the Sierra Club (est. 1892), and the Colorado Mountain Club (est. 1912) developed from the energies of people concerned about the preservation of America's natural treasures.

The need for protection of natural resources became more and more pronounced as time passed. A broader awareness of the need for preservation, not just in national parks but also in all natural and backcountry areas, began to grow during the late 19th century and throughout the 20th century. Rachel Carson's *Silent Spring* (1962) and Aldo Leopold's *A Sand County Almanac* (1949), among others, began to point to the perils of environmental neglect and pollution. These writers began laying the groundwork for a new environmental ethic, one promoting an ethic of environmental stewardship. The publication of *Silent Spring* actually is widely viewed as the birth of the modern environmental movement.

How you view the world—as a horn of plenty or as a finite vessel—dictates the ethic that you adopt in your relationship with the natural environment. In chapter 7, we learned that ethics is a code of conduct. Ethics involves three interdependent elements: an ideal, the precepts of rational ethics, and the imperfect self—us. The ideal in the case of someone who views the world as a finite vessel is ecological sustainability. As John Muir, Aldo

Leopold, Rachel Carson, and other denizens of the environmental movement would argue, the ideal relationship between humanity and the natural world is one of ecological harmony and balance. The ideal relationship between humanity and the natural world is based on an ethic of stewardship, so that we do not degrade the health of the natural environment and consequently our own health as humans. The precepts of rational ethics represent the code of conduct that enables us to achieve the ideal. We may never fully achieve the ideal of ecological sustainability, but the point is that we should be constantly striving to achieve it. We should all be striving to serve as responsible stewards of the natural environment.

In the case of outdoor leadership, we teach the seven principles of Leave No Trace for the sake of minimizing our impact on the environment. If we adhere to the code of conduct embodied in these seven principles, we can contribute to the ideal of ecological sustainability in our practice as outdoor leaders. We can help foster an ethic of ecological responsibility and environmental stewardship among program participants. If we do not adhere to this code of conduct, then we forfeit an opportunity to make a difference. We forfeit an opportunity to influence the way in which society views and interacts with the natural environment. One of the advantages that we have as outdoor leaders is that direct experience with the natural environment is one of the most effective ways to help people develop a caring relationship with the natural environment.

Environmental preservation continues to be a prominent concern, maybe more so today than at any other time in history. Prevalent issues in 2005 range from whether snowmobiles should be allowed into national parks to whether exploration and drilling for oil should be allowed in the Arctic National Wildlife Refuge (ANWR). Other controversial issues during the 1990s and the first decade of the 21st century include logging in the Pacific Northwest, restoration of fisheries and waterways through dam removals along rivers in both the eastern and western United States, and the preservation of roadless areas.

Caribou graze in the Arctic National Wildlife Refuge.

The debate over environmental preservation has come to extend beyond the debate over how national parks and public lands should be used (e.g., grazing, mineral, water, and logging rights). Debate has also come to extend beyond such hot-button issues as logging in Tongass National Forest and drilling for oil in ANWR. It has extended to a much more global concern, specifically, global climate change resulting from human activities. Concerns over pollutants that humans are generating, such as emissions from automobiles and coal-burning power plants, have taken center stage and have generated a great deal of debate.

Ecological Literacy

According to Matre, Public Law 91-516, the Environmental Quality Education Act, states, "The Congress of the United States finds that the deterioration of the quality of the Nation's environment and its ecological balance poses a serious threat to the strength and vitality of the people of the Nation and is in part due to poor understanding of the Nation's environment and of the need for ecological balance" (1990, p. 3). To what extent are citizens of the United States and other nations around the world aware of the dilemmas posed by environmental degradation? To what extent are people aware of their relationship to the natural environment? Where do the food in our refrigerators, the furniture in our houses, and the energy that powers our homes and cars come from? To what extent are people aware of the effects of environmental degradation on our lifestyles now and in the future? Natural resources play a critical role in the life of the United States and the world. This includes not simply those resources under the jurisdiction of our government and those on which we rely for outdoor education and recreation opportunities. It includes the health of the overall natural environment, the water that we drink, the air that we breathe, and the food that we eat.

Thomas Jefferson once famously commented, "Were it left to me to decide whether we should have a government without newspapers or newspapers without a government, I would not hesitate for a moment to prefer the latter. . . . But I should mean that every [person] shall receive these papers and be capable of reading them" (Boyd 1950, p. 49). Jefferson considered literacy an essential element of a successful democracy. Without the ability to remain informed about the affairs of society, individuals are unable to partici-pate in determining the direction of society. They are unable to govern themselves and instead must trust the decisions of others.

There are four basic forms of literacy: conventional literacy, functional literacy, cultural literacy, and critical literacy (Tozer, Violas, and Senese 1998). Conventional literacy is simply the ability to read and write a simple message in any language. According to the U.S. Census Bureau, nearly all Americans are considered to be literate under this definition of literacy (Tozer, Violas, and Senese 1998). Clearly, this definition has limitations.

Functional literacy is defined as the ability to use written and printed language to accomplish certain goals and to function in society. This definition creates a higher standard for literacy than conventional literacy, but it also has limitations.

Cultural literacy refers to more than a simple understanding of the written word for the sake of performing tasks or functioning in society. It refers to the ability to understand and communicate more broadly within or across particular cultural frameworks. Sharing a common language, heritage or ancestry, and customs and traditions are elements of participation in a cultural framework. Understanding what is meant by the phrase *Cinco de Mayo,* for example, would indicate a certain level of literacy within Mexican culture. This means understanding that *Cinco de Mayo,* the 5th of May, commemorates the victory of the Mexican army over the French army at the Battle of Puebla in 1862. This also means understanding the historical, economic, and political circumstances surrounding this battle.

Critical literacy is the most sophisticated of these definitions of literacy. It refers to more than the ability to understand what is written and to participate in a particular cultural discourse. It refers to the ability to critically analyze what is written as well as to critically analyze cultural frameworks and discourses. It refers not only to the ability to read but the ability to read between the lines about what is going on in a society for the sake of becoming a critical, conscientious participant in that society.

Ecological literacy is a form of critical literacy. It refers to our understanding of the natural world and our place within that world. It refers to the ability to make good decisions regarding our relationship with the natural world. It also refers to our ability to engage in intelligent action that allows us to avoid harming the environment. Ecological literacy can only be gained through

Learning Activity 14.1

1. Identify an environmental issue (e.g., forest management, wildlife management, soil erosion, pollution).

2. Explore the nature of the issue (i.e., history, contributing factors, stakeholders).

3. Brainstorm potential approaches to addressing the issue.

4. Decide on the best approach and develop an action plan. This plan can address the issue on a local, regional, national, or global level.

5. Implement the plan.

6. Evaluate the effects of the action.

a critical understanding of the environment. It cannot be gained if we allow ourselves to remain ignorant about the environment. In a democratic society such as ours, we each hold a responsibility as citizens to become aware of our relationship with our natural environment because we hold a responsibility to determine the nature of our relationship with the environment. Our environment is essentially our lifeblood. The future of the world will be determined greatly by the way in which we treat our environment. We are forfeiting our rights as citizens and neglecting our responsibilities to one another and to future generations if we neglect our responsibility to the environment.

Volk (1993) identifies five levels of learning for ecological literacy:

- Environmental sensitivity
- In-depth knowledge of issues
- Issue investigation skills (i.e., scientific-inquiry or problem-solving skills)
- Citizenship skills (i.e., civic responsibility to address environmental issues)
- Internal locus of control (i.e., the sense that you can make a difference)

Volk also identifies four curriculum levels that correspond to these five levels of learning. The first is the ecological foundation level, which involves "developing sufficient ecological knowledge to make sound decisions with respect to ecological issues." The second is the conceptual awareness level (issues and values), which refers to "how individual and collective actions influence quality of life and quality of the environment." The third is the investigation and evaluation level,

which refers to the "knowledge and skills necessary to investigate and evaluate problems and solutions." The fourth is the environmental action level, which involves "training in and applying skills necessary to take positive environmental action" (pp. 56-57).

Environmental Preservation Through Education

Outdoor leaders attempt to develop ecological literacy in program participants through two primary ways: environmental interpretation and environmental education. Our use of the phrase *environmental interpretation* in this text refers to both natural interpretation and cultural interpretation. Natural interpretation entails educating participants about the natural environment. Cultural interpretation entails educating participants about the human history of a particular area. Environmental education is aimed at "raising sensitivity, awareness, and understanding of linkages and interdependencies among human beings and the natural world in which they live" (Biderman and Bosak 1997, p. 93).

Environmental Interpretation

Jake offers a good example of the role of an outdoor leader as interpreter. Jake shares information about the natural and cultural history of the New River Gorge with his guests, enriching the quality of their experience. Wittingly or not, Jake is also helping his guests to develop a greater appreciation for the New River Gorge than they would without his interpretation of the natural and cultural history of the gorge. Developing this sense of appreciation for a place is essential to inspiring a sense of responsibility for the health of the place.

What Is Environmental Interpretation?

Interpretation is communication. It is the communication of technical information in nontechnical terms that a general audience can understand (Ham 1992). Interpretation is practiced in many fields. Lawyers interpret legal terminology and describe the workings of the legal system in ways that their clients can understand. Medical doctors interpret medical terminology and describe the workings of the human body in ways that their patients can understand. Religious leaders interpret scripture in ways that make it meaningful in the lives of their followers. Likewise, outdoor leaders interpret the surrounding environment in ways that make the outdoor experience more meaningful to their participants.

Sharpe (1976) defines interpretation as the communication link between an area's natural and cultural resources and the visitors to the area. The American Association of Museums defines interpretation as "a planned effort to create for the visitor an understanding of the history and significance of events, people, and objects with which the site is associated" (Alderson and Low 1985). Freeman Tilden, one of the first people to develop a philosophy of interpretation, defines interpretation as "an educational activity which aims to reveal meanings and relationships through the use of original objects, by firsthand experience, and by illustrative media, rather than to communicate factual information" (1977, p. 8). Though interpretation is based on factual information, effective interpretation involves revealing the relationship of those facts to the broader world in a way that helps the audience to establish a sense of connection to those facts. Tilden states that the true interpreter "goes beyond the apparent to the real, beyond a part to the whole, beyond a truth to a more important truth" (p. 8).

Origins of Interpretation

The practice of environmental interpretation developed during the 20th century, primarily within the National Park Service. In the 1920s, interpreters were commonly referred to as lecturers or nature guides (Knudson, Cable, and Beck 1999). Many of the original interpreters in national parks were college professors who spent their summers lecturing on the natural heritage of the parks. Enos Mills, who led the effort to establish Rocky Mountain National Park, used the term *nature guide* to describe his work in educating his clients about the Colorado Rockies on hikes to the top of Longs Peak near Estes Park, Colorado. Mills describes the role of the nature guide as follows:

> The nature guide is at his best when he discusses facts so that they appeal to the imagination and to the reason, gives flesh and blood to cold facts, makes life stories of inanimate objects. He deals with principles rather than isolated information, gives biographies rather than classifications. People are out for recreation and need restful, intellectual visions, and not dull, dry facts, rules, and manuals. What the guide says is essentially nature literature rather than encyclopedic natural history. (1920, pp. 186-187)

Mills (1920) further notes that nature guiding has been incidental to all other kinds of guiding. Distinguishing between nature guiding and other types of guiding, however, he states: "The hunter's chief aim is to kill the bear, while that of the nature guide is to watch the ways of the bear and to enjoy them. . . . A nature guide is a naturalist who can guide others to the secrets of nature" (1920,

Ralph White, manager of the James River Park System in Richmond, Virginia, leads an interpretive tour in the park.

This interpretive sign marks a trailhead along the Colorado Trail, which stretches from Denver to Durango.

pp. 244-245). Nature guiding was in its infancy in the 1920s, when it was established as a formal position in the newly created National Park Service. Mills and others accurately anticipated its growth as a profession, speculating that it would eventually rank alongside such professions as teaching and nursing.

Mills is one of the first individuals to use the terms *interpreter* and *naturalist* to describe the nature of his work in educating the public about the natural environment. The term *interpretation* grew in popularity in the 1930s as the practice grew to include historical and cultural interpretation as well as natural interpretation. The term *naturalist* became popular in the 1930s as well, when the Indiana State Parks system began using that term in place of the term *nature guide* (Knudson, Cable, and Beck 1999). Though the terms *naturalist* and *interpreter* are sometimes used synonymously, interpretation eventually became the dominant term in describing the practice. The creation of the Association for Interpretive Naturalists and the Western Interpreters Association in the early 1960s gave the term *interpreter* professional recognition (Knudson, Cable, and Beck 1999). These associations joined in 1987 to become the National Association for Interpretation. The Canadian counterpart to this organization is Interpretation Canada.

Goals of Interpretation

Environmental interpretation is an aspect of environmental communication whose goals are recreationally oriented. The goal of environmental interpretation is not to meet particular content objectives in sharing information with an audience but to rouse the interest of a noncaptive audience for the sake of inspiring further inquiry on the part of the audience. The goal of interpretation is to help people to better appreciate and enjoy the environments in which they live and travel. It allows people to better understand their natural and cultural heritage. Knudson, Cable, and Beck (1999) note that the primary purpose of interpretation is to enrich the recreational experiences of individuals. They also note, however, that another motive of interpretation "is to lead people to greater concern and intelligent action to sustain the natural and cultural environment in which people live" (1999, p. 6). They assert that "interpretation, properly carried out, serves as an indispensable tool to achieve successful, intelligent cultural and natural resource stewardship" (1999, p. 12).

Principles of Interpretation

Four basic principles lie beneath the practice of environmental interpretation: relating interpretation to experience, using facts to reveal a larger picture, drawing connections among disciplines, and stimulating the interest of the audience. These principles are based on the principles for interpretation developed by Tilden (1977) and Ham (1992). We see Jake employing all of these principles in his interpretive talk while raft guiding in the New River Gorge.

Relating Interpretation to Experience Interpretation should somehow relate the matter being interpreted to the experiences of the audience. Jake does this by framing the life of the New River Gorge in terms of the broader economic development of the nation. He presents a comprehensive story with which most audiences can identify. The Industrial Revolution was central to the economic development of the United States in the late 19th and early 20th centuries. By illustrating the role that coal from the New River Gorge played in the Industrial Revolution and in the lives of people who lived and worked in the gorge, Jake offers his guests a basis for connection to the history of the gorge.

Using Facts to Reveal a Larger Picture Interpretation is not based on facts alone, though it relies on facts to reveal a larger picture. Interpretive talks are not simply based on a series of unrelated topics but on an underlying theme that draws these topics together into a unified story. Knudson, Cable, and Beck (1999) discuss interpretive themes in terms of the principle of *genius loci.* *Loci* means place, and *genius* refers to what makes the place special or unique. Knudson, Cable, and Beck state the following:

> Each park, forest, museum, camp, historic building, and cave has its own characteristic value and uniqueness. A site may be representative of an ecological, geographic, historic, or architectural phenomenon. A visitor should have the central experience of understanding these special or representative values. The interpreter explains and translates the values to the visitor, thus enriching the experience by presenting the essence of the reason for the property's designation or existence. (1999, p. 148)

Jake integrates several strands of factual information together in bringing the New River Gorge to life in the minds of his guests. The underlying thread that draws all of these facts together, the genius loci on which Jake bases his interpretive talk, is coal.

Drawing Connections Among Disciplines Interpretation is based on multiple disciplines. In outdoor leadership, effective interpretation entails developing an understanding of the plant and animal life in particular ecosystems. It entails developing knowledge of the geologic history of an area for the sake of sharing information on the formation of landscapes and their geological features. It entails developing knowledge of the human, or cultural, history of an area for the sake of sharing information on the consequences of interactions between humans and their environment. Jake weaves together all of these disciplines

and more in telling the story of the New River Gorge.

Stimulating the Audience's Interest The primary goal of interpretation is to stimulate the interest and curiosity of the audience regarding the subject at hand. It is not educational in a formal sense. Jake attempts to determine the interests of his guests each day. Each group is different. Some are more interested in instigating water fights and telling jokes than in hearing about the history of the New River Gorge. Others are fascinated with the stories Jake tells and yearn for more. Jake tries to indulge the different interests of his guests, yet he tries to stimulate their interest in the gorge.

Interpretive Media

Three basic types of media are commonly used in environmental interpretation: personal media, written media, and audiovisual media. These types of interpretive media are often used to complement one another in an interpretive program.

Some of the more common forms of personal media in interpretation include desk duty in an information or nature center, interpretive talks (which are often accompanied by visual media such as slide shows), campfire programs, interpretive or guided hikes, and living interpretation (e.g., demonstrations, reenactments).

Written media in interpretation include such items as brochures, trail guides, campground bulletin boards, exhibits and displays, books, maps, newsletters, and newspapers. Written materials are scripts that tell the story of a place. Scripts

Learning Activity 14.2

1. Identify an important site in your region.

2. Make a list of the site's natural and historic features (i.e., the basis of its name, its history, and so on).

3. Identify at least one major theme (related to the genius loci of the place) that can be used to draw these facts into an interpretive program (i.e., a story of the site) with which people can identify and connect. What makes the place unique?

4. Develop at least two forms of interpretive media by which to convey your program (i.e., lecture, learning activities, self-guided media).

5. Create a list of interpretive activities (i.e., junior ranger programs, reenactments, slide shows).

6. Create a method for evaluating your interpretive program.

can be written for different types of presentations. They can be packaged in different ways and made to fit the particular form of media that the interpreter intends to use.

Video and audio recordings and combinations of the two are also frequently used as interpretive tools. Orientation videos, videos for auditoriums, and souvenir videos or audio recordings are all examples. Audiovisual interpretive programs are usually found in information and visitor centers. They can also sometimes be found along self-guiding trails.

Interpretation has been conducted for centuries through the writings of such individuals as Henry David Thoreau, Ralph Waldo Emerson, John Muir, Enos Mills, Aldo Leopold, Rachel Carlson, Edward Abby, and a host of others. Many people have learned to love and appreciate places that they have never seen through the inspirational accounts of such authors. Such authors have provided us with opportunities to experience places vicariously through their own experiences and insights. Modern interpretation, however, typically involves direct experience in the place that is the subject of interpretation. This is especially true in the case of outdoor leadership. Like Jake, the outdoor leader takes individuals into natural environments that are the subject of interpretation.

As an outdoor leader, you may think of yourself as limited solely to personal interpretive media—your voice—in conveying the significance of a place. Remember, however, that you have a powerful visual resource available: You have the environment in which you are traveling, the actual place that you are attempting to interpret. You may find yourself relying on your own voice as the primary means of interpretation, but you also have your surrounding environment as a visual complement. Jake sometimes finds himself parking his raft and exploring the ruins of the old ghost towns with his guests. They actually peer into the coke ovens that were used to refine coal that was mined from the gorge so many years ago. They see the foundation of Colonel Beury's house, which was destroyed by a fire in the 1930s.

You may also find yourself relying on written media in developing your knowledge of the area in which you are working. Jake read several books on the history and ecology of the New River Gorge to develop his knowledge of the area and to develop a script as the basis for his interpretive talk. In addition, the rafting company for which Jake works requires each of its guides to write an essay every year on some aspect of the cultural or natural history of the gorge. These essays are compiled into a collection that serves as a resource for guides in learning about the gorge.

Controversial Issues in Interpretation

Recognize the potential for controversy in your interpretive program. Native–nonnative issues, racial issues, environmental issues, religious issues, and political issues all provide fertile ground for controversy. It is often difficult to speak about a topic without bringing up controversial issues related to the topic. Be wary, though, in taking sides on controversial issues. Despite your personal beliefs, take an objective stance as a leader. You may otherwise create unneeded and unwanted barriers between you and your audience. This cautionary note is not to suggest that you should avoid discussing controversial issues. If you were to avoid controversial issues altogether, you would be left with little to discuss. The point is to discuss these issues in a moderate, tempered manner. Be careful not to alienate your audience through proselytizing or through taking a dogmatic view of an issue. Recognize and show respect toward opposing viewpoints before you take a stand. Show your rationale as well as your conviction in taking a stand.

Environmental Education

To this point, this chapter has focused on environmental interpretation as a means of inspiring a sense of responsibility for the environment in individuals. Another primary way to accomplish this goal is through environmental education. While environmental interpretation typically occurs in informal outdoor recreational settings, environmental education occurs in more formal educational settings. Examples of these settings include public and private schools, traditional outdoor programs such as Outward Bound and the National Outdoor Leadership School, and outdoor clubs and associations such as the Appalachian Mountain Club and the American Canoe Association. The remainder of this chapter focuses on environmental education as a tool for fostering a sense of ecological responsibility in individuals and promoting an ethic of environmental stewardship in our society.

What Is Environmental Education?

Sharpe (1976) states that it is difficult to distinguish between environmental interpretation and environmental education. He suggests that environmental education is an extension of envi-

This sign helps visitors to recognize and prevent further ecological damage in Rocky Mountain National Park.

ronmental interpretation: "Most writers strive to say that interpretation differs from education, yet is educational . . . the interpreter, although pedagogical, is not pedantic. Interpretation differs from schooling. Yet, people learn from it" (Knudson, Cable, and Beck 1999, p. 164). The difference is seen in their methods and in the contexts in which they are practiced. Matre defines a genuine environmental education program as "a carefully crafted, focused series of sequential, cumulative learning experiences designed with specific outcomes in mind" (1990, p. 17).

Ford (1981) notes that *conservation education* is the phrase most commonly used in outdoor education literature between 1930 and 1970 when referring to the concept of environmental education. The use of this phrase declined in the 1970s, however, because of its limited scope. Conservation education refers only to judicious use of natural resources. Environmental education is broader in scope, as the next paragraph explains.

As noted in chapter 1, Priest and Gass (1997) state that environmental education is concerned with two types of relationships: ecosystemic relationships and ekistic relationships. Ecosystemic relationships refer to the general interdependence of organisms within an ecological framework. Ekistic relationships refer more specifically to human interactions with the natural world, or the role of humans within the broader ecological framework. Ford defines ekistics as a way of life. She states, "It is a philosophy that incorporates understanding of natural resources, human resources, and culture as an interrelated whole. It is a way of looking at the interrelatedness of nature, humanity, and culture as a holistic concept that, when acted on, leads to world survival" (1981, p. 108). Environmental education is focused on how ecosystems function, the role of humans in those ecosystems, and what humans can do to create a healthier, sustainable role within those systems (i.e., how we can minimize our negative effects on the earth).

Goals of Environmental Education

As mentioned, a cautionary note for interpreters is to take care not to alienate audiences through sermonizing or proselytizing regarding controversial environmental and cultural issues. The environmental educator, on the other hand, may wish to take the opposite approach. Influencing and changing the attitudes and values of students may be exactly what the environmental educator hopes to accomplish. Teaching students to think critically about the environment and to make their own choices regarding environmental action may be the goal for some educators. Other educators may teach their students through indoctrination to prize the environment first and foremost. Ideally, ecological literacy makes its way into the curriculum at some point. Matre (1990) argues that the point of environmental education is change. He states, "Environmental education that just educates people about the environment, without asking them to make some changes in their own lives, is not environmental education, it's natural science" (p. 21). Within the context of outdoor leadership, environmental education is used to minimize ecological impact of humans in natural areas.

Approaches to Environmental Education

Hutchinson states, "Environmental education curricula and outdoor experiential programs constitute the largest proportion of attempts by educators to address environmental crisis and explore human/earth relations with students" (1998, p. 24). He identifies three primary approaches to environmental education: a supplemental approach, an infusionist approach, and an intensive experience approach. He argues that experiential education is the most appropriate method for teaching students about the environment.

Supplemental Approach Supplemental approaches to environmental education complement larger educational curricula in public and private schools and are used by teachers with experience in environmental education. They represent an attempt to incorporate environmental education into the curricula of schools. Project Learning Tree in the United States and Project Wild in Canada are two popular supplemental approaches to teaching environmental education. While many of these programs have gained a great deal of popularity, they are also criticized for failing to create focused environmental education programs that systematically address the subject (Matre 1990). The occasional environmental education unit presented by only a few conscientious teachers is not enough to address growing environmental problems around the world. Others argue that every little bit helps.

Infusionist Approach An infusionist approach incorporates environmental education into existing content areas (e.g., math, biology, and so on). This is a process-oriented approach to environmental education in which every part of the curriculum is drawn together under a concern for the environment. The environment serves as the overarching theme under which all subjects are taught. It is similar to the supplemental approach but is on a broader scale. Expeditionary Learning Outward Bound employs this approach through the thematic units that serve as the basis for teaching subject matter (for example, rainforests). This approach is criticized because it supposedly fails to offer "focused, sequential, cumulative environmental education programming" (Matre 1990, p. 5). It may be seen as a fragmented, diffuse, and scattershot approach to environmental education.

Intensive Experience Approach An intensive experience approach would consist of a multiday program focusing primarily on environmental education. Outward Bound, the National Outdoor Leadership School (NOLS), and the Wilderness Education Association (WEA) are examples

of organizations that use this approach. The environmental education components of NOLS and WEA are based on the principles of Leave No Trace.

Leave No Trace

Leave No Trace was established in 1990 as a joint endeavor between NOLS and the United States Forest Service (USFS) (Marion and Reid 2001). USFS commissioned NOLS to develop Leave No Trace as an experiential program focusing on environmental ethics. The first courses were taught in the Wind River Mountains of Wyoming in 1991. The curriculum proved a success, and in 1994 the Bureau of Land Management, the National Park Service, and the U.S. Fish and Wildlife Service joined the partnership. To reach a broader constituency and to become more economically viable, the Leave No Trace program eventually separated from NOLS and became an entity of its own based in Boulder, Colorado. It is now known as the Leave No Trace Center for Outdoor Ethics (the Center) and has since developed partnerships with land management agencies, outdoor equipment manufacturers, outdoor retailers, media, conservation groups, recreation groups, organizations, clubs, outdoor educators, and individuals who share a commitment to maintaining, preserving, and protecting natural lands. The mission of the Center is to promote and inspire responsible outdoor recreation through education, research, and partnerships.

The Center offers three types of courses and workshops: the master educator course, the trainer course, and awareness workshops. The master educator course is the most extensive of these. It is a course for those who intend to actively teach Leave No Trace to others. The course involves a classroom component along with 4 days of instruction in a backcountry setting. The trainer course is a condensed version of the master educator course. The trainer course is conducted by master educators and is designed for people who are interested in Leave No Trace principles and practices for backcountry use. Workshops are any session in the Leave No Trace principles and practices that are a day or less in length.

The primary purpose of the Leave No Trace curriculum is to promote the responsible use of natural resources for

A group gathers on a durable surface in the Colorado Canyons National Conservation Area.

Leave No Trace

1. Plan ahead and prepare.
2. Travel and camp on durable surfaces.
3. Dispose of waste properly.
4. Leave what you find.
5. Minimize campfire impacts.
6. Respect wildlife.
7. Be considerate of other visitors.

Figure 14.1 Leave No Trace ethics.

recreational purposes. The curriculum is based on seven principles (see figure 14.1).

- Plan ahead and prepare. A well-planned trip minimizes the chance of a crisis arising during the trip. This idea applies not only to personal safety of participants engaging in outdoor pursuits, it also applies to safety of the environment. The avoidance of personal injury can also help prevent damage to the environment that might result from a rescue situation where the welfare of humans typically trumps the welfare of the environment. A well-planned trip also entails knowing where you are going and exercising proper navigation so that you do not wander aimlessly off trail, compacting ground surfaces that would otherwise go untouched.

- Travel and camp on durable surfaces. One of the primary forms of ecological impact from recreational and educational use of natural environments is soil compaction and its consequent problems. This principle is aimed at minimizing compaction.

- Dispose of waste properly. Another primary form of ecological impact from recreational and educational use of natural environments is the introduction of nutrients, pathogens, and other pollutants into water sources. Proper waste disposal, whether it is food waste or biological waste, is aimed at minimizing this impact. It is also aimed at minimizing the risk of animal encounters, which could negatively affect both humans and animals.

- Leave what you find. This refers to flora, fauna, rocks, and so forth. The goal of this principle is to give other visitors the gift of discovery.

- Minimize campfire impacts. Outdoor leaders should encourage participants to avoid the use of fires in backcountry settings unless they are absolutely necessary for safety purposes. If campfires are built, proper protocol should be followed to minimize their impact.

- Respect wildlife. Another ecological impact resulting from recreational and educational use of natural areas is disturbance and sometimes death of wildlife. Disturbance can mean interruption of feeding, breeding, and other wildlife habits, which can negatively impact the welfare of wildlife. Death of wildlife results primarily from hunting, which is considered a recreational activity by many. Hunters who respect wildlife, however, are careful not to take careless shots at animals, shots that might simply wound an animal as opposed to killing it. Wounded animals are often difficult to track and find. Sometimes they are lost and suffer needlessly and their bounty goes unused. This principle is aimed at minimizing this impact on the environment.

- Be considerate of other visitors. One of the concepts addressed in the previous chapter is psychological carrying capacity. This refers to the effects of visitors on one another. This concept was also addressed in chapter 10 in the discussion of expedition behavior. This principle is aimed at minimizing our impact on one another as visitors to public areas.

Summary

One of the most powerful tools available to outdoor leaders in striving to fulfill the goal of environmental preservation is education. The two primary means through which outdoor leaders attempt to accomplish this goal are environmental interpretation and environmental education. The ultimate goal of both environmental interpretation and education is the development of ecological literacy in individuals. Ecological literacy is essential to becoming good stewards of the natural environment.

In considering your own development as a leader, ask yourself the following questions. What are your beliefs regarding the ways we interact with our natural environment? Do you

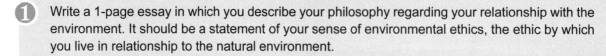

Professional-Development Portfolio Activities

1. Write a 1-page essay in which you describe your philosophy regarding your relationship with the environment. It should be a statement of your sense of environmental ethics, the ethic by which you live in relationship to the natural environment.

2. Create and lead an interpretive or environmental education activity during a scheduled class period. Receive feedback on the effectiveness of the activity from two of your classmates.

perceive the environment as a horn of plenty or as a finite vessel? What environmental issues are historically and currently significant in your area? How knowledgeable are you about these issues? What actions have you taken in addressing the issues? What impact do you have on your surrounding environment? What impact do you have on natural areas that you use for outdoor education and recreation activities? As an outdoor leader, to what extent do you incorporate the principles and practices of Leave No Trace into your outdoor education and recreation program activities?

Selected References

Alderson, W.T., and S.P. Low. 1985. *Interpretation of historic sites.* 2nd ed. Nashville: American Association for State and Local History.

Biderman, A., and W. Bosak. 1997. Environmental education in protected areas as a contribution to heritage conservation, tourism, and sustainable development. In *National parks and protected areas: Keystones to conservation and sustainable development,* ed. J.G. Nelson. Berlin: Springer.

Boyd, J.P., ed. 1950. *The papers of Thomas Jefferson.* Vol. 2. Princeton, NJ: Princeton University Press.

Carson, R. 1962. *Silent spring.* Boston: Houghton Mifflin.

Ford, P. 1981. *Principles and practices of outdoor/ environmental education.* New York: Wiley.

Ham, S. 1992. *Environmental interpretation: A practical guide for people with big ideas and small budgets.* Golden, CO: North American Press.

Hutchinson, D. 1998. *Growing up green: Education for ecological renewal.* New York: Teachers College Press.

Knudson, D.M., T.T. Cable, and L. Beck. 1999. *Interpretation of cultural and natural resources.* State College, PA: Venture.

Leopold, A. 1949. *A Sand County almanac.* New York: Oxford University Press.

Marion, J.L., and S.E. Reid. 2001. Development of the U.S. Leave No Trace program: An historical perspective. Leave No Trace Center for Outdoor Ethics Web site: www.lnt.org. Boulder, CO.

Matre, S.V. 1990. *Earth education: A new beginning.* Greenville, WV: Institute for Earth Education.

Mills, E.A. 1920. *The adventures of a nature guide.* Garden City, NY: Doubleday.

Priest, S., and M.A. Gass. 1997. *Effective leadership in adventure programming.* Champaign, IL: Human Kinetics.

Sharpe, G.W. 1976. Selecting interpretive media. In *Interpreting the environment,* ed. G.W. Sharpe. New York: Wiley.

Smith, G.A., and D.R. Williams. 1999. Re-engaging culture and ecology. In *Ecological education in action: On weaving education, culture, and the environment,* ed. G.A. Smith and D.R. Williams. New York: State University of New York Press.

Tilden, F. 1977. *Interpreting our heritage.* 3rd ed. Chapel Hill, NC: University of North Carolina Press.

Tozer, S.E., P.C. Violas, and G. Senese. 1998. *School and society: Historical and contemporary perspectives.* 3rd ed. Boston: McGraw-Hill.

Volk, T. 1993. Educating for responsible environmental behavior. In *Environmental education teacher resource handbook: A practical guide for K-12 environmental education,* ed. R.J. Wilke. Millwood, NY: Kraus International.

chapter 15

Program Management

© Sport the Library

" If you do not change, you can become extinct. " —**Spencer Johnson**

Chapter Concepts

- Program manager and program supervisor—This chapter uses these terms interchangeably. Outdoor leaders often have management responsibilities beyond leading trips in the field.
- Program management and program administration—This chapter uses these terms interchangeably. Both refer to the administrative procedures conducted by a program manager to ensure safe, enjoyable, and environmentally sound adventures.
- Program design—Program design refers to the larger program structure (macro program) within an outdoor organization. Program design on a macro level includes trips, activities, and other programming services that combine to form the larger programming structure.
- Trip plan or activity plan—This refers to the formal process of planning specific trips or activities (micro programs) within the context of the larger program design. Refer to chapter 17 for an in-depth discussion of trip planning.

The chapter concepts relate to the following core competencies:

- Program management (CC-6)—Outdoor leaders must be familiar with the skills of planning and implementing adventure experiences.
- Safety and risk management (CC-7)—Having the skills and knowledge to manage risks associated with adventure programs is an important part of outdoor leadership.

With his outdoor recreation degree in hand and 2 years of commercial guiding experience, Devon landed the perfect job. A large, for-profit organization offered him the position of adventure programming director. Devon could not believe his great fortune. Since his first year of college, Devon had aspired to work in a resort setting. When Bushwood, Inc., made the offer, he accepted without hesitation. Bushwood held the reputation as one of the oldest and most exclusive family mountain resorts in the Northern Rocky Mountains. Bushwood offered all the traditional activities such as golf, skiing, horseback riding, hiking, spas, fine dining, and social events. Devon was charged with instituting a new high adventure program, the first of its kind at Bushwood.

Devon's peers viewed him as a gifted technician. He had obtained technical proficiency in many areas. White-water boating came easily as well as technical rock climbing. Devon had no problems boating class IV white water or leading 5.10 traditional rock-climbing routes. He had been mountaineering since he was 12 and won the national junior championship in mountain biking. Devon's résumé of technical abilities far exceeded the average skill level of other applicants. The administration at Bushwood hired Devon based on this impressive array of skills. In addition, references verified Devon's leadership ability. Devon had acquired excellent trip-leading experience over the past 6 years.

He was perfectly poised to take on this exciting new position—or so he thought!

Devon's first day on the job began several weeks before the busy season. Meeting with his supervisor, Trish, was first on the agenda. Trish was the recreation director for the resort. Trish had accumulated many years of experience as a program administrator. While she knew little about white-water boating, climbing, mountaineering, and mountain biking, she was familiar with other adventure activities such as horseback riding and snow skiing. Trish depended on Devon to know the specifics of the new adventure activities. Trish first asked Devon his vision for overall program design and what documents he would need to compile. Devon looked puzzled and said he would have to think about that. Trish then asked what his format would be for staff training. Devon knew he would receive the assistance of three seasonal staff members but had not contemplated staff training or orientation. Trish followed with questions about equipment needs and an inventory system. Then she asked about national standards and which organizations might eventually accredit the program, and she asked about marketing and program promotion. Devon became less and less confident as questions were fired his way. Finally, Trish asked what system would best evaluate the success of his new program. Devon was at a loss for answers. He had no clue how to evaluate the program. In that

(continued)

moment, Devon felt completely inadequate as an outdoor leader.

At first, Trish was baffled by Devon's inability to answer. Then she realized that Devon possessed no program management skills. After making this realization, Trish relaxed and sensed Devon's devastation. Trish acknowledged that they needed to rethink Devon's program development strategy. Devon sat in disbelief that he would be responsible for these details. He explained that his academic preparation did not include program management. He spent his personal time perfecting technical skills, not administrative skills. He could create an expedition plan but had never designed a comprehensive program plan. Of course he had been through staff trainings and administered trip evaluations, but he never envisioned that one day he would be responsible for an evaluation system. He simply saw program evaluations as one of those bothersome jobs a leader must conduct at the end of a trip. Devon apologized for his lack of knowledge and asked, "Where do we go from here?"

Trish also apologized by stating that Bushwood human resource department focused solely on Devon's technical skills rather than his administrative ability. Bushwood fell into the trap of searching for the best technical expert for their guests, neglecting the administrative expertise necessary to operate the new program. Trish went on to explain that her supervisor expected all programs to be evaluated. Poor evaluations usually meant program elimination or restructuring. Positive evaluations meant more resource allocation and possible wage increases. Her supervisor also expected resort equipment to be inventoried for accounting and safety purposes. In addition, Devon would be expected to work with the resort marketing director to promote the new program. Devon began to see the big picture of skills needed to operate an adventure program. He realized that some important outdoor leadership skills were not to be found on the water, rock, or snow. Administrative skills compose a critical leadership function in outdoor programs.

Aspiring outdoor leaders should not dismiss the importance of program management. Quality outdoor programming requires leaders to exercise vital administrative functions. Most novice outdoor leaders find themselves attracted to professional positions glamorized by incredible adventures in wild places. The prospect of climbing remote mountains and paddling pristine rivers clouds the reality of leadership responsibilities. Most novice leaders do not think about the administrative duties necessary to implement safe, enjoyable, and environmentally sound outdoor adventures. As in Devon's case, critical administrative tasks are required to operate an outdoor program. Areas such as personnel management, record keeping, inventory systems, and program evaluation must be addressed on an administrative level. A leader's attention to these areas helps ensure quality programs. Competent outdoor leaders understand the importance of developing administrative skills along with technical skills. While unglamorous, administrative functions help facilitate a quality experience. Clients and leaders benefit in many ways from the structure of a well-organized program. Most importantly, well-organized programs are safer and are more likely to accomplish goals and objectives. Meeting goals and objectives provides concrete data to document program success.

This chapter discusses vital administrative functions in outdoor program management. Note that administrative duties vary dramatically throughout the industry. For example, an agency's organizational structure dictates how much administrative responsibility an outdoor leader holds. In Devon's situation, the agency expected him to develop and implement administrative duties as well as lead actual trips. Devon could have remained in a field position where all responsibility centered on leading trips with little administrative responsibility. However, basic trip-leading jobs tend to be seasonal and low paying compared to full-time programming positions. Aspiring outdoor leaders wishing to enter the profession as full-time employees should expect administrative responsibilities.

To gain a clearer understanding of program manager positions, two different organizational structures are provided in figures 15.1 and 15.2. Figure 15.1 represents the organizational structure of a commercial business like Bushwood, while figure 15.2 portrays the organizational structure of a typical not-for-profit organization that offers a variety of outdoor adventures. At the lowest level of both structures, trip leaders and seasonal staff can be found. These individuals do not typically oversee program management, although trip leaders must be familiar with

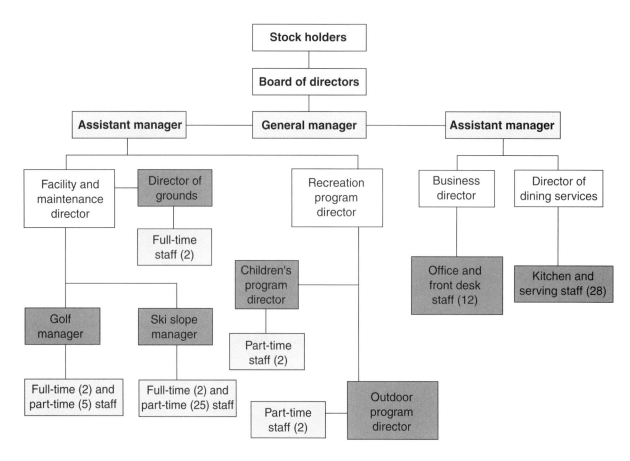

Figure 15.1 Organizational chart for a for-profit business.

administrative procedures in order to assist with implementation. However, outdoor leaders like Devon often find themselves in positions that require program management skills as discussed in this chapter.

This chapter does not indoctrinate the outdoor leader in business management strategies for outdoor organizations. Managing a for-profit business, nonprofit agency, or government-based outdoor program requires a body of knowledge beyond the scope of this text. Budgeting, marketing, public relations, human resources, long-range planning, and more compose management topics that require further study. This chapter focuses on selected program management topics that the average outdoor professional will encounter.

Administrative functions discussed in this chapter represent tasks common to most outdoor adventures. The first topic involves overall program design. Before an individual trip can be developed, the larger program must be put into place. Second, personnel management is discussed. Outdoor leaders may find them-

selves in a supervisory position; therefore, basic personnel management skills merit discussion. The third topic is documentation and record keeping. Outdoor leaders are expected to manage program paperwork. In addition, program marketing and equipment management are discussed as separate topics. Program managers typically oversee equipment needs for the larger programming structure. They also face the possibility of having to sell or promote their programs. Finally, programmers must know how to evaluate program services. Evaluation plays a huge role in documenting program success and instigating improvement.

Program Design

Before leading an outdoor adventure, certain administrative functions must be executed to ensure a safe, quality, enjoyable experience. Administrative procedures provide the organizational structure necessary to plan, implement, and evaluate a program. Program design forms

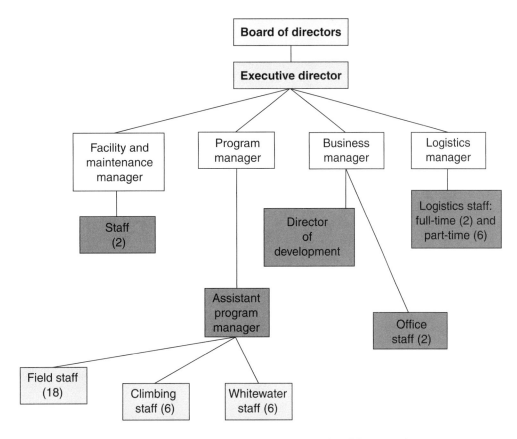

Figure 15.2 Organizational chart for a nonprofit business specializing in wilderness trips.

the cornerstone of program management. Program design influences staffing, budgeting, marketing, trip planning, equipment needs, record keeping, and evaluation systems. These administrative functions evolve in an interdependent process as programs are created. For example, marketing information assists program managers with vital information for program design. Market research that identifies teenagers as potential participants influences program design for youths. An older adult market influences program design another way. As is to be expected, program design varies tremendously throughout the industry based on the diversity of outdoor organizations.

In his new position, Devon was charged with program design and faced diverse programming options. Devon had many programming concerns to resolve on a macro level. **Macro programming** for Devon meant creating the entire adventure program structure. Devon may have been an expert trip planner, but he needed to establish the overall program before focusing on specific trip plans, or the **micro programming.** Trip plans or activity plans must be designed within the context of

larger programming goals and objectives. The outdoor programmer faces many considerations when designing the appropriate program. For example, Devon needed to address the following questions in order to plan on a macro level:

1. What adventure programming activities should he offer and why?

2. What programming formats would be appropriate? One-day or multiday trips? Guided recreation experiences or skill-development workshops?

3. Who is the experience for? Should he meet all ability levels with one trip format or offer specialized trips for beginner, intermediate, and advanced clients? Should experiences be designed for groups only or should private instruction be available?

Program Considerations

Devon had much to consider before planning the actual mountain-biking, kayaking, and mountaineering trips. He needed to create a larger program structure for the new adventure program. The diversity of North American outdoor organizations prevents the development of a generic program format for all programs. Programmers must take into consideration the context of their unique environment. However, generic considerations do exist to provide a framework for program development on a macro level.

Organizational Philosophy

All programs must consider organizational philosophy in the design process. Organizational philosophies differ dramatically based on the organization's purpose. The organizational philosophy is reflected in the organization's mission statement. A well-written mission statement serves as a guide for the development of program goals and objectives throughout the organization. For example, the Bushwood mission statement reads as follows: *Bushwood strives to provide the ultimate mountain vacation experience with special emphasis on family experiences.* Bushwood's philosophy would prompt Devon to provide adventure programs that maximize guests' vacation experience with a focus on relaxation and family enjoyment.

Let's look at another example for clarification. Leaders for a youth-at-risk program would focus on program design that builds self-esteem and appropriate socialization skills. A mission statement for such an organization might read as follows: *To facilitate developmental opportunities through adventure activities so that young people become healthy, functional, and productive members of society.* With a clear mission statement that reflects organizational philosophy, organizational goals and objectives can then be created.

Organizational Goals and Objectives

Programs should reflect overall organizational goals and objectives. Goals and objectives are designed to put organizational philosophy and mission into action. Program services typically form the measurable objectives associated with organizational goals. In Devon's case, Bushwood may have an organizational goal stating that it intends to provide guests with a wide variety of outdoor recreation opportunities. The adventure program becomes a specific program objective to accomplish the larger goal. Devon must first be aware of organizational philosophy and larger organizational goals and objectives before he

begins to create goals and objectives for his adventure program.

Additional Considerations

It should be clear at this point that program managers use organizational philosophy, goals, and objectives to guide their efforts in the programming process. Beyond these guides, programmers must consider other factors before putting together programs. The following list contains design considerations that program managers should take into account. These items also portray common practices of effective programmers.

- Programs should be designed that operate within an organization's budget. Organizations must acquire the financial resources to properly equip, staff, and insure programs. For example, programs that require massive amounts of equipment and large staffs may not be affordable for a small agency.
- Programs should be based on market research or extensive knowledge of the intended participants. Administering a needs assessment is one way to gain participant information. The intended participant population should be surveyed to discover program desires.
- Programs should be designed to be affordable for intended participants. Know the economic status of user groups and their willingness to pay for services.
- Programs should be planned based on participant developmental characteristics. Know the demographic characteristics of clients as well as ability levels.
- Programs should be planned based on current best practices within the industry. Program accreditation standards serve as an excellent source to establish programs.
- Programs should be designed to model the best environmental practices. Professionals planning programs that involve the natural environment have an ethical duty to minimize environmental impact of recreational use. For example, programs can be designed to follow Leave No Trace ethics by limiting the number of people taken to a particular area.
- Programs should be designed to be inclusive in order to facilitate participation by individuals of all abilities and backgrounds. This means making programs accessible and inviting to all potential clients.

Learning Activity 15.1

Design a summer program for Bushwood's new adventure program. Develop the program format to serve families in the areas of rock climbing, white-water boating, mountain biking, hiking, and mountaineering. Be creative in the types of services to be offered. For this exercise, do not factor in budget constraints.

Program Goals and Objectives

Organizational philosophy, organizational goals and objectives, and program design considerations all lead to the development of actual programs. Think back to the questions that Devon had to address on a macro level. They related to activity type, program format, and participant developmental level, all of which influence goal and objective development.

Devon can now answer these questions in the form of macro-level program goals and objectives. He has valuable information in the form of larger organizational goals to craft his vision. He can now make decisions about specific programs that are appropriate in a larger organizational context. He has information that will guide him on the number and types of activities his program will offer. Once the trips, events, and activities are in place, Devon and his staff will create trip and activity plans. Specific trip goals and objectives represent programming on the micro level. This is where Devon started when he first landed the job. He did not realize that so much has to be taken into consideration before programming on a micro level can occur. For a clearer perspective of the programming hierarchy starting with organizational philosophy, see figure 15.3. Keep in mind that this hierarchy reflects the process followed in a large organization with many other departments and services. The process may be less complex in a smaller organization with a limited mission and services.

Administrative Duties

Once the program manager designs the program, other administrative tasks will fall into place. Program managers are typically faced with administrative duties that are necessary to offer quality programs. As you might imagine, administrative duties vary greatly across organizations. However, competent outdoor leaders should be prepared to deal with fundamental administrative duties. Personnel concerns become important if an outdoor leader has supervisory duties. Staff qualifications, number of staff needed, and training needs must be determined. Type of record-keeping system and required documents become clear once a structure is in place. Safety systems, equipment needs, and marketing information must also be addressed on an administrative level. Finally, program evaluations should be created. Systematic evaluation provides data for program improvement and ultimately program success.

Staffing concerns, record keeping, equipment management, promotions, and program

Trip goals and objectives
Micro program goals and objectives

Larger program goals and objectives
Macro goals and objectives

Organizational mission and purpose
Organizational philosophy

Figure 15.3 Program goals and objectives hierarchy.

evaluations are discussed next. Competent outdoor leaders embrace the challenges of program management as a tool for program quality. Outdoor adventures supported by a strong administrative framework reflect sound professional practices.

Staff Selection

Program managers may find themselves in a position to hire staff members. This task composes a critical management function. Staff members make daily judgments that can affect participants' satisfaction with the organization. Staff members also can make judgments concerning safety of participants if they are in a technical-skills position. To manage risk and ensure program quality, staff selection and training need to be a central part of programming. The manager must carefully analyze each vacant position and determine the competencies and qualities desired. The core competencies outlined in this text serve as a good foundation to determine employee qualifications. A thorough job description must be designed based on the desired qualifications and characteristics. Program managers then work closely with human resource personnel to facilitate an appropriate hiring process. Time taken to select quality staff helps ensure program success and growth.

Personnel Management

Devon found himself in a supervisory position in charge of three seasonal staff members. Devon had not contemplated how he was going to manage his staff. This challenging administrative task requires a special set of skills to form a functional team. Personnel management is a complex process governed by state and federal laws. Creating job descriptions, screening, interviewing, developing benefit packages, and other personnel functions are typically handled by upper-level administrators. The average program manager may or may not play a role in the hiring process. Much depends on the size and organizational structure of the agency.

In Devon's case, the resort selected his staff team in advance. However, it is not uncommon for program managers to be part of the interviewing and selection process of new staff members. Program managers may be asked to assist with the development of job announcements and job descriptions based on their intimate knowledge of outdoor leadership. It is difficult to project how much personnel responsibility a program manager will receive. To operate safe, enjoyable, and environmentally sound outdoor adventures, aspiring outdoor leaders should at least be aware of fundamental supervisory functions. Program managers who have supervisory responsibilities typically address staff training and orientation. Once staff members receive proper training, supervisors face the challenge of maintaining employee health and morale.

Outdoor leaders who function as program managers must be prepared to orient and train staff members. Based on the seasonal nature of many outdoor activities, program managers face the challenge of preparing a new crew each time a new season begins. Agencies that hire leaders into full-time field positions also experience quick turnover due to the intense nature of fieldwork. Program managers find themselves preparing new full-time staff on a regular basis. In addition, once in these positions, employees require continuous training in order to maintain skills and knowledge. Designing and implementing new staff orientations and trainings require much time and energy. The following list of guidelines is designed to assist the program manager in developing orientation programs.

- Program managers work with other administrators to determine how much time and money will be needed to properly prepare staff for their jobs. Staff training can be expensive and time consuming. Do not shortcut the training process. Proper staff training is an important risk management practice and helps ensure quality programming.

- A comprehensive staff training program may not be enough in some cases. Consider implementing an apprenticeship program or assistant leader positions so that novice staff members work beside seasoned staff members before leading their own groups. Systems are created so that novice leaders are evaluated and approved by experienced leaders.

- Managers create a training schedule far in advance. This allows program managers to arrange for speakers and resources for the training period.

- Managers design the training program to foster team spirit so that the staff forms a healthy identity as an important part of the organization.

- Managers design the training so that staff members become well acquainted with organizational philosophy and purpose. Staff should feel that their work is important and meaningful.

- Managers create a training schedule to be sent in advance to all participating staff. This information allows staff to formulate realistic expectations and prepare properly for staff training.

- Managers create a realistic schedule that educates staff as well as allows time for team building and fun. See figure 15.4 for a sample training schedule that would be appropriate for Devon's situation.

Once staff training ends and the season begins, training responsibilities do not end. In-house or in-service employee training is an important component of continuing education. Professional organizations provide training in new methods and updated information that evolves within the industry. For example, river guides should receive periodic updates on rescue techniques. Rock climbers should receive rescue training so that emergency skills remain fine-tuned. Refreshers on customer service or equipment management are potential topics of in-house training. The following checklist of guidelines will assist

Time	Activity	Location
MONDAY		
9:00-10:00 a.m.	Introductions	Fall Wood Room
10:00-11:00 a.m.	Orientation	
BREAK		
11:15 a.m.-12:00 p.m.	Personal goal exercise	
LUNCH		Spring Café
1:00-2:00 p.m.	Facility tour	
3:00-6:00 p.m.	Policies and procedures	Outdoor Rental Shop
DINNER		
8:00-10:00 p.m.	Meet resort personnel	Kirk Ballroom
TUESDAY		
River orientation	Trips to local water resources	To be determined
8:00 a.m.-12:00 p.m.	Local lakes	
1:00-6:00 p.m.	Boating program orientation	
WEDNESDAY		
Climbing orientation	Trips to local climbing sites	To be determined
8:00 a.m.-6:00 p.m.	Climbing program orientation	
THURSDAY		
Mountain-biking orientation	Trips to local bike trails	To be determined
8:00 a.m.-6:00 p.m.	Biking program orientation	
7:00 p.m.-?	Dinner and social	Local restaurant

Figure 15.4 Sample training schedule.

the program manager in the development of in-house trainings.

- Managers are conscious of the timing and energy required to conduct an in-house training. During the busy season, staff may perceive in-house trainings as a burden rather than an educational opportunity. Program managers should poll staff to discover what they would like to see or what they need from in-house trainings before mandating a topic. Managers create realistic schedules so as not to overwork the staff. Managers must find time for in-house training that does not interfere with personal time off or with daily operations.

- Managers develop in-house training within organizational budget constraints. Consider compensating staff for additional training time. Also consider paying for certifications that are related to training rather than passing the costs to staff. For in-house trainings that are optional, consider rewarding staff members who choose to participate.

- Managers follow up in-house training with a social event such as a special meal or party. This helps foster a sense of community and cohesion among staff.

- Managers create a schedule of in-house trainings and disseminate in advance. Employees appreciate advance notice and this technique helps define agency expectations of employees.

Beyond orientation and training, effective supervisors pay close attention to staff health and morale. Attention to staff well-being promotes satisfied employees who lead quality programs. Especially in the outdoor recreation industry, field staff sometimes work 24 hours per day for weeks at a time. Outdoor professionals tend to be an enthusiastic group with great passion for their work. High salaries and attractive benefits do not attract them to outdoor work. Instead, outdoor leaders love the outdoors and enjoy working with people in wilderness settings.

Outdoor leaders typically find themselves in job situations that require time in the field away from friends and family. This lifestyle can interfere with establishing long-term relationships and maintaining a permanent home. As a result, outdoor leaders tend to be independent and self-reliant individuals who relish their freedom. While this is a stereotype, outdoor careers do create many of these lifestyle concerns, which is important for a supervisor to keep in mind. The following guidelines are designed for supervisors who work with outdoor leaders to assist supervisors in fostering a healthy, happy staff.

Scheduling

Managers should pay strict attention to scheduling concerns. Program managers can easily fall prey to the pressures of serving clients and meeting agency productivity goals. Do not overschedule field staff. Schedule appropriate days off and

Outdoor leaders-in-training discuss personal goals.

Learning Activity 15.2

Create a list of possible in-house trainings that would be appropriate for Devon to implement for his staff. Estimate the time and costs for each.

avoid scheduling trips back to back without breaks. Staff who lead multiday trips deserve multiple days off. Burnout is a common phenomenon in outdoor leadership. Help prevent burnout by allowing adequate time off.

Compensation

In general, salary and benefits tend to be minimal for field staff. Managers should consider creating a professional discount program so that staff can purchase personal outdoor equipment at significant discounts. Also, attempt to provide staff with equipment and clothing when working. Expensive personal outdoor gear receives excessive wear and tear when used at work.

Physical Health

Effective managers monitor staff physical fitness. Extended time in the field and repetitive physical activity are extremely hard on the body. Encourage staff to rest and relax to allow muscles, tendons, and ligaments to recover before they are permanently damaged. Try to arrange access to agency physicians or nurses because staff members may not be able to see their personal physician.

Emotional Health

Managers must monitor staff psychological and emotional health. Supervisors should make themselves open and available to all staff so that employees are able to share concerns. Encourage staff to take time off if signs of burnout appear such as chronic fatigue, irritability, reduction in performance, and change in personality and attitude. If possible, managers should arrange access to mental health professionals.

Staff Meetings

Managers should conduct periodic staff meetings within the context of the overall schedule. Checking in with the staff as a group allows a team to discuss and resolve work-related issues. Competent supervisors are able to facilitate productive staff meetings and appropriately deal with conflict.

Positive Feedback

Effective program managers recognize and praise staff members on a regular basis. Employees appreciate and need positive reinforcement for a job well done. Effective supervisors do this informally on a daily basis and also formally through such means as newsletter tributes, special ceremonies, and organizational publicity such as newspaper articles.

Outside Communication

Effective managers allow time for staff members to communicate with family and loved ones. Field staff who lead extended expeditions spend long periods of time away from personal support groups. Consider organizing events and periods of time for loved ones to visit and enjoy the resources of the organization. For example, Bushwood could allow Devon's family to visit and enjoy the resort at a significant discount. Policymakers should consider allowing staff to use cell phones in the field to communicate with loved ones. This should be done in private so as not to disrupt the participants' experience. Managers should attempt to arrange access to Internet and e-mail while field staff are in base camp or off work.

Documentation and Record Keeping

In addition to managing staff, program manager duties include documentation and record keeping. This function affects every aspect of programming. From a risk management perspective, accident reports, health records, assumption of risk forms, photo consents, and related forms document critical information demonstrating an appropriate standard of care. Registrations, evaluations, equipment logs, field logs, and other forms of documentation provide data to facilitate program quality. Organizations desiring to create long-range plans make more informed decisions if well-kept records provide decision-making data. Records allow agencies to study participant use patterns to make macro programming decisions. Documentation also allows outdoor leaders to make judgments regarding trip design.

For example, knowing a participant's medical background and participation goals enables the leader to plan accordingly. Clearly, well-kept records serve a multitude of purposes.

Outdoor leaders often perceive documentation as a bothersome task that detracts from program activities. The importance of record keeping cannot be overemphasized, however. Organizations rely on program managers and field staff to do their part. In extreme cases, proper documentation protects the physical well-being of staff members and program participants. For example, a staff member who documents the use of climbing equipment is recording use statistics. Equipment can be retired at the appropriate time before overuse causes a malfunction that could seriously injure a participant or leader. The following sections reflect generic records of outdoor organizations. This short list only reflects potential documents affecting program managers. Outdoor organizations will maintain many other documents and records not included in this list. A brief description of the document is followed by suggested uses.

Registration Records

Registration and enrollment forms provide valuable participant data. Accounting information such as fees, deposits, method of payment, and so on is found within registration records. Participant demographic information such as age, gender, and contact information is also obtained. In addition, information regarding specific dates, times, ability levels, goals, and so on can be recorded on registration forms. Outdoor leaders must have access to this information in order to properly plan a trip and to screen participants to determine if the activities are appropriate based on age, ability level, and personal goals. Agencies also use registration data to track use statistics. Use statistics involve discovering who the participants are (age, income, origin, gender). Use statistics also allow agencies to track which programs are in higher demand and to track program fluctuations based on total number of participants.

Health and Medical Records

Health records for participants and staff must be maintained. Leaders have to be aware of preexisting health conditions in order to program appropriate adventures. Awareness of medical conditions plays a key role in the prevention and treatment of illnesses and injuries. Medical records provide health care professionals with a historical record if someone requires hospitalization or a physician's care. Leaders are able to monitor medications and behavior with this information. Emergency contacts can be found on these forms if the agency needs to contact a family member in case of an emergency.

Photo Consents

Participants sign photo consents to give organizations or individuals permission to use trip photos in promotional materials, publications, and Web sites. In some cases, participants will not allow their images to be made available to the public. Program managers have a duty to inform participants when an agency desires to use photos and film footage.

Use Forms and Maintenance Records

Equipment check-out and check-in forms document what equipment is being taken into the field on any particular trip. These forms specify the condition of the equipment so programmers can monitor wear and tear. In some cases, organizations will hold participants responsible for equipment damage. Statements of responsibility and replacement cost may be included. Equipment forms document equipment condition before and after use. Equipment logs are additional documents used to monitor specialized equipment such as rock-climbing ropes. It is a common institutional practice to record the amount and type of use a rope receives. For example, after a certain number of hours, the rope is retired as a climbing rope and destroyed or used for other purposes. As equipment is cleaned, inspected, and repaired, these activities should be documented, which ensures that equipment is kept in excellent condition and allows substandard equipment to be taken out of commission.

Assumption of Risk Forms

Assumption of risk forms are risk management forms designed to fully inform participants of inherent risks. Activities and possible consequences are described in detail so that the participant is fully aware of the nature of the activity. In case of an injury, the agency can thus demonstrate that the client was aware of the inherent risks of the adventure activity.

Waiver of Liability Forms

Waivers of liability are risk management forms designed to protect the agency from lawsuits. Participants acknowledge inherent risks of participation and agree to hold harmless the agency and its agents. These forms are governed by law and vary in format based on regional legal statutes.

Incident and Accident Reports

These reports allow agencies to track **incidents** (near misses that could have resulted in a serious accident) or **accidents** (when injuries are sustained and medical care is rendered). Incident and accident reports provide valuable risk management data by tracking patterns so that future problems can be thwarted. For example, leaders record a series of foot injuries at a particular river crossing on a popular backpacking route. The agency sees a pattern and institutes a policy that boots, not river sandals, must be worn at this particular crossing due to the irregular bottom filled with sharp rocks from a nearby quarry. Accident reports must be maintained for a designated amount of time depending on the statute of limitations for that region.

Field Records

Agencies may require outdoor leaders to maintain field records that document specific events for each trip they lead. Weather, conflicts with participants, participant behavior, activities, logistical information, and so on can be kept in a journal or on a standard form. Agencies use this information to track trips for a variety of reasons. The information can be used as a tool to improve future trips. If accidents or incidents occur, there is a historical record that may help determine cause.

Permits and Permission

Permits obtained for public lands or permission obtained from private landowners must be maintained. Permits have to be updated. Proof must exist that the agency has permission to use a certain area. Copies of permits and permission are maintained in organizational files and a copy is typically carried by the leader in the field.

Trip Reports

At the end of a trip, leaders typically complete a trip report that summarizes the experience. Trip reports provide data regarding all events and activities associated with the trip. Leaders record activity type and locations, who led the trip, and accidents and incidents. Overall success of the trip is summarized and accompanied by suggestions for future trips. Agencies use these reports when necessary to obtain information about a particular trip months or even years later. This creates a convenient system when an agency sponsors numerous trips so that specific events can be reconstructed for risk management or evaluation purposes.

Contracts and Rental Forms

Program managers may rely on contractors or rental agencies for services. Knowing contract terms is important during trip operations. Program managers must be familiar with agreement details and where responsibility falls. For example, if an agency contracts with a river outfitter, the program manager must know all pertinent logistical information and liability information. Does the contracted service provide equipment, lunch, shuttles, permits, first aid kits, and so on? These details must be made clear for the purposes of program planning.

Program Promotion

Another area where program managers exercise management responsibility is marketing and promotions. Program managers may be held responsible for little or for all program promotion. In Devon's situation, he was responsible for assisting with the promotion of his programs. The resort employed a full-time marketing director and associated staff who promoted the resort to the general public. Devon's challenge was to attract current guests to the adventure program.

Program managers must first determine their level of marketing responsibility. Outdoor agencies with sophisticated marketing departments may require little assistance from program managers. At the very least, marketing departments may seek the assistance of program managers to proof materials for accuracy and realism. Program directors may also provide rough copy to assist in the development of brochures, flyers, and Web pages.

No matter the level of responsibility, program managers need basic knowledge of marketing techniques. An important risk management concern must be remembered when promoting high-risk activities. Program directors must accurately portray the reality of the activities. In addition to fun, challenge, and thrills there exists the possibility of serious injury. From a risk management approach, promotional materials cannot attest to the complete safety of adventure activities. However, activities are conducted in a professional manner by competent leaders to minimize and manage the risks. Accidents and injuries cannot be completely eliminated, but the activity can be managed to help reduce accident frequency and severity. Promotional material must be designed to attract as well as inform potential clients of this information.

When faced with marketing responsibilities, program managers should first determine if a marketing plan is warranted. If the organization has a formal marketing plan, program managers simply need to determine what role they play. If a plan does not exist, they determine whether a formal plan should be developed. A marketing plan provides a systematic approach to marketing, promoting, and advertising services.

The contents of marketing plans tend to be similar in most business settings. The following sections outline the basic ingredients of a marketing plan (Ford and Blanchard 1993). Program managers may find that many of the components are already in place. The challenge comes in adapting the plan to fit the context of a particular setting.

Marketing Objectives

First, managers should establish specific, measurable objectives in order to build an effective marketing plan. For example, Devon could have created the following objectives for his new program:

- Objective 1—Attempt to serve at least 400 guests within the first year of operation.
- Objective 2—Fill at least 90% of the single-day trips offered throughout the summer.
- Objective 3—Book at least 60% of the overnight trips offered during the first season of operation.
- Objective 4—Score above average in all areas on guest satisfaction questionnaires.

Market Assessment

A manager should assess the potential market by researching intended participant populations. Understanding participant lifestyle, economic status, leisure preferences, developmental level, and other characteristics determines how and where to focus promotions. This information also allows the program manager to design programs that solicit meaningful participation. In addition, managers should determine how the competition operates. Agencies that provide similar services provide invaluable marketing research in how they advertise and serve their clients. Consumers will compare and form certain expectations for outdoor programming services. For example, Devon may determine that Bushwood guests expect professionally guided experiences as opposed to experiential-based educational workshops. Bushwood guests might expect a certain standard of service due to the precedent set at other resorts in the region.

Program Profiles

Program managers must inventory all programs and services so that they know what needs to be marketed. A programmer can go back to initial program design and assess services. At Bushwood, white-water boating, mountaineering, rock climbing, mountain biking, and day hiking make up the primary activity base. These activities are divided into day trips and multiday trips. Within these categories there exist the options for group experiences and privately guided trips. In addition, Devon's program includes equipment rental so that guests can boat, canoe, and hike on their own. An array of rental gear is available to support personal excursions.

Target Marketing Strategies

Data from the overall marketing analysis will supply information for determining target markets. Within the market population there are identifiable groups. In Devon's situation, certain distinct groups make up Bushwood's guest population. Families make up 60% of the regular client base, older adults compose 20%, and corporate conferences make up the remaining 20%. Armed with this information, Devon has the ability to design programs to meet the needs of each population. He can then create promotional or advertising strategies to attract program participants. Common advertising methods include flyers, posters, brochures, newsletters, visual media, and word of mouth.

Budget

Marketing efforts must be based on a budget. Most marketing budgets are developed from specific marketing objectives. For example, if Devon proposed to serve 400 guests during the first year of operation, he would have to project the budget necessary to meet that goal. The money needed to finance flyers, posters, pamphlets, and so on would have to be projected. In some cases, program managers have little control and will find that their marketing budgets are determined by the organization's overall marketing budget. The programmer will supply the marketing director with information to market the program and not worry about calculating budget projections. In this situation, the program director has to operate under a dictated budget amount.

Implementation and Evaluation

After creating the initial components of the marketing plan, program managers must implement and evaluate their plans. Creating time lines, assigning responsibilities to others, adhering to budget constraints, and monitoring progress make up implementation procedures. Evaluation occurs throughout the process. During the season, program managers should attempt to discover the

Learning Activity 15.3

Consider the implementation of a marketing plan for Devon. Create an implementation strategy to promote adventure programming. Remember that 60% of the guests are families, 20% are older adults, and the remaining 20% are conference participants. In a resort setting where other recreation programs are offered, how should Devon go about promoting his program? Be creative and assume the resort has state-of-the-art technology, plenty of public spaces, and a large marketing budget. Also assume that there are many promotional tools in place advertising the traditional recreation programs. The adventure program could be included in these promotions.

most effective means of promotion. Asking clients how they learned about the program is a critical question, and the registration form is an excellent place to ask it. At the end of the season or programming period, goals and objectives are reassessed to determine levels of success.

Equipment Management

It should be apparent at this point how vital administrative functions are to the success of a program. Program design, staffing, record keeping, and marketing require much attention. Equipment management must also be added to the list of management responsibilities. For most outdoor organizations, equipment represents a significant capital investment. Improper care of equipment becomes a financial liability. Poor quality equipment is a safety hazard, and clients experience frustration and program dissatisfaction when buckles and straps are missing or when tents leak all night. Program managers have the responsibility to create an equipment management system. The fundamental components of such a system include an inventory system, a check-out and check-in system, and maintenance procedures. In the following material, each of these components is discussed in general terms, acknowledging that systems must be adapted for each unique setting.

Inventory Systems

Keeping track of outdoor equipment is a challenging task (Olson 1997). Developing an inventory system allows program managers to track individual items throughout the use cycle. Inventories exist in a variety of forms. Computer software programs, spreadsheets, and handwritten lists are all viable inventory methods. Inventory system design should provide the following data:

1. Dates purchased and retired. Record when equipment is purchased and removed from inventory. Knowledge of age allows managers to retire equipment in a timely fashion and assists in projecting when new equipment should be purchased.

2. Identification system. Equipment must be identifiable by name or item number. In large inventories, giving items an identification number provides a convenient method for identifying each piece of equipment. Identification numbers can be designated in a variety of ways, such as through a code. Coding systems vary depending on specific needs, computer program limitations, and so on. For example, one system for code development reflects the purchase date and item number. Tent number 20 purchased on July 14, 2002, would be given the following number: 020-0702. Permanent markers are commonly used to mark nylon equipment, while metal etchers work well on pots, pans, and other metal objects. Tape, paint, stickers, and other methods can also be used. Color coding equipment is another identification system. Program managers must determine what is best for their situation.

3. Equipment condition. Somewhere within the inventory records, the condition of the equipment should be documented so that program managers know exactly how functional items are within the inventory. Conditions may be updated frequently, such as after every use, or done once a year during annual inventory counts.

4. Amount of equipment. All inventories reflect the total number of items in possession. See figure 15.5 for part of an inventory system developed on a spreadsheet.

Equipment-Issuing System

Program managers should devise a way to check equipment out and in when outfitting trips. Check-out and check-in systems ensure accountability by tracking what goes into the field and what

Outdoor Equipment Inventory

By: Cindy Boater   RU Outdoors

Quantity	Item	Inventory #	Condition	Inventory date	Comments
12	U-Digit shovels	0103-1203	Good	4/15/2004	
12	U-Digit shovel covers	0103-1203	Good	4/15/2004	
5	Garden trowels	0101-0501	Poor	4/15/2004	
6	12-in. fry pans	0102-0602	Good	4/15/2004	
5	Bake pans & lids	0102-0602	Poor	4/15/2004	06 missing
13	Pot grips	0103-1303	Good	4/15/2004	
8	Strainers	0103-0803	Good	4/15/2004	
12	Spatulas	0103-1203	Good	4/15/2004	
12	Lg. spoons	0102-1202	Good	4/15/2004	
12	Polar Purs	0102-1202	Good	4/15/2004	7 new and 5 older
4	Fuel funnels	0103-0403	Good	4/15/2004	
8	Feather 400 stoves	0102-0802	Good	4/15/2004	06 lost fuel cap
10	Liter fuel bottles	0102-1002	Good	4/15/2004	
4	16 oz. fuel bottles	0102-0402	Good	4/15/2004	
9	Water bags	0103-0903	Good	4/15/2004	
6	10 × 12 tarps	0102-0602	Good	4/15/2004	
6	Summit XT tents	0102-0602	Excellent	4/15/2004	05 zipper repair
11	8 in. tent stakes		Excellent	4/15/2004	
14	Lg. nylon Stuff Sacs	0102-1402	Good	4/15/2004	
11	Sova Stuff Sacks	0103-1103	Excellent	4/15/2004	
10	Sova small duffels	0103-1003	Good	4/15/2004	
1	Pro. 3.0 first aid	103	Good	6/15/2004	replace medications
11	Whistles		Good	4/15/2004	
8	Sylva compasses	0102-0802	OK	4/15/2004	
11	BSA compasses	0103-1199	Poor	4/15/2004	all functional
10	Osprey packs	0103-1003	Good	4/15/2004	
3	small		Good	4/15/2004	04 needs new waist buckle
4	medium		Good	4/15/2004	
3	large		Good	4/15/2004	
	5000 ft. para cord		Good	4/15/2004	cut into pieces

(continued)

Figure 15.5 Sample inventory system.

Figure 15.5 Sample inventory system. *(continued)*

Quantity	Item	Inventory #	Condition	Inventory date	Comments
2	Tow sleds	0103-0203	Excellent	4/15/2004	
3	Throw bags	0103-0303	Excellent	6/15/2004	
15	Snowshoes	0103-1503	Excellent	4/15/2004	10 size 9s and 5 size 10s
8	4 gal. H_2O jugs	0103-0803	Excellent	4/15/2004	
9	Large canoe bags	0103-0903	Good	4/15/2004	3 new and 6 older
2	Small canoe bags	0103-0203	Good	4/15/2004	
4	Kitchen scales	0103-0403	Excellent	4/15/2004	
12	GPS	0102-1202	Good	4/15/2004	03 needs repair
6	Dagger canoes	0103-0603	Excellent	4/15/2004	
12	Canoe air bags	0103-1203	Excellent	6/15/2004	
12	Lash kits for flotation		Excellent	6/15/2004	installed 3/03

comes out. Computer programs exist that execute this procedure as part of the inventory system. Most organizations choose to use a simple form to record what equipment goes out into the field. Equipment-issuing systems should include type of item checked out, number of items checked out, date, condition of equipment at check-out and upon return, purpose of check-out, and person responsible for check-out and check-in. In some cases, the replacement cost of the equipment is recorded on a check-out form. See figure 15.6 for a sample check-out and check-in form created on a spreadsheet.

Maintenance and Care

Inventory systems and check-out and check-in systems provide information needed to maintain equipment. As equipment returns from the field, its condition is recorded. But what happens to the dirty or damaged equipment? A system needs to be devised to ensure timely repair or retirement. The person responsible for cleaning the equipment should repair the item on the spot. For more complex repairs, damaged equipment is deposited in a designated area and not mixed back into the functional inventory. An equipment bin designated for damaged equipment or a designated shelf in the logistics area might serve as the answer.

Program managers must ensure that someone is responsible for repairing equipment on a regular basis. Cleaning should occur immediately after a trip. Immediate cleaning reduces rusting, molding, odor buildup, mechanical malfunctions, and other damaging problems. Adequate drying space is necessary to ensure proper drying. Finally, proper storage is paramount to good equipment care. Most items, especially synthetics, should be stored in cool, dry spaces out of the sunlight. Storage spaces with shelves, hangers, lockers, hooks, and fire cabinets must be kept neat and organized. Marking these spaces with tags and labels helps ensure neat, organized storage.

Program Evaluation

If program design is the program manager's cornerstone, program evaluation is the rest of the foundation for quality program management. Program evaluations provide leaders, administrators, and organizational sponsors with vital information related to the accomplishment of goals and objectives. Evaluation data reveals specific, measurable criteria in the form of program objectives. Meeting a set of well-written objectives means that the corresponding goal is fulfilled. Evaluation systems based on goals and objectives provide program managers with concrete data to determine success. They give program managers who report to higher-level administrators or funding sources meaningful data to verify outcomes. As an accountability source, evaluation systems cannot be taken lightly when outdoor leaders must justify programming decisions, expenditures, staffing choices, and so

Equipment Check Out/In

Trip _____   Date: RU Outdoors

Item	Quantity	Inventory #	Condition	Notes	Check-in	Condition	Notes
U-Digit shovels							
U-Digit shovel covers							
Garden trowels							
12-in. fry pans							
Bake pans & lids							
Pot grips							
Strainers							
Spatulas							
Lg. spoons							
Polar Purs							
Fuel funnels							
Feather 400 stoves							
Liter fuel bottles							
16 oz. fuel bottles							
Water bags							
10 × 12 tarps							
Summit XT tents							
8 in. tent stakes							
Lg. nylon Stuff Sacs							
Sova Stuff Sacks							
Sova small duffels							
Pro. 3.0 first aid							
Whistles							
Sylva compasses							
BSA compasses							
Osprey packs							
small							
medium							
large							
5000 ft. para cord							
Tow sleds							
Throw bags							
Snowshoes							

(continued)

Figure 15.6 Sample check-out and check-in form.

240

Figure 15.6 Sample check-out and check-in form. *(continued)*

Item	Quantity	Inventory #	Condition	Notes	Check-in	Condition	Notes
4 gal. H$_2$O jugs							
Large canoe bags							
Small canoe bags							
Kitchen scales							
GPS							
Dagger canoes							
Canoe air bags							

Names:

_____   _____

_____   _____

_____   _____

_____   _____

_____   _____

_____   _____

on. In addition, professionals within the outdoor industry have an ethical duty to document outcomes of their programs. Well-documented outcomes help validate outdoor programs as an important part of an organization.

Program managers must not fall into the trap of interpreting the amount of participation with success. More participation does not necessarily translate into more program success. Perhaps there is only one outdoor program in town and participants do not have a choice and will take a mediocre program over no program. For this reason, participant satisfaction also serves as an evaluation tool, although high participant satisfaction does not necessarily mean program goals were met. For example, teenagers may have a fantastic time on a school camping trip but none of the curriculum goals are met. It rains the entire trip and the teenagers are able to socialize extensively at base camp but never learn intended rock-climbing skills. Program managers must design an evaluation system that encompasses several modes of data collection. Goals and objectives serve as the primary source for assessment. Quantitative data such as the number of users, user hours, number of trips, and revenue generated should also be collected in conjunction with participant satisfaction. Combining these sources provides program managers with valuable data to holistically interpret success. Program managers can then make more informed decisions to improve program services.

A variety of methods exist to collect data for program evaluation. Surveys, reports, debriefings, informal conversations, staff feedback, tests, and other assessments can be solicited. Implementation of these methods must also be planned into the overall evaluation process. Program managers must decide how, when, and where programs will be evaluated. It is common programming practice to institute a variety of approaches (Rossman and Schlatter 2000). Posttrip evaluations completed by participants and staff are routine. Formal debriefings with trip leaders and participants also provide valuable feedback. Informal conversations solicit information that does not always appear on formal evaluations. Surveys mailed or e-mailed to participants months after a trip help determine long-term effects and perceptions. The following two sections provide suggestions for instituting effective evaluation systems along with examples of such systems.

Program Evaluation Criteria

Program evaluation is a dynamic process that changes and improves as program managers test different methods until accurate information is obtained. Evaluation instruments should be based on intended outcomes. Formal questionnaires and survey questions are developed based on program goals and objectives (intended outcomes). As discussed, program goals and objectives vary dramatically throughout the outdoor industry. The following list of sample outcomes represents the diversity of intended outcomes.

- Commercial resort. Program evaluations might address guest satisfaction, amount of participation, and program quality in relationship to the service philosophy of the resort.
- School-based outdoor program. Program evaluations might address learning objectives developed in a formal lesson plan or mandated by state agencies or professional associations.
- Outdoor program for youth at risk. Program evaluations might include a standardized test to measure improvements in self-concept or socialization skills. For example, the Tennessee Self-Concept Scale (TSCS) could be administered pre- and posttrip to determine changes in self-concept. Long-term assessment might assess recidivism, grade improvement, or social skills.
- Wilderness schools. Program evaluations might assess leadership development, technical skill development, and participant satisfaction.
- University outing program. Program evaluations commonly assess participant satisfaction and are based on the total number of participants served.
- Environmental education center. Program evaluations might assess environmental knowledge gained or changes in attitude toward the environment.

To assess any of these outcomes, a number of methods could be instituted. Following are three global participant outcomes that program managers can focus on in the evaluation process: skill development, knowledge development, and attitudes and dispositions. Suggested methods and instruments demonstrate how these three global outcomes might be assessed.

Skill Development

Practical exams may be designed to assess participants' skills. For example, design a knot test or canoeing test to assess technical skills. Or, design the trip so that the culminating activity requires students to apply skills learned throughout the experience. Create a skills checklist that can be implemented any time during the trip. See figure 15.7 for a sample skills checklist for assessing basic camping skills during an outdoor leadership course.

Knowledge Development

Written tests, journaling, plant identification tests, oral exams, essays, debriefings, and informal conversations are common ways to assess knowledge. See figure 15.8 for a journal assignment designed to assess outdoor leaders' knowledge.

Attitudes and Dispositions

Journals, essays, surveys, standardized tests, debriefings, and informal conversations are common ways to determine whether an experience influences attitudes. Assessing participant satisfaction would fall under this category. Leader observations also serve as an evaluative tool. Once a participant learns something new, the leader observes to see if the participant is disposed to apply new skills and knowledge independently without prompting from leaders.

Participant-Centered Evaluations

Participant feedback is vital for program success by assisting leaders in program improvement. A variety of methods exist to solicit participant views. The following sections represent five participant-centered methods of program evaluations. The most effective evaluation system employs triangulation by using at least three different methods for assessment (Rossman and Schlatter 2000). Instituting at least three methods helps leaders solicit comprehensive data so that patterns can be established.

Trip Evaluation Forms

Trip or activity evaluation forms are designed to assess goals, objectives, and overall participant satisfaction upon termination of the trip. These forms are created in-house to reflect program goals and objectives. See figure 15.9 for a sample trip evaluation form for an outdoor leadership course.

Leader Evaluations

Participant forms designed to assess leadership performance are a common method of program evaluation. This assessment is implemented upon completion of a trip. Leaders use this information

Skill	Date	Instructor initials	Comments
Stove operation			
Breakfast			
Dinner			
Scratch dessert			
Baking			
Campsite selection			
Tarp pitching			
LNT fire			
Trail technique			
Time control plan			
Map interpretation			
Compass use			
River crossing			
Plant identification			
Bowline			
Trucker's hitch			
Taut-line hitch			
Square knot			
Figure 8			
Pack packing			
Rope mgt.			
Food protection			
Camp sanitation			

Figure 15.7 Sample skills checklist.

Wilderness Education Association Expedition Journal Assignment

Journaling is writing in a notebook about your experiences, including class notes, lesson plans, decision making, leadership, expedition behavior, environmental ethics, safety, and other reflections. The journal is a required component of the course. The journal accounts for a significant portion of your grade and serves as a primary learning tool. The purpose of the journal is threefold:

1. To provide the participant and instructor with specific documentation that learning has taken place and to show progress toward achieving the course outcomes.

2. To demonstrate to what degree the participants analyze their experiences.

3. To provide the participants with a historical record of their experiences.

Components of the Journal

1. Field and class notes—This section will help you compile information about what you're learning. One suggestion is to approach this section as if you would want to save this information as a reference for planning future outings. This section should contain the following:

   a. Class notes—Notes on various lessons taught by the instructors and other students throughout the expedition. This also includes notes on how you would or could adapt the lessons for future use.

   b. Lesson plans—Lessons that you develop and teach to the group.

   c. Field notes—Includes daily schedules (time, energy, control plans) and activities.

   d. Personal reflections and observations—Thoughts and perceptions about new knowledge learned and old knowledge revisited; how you feel about what you are learning and how you might apply it in the future.

2. Decision-making analysis—In this section you are asked to analyze at least one major decision every other day (you will have a minimum of 10 decisions to analyze). Be sure to clearly number your decisions so that the instructor evaluating your journal can keep a tally (i.e., D-1, D-2, D-3. . .D-10) Analyze decisions that are made by

   • you in your daily routine,

   • you or others as leader of the day (LOD),

   • the entire group, and

   • the course instructors.

As appropriate, address these questions in your decision analysis:

• What was the context for the decision, the reason for the decision, who facilitated, and were goals and objectives clarified?

• How did the decision-making process follow a model?

• Where or why did the decision-making process bog down?

• How was the solution finally reached (e.g., consensus, straw vote, dictated)?

• How was the decision implemented (e.g., smoothly, chaotically, no resistance)?

• What would you do differently next time?

3. Leadership style analysis—In this section you are asked to analyze leadership styles of at least seven different individuals while on the trip. Use the following system to number your entries in this category (L-1, L-2, L-3. . .L-7). You can analyze yourself, LODs, lesson plan facilitators, and course instructors.

• What leadership style was used? Describe.

• Why was the leadership style chosen?

• How was the style appropriate or effective?

• How did the group react?

• How did the individual's personality affect his or her performance as a leader?

• How did this person plan ahead?

• How did the leader manage conflict? Facilitate the decision?

• What teaching techniques did the leader employ?

• As a teacher or leader, what should be done differently next time or remain the same?

4. Expedition behavior analysis—On this subject you are asked to analyze what you have seen, what you have done, and how you feel about the expedition behavior and group dynamics you have observed. What did you and others do to contribute positively or negatively to the group's ability to work and get along?

5. Environmental ethics—On this subject you are asked to analyze what you have seen, what you have done, and how you feel about issues regarding environmental ethics. What did you or others do positively or negatively in regard to the environment and the practices taught to limit human effects?

(continued)

Figure 15.8 Required journal content for outdoor leadership students.

Adapted with permission of the Wilderness Education Association.

6. Safety analysis—On this subject you are asked to analyze what you have seen, what you have done, and how you feel regarding safety concerns. What did you or others do that reflected on the safety of the group? What are you learning from a leader's perspective about safety in the outdoors?

7. Personal reflections and observations—The purpose of this section is to encourage reflection about who you are, what you're like, and how you think. It might include the following:

- Perceptions about yourself and your thoughts
- How the course fits into your lifestyle and the world
- Drawings, poems, stories
- What you are learning about yourself by being part of a group
- Goals and objectives for the future
- Personal goals and objectives for the trip (how they may change throughout the trip and an ongoing analysis of accomplishing these goals and objectives)

Course Evaluation Questionnaire for an Outdoor Leadership Training Course

The purpose of this questionnaire is to aid the growth, success, and enjoyment of future programs. Please take your time in answering the following questions. Any additional comments or suggestions will be appreciated.

Sponsoring institution _____ Date of course _____

Location(s) _____

Instructor(s) _____

Course (circle one):   5 days   14 days   30 days

Did the course live up to your expectations? Explain.

Were there any activities that you think should have been covered in greater depth?

Did you have enough opportunities to develop or display your leadership abilities?

What additional types of opportunities do you recommend?

Was safety a major aspect of all judgment considerations regarding each subject area?

Do you feel your leadership ability changed as a result of the course? Explain.

(continued)

Figure 15.9   Sample trip evaluation form.

Figure 15.9 Sample trip evaluation form. *(continued)*

Was the trip evaluation process effective? Are there any improvements you might suggest?

- Your Midcourse Peer Evaluation

- Your Midcourse Instructor Evaluation

- Your Exit Interview Instructor Evaluation

- Your Ability Assessment Form

Do you feel your performance on the course was evaluated fairly?

What do you feel is the value of the Expedition Journal assignment?

Was the course flexible and sensitive to the needs of your specific group?

Please use the back for additional comments and suggestions.

Participant signature (optional) _____ Date _____

---

to improve leadership skills and agencies may use the information for promotion or merit pay increases.

Participant Satisfaction Surveys

Survey instruments designed in-house to assess participant satisfaction are common. Participant satisfaction is important to many agencies that seek to retain clients for future programs. As in Devon's case, participant satisfaction is critical to assessing overall program effectiveness. The quality of the resort vacation experience depends greatly on participant satisfaction.

Formal Debriefings

Many outdoor programs use group meetings or debriefings as an evaluation tool. Formal discus-

sions led by the leader solicit valuable information on all aspects of the program. Facilitated group discussions allow participants to verbalize feelings and thoughts that may be difficult to write. Group discussions tend to inspire individual perceptions as group members hear other members speak.

Informal Discussions

Leaders and program managers take the time to check in with individuals and groups in an informal context. For example, during a meal, while hanging out at the base of a climb, or during a rest break leaders have excellent opportunities to ask questions and informally discuss trip concerns. Leaders then share information with others through staff meetings or by integrating comments into formal reports.

Learning Activity 15.4

Design an evaluation system for Devon that he could present to his supervisor. Outline the methods and instruments to be used and describe the purpose of each strategy employed.

Leader-Centered Evaluations

In addition to participant-centered evaluations, leader perceptions are a critical piece of the evaluation process. Program managers must incorporate leader viewpoints into the evaluation mix. Leader recollections and interpretations provide a needed perspective to balance participant feedback. The following sections reflect common evaluation methods to solicit leader feedback.

Trip Reports

Formal reports written by trip leaders summarize the experience from the leader's perspective. Most organizations provide a form or standard format to guide the leader's thoughts. Leader perspectives may differ dramatically from participant perspectives. It is necessary for the agency to assess program effectiveness through the leader's eyes as well.

Peer Assessments

Staff members are often given the chance to provide coworkers with performance feedback. Trip leaders are provided the opportunity to give logistical staff, program directors, and other support staff feedback. Program directors, logistical staff, and others involved provide feedback as well. Peer assessments occur in written form and through staff debriefings. This is a critical form of evaluation to assess staff performance as well as program success.

Program Evaluations

Many organizations develop specific forms to solicit staff feedback regarding goal and objective accomplishment. Program evaluations may also occur in the form of posttrip leader debriefings. Program managers set aside a formal time after a trip to verbally evaluate the experience. Posttrip debriefings are an excellent format for discussing concerns.

A student reflects on her experience in a journal.

Summary

Outdoor leader preparation includes knowledge and skill development in program management. Novice outdoor leaders are understandably drawn to the profession with visions of paddling, climbing, and living in beautiful wilderness environments. Competent, well-rounded outdoor leaders, however, possess a balance of leadership, technical, and management skills. Management functions play a critical role in the implementation of quality programs. Outdoor leaders face a number of administrative responsibilities when serving as program managers. Management responsibilities vary throughout the industry depending on organizational structure. However, professional outdoor leaders should be familiar with certain key management functions.

Key functions discussed in this chapter include program design, personnel management, record keeping, marketing, equipment management, and program evaluation. Program design involves program planning on a macro level. Before actual

Professional-Development Portfolio Activity

Develop a program proposal on a macro level. Determine program context by establishing organizational structure (for-profit, nonprofit, or governmental) and the geographic location. Develop a mission statement, goals, and objectives for this new organization. Create a checklist of management forms necessary to help administer new programs.

trips and activities are planned, program managers must look at the larger program structure within the organization. Managers must look at organizational philosophy, client profiles, organizational resources, and other factors to determine overall program offerings. Managers must also develop and maintain proper documents and records to ensure sound risk management and to help assess program quality.

Many program managers serve as supervisors. Management of staff members poses an important challenge that requires specific planning and skills. Orientations and staff trainings must be planned and implemented, and supervisors must monitor staff health and morale to ensure quality leadership. Program managers may also be responsible for marketing programs. Knowledge of marketing plans and the ability to develop marketing initiatives are important administrative tasks. Also, most program managers carry much responsibility for equipment management. Creating inventory systems and procedures to maintain equipment is a necessary function to protect capital investments. Functional equipment is paramount to program safety and enjoyment.

Finally, program managers play an important role in evaluating programs. A comprehensive evaluation system must be in place as a sound evaluation system is the key to program improvement and safety. Outdoor professionals have a duty to assess goal and objective accomplishment. Quality evaluation data enable the outdoor professional to make numerous decisions that affect every aspect of an organization.

Program quality is contingent upon sound administrative practices. Aspiring outdoor leaders must develop administrative skills in order to be competitive in the job market. Potential employers are attracted to well-rounded outdoor leaders who possess management knowledge and experience. Novice leaders who focus solely on technical skills such as paddling and climbing limit their development. Aspiring leaders should seek internships, practicums, and in-service learning experiences that include administrative experience. Professional outdoor leaders must prepare themselves to participate in the entire programming process—including program management.

Selected References

Ford, P., and J. Blanchard. 1993. *Leadership and administration of outdoor pursuits.* 2nd ed. State College, PA: Venture.

Olson, J.R. 1997. *Facility and equipment management for sport directors.* Champaign, IL: Human Kinetics.

Rossman, R.J., and B.E. Schlatter. 2000. *Recreation programming: Designing leisure experiences.* 3rd ed. Champaign, IL: Sagamore.

chapter 16

Safety and Risk Management

"Too much safety results in killing students' souls. Too little safety results in dead bodies."
—Jasper Hunt

Chapter Concepts

- Risk in adventure experiences—Risk is an integral part of adventure experiences. Without risk, there is no adventure; with too much risk, there is misadventure, which can possibly result in injury or death. It is the outdoor leader's responsibility to find a proper balance between too little risk and too much risk.

- Legal aspects of risk management—While risk management is primarily a matter of quality assurance in outdoor programs, it is also a matter of protecting oneself from being sued because of an accident.

- Risk management process—Good risk management is essentially good program management. A series of steps in program management can be taken to minimize the risk of an accident occurring during an adventure experience.

- Emergency management—Risk management includes planning for emergencies.

The chapter concepts relate to the following core competencies:

- Self-awareness and professional conduct (CC-2)—Effective risk management by leaders involves an accurate sense of their abilities and limitations.

- Program management (CC-6)—Good risk management is essentially good program management.

- Safety and risk management (CC-7)—Every facet of this core competency is discussed in this chapter.

Watson and his students pulled up to a rocky beach next to the mouth of a stream flowing into Misty Bay. With tall mountains rising straight up from the bay and dense forests lining the shoreline, finding a suitable campsite was difficult. Evening was approaching and it was important to find a place to spend the night before much more time passed. It was the beginning of October and night would come early. The group was on a 3-day coastal kayaking trip in southeast Alaska. They were all excited about kayaking in the area in the month of October because humpback whales feed in southeast Alaska in October in preparation for their annual mating season in Hawaii in January. The group had seen plenty of whales while paddling that day. They had also seen sea otters, seals, and a wide variety of other sea life. Despite the thrill of the experience, the participants were becoming cold and tired. It was a rainy, wind-chilled day. Some were feeling seasick from the constant rocking motion of their kayaks as they paddled through the choppy waters. At the edge of the beach, just beyond a line of brush, was a stand of hemlock and Sitka spruce trees. Beneath these trees was a flat clearing that appeared to be a good site to set up camp.

Watson decided that this clearing was where the group would stay. The group beached their kayaks,

unloaded their gear, pulled the boats above the high-water mark, turned the boats over, and tied them to trees. The students immediately began to set up a tarp that would provide shelter for the group dining area, and once the dining area was established, individuals began to set up their tents. Once their tents were up, the students began to prepare dinner: stir-fry with rice, tofu, a mix of vegetables, and soy sauce.

Southeast Alaska is famous for its large population of brown bears. In some areas, there is one brown bear per square mile of land. Brown bears and grizzly bears are the same species of bear. Those living along the coast are called brown bears while those farther inland are called grizzly bears. Brown bears are typically much larger than their inland relatives because of their rich diet of salmon. There is nothing more threatening in the Alaskan bush than a sow (a mother bear) and her cubs. Sows are particularly aggressive when they feel that their cubs are in danger. Bear safety, or animal-encounter prevention, is a great concern in the coastal regions of Alaska. The group was conscientious about this as they established their camp for the night. They had been sure to pitch their tents at least 300 feet (91 meters) away from the cooking area in case the scent of the food drew bears during the night. After dinner, the group went about the task of hanging

(continued)

(continued)

bear bags. All food items, toiletries, clothing that had been worn while cooking, and any other items that might attract bears were placed in dry bags and hung in trees at least 12 feet (4 meters) from the ground for the night. The bear bags were hung at least 300 feet (91 meters) from the camp. Once this was done, the group settled in for the night. They crawled into their tents and sleeping bags early to ward off the chill of the early autumn night.

The group awoke to another misty, rainy day. They crawled from their sleeping bags and soggy tents, retrieved their bear bags, and prepared a breakfast of oatmeal, apples, and hot chocolate. After breakfast, the group decided to explore the surrounding area. The forest became fairly dense around the campsite, so the group walked out to the beach and began to follow the stream inland. The group had walked no more than 100 yards (91 meters) when Watson realized that he had forgotten an important consideration in choosing the campsite. He had forgotten that it was time for the annual silver salmon run. Bears are drawn to the streams and rivers of coastal Alaska during the annual salmon runs to feed on the easy prey of fish wallowing in streams as they attempt to spawn. The group had walked into a small meadow to find scores of salmon carcasses strewn in the grass. The carcasses were still fresh and mostly intact. The belly of each had been bitten away and consumed. Fresh bear scat and paw marks could be seen in the meadow. The grass was matted in the areas where bears had been fishing. Not wasting any time, the group returned their campsite, loaded their gear into their kayaks, and left the beach. As they paddled away from their campsite into the bay, they saw a sow and two cubs ambling along the shoreline not far from where they had camped. The group was lucky not to have stumbled onto the bears. Watson felt terrible about having overlooked the obvious risk of camping so close to a stream during a salmon run. He felt fortunate that this was simply a close call rather than a face-to-face encounter with a mother bear and her cubs.

There are many dangers that you might face while venturing into the wild outdoors. Some of these include hypothermia, insect-born diseases such as Lyme disease (ticks) and West Nile virus (mosquitoes), lightning, floods, falling rocks, animal encounters, poisonous snakes such as rattlers and cottonmouths, waterborne illnesses such as giardia, and so on. If ensuring participant safety in the outdoors is considered to be one of the three primary goals of outdoor leadership, why do we accept risk at all as outdoor leaders?

Risk is an integral aspect of outdoor education and recreation. Education itself is an inherently risky endeavor, though not always in a physical sense. In highlighting the role of risk in outdoor education and recreation, Hunt recounts a statement made by Willi Unsoeld, a famous philosopher, mountaineer, and outdoor educator:

> We used to tell them in Outward Bound, when a parent would come and ask us, "Can you *guarantee* the safety of our son, Johnny?" And we finally decided to meet it head-on. We would say, "No. We certainly can't Ma'am. We guarantee you the genuine chance of his death. And if we could guarantee his safety, the program would not be worth running. We do make one guarantee, as one parent to another. If you succeed in protecting your boy, as you are doing now, and as it's your motherly duty to do, you know, we applaud your watchdog tenacity. You should be protecting him. But, if you succeed, *we guarantee you the death of his soul!*" (1990, p. 123)

Hunt reiterates Unsoeld's point in drawing attention to a peculiar paradox in outdoor education and recreation: "Too much safety results in killing students' souls. Too little safety results in dead bodies" (p. 124). Ironically, Willi Unsoeld was killed in an avalanche along with one of his students from the Evergreen State College while mountaineering on Mount Rainer in 1979.

Adventure can be a profound source of personal growth. It is one of the reasons that the field of outdoor education and recreation is so appealing to so many people. The challenge for outdoor leaders and enthusiasts is to operate in a safe manner without compromising the excitement, the uncertainty, and the achievement of genuine adventure experiences. Risk should never be sought for its own sake, but it is integral to the adventure experience. Finding the proper balance between safety and risk is one of the primary tasks of any outdoor leader and any outdoor program. Continually managing risks and working to minimize the consequences of an accident should one occur is essential to this process. This does not mean eliminating risks altogether. It means

Risk is integral to all adventure experiences.

preparing to deal with risks through adequate trip planning, participant preparation and education, and so forth.

This chapter takes a look at safety and risk management from both a practical and a legal perspective. It offers a practical framework for considering risk management. It offers a general consideration of legal liability as an aspect of safety and risk management and then it takes a look at safety and risk management from a programming perspective.

Practical Aspects of Risk Management

This section presents a practical framework from which to consider risk management. Specifically, it addresses two concepts: the accident equation and the rescue curve. The accident equation helps us to understand how risk and accident potential arise. The rescue curve provides a framework for minimizing accident potential and the consequences of accidents, should they occur.

Accident Potential

An accident is an undesired, unexpected event resulting in an injury or a loss of some sort. Accidents in the outdoors typically result from a combination of two factors: human dangers and environmental dangers. **Human dangers** are those

dangers that originate in people who are venturing into the outdoors. They might include a lack of proficiency in the particular activity, a lack of preparation for the activity or the environment, poor decision-making skills, and a lack of judgment. **Environmental dangers** are those dangers that originate in the natural environment. Environmental dangers might include weather conditions, terrain, and wildlife. When human dangers and environmental dangers overlap, the potential for an accident arises. Human dangers plus environmental dangers equals accident potential. This formula is referred to as the **accident equation** (figure 16.1) (Hale 1984). When a person with little or no knowledge of the dangers associated with avalanches, for instance, enters into an avalanche-prone area while the danger of an avalanche is high, the potential of the person being caught in an avalanche rises. The greater the person's ignorance of avalanche danger and the greater the actual danger of an avalanche occurring, the greater the potential for an accident. This formula is useful to the outdoor leader because it illustrates the sources of most accidents in the outdoors and thus enables us to address those sources.

Human dangers and environmental dangers are often referred to as subjective dangers and objective dangers, respectively. Dangers can be considered in terms of variables. The only variables over which outdoor leaders exercise any control are subjective variables. We cannot control environmental variables, but we can

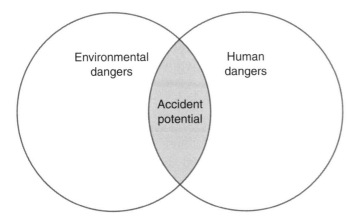

Figure 16.1 The accident equation.

Adapted by permission of Alan Hale.

control the nature of our interaction with those variables. The first step in controlling the nature of our interaction with environmental variables is developing an awareness of those variables, that is, educating ourselves and our participants about dangers that exist in the natural environment. The second step is preparing ourselves and our participants to interact in a safe manner with those dangers. Sometimes this means avoiding certain dangers altogether. Overlap of human dangers and environmental dangers typically results from human ignorance.

Reducing Accident Potential and Consequences

A useful framework for reducing accident potential and minimizing the consequences of accidents is the **rescue curve** (Kauffman and Carlson 1992). The rescue curve posits that there are four steps between an individual engaging in an adventure experience and winding up dead as a result of an accident while participating in that activity. These steps include accident prevention, self-rescue, rescue from within a group, and rescue from an outside party (see figure 16.2). The rescue curve also posits that as time increases in responding to a life-threatening accident, the chances of survival decrease.

Accident Prevention

Accident prevention is based on the idea of effective preparation. The saying, "An ounce of prevention is worth a pound of cure," speaks to the idea that effec-

tive preparation is one of the best ways to reduce the potential for an accident to occur during an adventure experience. Preparation entails everything from having an adequate trip plan to having the technical competency to travel or perform safely in the environment into which you are traveling. It entails knowledge of terrain conditions, knowledge of weather conditions, proper clothing and shelter for the conditions, proper equipment for the activity, and a variety of other considerations. Many of the considerations involved in ensuring adequate preparation are covered in chapter 17.

Self-Rescue

Self-rescue entails solving any mishaps that might befall an individual without the assistance of others. For example, in April of 2003, Aron Ralston ventured into a canyon in southeastern Utah. As Ralston was climbing down through a narrow slot canyon, a large boulder shifted and trapped his arm. Alone and unable to move the boulder, Ralston was literally caught between a rock and hard place. He remained in the canyon for the next 6 days with little water, food, or shelter. Faced with certain death, Ralston made an agonizing decision. He cut off his arm to free himself. Since he had ventured into the canyon alone and had not told anyone where he was going, he would not have survived if he had not had the willpower to cut off his own arm. Fortunately, this is an extreme case in self-rescue. In most cases, self-rescue is a much simpler act.

A person's line of defense against injury, damage, or loss include:

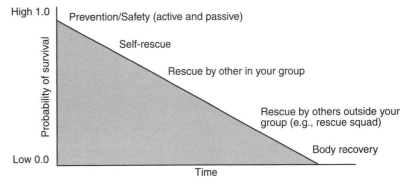

Figure 16.2 The rescue curve states that once an incident occurs that can result in injury, damage, or loss, as time increases and without intervention the probability of survival falls from near certainty (1.0) to zero.

Adapted, by permission, from R. Kauffman and G. Carlson, 1992, "The rescue curve: A race against time," *American Canoeist* (March): 10-13.

In kayaking, for example, the first form of self-rescue is known as a bracing stroke. When kayakers begin to lose their balance, the first thing they should do is perform a bracing stroke to stay in an upright position. If the brace fails and the kayak capsizes, a second form of self-rescue is a maneuver called a kayak roll. A third form of self-rescue in kayaking involves performing a wet exit (exiting the boat while it is upside down), recovering your equipment, and reentering the kayak without the assistance of others.

If you are on your own and you exit your kayak while far from shore and are unable to reenter your kayak or to swim to shore, you face a number of dangers. The most prevalent of these is hypothermia, loss of body heat. In the cold waters of the Pacific Northwest, for example, especially if you are inadequately dressed, hypothermia will set in rapidly. Without assistance, the probability of your survival is small.

Rescue From Within a Group

The rule of thumb for the size of any group venturing into the outdoors is to travel in a group of at least four. Traveling in a group is especially important should things go wrong. If you are in trouble and unable to help yourself, other members of the group can provide assistance. If outside assistance is needed, one person can stay with the victim and two can go for help. Ralston's mistake was traveling alone into a remote backcountry setting without informing anyone of his whereabouts. When things went wrong, there was no one around to help. Had he traveled in a group, he would have spared himself the ordeal of 6 days trapped in a slot canyon and the ultimate agony of having to cut off his arm to survive.

In mountaineering, there are a number of ways to ensure rescue from within a group. One of the most basic ways when traveling on steep snow and ice slopes or glaciers is traveling in rope teams. Should one climber fall and fail to self-arrest, other members of the rope team can attempt to arrest the fall of their fellow climber. Self-arrest is a technique used to avoid sliding into crevasses or even off mountains. The technique involves using an ice axe to stop your descent. When traveling in a rope team, climbing partners can help arrest the falls of fellow climbers by using their ice axes as braking devices and allowing the rope to stop the fall of a partner. Should this fail, an entire team can be pulled down a mountain, into a crevasse, or over a cliff. Another basic form of assisted rescue in mountaineering and other backcountry winter sports is the use of avalanche beacons, probes, and shovels to rescue fellow travelers who may be buried in an avalanche.

Rescue From an Outside Party

One essential piece of safety equipment that Watson always includes in his safety gear when kayaking in southeast Alaska is a VHF radio. A VHF radio serves a number of purposes for kayakers, sailors, and other outdoor enthusiasts who travel into remote areas. It serves as a weather radio, as a means to communicate with base camp, and most importantly as a means to communicate with the U.S. Coast Guard and local search and rescue groups. Should an event occur that Watson and his group were unable to remedy on their own, they could call the Coast Guard to perform a rescue. Had his near miss become an actual encounter with the sow and her cubs and he or one of the participants had been mauled by the bear, they might have called the Coast Guard to perform a medical evacuation.

The Coast Guard is typically glad to offer rescue

A helicopter performs a medical evacuation.

© DavidSandersphotos.com

services in life-threatening situations. However, some locations have encountered so many search and rescue situations that public resources have worn thin. As a consequence, public agencies that participate in search and rescue operations have begun to charge for their services. Colorado actually offers insurance to people who enter the backcountry. The fee for hunting and fishing licenses in Colorado includes an insurance policy that covers the costs of a rescue should you find yourself in a rescue situation. This insurance policy can be purchased independently of hunting and fishing licenses as well.

The rescue curve is a useful framework for thinking about the practical aspects of risk management. It outlines a series of steps, things that you can do as an outdoor leader or outdoor enthusiast, to enhance the probability of your survival should an accident occur. There are several instances where individuals engaged in recreational activities have found themselves in life-threatening situations due to inadequate preparation, an inability to perform a self-rescue, or a lack of rescue from within their group. Individuals who venture alone into remote settings immediately place themselves at a greater risk than those traveling in parties of four or more. If a self- or assisted-rescue fails, then the ultimate consequence of an accident is death.

Legal Aspects of Risk Management

We must consider risk management not only from a practical perspective but also from a legal perspective. Why is this? The simple answer is that we might find ourselves in a court of law defending our actions as an outdoor leader should any of our clients suffer a loss resulting from an accident during one of our programs. Familiarity with the law is essential in guarding ourselves against lawsuits and to ensure that we are providing the highest level of care possible to our program participants. It is a matter of offering quality assurance within programs.

Standard of Care

Whether or not an outdoor leader is offering an adequate level of care to program participants is determined according to the general **standard of care** offered by other professionals in the industry. Most commercial rafting companies, for instance,

require their clients to wear helmets to protect against potential head injuries should they fall out of their raft and hit their heads on rocks. A rafting company that fails to require its clients to wear helmets runs the risk of being held liable, or accountable, for such an injury because it failed to require its clients to wear helmets. The standard of care in a particular industry is determined according to what other *reasonable and prudent professionals* would do in similar situations. The court will rely on other professionals, or expert witnesses, to determine what you as a reasonable and prudent professional should have done in a particular situation in order to meet the standard of care in the industry. The standard of care within an industry is sometimes referred to as the industry standard or the industry norm.

Tort Law

There are two general types of law in the United States: criminal law and tort law. Criminal law is the body of law under which individuals are held accountable for criminal acts, or acts of wrongdoing against the general public. Criminal lawsuits are tried under federal or state penal codes and are always initiated by government prosecutors. Criminal convictions result in a fine, incarceration, or both, and in some instances criminal convictions for severe crimes result in the death penalty.

Tort law, commonly referred to as civil law, is the body of law that deals with the private rights of citizens rather than with crimes. Tort law is intended to remedy civil wrongs through some form of compensation, usually financial. There are several kinds of torts, or infringements on the private rights of citizens, including trespassing, product liability, and **negligence,** to name a few. Civil lawsuits are always initiated by an individual, group, or organization against another individual, group, or organization. Civil litigation never results in incarceration. Judgments against defendants in civil suits typically result in reimbursement or monetary compensation for losses suffered by the plaintiff.

As in criminal law, the burden of proof in a civil suit is on the plaintiff. The standard of proof in a civil lawsuit is lower than in a criminal case, though. In a civil suit, the plaintiff must simply show that there is more than a 50% probability that the defendant is responsible for a loss or an injury to the plaintiff. The standard in a criminal case is much higher. A defendant is considered guilty in a criminal case only if the evidence proves guilt beyond a reasonable doubt. Though this standard is difficult to quantify, it is generally considered to be equivalent to approximately a 98% probability that the defendant is guilty.

Lawsuits brought against outdoor leaders for injuries or losses to participants as a result of an accident are always filed under tort law. A plaintiff who brings a lawsuit against an outdoor leader must show that the outdoor leader was negligent in order to hold the leader liable for losses resulting from an accident. Volunteers and interns are held to the same standard of care as paid professionals in rendering services to clients or program participants.

Negligence

Four conditions must be met to prove negligence: duty to act, breach of duty, proximate cause, and actual loss. Duty to act refers to the duty of outdoor leaders to provide a certain level of care to the program participant. It refers to the duty of outdoor leaders to meet the standard of care in the industry, or to act as other reasonable and prudent professionals would in similar situations. There is a legal basis for the duty to act, usually in the form of a contract for services. Such a relationship exists between leaders and paying customers, between teachers and students, between park administrators and park visitors, and so forth. If there is no legal relationship between two parties, then there is no duty to act and, therefore, no negligence.

Breach of duty refers to the failure of a leader to meet the industry's standard of care in providing services. If the leader fails to meet the standard of care in providing services and consequently fails to prevent a foreseeable accident, then the leader could be found to be negligent. Breach of duty can result from acts of omission, or a failure to perform duties that should have been performed. Breach of duty can also result from acts of commission, in which leaders do something they should not have done or perform a particular duty incorrectly.

Proximate cause means that the breach of duty was the cause of the accident. There needs to be a causal connection between the breach of duty and the accident. The cause could be either an act of omission or an act of commission. Unless there is a direct connection between the breach of duty and the accident, however, negligence does not exist.

The fourth condition refers to whether an actual injury or loss resulted from the event. Injuries

and losses can take a variety of forms. Individuals can suffer physical injuries such as broken bones, lacerations, illnesses, and heat or cold injuries. Individuals can suffer emotional injuries such as emotional trauma, embarrassment, and mental anguish. Individuals can also suffer financial losses as a result of physical or emotional injury. Financial losses might include the cost of medical treatment, loss of income because of an inability to work due to an injury, and loss of valuable equipment during an accident. The ultimate loss that an individual might suffer is the loss of life. In this case, an individual's family or heirs might file a suit to claim damages against a leader and anyone else who might be held accountable for the death of their loved one. If there is no actual injury or loss, then negligence does not exist.

Process of Risk Management

Good risk management is essentially good program management. Following are a number of steps you can take to ensure that you are effectively managing risks as a program administrator and an outdoor leader.

Adherence to Published Guidelines

Documentation is an essential part of risk management and consequently an essential part of program management. Appropriate documentation can show that you and your program are meeting industry standards, or operating according to industry norms, which is important should you find yourself the defendant in a lawsuit. Appropriate documentation indicates how you operate as a practitioner in the field and the standards to which you adhere in your conduct as a practitioner.

A primary form of documentation is program manuals. Program manuals should document every aspect of the policies and procedures under which a program operates. Such documentation includes a description of the program's mission, goals, and objectives as well as a detailed description of the program's organizational structure and operational procedures. It will also include such items as equipment checklists, menu lists, trip plans, waiver of liability or assumption of risk forms, participant health history forms, photo release forms, incident report forms, and accident report forms. Most importantly, it will include a description of the organization's safety management plan.

Perform a safety analysis for a specified adventure activity (such as a backcountry ski trip, a caving trip, a ropes course program, and so on). During class, get into a group of three or four. Present your safety analysis to one another for peer review. Each presentation and review should require no more than 10 to 15 minutes. Submit your analysis with peer comments in writing to the instructor.

Along with a program manual of policies and procedures, every program should have an instructor handbook that leaders can access while in the field as a reminder of program policies and procedures. Such handbooks document the protocol to which leaders must adhere to ensure that they are meeting the industry standard as they conduct programs. Such handbooks document program policies and procedures that are relevant to the performance of leaders while in the field.

When there is an absence of guidelines in a program's own literature, the program should defer to guidelines that are published by various professional associations within the industry for safely conducting activities. Examples include the Association for Experiential Education (AEE), the American Canoe Association (ACA), and the American Mountain Guides Association (AMGA). Each of these organizations has established guidelines for safely conducting activities in their respective areas of expertise. Your program's guidelines may exceed those of organizations such as these, but they should never be less rigorous.

Program Review

One way to ensure that your program is meeting the industry standard is through continual review of program policies and procedures. Program review should be conducted through self-review as well as peer review.

Peer Review

A peer review involves opening your program to review by other professionals in the field or experts on specific aspects of your program's operations and procedures. These professionals and experts gauge the quality of your program. Following are two approaches to peer review.

Risk Management Advisory Committee One mechanism for performing peer reviews is the development of a risk management advisory committee (RMAC). An RMAC is typically comprised of individuals from the community who represent different areas of expertise that are significant in outdoor education and recreation. For instance, you might include a lawyer on your RMAC to provide counsel on the legal aspects of your program's risk management policies and procedures. You might include a medical doctor on your RMAC to provide advice on policies and procedures for managing medical emergencies as a part of your program's risk management plan. Members of your local search and rescue groups can offer advice and expertise in developing and maintaining an effective risk management plan for your program and could be included on your RMAC. You might also include representatives of various professional associations (e.g., ACA, AMGA) that represent different skill areas (e.g., kayaking, rock climbing) on which you rely to conduct programming. The idea is that you are relying on the collective experience of individuals in your community to assure that your program is meeting the highest level of quality possible in its design and function. An RMAC typically meets once annually to review program policies and procedures as well as incident report forms.

Program Accreditation The AEE is unique in the field of outdoor education and recreation because it is the only professional association that currently offers accreditation to outdoor programs. **Program accreditation** speaks to the general level of competence under which programs are operated. Accreditation indicates that a particular program is meeting or exceeding industry standards. A central part of the accreditation process is an objective peer review. The AEE assigns a committee of reviewers to determine whether a program is meeting the criteria required to obtain accreditation. Once accredited, programs must undergo periodic reviews to ensure that they are continuing to adhere to industry standards.

Learning Activity 16.2

Conduct an incident review session using incident report forms from your college's outdoor program or using incidents reported in various professional venues (such as American Alpine Club's *Accidents in North American Mountaineering*, American Whitewater's Whitewater Accident Database, and so on). Identify lessons learned in each incident.

One of the benefits of AEE accreditation is reduced cost of liability insurance. Insurance companies recognize that organizations that achieve this accreditation are striving to meet the highest standards possible in the practice of outdoor leadership and to reduce the risk of accidents. Reduced risk is rewarded with a reduction in the cost of insurance.

Review of Trip Plan

A written trip plan should be developed for every trip, expedition, or activity that an outdoor program sponsors. Plans for new trips should be submitted to the program director or coordinator for review before the trip. Plans for established trips should also be reviewed and updated before each trip. Trip planning is addressed in detail in chapter 17, but here we'll cover contingency planning and safety analysis.

Contingency Planning All trip plans include an itinerary of daily activities as well as terrain and route descriptions that represent plan A. All trip plans should also include alternative itineraries of daily activities and trip routes that represent plan B should plan A prove impossible or too risky.

Safety Analysis In addition to a contingency plan, your trip plan should include a safety analysis. This safety analysis should address three concerns: expected weather conditions, expected terrain conditions, and other potential hazards. In addressing each of these three concerns, your safety analysis should determine potential no-go conditions. For instance, in addressing expected weather conditions, to avoid the risk of hypothermia you might decide to cancel a white-water kayaking class or a rafting trip if the combined air and water temperature is less than 110° Fahrenheit (43° Celsius). You might decide to cancel a backcountry snowboarding trip if a severe winter storm is forecast. Under terrain conditions, you might decide to cancel a white-water kayaking class or rafting trip if the river or stream that you plan to use is flooded. You might decide to cancel a backcountry snowboarding trip when the snow conditions

are unstable and avalanche danger is high. Under other potential hazards, you might decide to avoid hiking along certain rivers in the Pacific Northwest during salmon runs to avoid potential encounters with brown bears that rely on the salmon runs as a primary part of their diet. In the case of Watson's kayaking trip with his students in southeast Alaska, he might have decided to avoid camping at the mouth of a stream during the salmon run to minimize the chance of encountering brown bears.

Review of Incident Reports

Whenever outdoor leaders experience an accident or a close call during a trip, they should complete a written report documenting the incident. Accidents are those incidents that result in injury, illness, loss of person, or fatalities. Close calls are incidents in which any of these events could potentially have occurred but by chance did not. Accident report forms and close-call report forms should be carried on every trip. The first aid kit is a good place for these forms. They should be completed as soon as possible following an incident while memories of the incident are still fresh. These reports should later be reviewed by the trip staff and by other program staff members to determine if any changes are needed in programming procedures to prevent the likelihood of such incidents occurring again. All incident reports should also be kept in a file that can be periodically reviewed as part of a general program review to determine if any patterns exist that may be contributing to the repetitive occurrence of close calls or accidents. These forms are an important source of data in determining whether the program is operating in a safe manner.

Personnel Training and Development

Safety is an integral part of the training of outdoor leaders. One of the things that this text emphasizes most is to know your limitations, or, to repeat an oft-used saying, "Know what you know and know what you don't know." This is especially important for outdoor leaders when it comes to safety and risk management. Outdoor leaders who do not know their limitations run the risk of getting themselves as well as their group in over their heads. This is usually the case when it comes to technical skills, but it can also be the case in the emotional realm as well. Before hiring a leader or promoting a trainee to a leadership position, program administrators should be sure that the prospective leader is technically proficient. They should also be sure that the prospective leader has the maturity and wisdom to recognize personal limitations in a leadership position. All leadership training should include safety as an underlying theme. Leader proficiency ultimately amounts to ensuring the safety of program participants.

Including Participants in Risk Management

Program participants should be included in the risk management process from the moment they sign up for a trip. There are numerous ways to include program participants in the risk management process. We cannot mention them all here, but following are a few of the common ways that this inclusion is achieved in outdoor programming.

The first step in involving program participants in the risk management process is to make them aware of the risks associated with the program. One of your first opportunities to do this is to have participants complete waiver of liability and assumption of risk forms. These forms serve as an initial opportunity to make participants aware of the risks that they may encounter as part of the program activity. Introduce this form to program participants at their pretrip meeting; for instance, Watson explained to participants that they would confront a variety of risks during their 3-day kayaking trip in southeast Alaska. They would confront the risk of cold water immersion, hypothermia, sunburn, encounters with bears and marine life, drowning, and so forth. To participate in the kayaking trip, the participants must first acknowledge these risks, assume responsibility

for any loss that might result due to these risks, and waive the trip leader and the program of any liability for possible losses.

Participants signify their agreement to assume risks by signing the form. Participants typically complete these forms when signing up for a trip or when attending a pretrip meeting. The forms should not only be read and signed by the participants, they should be explained to the participants by the outdoor leader. Waiver of liability and assumption of risk forms should be a standard part of any outdoor program's risk management procedures.

Another way to include program participants in the risk management process is to offer them adequate training in the technical skills they will have to use during a program activity. Watson, for instance, offered his participants basic instruction in coastal kayaking in a heated indoor pool before their trip. He taught them how to perform wet exits, Eskimo rescues, Eskimo rolls, and a variety of other assisted and unassisted rescue techniques. As a consequence, his participants were prepared to take an active part in ensuring their own safety during the trip rather than becoming hapless victims relying solely on their leader to bail them out should they experience a mishap. Teaching participants how to ensure their own safety and how to help ensure the safety of others is a key aspect of risk management.

Safety is an integral part of training people to use the outdoors for recreation on their own. Safety should be in everything you teach your program participants, whether you are teaching basic backcountry living skills like stove use or whether you are teaching how to competently engage in a high-risk adventure pursuit like winter mountaineering. Safety is an attitude that you should constantly strive to impart to participants. Watson swallowed his pride and acknowledged his mistake to his participants so that they would learn from his mistake and hopefully exercise better judgment in choosing campsites of their own in the future.

Learning Activity 16.3

Get into a group of three. Each member should practice giving a 10- to 15-minute "safety talk." This talk should focus on making the audience aware of risks associated with participating in a specified adventure activity (such as rock climbing, backpacking, white-water rafting, and so on). The talk should also include an introduction to a waiver of liability form and a health history form.

Emergency Management

Paul Petzoldt is noted for his many maxims that speak to the realities outdoor leaders face on a daily basis. One of these addresses the prospect of being caught in survival situations: "If you're dumb enough to get yourself into the situation in the first place, you're probably not smart enough to get yourself out of it." On the basis of this rationale, Petzoldt avoided teaching outdoor survival to the many leaders and program participants he trained and worked with over the years. He suggested that survival situations should be avoided altogether. This text does not address outdoor survival specifically, but it does address important considerations should a group find itself in an emergency situation. An important aspect of a program's overall safety management plan and of every trip plan is an emergency management plan. Every safety management plan and every trip plan should include emergency management as one of its components. There are several considerations involved in creating an emergency management plan.

Roles and Responsibilities

One consideration in developing an emergency management plan concerns the roles that program staff members and participants will play throughout an incident. The leader of a particular trip is ultimately responsible for decisions in an emergency. Program personnel who are not in the field, a program administrator, for instance, should avoid making decisions or attempting to influence the course of actions of individuals in the field during an incident. People who are not present in the field are unaware of the variables at play in the situation and therefore cannot make a qualified decision about the situation. The leader of the trip is responsible for managing and making decisions about the situation.

A key aspect of managing an emergency situation is delegating responsibility for specific tasks. For instance, a leader might assign a party of individuals to seek help in the absence of communication with the outside world. A leader might assign the person who is most qualified in administering first aid or life support the task of tending to the medical needs of an injured person. Often the leader is not the most qualified group member in this area or must assign this task to another individual in order to better manage the incident. The leader might assign members of the group to construct a litter for transporting an injured person from the field. A number of roles and tasks must be performed in an emergency situation. Identifying who is best suited to perform these various tasks is an important part of an emergency management plan.

Evacuation Plans

Every trip plan should include evacuation plans. An evacuation plan simply details the most expedient way to get an injured person out of the backcountry to advanced medical care. This entails identifying potential routes for evacuating a victim from an area and identifying means of transportation by which an individual might be evacuated (e.g., via land, water, or air). If the possibility of evacuation via helicopter exists, then an evacuation plan should identify potential landing sites for a helicopter. If there is a possibility for evacuation from a river, then the plan should identify the nearest vehicle access points along the river. If there is a possibility for evacuation by foot, an evacuation plan should identify the nearest trailheads or roads that serve as vehicle access points.

Emergency Contacts

Another consideration in the case of a serious incident is notification of program administrators that an incident has occurred. Your trip plan should include a list of individuals within the program that you must contact in case of an emergency. It should also include a list of organizations or agencies outside of your program that you might contact (e.g., local sheriff's office, local hospital, land management agencies, local search and rescue groups). Calling for help is sometimes as easy as dialing 911. Other times it is useful to have specific contact numbers for particular organizations and agencies.

In developing an emergency management plan, be sure to consider how you intend to communicate with the outside world in case of a serious incident. Cell phones work in many areas that are close to urban centers, while VHF radios are a method for communication in more remote settings. Occasionally, you will find yourself entering areas where modern communication devices such as cell phones and VHF radios do not work. It is necessary when traveling in these areas to identify the location of the nearest telephone or the nearest cell phone or radio towers. Program personnel or participants can be sent to these locations to call for assistance. In some areas, radio messages can be relayed from one radio operator to another until the messages reach their intended destination, usually rescue personnel.

Media Contact

Contact with the media is another consideration in an emergency management plan. Leaders should avoid offering information directly to the media. Any information given to the media should be filtered through an appropriate representative of your program, usually your program director or administrator. Newsworthy incidents will capture the attention of local and national media, and the media will attempt to obtain information from rescue personnel, witnesses, program participants, and any other potential sources. As the leader, you should instruct your staff and program participants to avoid communicating directly with the media. The reason for this is to avoid the possibility of spreading misinformation or rumors about the nature of the incident. The relatives of victims or lost persons as well as other members of your group should hear an accurate account of the incident from an appropriate program representative rather than hearing misinformation and speculation through the media. Names of victims and information about the nature of the incident should be released only to the proper authorities and program personnel.

Judgment and Decision Making in Risk Management

Another quote from Paul Petzoldt that speaks to the heart of safety and risk management is his statement, "Rules are for fools!" There are two general approaches to decision making in the outdoors, a rules-based approach and a judgment-based approach. A leader who relies solely on a rules-based approach to decision making is one who refers solely to the instructor field manual, the program policies and procedures manual, and other sets of guidelines for insight on how to approach problematic situations. Petzoldt's point is that no set of rules can address every potential problem that a leader might encounter. While rules and guidelines are useful, they should represent only one part of a more comprehensive approach to safety and risk management. Those

You will not often find stop signs in the wild. More often, you'll have to rely on your own judgment to assess risks.

who rely solely on rules or guidelines as a basis for decision making will eventually find themselves in a situation for which they are ill-prepared and for which the guidelines come up short. Rather than a strictly prescriptive rules-based approach to decision making, Petzoldt advocates a judgment-based approach as an integral competent of outdoor leadership.

The difference between the two approaches can be exemplified through the experience of a rock-climbing instructor who has been trained to manage a particular climbing site for her outdoor program. The program uses the same site for all of its climbing programs and it trains its instructors specifically for this site. The instructor is familiar with all of the climbing routes, anchor points, setups, and safety concerns at the site. It is the only site at which she has worked, however, and she is unfamiliar with many of the general principles of rock climbing. Imagine asking this instructor to lead a group of students in climbing at an unfamiliar site where she must identify all climbing routes, anchor points, and safety concerns. Because of this program's prescriptive approach to training, its leaders are not equipped to ensure the safety of program participants in areas with which they are unfamiliar. These leaders have not been given the tools—the experience and knowledge—to exercise good judgment regarding the safety of their participants in unfamiliar settings.

While program policies, procedures, and guidelines are integral to effective program management and consequently to effective risk management, the importance of instructor judgment should not be overlooked. As we learned in chapter 6, judgment is an informed opinion based on past experience. We also learned that decision making is the process of choosing the best option from a collection of options. A leader with good judgment and extensive experience has a much greater chance of selecting the best option in a problematic situation than a leader who simply relies on preset rules or guidelines in approaching the problem.

Summary

One of the main reasons for adhering to industry standards is not to avoid the prospect of being sued, though this is a primary concern. A more important concern, however, is ensuring that you meet the highest level of care possible in providing services to program participants. The goals of outdoor education and recreation are generally focused on personal and interpersonal growth among individuals. There is not much growth in getting hurt or killed as the result of an accident in the outdoors. Quality assurance in what we do as outdoor leaders is one of the primary reasons for developing and implementing an effective risk management plan.

Selected References

Hale, A. 1984. Safety management for outdoor program leaders. Unpublished manuscript.

Hunt, J.S. 1990. Philosophy of adventure education. In *Adventure education,* ed. J.C. Miles and S. Priest. State College, PA: Venture.

Kauffman, R.B., and G. Carlson. 1992. The rescue curve: A race against time. *American Canoeist* (March): 10-13.

Priest, S., and T. Dixon. 1990. *Safety practices in adventure programming.* Boulder, CO: AEE.

Van der Smissen, B. 1990. *Legal liability and risk management for public and private entities.* Cincinnati: Anderson.

Professional-Development Portfolio Activity

Complete a self-assessment in which you identify your abilities and limitations as an outdoor leader. The core competencies in outdoor leadership (see page xiv) should serve as the criteria for your assessment. Identify particular goals for continued growth and development. Develop a plan for achieving these goals, including a time line. Identify potential barriers to the achievement of these goals.

chapter 17

Expedition Planning

" 'I think,' said Christopher Robin, 'that we ought to eat all our provisions now, so that we shan't have so much to carry.' " —A.A. Milne

Chapter Concepts

- Trip planning or expedition planning—These terms are used interchangeably to denote a formal planning process for outdoor adventure activities such as backpacking, canoeing, mountaineering, and so on.
- Logistics—Logistics are a support system devised to assist in the execution of an expedition.
- GO PREPARE—This is a systematic approach to planning and implementing expeditions.

The chapter concepts relate to the following core competencies:

- Program management (CC-6)—An outdoor leader must be able to manage logistics.
- Safety and risk management (CC-7)—Trip planning requires the ability to manage risks.
- Technical ability (CC-8)—Trip planning is one of many technical competencies an outdoor leader must possess.

An incredible opportunity had fallen into Juan's lap. Juan's dream was to obtain an outdoor leadership position so that he could lead others into the outdoors. A local youth director, Liz, knew of Juan's interests and approached him to lead a group of inner-city teenagers on a 5-day backpacking trip. Juan had no formal outdoor leadership experience but had spent many summers backpacking in the nearby Pisgah National Forest with his friends. Liz provided Juan with a budget and a participant contact list. Liz also requested that Jennifer, an agency employee, serve as an assistant leader for the group. Jennifer had excellent leadership skills and knew the teenagers but lacked outdoor experience.

Juan immediately developed a personal clothing and equipment list for the group. Much time was allotted to planning the most scenic route. Juan chose a route he had taken once before and anticipated that it would make a big impression. He rented group gear such as tents, backpacks, sleeping pads, and cooking gear from a local outfitter, and he purchased food at a local grocery store.

Juan met Jennifer and the group at the designated time and place. Everyone buzzed with excitement fueled by anticipation of the unknown. The 10 teenagers ranging from 14 to 16 years of age had never slept outdoors. Juan felt a bit uneasy as he looked at the inappropriate personal equipment strewn about the parking lot. He began to lecture the group on the advantages of synthetics and wool over cotton as well as the importance of layering. Half the group had sleeping bags and others had brought blankets

and sheets. Most wore sneakers but all had at least a poncho for rain protection. Juan gave a quick packing demonstration and the participants then packed their bags in similar fashion.

The bus dropped the group off at the trailhead at 1:00 in the afternoon. Juan felt confident that the teenagers would have no problem with the 4-mile (6-kilometer) hike. Jennifer was impressed with Juan's knowledge of the forest and with his high-tech gear. She inquired about a map and trip route as they hiked, and Juan explained that a map was not needed. He knew all routes based on previous trips and all trails were clearly marked with colored blazes and information signs. He had decided not to purchase maps and instead invest in higher quality food. Juan excitedly shared that he had purchased smoked oysters, specialty cheeses, macadamia nuts, and other delicacies. Jennifer looked at Juan with concern and told him she thought several kids had food allergies. Jennifer knew all the participants from previous agency activities but had left their medical information back at the office where it would be safe.

Juan and Jennifer stopped for a moment to look back at only half of the group. Many of the teenagers lagged farther back, struggling up the slope. He promised the views at the top would make it all worthwhile. Juan had only hiked this particular trail from the other direction and did not really remember the steep grade. A map would show the group gaining 1,000 feet (305 meters) in about a mile then leveling off for another mile before going down. When the group finally reached the halfway point, 5 hours later, two

(continued)

were crying and the rest were clearly irritated. At the first overlook and break, they all threw their packs down and reclined on the rocks with little interest in the view. Several asked when the hike would be over for the day. Juan wanted to do the last half of the hike, all downhill, but remembered a campsite just a mile away. The group struggled to the campsite, but with several consequences. One boy pulled his boots off to display two large blisters on his feet. Another participant limped into camp on a sore knee from years of soccer playing.

Juan talked to Jennifer about getting the tents up and starting dinner. Jennifer did not know how to erect the tents or light the stoves but was willing to learn. It was a dry camp, and they would have to hike to the next campsite a mile away to find water. Everyone was exhausted and unwilling to walk with Juan to collect water. Juan emptied his pack and gathered each person's empty water bottle, which made him realize how dehydrated the group had become. He wished he had larger containers for collecting water. He had always camped by water before so obtaining adequate water for the night was never a problem.

Juan spent 2 hours hiking to the water source and hauling what he could back to camp. Most of the kids wanted to drink the water immediately, but he was able to keep a little to cook the meal. After dinner, spirits were rejuvenated. Juan noticed a few clouds building up to the west but did not think much of it when questioned by Jennifer. Juan double-checked the tents and hung the food before going to bed. As he was hanging his food, he spotted where someone had gone to the bathroom without burying it. He realized that in his haste to set up camp he had not properly briefed the group in such matters.

The group awoke in the middle of the night to flashes of lightning and the pounding of thunder. The torrential downpour penetrated a few leaky tents and soaked blankets and sheets, and a slow drizzle continued through the morning hours. An unseasonable cold front was coming through and the wet teenagers were miserable and sullen. On top of the attitude problem, they had a more serious problem. The young woman with the sore knee could not walk. Her knee had become so swollen and painful it was impossible to put any pressure on it. Juan could not believe he was faced with a possible evacuation. By this time, Jennifer had become impatient and asked where the nearest road was located. Juan thought there might be a gravel road not too far east of their location but was not sure. Jennifer had her cell phone but could not access service at their present location. Even if the phone worked, they were not sure where to call for help. Juan sat down on a log and realized he was in this predicament because of poor planning.

Juan's story portrays the reality of misadventures when leaders lack planning skills. The inability or lack of knowledge related to expedition planning results in a multitude of problems. Accidents and injuries are the most obvious and dramatic consequences. The probability of a serious accident resulting in injury increases relative to the poor quality of a trip plan. If participants are lucky enough to avoid injury during a poorly planned trip, they still face the high probability of a miserable experience. Excessive discomfort resulting from poor planning tends to dissuade people from participating in future outdoor activities, and leaders who do not properly plan may inadvertently teach people to dislike the great outdoors. Finally, another problem can arise from poor planning that few people realize—poor planning is detrimental to the natural environment. Damage to the environment occurs in many forms as a result of poor planning. Leave No Trace ethics profess the need for proper planning as one of their seven guiding principles (see page 221 for a list of all seven principles).

This chapter focuses on proper expedition planning so that leaders will minimize accidents, ensure a quality experience, and protect the environment. To assist the aspiring outdoor leader in developing appropriate planning skills, the **GO PREPARE** system of expedition planning is presented. The first portion of this chapter discusses the GO (goals and objectives) aspect of the trip plan. Goal and objective development based on organizational philosophy is analyzed. Sound goals and objectives guide outdoor leaders as they develop a trip plan. Next, the remainder of the trip plan is discussed in detail using the PREPARE portion of trip planning. An outdoor leader must take into consideration the following planning components by answering the related questions:

P = Participants (Who are the participants?)

R = Resources (What resources are available to support an expedition?)

E = Equipment and clothing (What equipment and clothing will be needed?)

P = Plan (What is the itinerary and time control plan?)

A = Access (How does the group obtain proper access?)

R = Rationing (How will the menu be determined and food packed?)

E = Emergency plan (What is the emergency plan?)

Each aspect of the GO PREPARE system will be discussed at length to give the aspiring outdoor leader the tools to design a comprehensive expedition plan. The last part of this chapter discusses the final aspect of the GO PREPARE process: logistics. All trips require some level of logistical support. Logistics include transportation to and from the program site, food drops, equipment exchanges, shakedowns, and procedures for trip termination. Smooth, well-planned logistical support ensures that the trip plan is conducted in a competent manner.

Trip Purpose

The foundation of an effective trip plan is well-defined program goals and objectives. Outdoor leaders must understand their organization's philosophy and program goals before attempting to develop a plan. Juan's first mistake was not taking the time to discover why the youth director was sponsoring the trip. Juan should have learned what specific program goals and objectives Liz wished to accomplish through outdoor programming. Juan designed the trip from an assumption that the teenagers wanted a view. His personal agenda influenced his choices, such as his desire to experience a particular part of the forest. Juan fell into the trap of basing all planning decisions on limited, personal experience.

Organizational philosophy and program goals vary significantly among agencies. A competent outdoor leader is able to operationalize philosophy and goals through the expedition plan. The following examples represent three different organizations' philosophies of outdoor programming.

Organization 1: Teen Power

Teen Power serves youths from 14 to 19 years of age. The organizational philosophy focuses

Leaders who don't plan often deal with hurt, hungry, tired groups.

on building self-confidence and self-esteem. This organization believes that young people need challenging experiences to foster character development because character development establishes the foundation for self-identity and discovering the true self. Through identity development young people can build self-esteem and confidence. Teen Power uses extended wilderness trips to accomplish this developmental process. Based on organizational philosophy and principles, Teen Power integrates the following elements into their trip plans.

- Physically demanding experiences such as long strenuous hikes on and off trail, challenging peak climbs, and a solo experience are all incorporated. Clients spend 20 days in the wilderness without exposure to modern facilities and conveniences.

- Daily debriefings and other tools such as journaling are integrated into the schedule for personal and group reflection so that clients may process the psychological dynamics created by the extreme physical challenges.

- Technical skills are taught only to the point that clients can safely engage in the adventure activities. It is not an organizational goal to produce technically competent backpackers or mountaineers.

Organization 2: Big Adventure

Big Adventure teaches technical outdoor skills to adults 18 years of age and older. Big Adventure promotes outdoor adventure activities as a way to improve health and general well-being. The organization believes in promoting lifetime leisure activities through adventure recreation. It integrates the following global elements into trip plans.

- Technical skills instruction is offered according to individual abilities. Trips are designated as beginner, intermediate, or advanced.

- Significant amounts of time are programmed for teaching and practicing skills.

- Breaks are scheduled throughout the program for hot showers, cooked meals, machine washing of clothes, and so on.

Organization 3: Quest, Inc.

Quest serves individuals of all abilities through wilderness experiences. Quest believes that individuals of all abilities have the right to experience wilderness adventures. It provides opportunities for all people to explore the great wilderness areas of the world. It believes in protecting natural resources for all to enjoy. Quest integrates the following elements into its trip plans.

- A mix of challenging and relaxing activities are provided so that clients can focus on the natural environment.

- Time is devoted to studying the natural environment. This includes scheduling evening discussions on the environment.

- Technical skills are taught so that participants can travel comfortably through the wilderness. Much time is devoted to teaching Leave No Trace skills.

These examples provide insight into a variety of philosophical perspectives that outdoor-oriented organizations may embrace. Of course, there are many more philosophies in the outdoor industry. The objective is to demonstrate how basic programming structure varies based on organizational philosophy. After gaining an understanding of organizational philosophy, the leader must next operationalize a philosophy through the development of goals and objectives. Comprehensive trip plans contain specific goals and objectives that provide guidance as outdoor leaders make planning decisions.

Trip Goals and Objectives (GO)

Developing expedition goals requires the same thought process used to create goals for any program or educational lesson. Goals represent broad, intended outcomes to be experienced by clients as a result of participation. Trip goals reflect larger program goals, which are guided by the organization's philosophy. Therefore, expedition goals should reflect the purpose of the organization by putting the philosophy into operational terms. Goals provide direction for outdoor leaders and participants as they engage in a trip experience. Several objectives, or specific, measurable outcomes, should be created to accompany each goal. Outdoor leaders are encouraged to use the SMART (specific, measurable, achievable, realistic, time-bound) method of objective development (Priest and Gass 1997). For an in-depth discussion on creating SMART objectives, refer to chapter 12. Objectives serve as targeted outcomes to assess goal accomplishment. Well-developed goals and objectives create measurable criteria necessary for program evaluation. Trip success and improvement can be determined through well-written goals and objectives. For a clear understanding of the goal and objective hierarchy, refer to chapter 15, figure 15.3 (page 229).

Outdoor leaders must take the time to craft quality goals and objectives when developing their trip plans. Well-written goals and objectives serve the same purpose as a good map. Leaders are able to focus on a specific path or direction as they create and execute a trip. If leaders are forced to make tough programming decisions during the trip, goals and objectives will assist in the decision-making process. For example, a primary goal is to develop the participants' kayaking skills to be competent in class II white water. The leaders thus decide to add an extra day to the schedule for kayaking because the group did not develop class II paddling ability. Time will be shaved from the backpacking portion of the trip without negatively affecting goals and objectives associated with backpacking.

To provide a clear picture of specific goals and objectives that could be integrated into a trip plan, Teen Power will be revisited. Examples of specific goals and objectives are provided to guide the aspiring outdoor leader in developing this important planning skill.

Creating Goals and Objectives

Creating goals and objectives requires leaders to put thought and time into the expedition's purpose. In order to model goal and objective development, Teen Power, as described on page 266, will be used as an example.

Teen Power's purpose emphasizes the building of self-confidence and self-esteem in teenagers. This organization's philosophy is based on the belief that young people need challenging personal and social experiences to foster character development. Character development promotes a healthy sense of self, or self-identity. Through identity development, youths can then strengthen their self-esteem and confidence. Teen Power uses extended, 20-day wilderness trips to accomplish this developmental process. Teen Power is located in an area conducive to backpacking and mountaineering. The following are goals and corresponding objectives that could be used to form a trip plan for a 20-day expedition.

Goal 1

Provide challenging adventures that promote the development of participant self-confidence.

- Objective 1: Offer a backpacking trip lasting 20 days that becomes progressively more difficult as the participants acclimate and develop skills.
- Objective 2: Provide the opportunity to attempt climbing at least one mountain peak over 16,000 feet (4,877 meters) during the backpacking expedition.
- Objective 3: Provide the opportunity to engage in technical rock climbing so that participants are challenged at their personal ability level.
- Objective 4: Challenge all participants with a 13-mile (21-kilometer) cross country run at the end of the trip.

Goal 2

Provide ample opportunities for personal reflection in order to promote the formation of self-identity.

- Objective 1: Provide a 48-hour (minimum) solo experience for each participant that includes at least two self-reflection exercises.
- Objective 2: Require that each participant maintain a personal journal throughout the experience that includes assignments and exercises to promote self-reflection.
- Objective 3: Provide a minimum of 30 minutes per day for individuals to be alone for personal reflection and journal time.
- Objective 4: Provide the opportunity for each individual to have a personal interview with the leaders at the end of the trip to discuss personal growth and discoveries as a result of the experience.

Goal 3

Facilitate positive group experiences to enhance character development through social interaction.

- Objective 1: Facilitate formal group debriefings at least once per day to discuss group concerns.
- Objective 2: Encourage participants to share their personal story with the rest of the group to promote empathy and tolerance for diversity.
- Objective 3: Facilitate daily activities such as cooking, cleaning, shelter building, hiking, and so on so that these tasks are accomplished through a group-centered process rather than an instructor-centered process.

- Objective 4: Teach basic lessons in group dynamics and communications to foster effective group communication.

Goal 4

Provide a positive, enjoyable experience to enhance personal growth and self-discovery.

- Objective 1: Design a progression of activities and skills so that participants obtain a mastery of skills to enjoy the adventure activities.
- Objective 2: Take time to celebrate accomplishments by designing ceremonies and special activities that promote laughter, camaraderie, and sense of accomplishment.
- Objective 3: Allow properly prepared participants the opportunity to engage in a final expedition (last 2 days of the trip) to hike out of the mountains without the leaders' assistance.
- Objective 4: Integrate games and team-building activities throughout the experience to enhance positive group interactions.

These sample goals and objectives provide a clear program format for trip design and facilitation. The goals and objectives are specific and yet remain flexible from a programming standpoint. For example, some groups may have the desire and ability to climb more than one 16,000-foot (4,877-meter) peak. Also, the leaders reserve the right to extend the solo time if the conditions are appropriate. These goals and objectives are designed so that options exist within the structured framework. The goals and objectives also represent measurable outcomes. Specific program components such as games, personal stories, debriefings, journals, and other elements can be documented. Specific numbers such as a 16,000-foot peak attempt or a 48-hour solo serve as quantitative outcomes. Leaders can now take these goals and objectives to create a more detailed itinerary and solidify other aspects of the trip plan. We can now see how well-designed goals and objectives provide the foundation for an effective trip plan. The next step in the planning process is to PREPARE!

PREPARE System

Once the outdoor leader establishes trip goals and objectives, the leader must PREPARE for the expedition by engaging in a formal planning process. As learned earlier, a proper trip plan ensures safe, quality, and environmentally sound experiences. An actual trip plan should be compiled that addresses participants, resources, equipment and clothing, access to the trip area, rationing, and emergencies—the seven elements of PREPARE. Addressing these components will alleviate many potential problems during the expedition. Seasoned leaders work on the components simultaneously to bring the entire plan together as information falls into place. In some cases, trip planning may require the leader to begin several years in advance. For example, obtaining a permit for a trip location can take years if a waiting system or permit lottery is in place. However, the planning process may only take several days if components of the PREPARE system are in place. For example, an outdoor leader working for an established wilderness camp may experience the benefit of administrative support and a well-established program. In this scenario, participant information, food, permits, routes, and emergency procedures may already be in place. This wilderness leader simply needs to gather equipment and follow the standardized program format.

The amount of necessary trip planning varies in any situation. The competent outdoor leader fully understands the GO PREPARE system of planning and creates a planning document. If we reflect back on Juan's planning process, his efforts were not systematic. Juan lacked proper planning skills to create a 5-day trip plan for the teenagers. Juan would benefit from formal training and institutional planning experience. The following sections encompass the PREPARE system of

Learning Activity 17.1

Using the organizational philosophy of Big Adventure, Quest, Inc., or any other philosophy, create the framework for a trip by developing appropriate goals and objectives.

trip planning and each of the seven components, which should all be included in a trip plan.

Participants

Who are the participants? Any outdoor leader involved in the planning process must ask this critical question. Many of the trip's parameters hinge on this important question. The competent outdoor leader views this question on several levels. An analysis of participant characteristics includes age, group size, gender, health, prior experience, and motivational level. Participant cultural backgrounds may also be pertinent, as an understanding of religious practices, food restrictions, gender roles, and so on assist the outdoor leader in the planning process. In addition to cultural background, leaders may need to know participants' physical and mental abilities so that accommodations can be made during the planning process to make trips inclusive. Careful consideration of all these factors enables outdoor leaders to design the appropriate trip. Applications, interviews, and personal correspondence with clients before the trip begins allow leaders to obtain this vital planning information.

Age

Developmental level by age is a logical consideration. Experiences designed for teenagers will be different from experiences designed for older

adults. For example, the outdoor leader might keep the itinerary packed with numerous activities in order to keep teenagers engaged. Older adults, on the other hand, might appreciate a less structured schedule with more opportunity to control their own time and pace. Outdoor leaders without knowledge of human developmental levels would benefit from further research in this area.

Group Size

The number of participants is a critical planning factor. Group size dictates equipment decisions, food amounts, permit restrictions, and so on. Group size also influences environmental factors. Larger groups should not be led into environmentally sensitive areas to help prevent such problems as vegetation trampling and perceptions of overcrowding. Large groups (20 or more) can be split into patrols to increase hiking efficiency. This technique requires more leaders and first aid kits.

Gender

Gender characteristics of a group also influence planning decisions. Is the group all males, females, or coed? Serving a coed group (especially youths) may require the leadership team to be coed. Coed groups influence risk management and equipment decisions as well as things like tenting arrangements. Also, food purchased for a group of teenage boys may vary from the quantity and type of food purchased for a group of adult women.

Health

Leaders must know the physical and mental condition of their participants. Medical and personal data forms contain this information. Leaders should have access to these forms during the planning process. Information such as physical limitations, diet restrictions, medications, and past medical history will influence all aspects of the trip plan. For example, if a participant has a documented physical restriction, the outdoor leader may have to adapt an activity or modify equipment to meet individual needs.

Prior Experience

Knowing a participant's prior experience allows the leader to make informed decisions in all aspects of

Two teenagers work together to pitch a tent.

planning. For example, a known group of experienced white-water canoeists might allow a leader to design a paddling trip at an advanced level. Beware, though; leaders must have an accurate screening system to predetermine experience. Participants who underestimate or overestimate their own ability provide poor information when it comes to designing the ideal trip.

Motivational Level

Knowing a participant's motivational level helps when designing a trip. Many leaders will ask participants well before the trip to describe their personal goals and reasons for participation. Trips can then be designed around personal needs. Many organizations institute an admissions or screening process. If a participant's goals and motivations are not congruent with trip goals, other experiences and organizations can be recommended.

Resources

In most cases, resource availability helps determine trip design. A trip budget should be reflected in the trip plan. Minimally, competent leaders create a simple budget to account for anticipated expenditures (see figure 17.1). In addition to budgeting, creativity is also a handy skill for compiling resources. Equipment may be borrowed, traded, or rented to supplement trip resources. For example, some organizations do not have the resources to purchase specialized outdoor equipment, so they require participants to bring specialized equipment such as personal kayaks or mountaineering equipment. Or, one agency may trade specialized equipment with another agency such as vertical caving gear for snowshoes as opposed to investing and maintaining an inventory of both items. Outdoor leaders must take into consideration all possible resources in order to execute fiscally sound expeditions. One final word of advice on participant resources: Participants of all socioeconomic backgrounds participate in outdoor adventures. Consider stockpiling extra clothing and equipment to assist clients who may be in need.

Equipment and Clothing

A quality trip plan includes a personal clothing list. Leaders should determine the appropriate clothing and equipment for any given trip and

Sample Trip Budget

The following budget reflects potential costs associated with Juan's trip. Juan's budget reflects 10 participants and 2 leaders for 5 days. While budgets vary, the following exemplifies a typical trip budget. Be sure to include a miscellaneous category for unforeseen expenses.

Budget item	Estimated expense
Food ($4.00/day/person)	240.00
Transportation (200 miles @ .43/mile)	86.00
Instructor salary and fees	600.00
Equipment rental	900.00
Maps	20.00
Permit	100.00
Fuel and supplies (i.e., gas, first aid, cord)	75.00
Final banquet expenses	150.00
T-shirts	150.00
Miscellaneous	50.00
Total expenses	**$2,371.00**

Figure 17.1 Example of a basic trip budget.

distribute a recommended personal clothing and equipment list to participants. The Dress **WISE** layering system serves as the primary guide for clothing selection:

W= Wicking layer—This layer is worn next to the skin to wick moisture away and to insulate. It includes long underwear, liner socks and gloves, and stocking caps.

I = Insulation layer—This layer traps warm air against the body to ensure adequate warmth. It includes wool or fleece pants, fleece jackets, and gloves.

S = Shell layer—This layer consists of a water- and windproof outer shell such as rain and wind gear made of treated nylons or breathable, waterproof fabrics.

E = Extra clothing—Extra layers should be packed according to environmental conditions and types of activities.

Trip equipment falls into two categories: personal equipment (see figure 17.2) and group equipment (see figure 17.3). A quality trip plan includes both lists. The content of these lists varies depending on organizational philosophy

Personal Equipment List

The following is a personal equipment list for backpacking.

Qty.	Wicking layer
2	pair long johns (synthetic, wool or silk, tops and bottoms)
1	pair lightweight synthetic gloves
2	pair underwear (synthetic or silk, quick drying)
3	pair synthetic liner socks
	Insulation layer
1	lightweight long-sleeved shirt (synthetic, polyester for insects and sun protection)
1	pair lightweight long pants (loose-fitting, synthetic; no jeans)
1	lightweight wool shirt, sweater, or synthetic layer such as fleece
1	fleece jacket
1	pair fleece or wool pants
3	pair socks (no cotton; should be wool or synthetic)
1	wool or synthetic stocking-type hat
1	pair fleece or wool gloves
	Shell layer
1	pair sturdy hiking boots
1	rain gear (breathable, waterproof fabric recommended, no ponchos, *must* have parka with hood and pants)
	Extra clothing and equipment
1 or 2	pair shorts
1 or 2	short-sleeved shirts (synthetic T-shirts recommended)
3	bandannas
1	pair lightweight camp shoes
1	headlamp with extra bulb and batteries
	sunscreen
	insect repellent
	sunglasses (UV protection)
	personal hygiene items
1	brimmed hat

Figure 17.2 Sample personal equipment list using the WISE system.

Group equipment	Qty.	Condition	Notes	Check-in	Condition	Replacement price/item
Spatula						$5.00
Lg. cook spoon						$2.00
Pocketknife						$12.00
Pot grips						$4.00
Stove						$54.00
Fuel bottles						$16.00
Funnel						$3.00
Water bag						$6.00
Water filter						$30.00
Iodine						$6.00
Cook kit (pots with lids)						$21.00
Baking/frying pan and lid						$28.00
Tarp						$75.00
Cord						$2.00
Tent						$250.00
Compass						$16.00
Duffel bags						$25.00
Food-hanging rope						$15.00
Shovel						$15.00
Stuff sacks						$5.00
Whistle						$2.00
Maps						$8.00

Figure 17.3 Group equipment list and logistical check-out system. Prices are given for each item so that participants are aware of replacement costs if held responsible for lost or damaged items.

and resources. For example, some organizations believe standard gear should be issued to all participants to alleviate any feelings of inequity. Feelings of inadequacy are reduced if everyone has the same rain gear, sleeping bag, and backpack, for example. Other organizations maintain no equipment inventories and require participants to supply all equipment.

Outdoor leaders know that weather plays a major role in expedition planning. Leaders must research the weather patterns for a given area. This information is easily accessible on the Internet—you can discover record temperature highs and lows,

wind speeds, and averages. With this information, leaders anticipate the absolute worst- and best-case weather scenarios and prepare properly. A leader who plans a trip based on a current long-term forecast is asking for trouble. Leaders should not forget to check current environmental conditions, too. Snow pack, water level, fire hazard, and so on also affect equipment and clothing choices. For example, neglecting to bring snowshoes and gaiters when needed could adversely affect the trip. The worst should always be anticipated. See figure 17.4 for a winter travel list issued to students attending a university-sponsored trip in the

Mandatory Equipment List for Winter Trips

The outdoor program will provide the following gear to all students:

- Snowshoes or skis, depending on course and snow conditions
- Sleeping bags, tents, stoves, snow shovels, backpacks, and cooking gear
- Plastic boots
- Wool pants
- Expedition gear (insulated pants and jackets with hoods)
- Gaiters
- Insulated sleeping and sitting pads
- Face masks

Students are responsible for the following equipment:

- Eating utensils: Cup, bowl, spoon. Insulated mugs work well.
- Sweaters (2): They must be wool or pile. Check the attic, basement, or secondhand stores for good sweaters. They must be fairly roomy.
- Wool or pile hat (1): A ski hat or stocking hat is fine. It must cover your ears. Bring a face mask if you don't have a hat that will pull down to cover your face. You are attempting to eliminate exposed skin.
- Gloves or mittens (several pairs): Should be wool, pile, or polypropylene gloves and mittens.
- Wool socks (2-3 pair): *Not cotton!*

- Long underwear pants (1 pair): Must be made of polypropylene, Capilene, Thermax, wool, or similar material, *not cotton!*
- Long underwear shirt: You may use a fine wool sweater or one made of polypropylene, Capilene, or Thermax. Many participants like zippered turtlenecks.
- Wind parka: Should be lightweight nylon or insulated winter jacket. *No cotton lining.*
- Pants: Should be wool, pile, or polyester-blend pants. *No jeans or cords.*
- Rain jacket: Should be lightweight waterproof jacket (yes, it can rain in the winter and the course will still run).
- Water bottles: Wide-mouth quart bottles are fine (small-mouth bottles tend to freeze easily).

Optional equipment (highly recommended):

- Compass
- Lighter
- Pocketknife
- Liner socks and gloves (nylon, silk, or polypropylene): Nylon dress socks work well.
- Vapor barrier, a layer between liner and insulating sock to keep outer socks and boot liner dry from sweat
- Extra gloves, mittens, layers of clothing

Figure 17.4 Winter travel list for a trip in the Adirondacks.

Adirondacks of New York. For another perspective of proper preparation for diverse environments, see figure 17.5 for a kayaking equipment list used by the outdoor program at San Diego State University in California.

One final thought regarding equipment and the environment needs to be addressed: Proper equipment preparation ensures that groups practice Leave No Trace methods. For example, stoves minimize fire impacts. Gaiters allow participants to walk through puddles rather than skirting around them only to widen the trail. Carrying large, lightweight, collapsible water bags reduces trips to water sources that could be damaged by heavy traffic. Earth-tone tents and tarps reduce social impact on others. It should be apparent that equipment decisions made before the trip have a profound effect on the experience and environment.

Plan

A quality trip plan includes both an itinerary and a **time control plan.** Itineraries vary in detail and length. The leader's objective is to provide a basic overview of trip flow through these tools. Some leaders create a detailed, daily schedule delineated by a time line of all activities. Others create a broad overview of activities on a daily basis without time constraints. A quality trip plan includes some form of schedule to guide everyone involved in the process such as leaders, participants, administrators, parents, emergency contacts, permit providers, and so on.

The time control plan is a critical component of the trip plan. It involves map reading and understanding the details of a route. Quality time control plans provide insight into the amount of energy and time required to complete a specified

Sea Kayak Expedition, Baja, California
Personal Equipment and Clothing List (Summer)

Note: All items marked with ** can or will be provided by the course as part of the overall cost.

Personal items

- Sunscreen, lip balm, and hand lotion
- Sunglasses with retainer strap: The sun can be extremely bright at times. A good pair of glasses that offers UV protection with polarized lenses is recommended.
- Small towel and toiletries: Bring what you need to feel comfortable. Fresh water will be at a premium, so bathing will be limited (try baby wipes).
- Ziplock bags and heavy trash bags: 6 to 12 bags come in very handy throughout the trip for numerous uses, such as for personal garbage, wet gear, and so on.
- 1-quart (1-liter) water bottles: Bring a minimum of 2. Nalgene and Gatorade bottles are excellent because they will withstand someone stepping on them. Soda or bottled water containers are unacceptable.
- Water bags and hydration-hose systems: These are wonderful when paddling because they allow hands-free access.
- Flashlight or headlamp with spare batteries.
- Cup, bowl, fork, and spoon: Stainless steel seems to clean up better than plastic when cooking with butter and oils.
- Daypack or fanny pack: Great for day hikes.
- Toilet paper in Ziplock bag.

Miscellaneous items

- Camera and film (waterproof disposable cameras work great)
- Binoculars
- Pocketknife
- Matches and lighter in waterproof container
- Wristwatch (waterproof)
- Note pad, pocket sized (for keeping notes on trail)
- Journal organizer: A hard-shell nylon case will protect your journal from the elements and hold other important documents and identification.
- Fishing rod and light tackle: Supplement your rations with some fresh triggerfish or bass.

Equipment list

- 2- or 3-person freestanding dome tent with rainfly
- 40° mummy sleeping bag with plastic-lined stuff sack
- Ensolite pad or Thermarest sleeping pad
- Plastic or nylon ground tarp
- Camp chair
- ** Dry bags (4) for storing *all* of your gear in your kayak

- ** Deck bag for storing your sunscreen, snacks, water, paddling jacket, and so on for easy access while paddling

Clothing list

Head:

- Shade hat: Side-brimmed is best. A baseball cap with bandanna covering the back of your head and neck will work in a pinch.
- Warm hat: A wool or fleece stocking cap or balaclava is wonderful if you are a "cold" sleeper or for wearing in the evening when it is cool and windy.

Upper body:

- Cotton T-shirt: Cotton is wonderful to put on after a long day of paddling.
- Lightweight long-sleeved shirt: This is mandatory for sun protection.
- Synthetic long underwear top: Lightweight (Capilene, polypropylene) top will keep you warm even when wet. It's nice to wear under your spray jacket as added insulation.
- Lightweight wool sweater or fleece jacket or pullover: Great for in camp or if conditions get cold.
- Windbreaker or rain jacket: This will keep you warm in the evenings.
- ** Paddling jacket: This jacket is for keeping the wind and water spray off your fragile body.

Lower body:

- Nylon shorts: These are better than cotton because they dry quickly.
- Synthetic long underwear bottoms, medium weight
- Lightweight, light-colored, quick-drying long pants: Must have these for sun protection.
- Bathing suit
- Underwear

Hands:

- Paddling gloves (weight-lifting or cycling gloves will substitute): Some people like them to prevent calluses and blisters.

Feet:

- Sport sandals or neoprene booties: The terrain around camp is very rugged. In warmer weather sport sandals are nice to wear all the time.
- Hiking shoes: Essential for day hikes.
- Hiking socks: Wool or wool–nylon blend.

Group gear

Tents, dry bags, stoves, fuel bottles, cook pots, and large cooking utensils will be supplied. If you would like to bring your own, you are more than welcome. Most participants wind up using the group gear instead of putting wear and tear on their own.

Figure 17.5 Sea-kayaking equipment list for a desert environment.

Participants pack for an expedition.

route in a safe fashion. Such plans also provide an opportunity to develop topographic map interpretation skills. A competent leader develops a time control plan that matches the goals and ability level of the group. Time control plans can be developed for any adventure travel mode such as canoeing, backpacking, mountain biking, and so on. This chapter discusses time control plan in the context of foot travel only. Adaptations can be made to create plans for other travel modes. Time control plans typically include the following (see figure 17.6):

- Start time: The estimated time the group will start a hike.

- Estimated walking pace: This is the estimated distance to be covered in an hour. This calculation reflects many factors such as the group's level of fitness, weight of packs, weather, experience, and so on. Average hiking speeds for a group of beginners with moderate levels of fitness and pack weights range from 1 to 2 miles (1.6 to 3 kilometers) per hour.

- Linear miles to be covered: Route mileage is estimated using trip maps.

- Elevation gain and loss over the hike: The total amount of elevation gained and lost over the length of the hike is calculated. As a general rule, an hour should be added to the total hiking time for every 1,000 feet (305 meters) gained and half an hour added for every 1,000 feet lost (Ford and Blanchard 1993). This calculation allows leaders to take into account

the amount of energy required to hike over rough terrain. The amount of energy used is interpreted in **energy miles.** Another method used to determine actual energy miles is to add a mile for every 1,000 feet gained and half a mile for every 1,000 feet lost over the length of a hike. Note that high altitude will affect this estimation and typically increase hiking time as groups gain altitude over 10,000 feet (3,048 meters). See figure 17.6 for applications of both formulas to calculate total hiking time.

- Break time: Average amount of break time expected per hour as well as additional breaks for food or other activities.

- Potential campsites: Daily destinations with backup options along the way.

- Hazards and attractions.

- Ending time: The anticipated ending time for the hike allows leaders to estimate the total amount of time required to accomplish the hike.

Access

An important piece of any trip plan is legal access to the intended area. Appropriate permission must be gained to travel on public or private lands. Leaders are responsible for ensuring that legal access is obtained. This important task must occur far in advance to allow for adequate communication and administrative procedures. Fostering healthy relationships with land agencies and private landowners is a critical leadership function. The following tips will help ensure excellent public relations with private and public land managers:

- Personally call or meet appropriate representatives to inquire about access.

- Complete all paperwork in ample time so as not to inconvenience or pressure land administrators.

- Pay appropriate fees and maintain copies of all permits and letters of permission.

- Offer to send the agency or landowner a copy of your trip plan if it's not required.

- Thank individuals for their time as opposed to arguing if permission cannot be obtained.

- Strictly adhere to all regulations and wishes of the agency or landowner.

- Follow up with a thank-you note once the trip is complete.

Sample Time Control Plan

The following time control plan reflects the route Juan chose for the first day on the trail. Remember, Juan was leading a group of 10 individuals with no experience and full backpacks. He was not familiar with their physical condition and most members of the group were not prepared. If Juan had taken the time to estimate the following conservative time control plan based on the group's ability, he would have discovered the difficulty and time commitment of this route. Example 1 represents application of the following formula: Add 1 hour for every 1,000 feet (305 meters) gained and add 1/2 hour for every 1,000 feet lost. The second example applies the following energy formula: For every 1,000 feet (305 meters) gained add 1 mile (1.6 kilometers) and for every 1,000 feet lost add 1/2 mile (.8 kilometer).

Example 1

Route statistics	Hiking time
4-mi. route (4 mi. ÷ 1 mi./hr pace)	4 hr
Total elevation to be gained (1,000 ft or 305 m)	1 hr
Total elevation to be lost (2,000 ft or 610 m)	1 hr
Total hiking time, no breaks	**6 hr**
Anticipated average break time (10 min/hr)	1 hr
Anticipated lunch break	.5 hr
Est. total time to complete route	**7.5 hr**
Group's start time	1:00 p.m.
Est. time of arrival at camp	**8:30 p.m.**

Example 2

Route statistics	Energy miles
4-mi. linear route	4
Total elevation to be gained (1,000 ft or 305 m)	1
Total elevation to be lost (2,000 ft or 610 m)	1
Total energy miles	**6**
	Hiking time
6 energy miles ÷ 1 mi./hr pace	6 hr
Anticipated average break time (10 min/hr)	1 hr
Anticipated lunch break	.5 hr
Est. total time to complete route	**7.5 hr**
Group's start time	1:00 p.m.
Est. time of arrival at camp	**8:30 p.m.**

Figure 17.6   Two methods for developing a time control plan.

Students rappel into a vertical cave entrance.

Rationing

Planning and packing appropriate food rations can dramatically affect the success of an expedition. Participants typically burn many more calories on an expedition compared to everyday life activities. Ensuring that participants have enough calories and nutritional balance helps maintain energy levels as well as positive attitudes. Well-nourished expedition members consistently make better safety-related decisions as opposed to chronically tired, hungry participants. Mealtime with great-tasting food promotes relaxation and a sense of community. Great satisfaction comes when participants develop their culinary skills and share with others. A competent outdoor leader is able to develop an appropriate rationing system.

The planning taken to ensure proper rations should increase as trip length increases. An outdoor leader must keep basic nutrition rules in mind. The average person consumes 2,500 to 3,000 calories per day when participating in outdoor activities such as moderate backpacking or canoeing. Strenuous activities such as difficult backpacking or snow camping require consumption of 3,000 to 3,700 calories per day. Very strenuous activities such as mountaineering or extended time spent in cold weather requires 3,700 to 5,000 calories per day. Leaders ensure nutritional needs by adhering to the following guidelines: The average intake per person per day should be 50 to 80% carbohydrates, 10 to 15% proteins, and 30% fats, of which only 10% should be saturated fats (Pearson 1997). Two different rationing systems lend themselves to sound trip planning: menu planning and bulk rationing.

Menu Planning

Most people tend to be familiar with menu planning. Leaders systematically plan the contents of each meal over the course of a trip. Advantages of the menu system include having outlines of all meals to avoid confusion, an organized guide to prepare each meal, and a convenient way to plan short trips (2 to 5 days). Leaders will discover that calculating calories and ensuring appropriate nutritional breakdown is more difficult when menu planning.

Bulk Rationing

Bulk rationing involves buying food in bulk based on the amount (weight) of food consumed per day. Food purchased in bulk would include items such as pasta, beans, rice, flour, cereals, nuts, dried fruits, cheese, sugar, soup bases, spices, and so on found at a local grocery store or food co-op. Advantages of bulk rationing include avoiding extensive menus for long trips, opportunities for cooking creativity, and easier caloric and nutritional calculations. Using this system, participants consume anywhere from 1.5 to 2.5 pounds (680 to 1,133 grams) of food per person per day. Average activities require 1.5 to 2 pounds (680 to 907 grams) per person per day. Strenuous activities require from 2 to 2.25 pounds (907 to 1,021 grams) of food per person per day. Very strenuous activities range up to 2.5 pounds (1,133 grams) of food per person per day (Pearson 1997). Bulk food must be repacked into clear plastic bags to reduce packaging and additional waste generated in the field. Repackaging consolidates food into a more manageable system of transport. A convenient way to plan rations using the bulk method is a spreadsheet (Drury and Holmlund 1997). (See figure 17.7.)

Food item	Cals per lb	Total lbs	Total cals	Cost per lb	Total cost
Dairy products					
powdered milk	1650	6	9900	$5.60	$33.60
powdered eggs	2700	16	43200	$6.60	$105.60
margarine	1900	8	15200	$0.60	$4.80
cheddar cheese	1760	14	24640	$1.91	$26.74
colby cheese	1760	14	24640	$2.35	$32.90
mont. jack cheese	1600	14	22400	$1.77	$24.78
parmesan cheese	1800	3	5400	$3.99	$11.97
Grains and starches					
flour, white	1650	20	33000	$0.17	$3.40
flour, wheat	1500	16	24000	$0.19	$3.04
pancake mix	1850	16	29600	$0.50	$8.00
cornmeal	1610	7	11270	$0.18	$1.26
rice, white	1650	14	23100	$0.27	$3.78
rolled oats	1750	16	28000	$0.86	$13.76
cream of wheat	1750	3	5250	$0.88	$2.64
bagels	1200	12	14400	$1.75	$21.00
potato flakes	1650	8	13200	$1.25	$10.00
potato	1624	15	24360	$0.28	$4.20
pasta noodles	1700	25	42500	$0.70	$17.50
Legumes					
lentils	1550	3	4650	$0.69	$2.07
couscous	1500	4	6000	$0.88	$3.52
pinto beans	200	7	1400	$0.46	$3.22
veg. burger mix	1700	7	11900	$2.22	$15.54
chili base	1600	7	11200	$4.43	$31.01
soup mix	2000	8	16000	$3.40	$27.20
Meats					
bacon bits	2836	2	5672	$2.40	$4.80
pepperoni	2250	8	18000	$3.03	$24.24
salami	2050	8	16400	$2.00	$16.00

(continued)

Figure 17.7 Ration plan using the bulk method.

Figure 17.7 Ration plan using the bulk method. *(continued)*

Food item	Cals per lb	Total lbs	Total cals	Cost per lb	Total cost
Trail foods					
dried apricots	1100	6	6600	$2.55	$15.30
mix dry fruit	1250	6	7500	$1.50	$9.00
raisins	1400	12	16800	$1.25	$15.00
salted peanuts	2650	10	26500	$1.65	$16.50
peanuts, roasted	2500	10	25000	$1.69	$16.90
cashews	2500	6	15000	$3.26	$19.56
walnuts	2450	6	14700	$3.00	$18.00
M&M's	2133	26	55458	$1.83	$47.58
prunes	1550	8	12400	$1.50	$12.00
Sweets					
honey	1300	7	9100	$1.20	$8.40
sugar, white	1700	12	20400	$0.39	$4.68
sugar, brown	1700	6	10200	$0.50	$3.00
choc. chips	2100	5	10500	$1.96	$9.80
cocoa	1650	1.2	1980	$3.81	$4.57
cookies	2200	12	26400	$1.00	$12.00
brownie mix	1800	5	9000	$1.50	$7.50
Condiments					
jelly	1200	7	8400	$0.75	$5.25
peanut butter	2580	17	43860	$1.30	$22.10
maple syrup	1222	3	3666	$3.58	$10.74
salad dressing	500	1	500	$3.40	$3.40
soy sauce	240	3	720	$1.10	$3.30
BBQ sauce	240	2	480	$2.10	$4.20
Drinks					
tea bags	0	1	0		$7.50
coffee	0	2	0	$7.72	$15.44
hot cocoa mix	1650	15	24750	$1.18	$17.70
juice mix	1950	21	40950	$3.50	$73.50
Spices					
pepper	0	2	0	$4.96	$9.92
salt	0	3	0	$0.25	$0.75

(continued)

Figure 17.7 Ration plan using the bulk method. *(continued)*

Food item	Cals per lb	Total lbs	Total cals	Cost per lb	Total cost
Spices *(continued)*					
cinnamon	0	1	0	$4.00	$4.00
garlic powder	0	1	0	$2.88	$2.88
oregano	0	0.5	0	$9.28	$4.64
chili powder	0	1	0	$3.20	$3.20
onion powder	0	1	0	$2.40	$2.40
curry powder	0	0.75	0	$4.80	$3.60
red pepper	0	0.5	0	$4.80	$2.40
Tabasco	0	0.75	0	$1.76	$1.32
baking powder	0	1.5	0	$1.40	$2.10
beef bouillon	0	1.25	0	$2.40	$3.00
Miscellaneous					
yeast	0	1.5	0	$1.50	$2.25
olive oil	4000	6	24000		$0.00
vegetable oil	4000	6	24000	$0.90	$5.40
granola bars	1760	12	21120	$0.89	$10.68
dairy creamer	3750	1.5	5625	$0.90	$1.35
ketchup	400	0	0	$2.00	$0.00
tomato sauce	109	8	872	$0.48	$3.84
popcorn	1650	7	11550	$0.43	$3.01
produce bags (700)	0	0	0		$0.00
borax	0	0	0		$0.00
		547.45	963,313		$906.23

10 people (8 participants and 2 instructors)
25 days
250 people days
2.19 pounds per person per day
3853.25 calories per day
$4.53 cost per participant per day

A short discussion comparing freeze-dried food and bulk rationing is merited in case you ever face the choice. Prepackaged freeze-dried meals allow for quick preparation with minimal skills and time. They tend to be very expensive ($4.00 to $10.00 per packaged meal) but also very light if carried in a backpack. Beware that a prepackaged meal for four may actually satisfy only two hungry people.

The bulk rationing system is cheaper ($3.00 to $6.00 per person per day). Participants can get by with plenty of delicious food on $3.00 a day and eat extremely well on $6.00 a day. Bulk rationing tends to be more financially feasible for institutional budgets and participant pockets. Prepackaged freeze-dried food doubles or even triples food costs and tends not to be as nutritious.

Students pack food using bulk rationing for a 30-day expedition.

Fuel

When using camp stoves, fuel calculations vary depending on climate, altitude, size of group, food type, and stove type. Leaders should start by checking the manufacturer's recommendations. For example, using a white-gas stove at high altitude in the snow requires much more fuel as opposed to using the stove on a summer backpacking trip in the Great Smoky Mountains. A general rule for a typical white-gas backpacking stove is as follows: Pack 1/2 quart (1/2 liter) of fuel per day for a group of three people backpacking in the summer under moderate conditions (Harvey 1999).

Emergency Plan

Competent outdoor leaders include emergency protocol within a functional trip plan. Formalized emergency procedures create the framework for a quick, smooth response to any emergency situation. Of course, the best preparation for an emergency is prevention. Proper trip planning and quality leadership are two of the best defenses against emergencies. However, incidents do occur during outdoor expeditions. Leaders must have a formal plan to guide them through intense decision-making situations. Emergency protocol varies depending on the specifics of an organization's risk management plan. There are, however, fundamental components to an emergency plan. The following items are typically addressed in an emergency plan.

Emergency Contact List

Names, titles, primary phone numbers, and alternative phone numbers for all potential emergency contacts must be compiled and carried during the trip at all times. Contacts should include emergency rescue services for the area, the local sheriff, the land management agency or landowner, organizational emergency contacts, support staff, contractors, and the nearest hospital or medical services. This list should be duplicated, waterproofed, and carried in the first aid kits and by the leaders.

Evacuation Procedures

If an evacuation is required, leaders must decide if outside assistance is needed or if self-evacuation is feasible. Protocol for either decision must be developed before the trip. For assisted evacuations, protocol might cover the process for landing a helicopter, how information is relayed over a phone or radio, how teams of messengers are managed, and how jobs are assigned to group members during the situation. For self-evacuations, protocol might reflect when to use a litter and how to protect other members of the group. It should be clear who will pay for an assisted evacuation. Knowing this upfront will avoid confusion and allow leaders to obtain the appropriate resources. For example, some organizations require participants to obtain additional insurance to cover costs of evacuation.

Evacuation Routes

At all times during a trip, leaders must be aware of the nearest evacuation route. Topographic maps, guide books, and research will provide this information. Document evacuation routes by marking each location on a map.

Communications

Contingency plans must be made to contact the appropriate authorities in the event of an emergency. Satellite and cell phones may not always work. Backup plans must be developed so that leaders are not totally dependent upon technology. Along with evacuation routes, knowing where the nearest landlines are is important.

Learning Activity 17.2

Using organization 2 (Big Adventure) or organization 3 (Quest, Inc.), outline a trip plan based on the PREPARE system. (Note: If the class using this text can actually participate on an actual trip, the GO PREPARE process as well as logistics should be developed by the class.)

First Aid Procedures

Competent outdoor leaders seek training in wilderness medicine. Most outdoor leaders possess one of the following certifications: Wilderness First Aid, Wilderness First Responder, and Wilderness Emergency Medical Technician. Outdoor leaders should follow the protocol learned during this training and provide first aid at the level dictated by their training. The number of first aid kits and their contents should reflect the type of trip, environmental conditions, and caregiver's expertise. For example, a leader not trained to inject epinephrine for anaphylactic shock should not carry syringes in the first aid kit.

Record-Keeping Procedures

Accident reports must be maintained by trip leaders. These documents are designed to be used in a variety of ways as discussed in chapter 16. Leaders are responsible for completing and maintaining the forms in the case of an emergency. In some cases, copies of the forms are sent out with runners during a self-evacuation to properly inform

Students practice a litter carry evacuation.

response teams of the emergency. These forms typically are carried in the first aid kits.

Additional Considerations

Emergencies will be handled in a smooth, efficient manner if leaders are aware of all emergency-related protocol. As stated earlier, protocol will vary among agencies. Competent outdoor leaders have knowledge of protocol for the following: severe weather, loss of life, sexual harassment, misconduct, and evacuations. Copies of the trip plan should be left with the appropriate individuals back home so that others have comprehensive information to assist when needed.

Logistics

Finally, GO PREPARE, but don't forget about logistics! Once a leader establishes a quality trip plan based on the GO PREPARE system, trip logistics are required to carry that plan out. Logistics involve administrative concerns, transportation, food drops, equipment transport, and posttrip procedures. A successful expedition relies on well-planned logistical support. Leaders may be able to manage their own logistics during a shorter, less complex trip. Longer trips that integrate numerous adventure activities over a long period of time require more complex logistical support. Some organizations specifically hire staff to serve in a logistical role. Logistics staff duties may include purchasing and packing food, issuing and cleaning gear, and transporting participants and equipment. Logistics staff sometimes conduct food drops during long expeditions. For example, a 30-day expedition may be divided into three 10-day food rations. Once the group nears the end of a ration period, logistics staff may horsepack food to a designated meeting point or meet the group at a convenient location.

Leaders who arrange their own logistics must plan accordingly. If there are multiple ration drops, for example, food can be hidden in a cache to be picked up along the route later. If leaders serve as transportation drivers, perhaps secure places exist to leave vehicles and equipment at the trailhead. With no outside logistical support, leaders may have to design a trip so that the group loops back to vehicles. Private shuttle services can also be contracted to meet transportation needs. The point is that leaders must design appropriate logistical support to execute trip plans. Goals and objectives, resources, route choices, itineraries, equipment needs, and other planning components affect logistical choices. For example, leaders may simplify a trip plan to minimize logistical costs.

Transportation, equipment, and food considerations compose three critical logistical concerns. The following considerations are stated in the form of questions. No exact answer will exist for each question. Leaders must put each question into the context of their situation to arrive at an appropriate solution.

Transportation

1. What resources are available to transport participants and equipment? Do leaders have access to agency buses or vans? What is the vehicle carrying capacity and does this number affect group size? Does the option exist for participants to transport themselves to the area? Are trailers or other modes of transportation available to carry equipment?

2. Who will drive? Are specific qualifications and training required to drive vehicles? Is it possible for qualified participants to serve as drivers on long road trips? If a shuttle service is contracted, are they reputable and safe?

3. What will be the status of vehicle access and security? Will vehicles be parked at trailheads and be accessible during and after the trip? Will these vehicles be secure if left unattended for long periods of time? If vehicles are not left at trailheads, how will transportation be arranged?

Equipment

1. How are equipment needs to be met before the trip starts? Who will inventory, organize, and issue equipment before the trip? Who will ensure proper equipment functioning before equipment is taken into the field? Do leaders conduct a visual inspection of participants' personal gear before the trip to ensure preparedness?

2. Who is responsible for equipment during the trip? Who will pay for damaged or lost equipment during the course of a trip? If the trip consists of numerous adventure activities, how will kayaks, caving gear, climbing gear, and other specialized equipment be available when needed? How will personal and group equipment be transported to the trip site? See figure 17.3 (page 273) for a sample group equipment check-out form.

3. How will equipment be dealt with after the trip? Who will inventory, clean, repair, and store equipment once the trip is over? How will lost or damaged equipment be replaced and made ready for the next trip?

Food

1. How will food acquisition and preparation be handled? Who conducts initial menu or bulk ration planning? Who purchases the food? Where is the best place to purchase needed items? Who will organize and repackage food? How will food be distributed to participants? If a long trip requires multiple rations, how will the food be divided, packaged, and stored?

2. How will food be handled during the trip? Will the participants be divided into smaller cooking groups or will cooking occur in one large group? How will the food be divided and carried during the trip? How will food drops be arranged during the trip if needed? What will be done with leftover food at the end of a ration period or trip?

Pretrip Considerations

Beyond the major concerns of transportation, equipment, and food, outdoor leaders have other logistical concerns. For one, administrative functions influence logistical considerations. Leaders must obtain and review participant information as discussed in the GO PREPARE system. This information can be obtained from medical forms or participant applications. Participant information and special needs influence logistical decisions. For example, a participant with unique needs may require the leader to adapt or modify equipment in advance. Dietary restrictions will influence food planning.

Learning Activity 17.3

Using organization 2 (Big Adventure) or organization 3 (Quest, Inc.), outline logistical support into the draft trip plan created in activity 17.2. Be sure to include pre- and posttrip considerations.

Leaders typically conduct some type of participant orientation before going into the field. Pretrip meetings, telephone interviews, and information packets are common orientation techniques. Once participants arrive, leaders should consider inspecting participants' personal gear. Double-checking participants' clothing selection, sleeping system, hiking boots, and so on allows leaders to spot inappropriate or unsafe equipment. Arrangements for additional clothing or new gear can be made before entering the field.

Many programs integrate a **shakedown** into the programming before the actual trip begins. Shakedowns involve taking participants into the field for a short period (1 to 7 nights) to test gear, experiment with clothing, and develop initial skills before embarking on a full-blown expedition. Leaders identify faulty or inappropriate equipment that can be exchanged while equipment remains accessible. Participants learn quickly if rain gear, footwear, and other personal items are adequate. Participants also have the opportunity to experience the rations during a shakedown. Some organizations require the participants to package their own rations after the shakedown. Exposure to the food during the shakedown allows the participants to make more informed decisions about food packing. Better decisions regarding food choices, quantities, and packaging techniques can be made. Before starting a shakedown or trip, it should be made clear who will be responsible for lost or damaged equipment. Leaders can prevent misunderstandings by addressing this responsibility upfront. For example, some organizations check equipment out to individuals and hold them responsible for each issued item, and some allow groups to share in the cost of lost or damaged equipment. Others absorb the costs based on budgeting techniques to account for damaged and lost equipment. Finally, do not forget to leave a copy of the trip plan with logistical support, which includes individuals who remain out of the field to support the trip

(e.g., hired logisticians or volunteers). The plan serves as a handy reference for meeting deadlines and for problem solving when necessary.

Posttrip Considerations

Finally, leaders need to account for logistical concerns once the trip ends. How will the leaders handle final evaluations? For example, an organization requires that all participants complete a course and instructor evaluation. Leaders must arrange access to evaluation forms and schedule an appropriate amount of time for completion. Leaders must also consider the logistics of a closing ceremony and the supplies needed to conduct the ceremony. Let's say certificates and patches will be awarded to the participants. How will leaders obtain these supplies and when and where will the ceremony be conducted? Leaders may want to consider a closing banquet. Whether it means visiting a restaurant or purchasing fresh food, these arrangements must be considered. Many times participants wish to have member contact information upon trip completion. Leaders should consider facilitating this process so that participants can foster bonds developed during a trip.

Of course, equipment and leftover food must be dealt with in order to support logistical planning for the next trip. Equipment must be inventoried, cleaned, and stored properly, and adequate washing and drying space must be made available. Participants may or may not be part of the cleaning process. For example, at the end of an outdoor leadership training experience, an educational objective might be for students to have this important experience with equipment. At the end of a guided commercial trip, on the other hand, equipment cleaning and repair would be the guide's responsibility. Finally, if additional fees need to be collected for equipment damage, trip photographs, T-shirts, mugs, and so on, they must be factored into the overall logistics.

Summary

A competent outdoor leader is guided by the mantra, "Proper planning prevents poor performance." Proper planning ensures safe, enjoyable, and environmentally sound outdoor adventures. Remember Juan's predicament as he slumped on the log wondering what to do next? Juan would have never put himself or the group in that situation if he had practiced the GO PREPARE method of trip planning. The GO PREPARE system serves as an outdoor leader's guide to proper planning. The foundation of a good trip plan rests on the established purpose of a trip. Leaders must develop sound goals (G) and objectives (O) to guide the development of a trip plan. Goals are intended outcomes supported by specific, measurable, achievable, realistic, and time-bound objectives. Well-written objectives allow leaders to assess the accomplishment of goals. An understanding of trip purpose allows leaders to PREPARE an appropriate trip plan.

The GO PREPARE system of trip planning can be a complex process depending on the length and purpose of an expedition. Competent leaders actually develop a formal trip planning document based on the GO PREPARE system. The following components make up the well-PREPAREd trip plan:

- Participants: An outdoor leader makes plans based on participant characteristics such as health, physical abilities, goals, ability level, experience, developmental characteristics, and group size.

- Resources: An outdoor leader makes plans based on budget constraints and availability of resources such as equipment and logistical assistance.

- Equipment and clothing: An outdoor leader carefully plans the type of equipment and clothing needed to execute a successful trip.

- Plan: An outdoor leader develops an itinerary and time control plan. Time control plans assist in choosing appropriate levels of activity to meet participant needs.

- Access: An outdoor leader obtains proper permission from public or private landowners.

- Rationing: An outdoor leader plans for enough food to feed participants nutritious meals that are appropriate for the activity.

- Emergency plan: An outdoor leader creates an emergency plan so that accidents and injuries are confronted in a professional, efficient manner.

Competent leaders GO and PREPARE properly for trips but do not forget about logistics! Logistics serve as the backbone of a good plan. Transportation, food, and equipment are three major tasks that require logistical considerations. How participants and equipment are transported must be carefully orchestrated. Purchasing and packing food for a long expedition takes considerable thought. Properly preparing and issuing equipment must be done in an organized fashion. Logistics also involve pretrip considerations. Leaders must obtain participant information before the trip to plan appropriately. Equipment may have to be modified or adapted or special diet restrictions addressed. Leaders should consider providing some type of pretrip orientation to reduce mistakes. Shakedowns are one way of testing equipment and clothing before an extensive trip; they avert major problems once a group loses access to additional food and equipment. Finally, leaders must consider posttrip logistical considerations. How will equipment be inventoried, cleaned, and stored upon trip completion? Evaluations, ceremonies, and other posttrip activities must be worked into the overall schedule. Access to

Professional-Development Portfolio Activity

Develop a comprehensive, 5-day trip plan for 10 people in the environment of your choice. Or, create a trip plan for an actual trip to be conducted as part of a class.

supplies for closing activities should be arranged in advance. The importance of trip planning cannot be overestimated. The best outdoor leaders are also the best trip planners.

Selected References

Drury, J., and E. Holmlund. 1997. *The camper's guide: To outdoor pursuits.* Champaign, IL: Sagamore.

Ford, P., and J. Blanchard. 1993. *Leadership and administration of outdoor pursuits.* 2nd ed. State College, PA: Venture.

Harvey, M. 1999. *The National Outdoor Leadership School's wilderness guide.* New York: Simon & Schuster.

Pearson, C. 1997. *NOLS cookery.* Mechanicsburg, PA: Stackpole Books.

Priest, S., and M.A. Gass. 1997. *Effective leadership in adventure programming.* Champaign, IL: Human Kinetics.

Appendix

As you read this text, you encountered a number of different professional associations, companies, and other organizations that are significant in the field of outdoor leadership. This appendix provides you with a reference list of each of these organizations. The list includes a description of the organizations and their Web site addresses. These organizations will be useful resources to you as you continue to develop as an outdoor leader.

AAHPERD: American Alliance for Health, Physical Education, Recreation and Dance

www.aahperd.org

AAHPERD promotes healthy lifestyles through quality programs in health, physical education, recreation, dance, and sport.

ACA: American Camp Association

www.acacamps.org

The American Camp Association is a community of camp professionals dedicated to enriching the lives of children and adults through the camp experience.

ACA: American Canoe Association

www.acanet.org

The mission of the American Canoe Association is to promote the health, social, and personal benefits of canoeing, kayaking, and rafting and to serve the needs of all paddlers for safe, enjoyable, and quality paddling opportunities.

ACCT: Association for Challenge Course Technology

www.acctinfo.org

The purpose of the ACCT is to provide leadership in the promotion and use of challenge course programs. ACCT is a professional trade association whose mission is to establish and guide the implementation and compliance of standards that promote quality and safety for challenge courses.

Its commitment is to develop and advance challenge course technology through the research of industry and member resources.

AEE: Association for Experiential Education

www.aee.org

AEE is a professional association for experiential educators in outdoor and adventure contexts. Its mission is to develop and promote experiential education. It supports professional development, theoretical advancement, and evaluation of experiential education worldwide.

AMC: Appalachian Mountain Club

www.outdoors.org

Founded in 1876, the AMC is the United States' oldest conservation and recreation organization. It promotes the protection, enjoyment, and wise use of the mountains, rivers, and trails of the Appalachian region. It fulfills its mission through conservation, education, and recreation.

AMGA: American Mountain Guides Association

www.amga.com

AMGA is a nonprofit organization that seeks to represent the interests of American mountain guides by providing support, education, and standards.

AORE: Association of Outdoor Recreation and Education

www.aore.org

The mission of AORE is to provide opportunities for professionals and students in the field of outdoor recreation and education to exchange information, promote the preservation and conservation of the natural environment, and address issues common to college, university, community, military, and other not-for-profit outdoor recreation and education programs.

BOW: Becoming an Outdoors-Woman

www.uwsp.edu/cnr/bow/

BOW offers outdoor skills workshops to women throughout North America. Programs are usually offered through a state's department of natural resources or a state university.

BSA: Boy Scouts of America

www.scouting.org

The mission of the Boy Scouts is to prepare young people to make ethical and moral choices over their lifetime by instilling in them the values of the Scout Oath and Law.

Camp Fire USA

www.campfire.org

Camp Fire USA builds caring, confident youth and future leaders.

Council of Outdoor Educators of Ontario

www.coeo.org

The Council of Outdoor Educators of Ontario (COEO) is a nonprofit, volunteer-based organization that promotes safe and high-quality outdoor education experiences for people of all ages. It also acts as a professional body for outdoor educators in the province of Ontario. These aims are achieved through publishing *Pathways: The Ontario Journal of Outdoor Education* as well as an electronic newsletter, running an annual conference and regional workshops, maintaining this Web site, and working with kindred organizations as well as government agencies.

Girl Scouts of the USA

www.girlscouts.org

The mission of the Girl Scouts is to inspire girls with the highest ideals of character, conduct, patriotism, and service so that they may become helpful and resourceful citizens.

LNT: Leave No Trace

www.lnt.org

The Leave No Trace Center for Outdoor Ethics is a nonprofit organization dedicated to promoting responsible outdoor recreation through education, research, and partnerships. Leave No Trace builds awareness, appreciation, and respect for the outdoors.

The Mountaineers

www.mountaineers.org

The goal of the Mountaineers is to be the premier northwestern outdoor recreation club, dedicated to the responsible enjoyment and protection of natural areas.

NAI: National Association for Interpretation

www.interpnet.org

The NAI inspires leadership and excellence to advance heritage interpretation as a profession.

NOLS: National Outdoor Leadership School

www.nols.edu

The mission of NOLS is to be the leading teacher of wilderness skills and source of leadership that serve people and the environment.

NRPA: National Recreation and Park Association

www.nrpa.org

The mission of NRPA is to promote parks, recreation, and conservation efforts that enhance quality of life for all people.

OB: Outward Bound

www.outwardbound.org

Outward Bound's goal is to conduct safe adventure-based programs that inspire self-esteem, self-reliance, concern for others, and care for the environment.

PA: Project Adventure

www.pa.org/index.php

Project Adventure was one of the first nonprofit adventure-based organizations to use challenge courses.

PRCA: Professional Ropes Course Association

www.prcainfo.org

PRCA is a professional association for challenge course professionals.

WEA: Wilderness Education Association

www.weainfo.org

The mission of WEA is to promote outdoor leadership and thereby to improve the safety of outdoor trips and to enhance the conservation of the wild outdoors.

Glossary

abdicratic or laissez-faire leadership style—Allows the group to operate on its own. The leader provides information when asked, but otherwise stays out of the group process. The leadership style that a person chooses to express will depend on that person's orientation to the dimensions of task and relationship.

accident equation—Human dangers plus environmental dangers equals accident potential. This equation helps us to understand how risk and accident potential arise.

accident—An undesired and unexpected event resulting in an injury or a loss of some sort.

adventure education—Education that relies on adventure experience as a catalyst for personal and interpersonal growth.

adventure therapy—Using adventure-based activities to promote treatment for physical, psychological, emotional, or social problems.

analytic model of decision making—Most decision-making models are linear, analytic models. Most of these models include some or all of the following steps: Define the problem, gather relevant information, consider priorities, consider options, list solutions, evaluate solutions and consequences, implement a decision, and reevaluate.

authentic leadership theory—Authentic leadership is based on the principles of dwelling, freedom, justice, participation, love, and responsibility. Leaders must live, and impel others to live, according to these authentic principles. It is through living out the principles that leaders can model a way of being that is an authentic and ethical engagement with the world. This model of leadership has transformative potential for both followers and leaders.

autocratic or authoritarian leader—A leader who is highly directive and does not allow input from group members. The leader rarely reveals reasons behind his decision making or actions and believes that participants should do as they are told.

axiology—The branch of philosophy that seeks to help us answer the question "what is of value?"

belay—Safety system to protect climbers in the case of a dangerous fall.

biological carrying capacity—Actual physical impact a natural resource can sustain before damage occurs.

bulk rationing—System of food management and preparation used during extended expeditions.

carrying capacity—Amount of human traffic an area can withstand before being adversely affected by that traffic. Includes biological carrying capacity and psychological carrying capacity.

challenge by choice—Group facilitation technique used to empower participants who participate in adventure-based experiences. Participants can choose their level and type of challenge.

challenge course—Series of challenge activities that typically consist of games, initiatives, low elements, and high elements designed to facilitate group and individual adventure experiences. Also known as a ropes course.

charismatic leadership theory—Throughout history, charismatic leaders have played a significant role, politically, economically, and socially. A consideration of the influence of Martin Luther King, Jr., Adolf Hitler, or any number of celebrities, actors, musicians, and politicians helps to illustrate the impact of charismatic leaders. Charismatic leaders do not merely inspire; they generate unusually passionate reactions in their followers.

complex decisions—Complex decisions are characterized by uncertainty in terms of the information, the options, or the outcome.

conditional outdoor leadership theory (COLT) model—Priest and Gass further developed the situational leadership model and adapted it specifically for outdoor leaders. The COLT model postulates that outdoor leaders must go beyond the dimensions of relationship, task, and group readiness and look at the level of conditional favorability to dictate their behavior toward a group. Conditional favorability is based on five factors: environmental dangers, individual competence, group unity, leader proficiency, and decision consequences.

consequentialist theory of ethics—This ethical theory focuses on the end result of any given action. If a certain act results in "bad" consequences, than the act is a "bad" act. If a certain act results in consequences that are "good," then the act itself is deemed to be a "good" act.

contingency leadership theory—Contingency theory explains leadership in terms of an individual's style of leadership and the response of the group he is leading. Fiedler suggested that a leader is motivated from either a task orientation or a relationship orientation. The contingency theory of leadership is based on the premise that leadership is dependent upon the appropriateness of the leader's style to the task.

core competency—Proficiency at a task or activity that is central to a practice, in this case outdoor leadership.

creative decision-making model—A nonlinear model, but the level of structure and the approach that is employed will depend upon the situational variables. This model involves the use of inductive and deductive reasoning in the decision-making process. Creative decision making is based on the recognition of patterns, reflective thinking, simulation, and extended brainstorming

debriefing—An experience is relived with all of its emotion and dynamism. Learning comes from doing and making sense of the experience.

democratic leadership style—Emphasizes the need for group members to be involved in decision making. The group may vote on decisions or may base decisions on the majority opinion.

designated leader—A person who is appointed as a leader is generally referred to as a designated leader.

dispersed use—Dispersing the effects of visits to parks and protected areas by limiting human traffic in a particular area and encouraging use of less popular areas.

Dress WISE—See *WISE.*

dude ranches—Ranches in the American West that accommodate tourists.

ecological literacy——Form of critical literacy that is essential to making good decisions about the environment. Ecological literacy is developed through environmental education.

ecosystemic relationships—Relationships of organisms within an ecological system. Examples include the food chain, the pyramid of life, and so on.

ekistic relationships—Relationship of humans to the natural world; the role of humans within their environment. Ekistic relationships involve the effects of humans on their surrounding environment and subsequently the effects of the surrounding environment on human quality of life.

elected leader—Leader who has become the leader through an election process, most often through a process of voting. Elected leaders are therefore often admired by those who follow.

emergent leader—On occasion the appointed leader has never led any group and may be unable or unwilling to carry out the role. In such a case, one person will often emerge as the leader from within the group. This person is referred to as the emergent leader.

energy miles—Mileage used to calculate time control plans that includes elevation gain and loss in addition to linear miles.

environmental dangers—Dangers that originate in the natural environment (e.g., weather, terrain, wildlife).

environmental education—The practice of educating audiences about the natural environment and the relationship of humans to that environment. The goal of environmental education is ecological literacy.

environmental interpretation—Communicating the significance of natural and cultural environments to audiences using written, visual, and auditory media.

epistemology—The branch of philosophy that studies the nature, sources, and validity of knowledge. Roughly translated, epistemology means "ways of knowing." It seeks to answer such questions as "what is true?" and "how do we know?"

ethic of care—An ethic based on relationships. One person responds to another out of love or natural inclination.

ethic of justice—Operates upon the principles of fairness and reciprocity, focused on the summum bonum.

expedition behavior—Refers to a variety of relationships in an outdoor group. They include individual to individual, individual to group, group to individual, group to group, individual/group to local populace, and individual/group to managing agencies.

experiential education—Hands-on teaching and learning process that integrates reflection, analysis, and active experimentation. The assumption is that experience, no matter how subtle or basic, provides substance for thought, while thought gives perspective to experience and its consequences.

expert power—Influence based on what a person knows or the person's abilities. The power comes from the fact that the leader or group member has an expertise that is important to the group.

facilitation—The process of moving a group or individual toward a desired outcome.

feminist leadership—Theories that have focused on specific aspects of organizational structure change. Within a feminist model of leadership, there would be attention paid to both process and product and traditional notions of power would be reconsidered, allowing all people to experience the same potential for success. All persons would additionally have the same potential to become leaders. A feminist transformative perspective to leadership would regard communication as upward, downward, and lateral.

feminist model of outdoor leadership—Proffers a vision of a more egalitarian approach to outdoor leadership—one that encourages that women have equal rights in outdoor participation, equal opportunities to become outdoor leaders. Warren and Rheingold suggest that leaders act on the following principles: work to minimize power differentials, value students' personal experiences, advocate for female learners and use various teaching methods that address diverse learning styles, create organizational structures that prevent the marginalization of women, and develop a critical consciousness about outdoor leadership.

framing—A technique used in group facilitation to make conscious the purpose and goals of an activity. Framing typically occurs to set the stage for an activity.

frontloading—Prebriefing or setting the stage before a group attempts an activity.

full-value contract—Group facilitation technique used to develop and maintain appropriate group norms. Also used to gauge the level of commitment in a single activity or for a whole experience, it makes everyone aware that the group's success will take everyone's cooperation.

future pace—Any learning that occurs needs to be knowledge that will be used by the individual in the future.

GO PREPARE—System for trip planning that includes the following considerations: goals, objectives, participants, resources, equipment and clothing, trip plan, access, rationing, emergencies, and logistics.

grasshopper method—Teaching method used by outdoor leaders to systematically cover curriculum content over an extended period of time while in the field.

great men theory of leadership—According to this theory, certain men were predestined to be leaders based on factors such as birth order, family background, education, and upbringing. Leadership was predominantly a monopoly of the aristocracy. It was historically understood that the world was shaped by the leadership of great men, such as Moses, Winston Churchill, Thomas Jefferson, and Lenin.

halo effect—Sometimes a person who emerges as a leader in one group or situation, and experiences success, will be expected to be a leader in other groups and situations in which she is involved. Deb Jordan calls this the halo effect. "The halo effect refers to how certain attributes or thoughts about a person are carried over into other situations" (Jordan, 1996, p. 25).

hegemony—Hegemony suggests that as a culture develops, systems of meanings and values are actively created by both groups and individuals. Hegemony explains how dominant meanings and interests, which are inherited from past tradition, explain our present condition and provide an understanding of certain "taken for granted" assumptions about what makes a good leader, what leadership qualities are valued, how we define leadership, and the sources of that knowledge.

high elements—Activity-based experiences found on challenge courses, usually 10 feet (3 meters) or more above the ground, that require belay safety systems.

human dangers—Dangers that originate in the members of a group or in individuals who are venturing into the outdoors (e.g., poor judgment, lack of knowledge).

incident—Close calls, or situations in which an accident could potentially have occurred but by chance did not.

inclusion—Allowing anyone who wants to be involved to be involved.

Kohlberg's six stages of moral development—Includes the following stages: the preconventional level, wherein the preadolescent is oriented toward punishment, defers to superior power, and sees proper actions as those that satisfy mainly one's own needs, the conventional level which emphasizes conformity and gaining others' approval, and the postconventional level whereby a person's moral orientation is more principled and logical and takes the needs of others into account.

land resources—Forests, grasslands, deserts, snow and ice areas, and tundra.

leadership traits and qualities—A trait is basically a distinguishing characteristic or quality. In general, people believe that a leader is someone who has many positive qualities. Studies have suggested that those qualities include: creativity, positive mental attitude, high expectations, integrity, sense of responsibility, courage, authenticity, self-awareness, and a high ethical standard.

learning styles—Specific methods and preferences of learning. Outdoor leaders teach to different learning styles in order to develop knowledge, skills, and dispositions in all participants.

legitimate power—The influence a person has because of being elected, appointed, or selected to direct others. This power is inherent in the leader's position.

leisure—Nonwork activity into which people enter voluntarily for enjoyment. The ultimate goal of leisure activity is cultivation of the self. Leisure involves three elements: perceived freedom, intrinsic motivation, and a positive outcome.

living resources—All forms of plant and animal life.

low elements—Activity-based experiences found on challenge courses that do not require the use of belay safety systems. Spotting is usually practiced to ensure participant safety.

macro programming—Program development and planning on an organizational level that is driven primarily by organizational goals and objectives.

maintenance behaviors—Behaviors that keep relationships in the group positive, such as group members supporting one another or doing their fair share of the work.

metaphors—Applying a word or phrase to somebody or something that is not meant literally but to make a comparison.

micro programming—Program development and planning for daily program operations.

motivational needs theory—Emphasizes the need for outdoor leaders to identify the motivation and needs of the group as well as the individual motivation and needs of the leader. He encourages leaders to evaluate the following: the need for achievement, the need for authority and power, and the need for affiliation.

multiple intelligences—Term developed by Howard Gardner to describe nine distinct learning styles.

multiple use—Resource management principle aimed at drawing a balance between the interests of various groups competing for the same resource.

natural decision-making model—Most experienced outdoor leaders rely on a process of systematic thinking, common sense, intuition, and experience-based judgment in the decision-making process. Kosseff refers to this process as natural decision making, suggesting that the analytic model of decision making is more conducive to confirming decisions that have already been made. The natural decision-making model is nonlinear and relies on a person's ability to think systematically, listen to and apply anecdotal information, and use common sense and natural intuitive ability alongside experience-based judgment in the decision-making process.

natural resources—Natural resources are divided into three basic categories: land resources, water resources, and living resources.

negligence—When a professional, such as an outdoor leader, fails to fulfill the standard of care in a given practice and that failure results in an actual injury or loss to the client.

nonconsequentialist theory of ethics—The nonconsequentialist approach to ethics is concerned with the acts themselves—the means. Acts within this tradition are predetermined to be "good" or "bad" based on the standard set by the summum bonum. For example, telling lies is "bad," regardless of the end result of the lie.

norm—Parameter that defines acceptable behavior in a group.

outdoor education—Education comprised of two disciplines, environmental education and adventure education.

outdoor leadership—Practice of leading individuals and groups into natural settings on safe, enjoyable, and environmentally sound excursions.

outdoor recreation—Recreation activities that occur in natural settings.

Outward Bound process model—Developed by Walsh and Golins, this is probably one of the most influential models that is used in outdoor programming to describe the key elements of an adventure experience. The seven key elements include: the learner, the prescribed physical environment, prescribed social environment, characteristic set of problem-solving tasks, a state of adaptive dissonance, mastery or competence, and the transfer of new learning.

preservation—Conservation practice aimed at protecting nonrenewable resources from neglect and destruction.

principle ethics—Ethics that are guided by a proactively determined set of rules, often determined by a governing professional organization or by the current professional standards of behavior. Hunt refers to this as ethical objectivism.

program accreditation—Speaks to the level of quality under which programs are operated. Accreditation indicates that a program is meeting or exceeding industry standards.

psychological carrying capacity—Effects of visitors on one another in the outdoors.

recognition of patterns—Involves the development of a "sixth sense." You will begin to recognize certain patterns as you lead more and more wilderness trips. These patterns will include: weather prediction, your ability to "read" participants, the average distance that a group paddles in a day, and how much pasta to pack for a group of ten people. The more experience that you have, the greater the recognition of these patterns will become. This process is also called *inductive reasoning*. Inductive reasoning is used to develop general concepts from specific experiences.

recreation—Form of leisure in which individuals exert energy through some form of physical activity.

recreation ecology—Both positive and negative environmental effects of recreational use of natural areas.

referent power—The influence a person has because others identify with that person or because their contributions are most valued by group members. This form of charismatic power may impel group members to work harder to please the leader.

reflective thinking—Employed when a situation is ambiguous, when it presents a dilemma, and when there are alternatives available. When uncertainty is present and information is missing, then a person must rely on her memory of general concepts, composing specific predictions to fill in for uncertainties. This represents the process of deductive reasoning.

rescue curve—A useful framework for reducing accident potential and minimizing the consequences of accidents. The rescue curve posits that there are four steps between an individual engaging in an adventure experience and winding up dead as a result of an accident while participating in that activity. These steps include accident prevention, self-rescue, rescue from within a group, and rescue from an outside party. The rescue curve also posits that as time increases in responding to a life-threatening accident, the chances of survival decrease.

reward power—Reward power is the influence that comes from a person's ability to provide a benefit that is valued by another person. It is achieved by giving a reward for effort. A person can use punishment power by withholding favors as well. This is often referred to as *coercive power* and usually follows the failure of reward power to influence a person.

risk management—Systematic process of reducing the potential occurrence of an accident during an adventure experience.

role—Set of expected behaviors associated with a position in a group.

self-efficacy—Perception about what we can or cannot do. It is developed from direct and indirect experience.

servant leadership theory—This model of leadership is based on the ideal that a leader's main role is to serve others. One who acts as servant first, either leader or follower, is always searching, listening, and not only believing but expecting that there is hope for the future. The practice of this theory manifests itself in an ethic of care, whereby the leader, who is servant first, ensures that other peoples' highest priority needs are being met.

shakedown—Initial part of an outdoor expedition that enables groups to test and refine equipment and systems before committing to a serious expedition.

shared leadership—Occasionally, no single person takes on the responsibility to lead and several members of the group share the leadership role. Shared leadership often works well when there are several group members who are skilled in the tasks necessary to lead the group.

simple decisions—Simple decisions have fewer variables, limited consequences, and outcomes that are relatively predictable.

situational leadership model—Hersey and Blanchard's research of situational leadership is based on the premise that most leader activities can be classified into either task or relationship orientations. The key assumption of the situational model of leadership is that the leader is both able and willing to adapt her leadership orientation to the group's situation based on the readiness level of the group and the group's orientation to the dimensions of task and relationship.

situational leadership theory—Situational theories are models of leadership that take into account the leader, the followers, and the situation and explain leadership as emerging based on the situation. Situational leadership accounts for two ideals: 1) any situation plays a large part in determining leadership qualities and the leader for that situation and 2) the leadership qualities of an individual are themselves the product of a previous leadership situation that have molded that individual.

SMART system—Method used to develop goals and objectives for programs or lesson plans that are based on specific, measurable, achievable, realistic, and time-based criteria.

social learning theory—People learn new behaviors from observing others and patterning their behavior after that of others. This is called modeling.

standard of care—The standard of care in a particular industry is determined according to what other reasonable and prudent professionals would do in similar situations.

summum bonum—One of the most common approaches in determining right from wrong is to make judgments in terms of the highest good. "In ethical language, the search for the highest good is the search for the summum bonum" (Hunt 1994, p. 14).

sustainable use—Conservation practice that aims to balance use of natural resources with replenishment of those resources.

task behaviors—Behaviors that move a group toward accomplishing goals.

teachable moments—Taking advantage of unforeseen opportunities to teach that present themselves during the course of an outdoor experience.

time control plan—Plan used to calculate the time and energy needed to move from point to point through the natural environment when engaged in activities such as backpacking, mountaineering, or paddling.

tort law—Lawsuits brought against outdoor leaders for injuries or losses to participants as a result of an accident are always filed under tort law. Commonly referred to as civil law.

trait theory of leadership—According to the trait theory of leadership, leaders are born not made. Trait theory has been used to describe a leader as one who exhibits a certain set of characteristics: physical, intellectual, and interpersonal. Characteristics of this traditional leader would be an individual who shows good posture, is attractive, speaks firmly, acts confidently, is task-oriented, and is assertive.

transactional leadership—For Burns, the transactional leader approaches followers with an eye to exchanging one thing for another. Transactional leadership applies to those leaders who are task-oriented and able to direct their groups in specific ways to accomplish finite goals. Transactional leaders work at gaining their group's compliance through various approaches: offering rewards, threatening punishment, appealing to group members' sense of altruism, or appealing to followers' rational judgment in order to accomplish a particular goal.

transfer of learning—Taking an experience and applying that learning elsewhere. It represents the integration of learning from the experience to life back home.

transformational leadership—Considers the affective, intellectual, and action traits of the individual, as well as the specific conditions under which the individual operates. Leadership is seen to be contingent on a condition of traits and situations involving an exchange between the leader and the led. The transformational leader asks followers to transcend their own self-interests for the good of the group, organization, and society.

utilitarianism—A consequentialist theory of ethics that maintains that an act is good only if it brings about the greatest good for the greatest number.

virtue ethics—Ethics that are guided by the particular virtues associated with being a moral outdoor leader rather than the principles of being ethical. According to this ethic, an individual must examine the particular factors and influences of each act, maintaining that the "right" decision is defined by each specific situation and cannot be linked to any decision made in other situations. Hunt refers to this as ethical subjectivism.

water resources—Rivers, bays and estuaries, wetlands, coastal areas, and lakes and reservoirs.

WISE (Dress WISE)—Outdoor clothing system that includes a wicking layer, insulation layer, shell layer, and extra clothing.

Index

Note: Page numbers followed by an italicized *f* or *t* refer to the figure or table on that page, respectively.

About the Authors

Bruce Martin, PhD, is an assistant professor in the School of Sport and Exercise Science at the University of Northern Colorado in Greeley, Colorado. He developed and implemented an accredited baccalaureate degree program in outdoor leadership at Sheldon Jackson College in Sitka, Alaska, and has five years of experience teaching both theoretically oriented and practically based outdoor leadership courses at the college and university level. He has worked as a camp counselor, professional river guide, and Outward Bound instructor. Martin is a member of the Wilderness Education Association, the American Canoe Association, and the Association for Experiential Education. He serves as the Rocky Mountain Region chair for the latter association. Martin is a whitewater kayak instructor trainer for the American Canoe Association, and he is a master educator for Leave No Trace, Inc. He also is the author of *Wayside Attractions: The Negotiation of Aspirations and Careers Among African-American Adolescent Males in an Urban Alternative School.*

Christine Cashel, EdD, is a professor of leisure studies at Oklahoma State University in Stillwater, Oklahoma. She has taught elementary, middle school, and college students for 33 years and has taught outdoor leadership courses for the Wilderness Education Association for 23 years. She is also a master educator for Leave No Trace, Inc. She regularly presents at various national conferences and has presented papers four times in Japan in the last six years. She is most proud of her students who have continued to inspire others through the power of the outdoors.

Mark Wagstaff, EdD, is an associate professor in the department of recreation, parks and tourism at Radford University in Radford, Virginia. He has taught outdoor leadership and adventure education in the college setting for 13 years and has served as a professional river guide for more than 10 years. He has been an instructor for Outward Bound and Wilderness Education Association and has led outdoor adventures in Costa Rica, Ecuador, and Nepal. Wagstaff managed the outdoor program at Oklahoma State University for five years and is a master educator for Leave No Trace, Inc. He has developed curriculum and instructed for Wilderness Education Association and served as that association's executive director for three years. He is also a member of the American Canoe Association and the Association for Experiential Education.

Mary Breunig, MS, has been involved in outdoor and experiential education for 16 years. She spent 7 of those years leading outdoor wilderness trips year-round. Currently, Breunig is a PhD candidate in the educational studies program at Lakehead University in Thunder Bay, Ontario, where she teaches full-time in the School of Outdoor Recreation, Parks and Tourism. She teaches courses in outdoor leadership, outdoor education, and experiential education, in addition to a number of field-based courses. Breunig's research interests include the study of integrated wilderness trip programs and issues of social justice in outdoor education. Her research examines the intersection of the fields of experiential education and critical pedagogy. She is co-editor of the *Journal of Experiential Education.* Breunig lives in a cabin in the woods with her husband, Tim O'Connell, and their dog, Ridge.

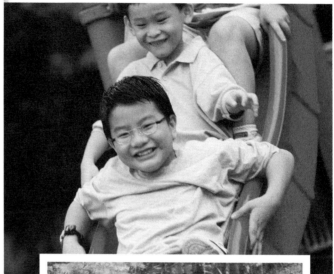

You'll find other outstanding recreation resources at
www.HumanKinetics.com

In the U.S. call 1.800.747.4457
Australia 08 8372 0999
Canada. 1.800.465.7301
Europe . . . . . .+44 (0) 113 255 5665
New Zealand 0800 222 062

HUMAN KINETICS
The Information Leader in Physical Activity & Health
P.O. Box 5076 • Champaign, IL 61825-5076